The Sufi Muslim orders to which the vast majority of Senegalese belong are the most significant institutions of social organization in the country. While studies of Islam and politics have tended to focus on the destabilizing force of religiously based groups, Leonardo Villalón argues that in Senegal the orders have been a central component of a political system that has been among the most stable in Africa. Focusing on a regional administrative center, he combines a detailed account of grassroots politics with an analysis of national and international forces to examine the ways in which the internal dynamics of the orders shape the exercise of power by the Senegalese state. This is a major study that should be read by every student of Islam and politics as well as of Africa.

Islamic society and state power in Senegal

African Studies Series 80

Islamic society and state power in Senegal

A list of books in this series will be found at the end of this volume.

Islamic society and state power in Senegal

Disciples and citizens in Fatick

Leonardo A. Villalón

The University of Kansas, Lawrence

CAMBRIDGE
UNIVERSITY PRESS

Published by the Press Syndicate of the University of Cambridge
The Pitt Building, Trumpington Street, Cambridge CB2 1RP
40 West 20th Street, New York, NY 10011-4211, USA
10 Stamford Road, Oakleigh, Victoria 3166, Australia

First published 1995

Printed in Great Britain at the University Press, Cambridge

A catalogue record for this book is available from the British Library

Library of Congress cataloguing in publication data
Villalón, Leonardo Alfonso, 1957–
Islamic society and state power in Senegal: disciples and
citizens in Fatick / Leonardo A. Villalón.
    p.   cm. – (African studies series: 80)
Includes bibliographical references.
ISBN 0 521 46007 7
1. Islam and state–Senegal–Fatick (Region)   2. Tījanīyah–
Senegal–Fatick (Region)   3. Senegal–Politics and government.
I. Title.   II. Series.
BP64.S42F388   1995
320.5′5′09663–dc20   94-13358   CIP

ISBN 0521 460077 hardback

SE

For Fiona

Contents

x   Contents

Tables

Acknowledgments

At the risk of some inadvertent omissions, I would like to take the opportunity to thank some of the individuals who have helped make this book possible.

My debt to the people of Fatick will be apparent to any reader of this work. I owe a special thanks to the various men of religion in the town, in particular the four local marabouts who figure most prominently in the pages that follow. Without their patience and sincerity in response to my questions this work would not have been possible. I must also thank the various officials who represent the state in Fatick. Their openness to a foreign researcher is a testament to the exceptional qualities of the Senegalese state. I cannot list the innumerable ordinary citizens who enriched my stay in Fatick, and among whom I count many friends, but neither can I refrain from mentioning several. In the household of Cheikh Guèye and his wives Marie Touré and Soukay Ndiaye I was made to feel a member of the family, and I am grateful and honored to have shared their celebrations, holidays, and sorrows. Souleymane Gaby Bâ, El Hadji Arfang Diouf, Amadou Faye, Théophile Sonar Ngom, and Thierno Seydou Sall were all not only teachers, but friends, as was my neighbor Abal Diallo, tragically killed on the Dakar road in 1992. The late Djibril Ndiaye, Rokhaya "Daba" Ndour, and the young Cheikh Thiam contributed much more than they can know. Senegal is a poor country, and Fatick is a poor town. The generosity with which I was received by people there, and which has been shown in subsequent visits, is humbling. *Yàlla na leen Yàlla may jàmm.*

Resisting the temptation to elaborate in each case, I would like to simply thank the many who provided logistical support, intellectual stimulation, and friendship during my initial period in Dakar, and on occasional forays there from Fatick: Jess Baily, Phil Burnham, Horma "Pape" Diouf, Jérôme Faye, Khady Guèye, Sean Kelly, Babacar Mboup, Alé Ndiaye, John and Salimata Peterson, Helen Picard, Capie Polk, Suzanne Prysor-Jones, El Hadj Sarr, Ibou Sarr, Mark and Karen Schoonmaker-Freudenberger, Jim Searing, and Leigh Swigart, as well as Lillian Baer, Gary Engleberg, and my

Wolof teachers at the Baobab Center. At the Université Cheikh Anta Diop de Dakar I am especially indebted to Professors Mohammed Mbodj and Mamadou Diouf for their good advice. The family of El Hajj Moustapha Ndiaye received me warmly as their guest in Touba at the occasion of the *grand màggal* in two successive years. I would especially like to thank a son of that family, Touba Ndiaye, for his help. My intellectually exciting friendship with Ousmane Kane began in Senegal, and I am glad to have had the occasion to develop it since. I learned a great deal from Professor Donal Cruise O'Brien – not only about Senegalese Islam – when I had the opportunity to work with him for a two week period during which we traveled to various parts of the country. The hospitality of Charles and Sévrine Stewart made possible a visit to Mauritania during which I learned much about Senegal's ties to the north. Catherine Bicknell brought remarkable enthusiasm on visits to Fatick, and her untimely death has saddened her many friends there and elsewhere.

Many teachers, intellectual precursors, and colleagues will recognize their input in this work, and several deserve special note: Lucie Colvin Phillips, who first nurtured my interest in Senegal, Michael Schatzberg, who first planted the idea of conducting research at the local level, and James Bill, who provided much-needed guidance at early stages of this project. More directly, Clement M. Henry, Charles Stewart, and especially Catherine Boone and Robert Hardgrave offered invaluable help in improving both the substance and the style of the manuscript. I benefited enormously from the intense and stimulating conference, "Etat et Société au Sénégal: Crises et Dynamiques Sociales" which united numerous Senegalese scholars and scholars of Senegal at the Institut d'Etude d'Afrique Noire in Bordeaux in October 1991. My thanks to all participants at that conference, and particularly to Christian Coulon for the invitation to take part.

The primary field research on which this work is based was made possible, like so many other studies of Africa, by funding from the Fulbright-Hays Program and from the Joint Committee on African Studies of the Social Science Research Council (SSRC) and the American Council of Learned Societies, with funds provided by the Rockefeller Foundation and the William and Flora Hewlett Foundation. Follow-up research in 1993 was funded in part by the New Faculty Research Program of the University of Kansas. I am grateful for the support of all of these organizations.

The substance of the section on ritual ceremonies in chapter 5 and a version of some of the material in chapter 7 have already been published in two articles, "Sufi Rituals as Rallies: Religious Ceremonies in the Politics of Senegalese State-Society Relations" in *Comparative Politics* 26:4 (1994) and "Charisma and Ethnicity in Political Context: A Case Study in the Establishment of a Senegalese Religious Clientele," in *Africa* 63:1 (1993). I gratefully acknowledge permission to reprint from the editors of those journals.

The contribution of my (extended) family to this work has been indirect, but fundamental, and I would like to name the most immediate here: my late father, Leonardo A. Villalón, my mother, Isabel María Villalón, and my siblings and their spouses: Alejandro, Gonzalo, Miguel, Annalisa, and Isabel Villalón and Leonardo Zavarse. I dedicate this book to my wife Fiona Mc Laughlin; in many ways it is already as much hers as mine.

A note on spelling

The transliteration of Senegalese terms and names is complicated by two factors. French orthography, which is not well adapted to the phonemics of Senegalese languages, has resulted in conventions which may be difficult for English speakers to decipher. For example, the French spelling of the village "Diouloulou" might more clearly be rendered "Jululu." Secondly, there are many words of Arabic origin that have been borrowed into Wolof whose common pronunciation has been modified in accordance with Wolof phonology. For example, the Arabic term *ziaara* has become the Wolof *siyaare*. In this work I have opted for a pragmatic approach, attempting to be linguistically accurate while avoiding excessive pedantry. For the names of people, places, and organizations or groups I have conformed to the most widely accepted usage in Senegal and in the literature, while less commonly known words are written in accordance with the spelling now prefered by linguists. Thus I have referred to the pre-colonial state and the later administrative unit in which Fatick is located as "Sine," while in spelling the term for the people of the region I have opted for the more accurate *Siin-Siin*.

Due to differences in dialects and disagreements among linguists I have followed whenever possible the spelling found in the *Dictionnaire Wolof-Français* compiled by Arame Fal, Rosine Santos, and Jean Léonce Doneux (Paris: Karthala, 1990). A few points on that orthography may help English speakers. Vowels are generally pronounced as in Spanish or Italian (accents can usually be ignored without great inaccuracy), and double vowels are simply lengthened. Most consonants are pronounced as in English, although the following conventions should be noted:

c = ch in cherry
x = ch in German Bach
j = j in jam
g = g in great
ñ = ñ in Spanish *niño*

Geminate (double) consonants are treated as in Italian. With the exceptions of the term *shaykh* (Wolof *séex*) and *baraka* (Wolof *barke*) I have preferred

Wolofized terms to the original Arabic; hence *tarixa* rather than *tariqa*. Arabic words and names are transliterated in a simplified form of the anglicized convention, although given its frequency as both a title and a proper name in Senegal I have preferred the French transliteration El Hajj to al-Hajj. In all cases plurals have been made simply by adding an "s."

For the name of the language and the largest ethnic group in Fatick I have opted for the simplified spelling "Serer" rather than the more frequent French spelling "Sérère" or the linguistically accurate – but perhaps less readily recognizable – "Seereer."

Glossary

addiya	A gift or contribution to a marabout, usually made yearly on the occasion of a visit.
baraka	(Arabic; Wolof *barke*) Grace; blessing; spiritual benefit. Used in particular to describe a quality of a marabout or in an oath, as in *Barke Sëriñ Touba!* (By the grace of Amadou Bamba!)
buur	Title of the monarch of various pre-colonial Senegambian kingdoms. *Buur-Siin*: King of Sine.
daara	A Qurʾanic school; the house of a marabout. Among the Mourides also used for an agricultural community of young men in the service of a marabout.
daaira	A local "cell" or organizational unit of a Senegalese Sufi order or of the followers of a specific marabout.
gàmmu	Originally a traditional celebration held before the start of the rainy season. Today a religious ritual celebration, especially that held on the occasion of the prophet's birthday (*Mawlud*) by marabouts of the Tijaniyya order.
griot	French term for the caste of praise-singers and genealogists found among most Sahelian ethnic groups. This socially important but low-status caste (known as *géwél* in Wolof) occasionally plays a role within Senegalese Islamic structures.
jàkka	A mosque. Used in particular for a smaller neighborhood mosque to distinguish it from a Friday mosque (*jumaa*).
jàng	Literally to learn or study; also to read or recite. Used as a noun for a religious chanting ceremony, especially those held weekly by *daairas*.
jébbalu	To declare allegiance or submission to a marabout; used in particular by the Mourides. The noun form, *njébbal*, refers to the formal act of declaring submission.
jumaa	A Friday mosque; i.e., a mosque where communal Friday prayers are said.

Korite
: (Arabic *'Id al-fitr*) The feast marking the end of the fasting month of Ramadan (*weer-u koor* in Wolof).

màggal
: Literally to celebrate or exalt. More commonly, as a noun, a Mouride religious ritual celebration. The *grand màggal* is the major annual celebration of the Mouride order held in the holy city of Touba.

marabout
: The generic French term used throughout north-west Africa for a Muslim religious leader. In Senegal it now refers more specifically to a religious leader within the Sufi orders. See *sëriñ* and *shaykh*.

Mawlud
: The celebration of the prophet's birthday. A major *gàmmu* is held at Tivaouane, as at most other Tijan *zawiyas*, on this occasion.

muqàddam
: An individual of standing in the Tijan order, usually referring to a representative of an important marabout or someone capable of transmitting the *wird*.

ndigal
: An order, directive, or instructions. When used in reference to a maraboutic command it connotes Mouride marabouts.

saltigi
: (Serer; Wolof *saltige*) Seer or healer. With Islamization the social role of this traditionally important group has blurred with those of local marabouts among the Serer.

sëriñ
: Marabout; Sufi religious leader.

shaykh
: (Wolof *séex*) Title for a Sufi leader; marabout. In Senegal used in particular by the Mourides and Qadirs as a parallel to a Tijan *muqàddam*.

sikar
: A litany or recitation of the names of God, or the repetitive chanting of one or more of these names. Performed with special frequency in Senegal by the Baye Fall sect of the Mourides, and thus often used to refer to a Baye Fall ritual.

siyaare
: (Arabic *ziaara*, a visit) To visit a marabout, and by extension any religiously associated visit. As a noun refers to an organized group visit or ritual at a maraboutic center. Used in particular today by the Dahiratoul Moustarchidina wal Moustarchidaty movement to refer to the annual celebration in Tivaouane at the feast of Tamxarit.

Tabaski
: (Arabic *'Id al-adha*) The feast which commemorates Abraham's sacrifice. Celebrated by those who can afford it with the slaughter of a ram.

Tamxarit
: (Arabic *'Ashura*) The holiday for the Muslim new year.

Glossary

tarixa	(Arabic *tariqa*) A Sufi "path" or order. Also translated at times as "brotherhood."
taalibe	A disciple of a marabout or student in a Qur'anic school.
wird	The unique litany of prayers of a Sufi order. The transmission or teaching of the *wird* is part of the initiation into an order, and establishes a tie of spiritual indebtedness to the teacher.
xalifa	(Arabic *khalifa*, "caliph") The successor to a marabout's position. The Franco-Wolof term *xalifa-général* (Wolofized as *xalifa-seneraal*) is used to refer to the successors of the founders of the most important maraboutic dynasties in Senegal, especially the leader of the Mouride order in Touba or the heir to the Tijan El Hajj Malik Sy in Tivaouane.
zawiya	A Sufi center usually organized around the tomb of a saintly figure or marabout; the home base of a maraboutic dynasty. Although the term is not frequently used at the popular level, to the extent to which it is known it tends to connote a Tijan locale centered around a mosque.

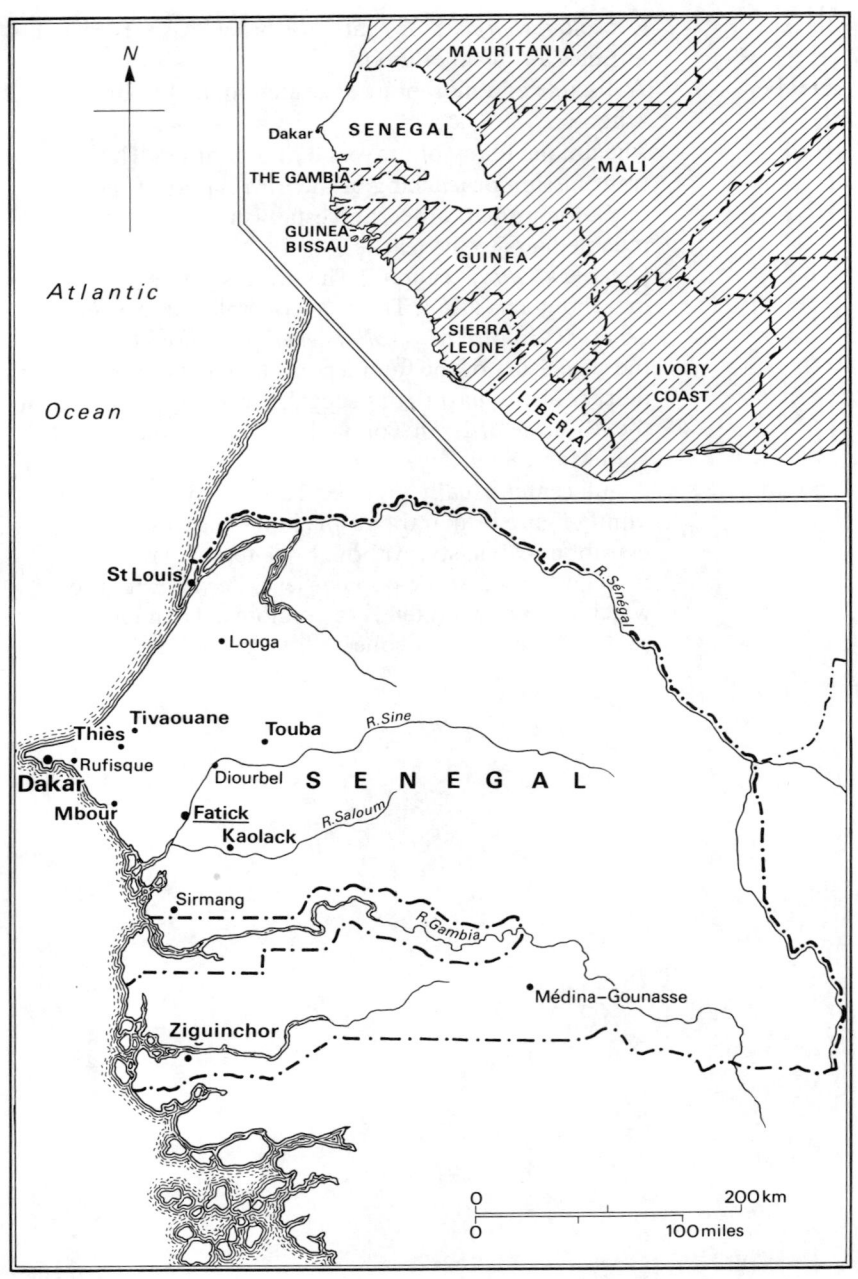

SENEGAL
Location of Fatick and other sites referred to in the text

Introduction: good Africans, good citizens, good Muslims

Two dimensions of Senegalese exceptionalism: religion and politics

Shortly after arriving in the town of Fatick I made a series of courtesy visits to introduce myself to local marabouts, religious leaders of the Islamic Sufi orders. Without exception I was warmly received, and all of these men indicated their willingness to discuss their religion with me, evidently pleased by my interest. Embarking on this task immediately, one offered to lend me a cassette recording of a speech by one of Senegal's most important marabouts of the Tijaniyya Sufi order; he would bring it to me personally as soon as he recovered it from the local Catholic priest to whom he had previously lent it. This cross-religious connection in itself was rather surprising. Then listening to the speech a few days later, I was startled to hear the marabout proclaim: "Senegalese Muslims are not only Muslims. They are also the citizens of a republic, the activists of a party. They are also negroes. And that which Islam requires of them is that they be at the same time very good negroes, very good citizens, and excellent activists."[1]

Certainly not all marabouts would say the same, as I was to learn. Indeed, the same marabout at different times has struck a notably different tone. Yet the fact that the statement would be made by an important and well-known religious figure nevertheless underscores one of the most salient features of Senegalese Islam. In James Piscatori's terminology, Islam in Senegal has been paradigmatically "conformist," capable of accommodating itself to the "prevailing political reality" of the modern nation-state.[2] Indeed, as the marabout's statement indicates, Senegalese Islam has – at least at times – done much more than conform; it has been willing to embrace not only state and party, but even the controversial notion of race enshrined in the cultural philosophy of "Négritude" advocated by Senegal's first president.[3] For many scholars of Islam, mindful of the theoretical unity of the Muslim *umma* and the lack of legitimacy of any other division of the faithful in classical Islamic thought, that adaptability in itself is anomalous. But even for those persuaded by Piscatori's argument that "conformists" outnumber "non-conformists" in the contemporary Muslim world, the specific pattern of interaction of religion and politics in Senegal proves intriguing, and puzzling.

1

Islam is, on the one hand, clearly central to the political sociology of Senegal: the religious elite carry great weight in national politics; political discourse is replete with references and appeals to Islam; Islamic symbols are omnipresent, and a myriad of popular organizations centered around Islam are flourishing. At the same time, however, there is little evidence of the social phenomena which might be expected to accompany the politicization of Islam: socio-political cleavages based on religion, whether between Muslim and non-Muslim or between Sufi orders, are virtually non-existent; and outside a very small urban minority there is virtually no opposition to the much-touted principle of *l'état laïc*, the secular state. The political role of Islam in the country is clearly not that which much of the recent literature on Islam and politics would lead one to predict.

Alongside this religious peculiarity, the Senegalese political system has also provided an exceptional case in Africa for its stability and relatively non-repressive character. There is, indeed, a reasonable basis to Senegalese claims of having one of the rare functioning democratic systems on the continent.[4] To be sure, it is a rather imperfect democracy. Most significantly, it has not passed the crucial test of producing an alternation in power via the ballot box. This shortcoming has at times threatened the very continuance of the system, as when the frustration of sectors of the urban population – most notably unemployed youth – exploded into violent protests and riots following the announcement of the 1988 election results. And the failure once again of the opposition to displace President Abdou Diouf or the ruling Parti Socialiste in the 1993 elections, despite a series of significant governmental concessions on electoral procedures, has clearly eroded popular confidence in the capability of the system to yield an alternation in power, and consequently undermined the system's legitimacy.[5] While democracy in Senegal thus still exhibits some noteworthy limitations, the country has nevertheless not only experienced a remarkable stability since independence in 1960, but its people have enjoyed the benefits of a relatively benevolent relationship with the state. The Senegalese state's capacity for governance, understood in Goran Hyden's words as "the conscious management of regime structures with a view to enhancing the legitimacy of the public realm," has at the very least ensured that Senegalese society has never been subjected to the repression, exploitation, arbitrariness, or indeed terror at the hands of the state known by all too many of its neighbors.[6]

This book explores the relationship between these two central traits of the Senegalese political system. It recognizes, as many others have, that there is a close link between the role of Islam in the country and its political system. In attempting to specify precisely what the relationship is, however, the approach I take and the interpretation I propose differ substantially from various other models that have been suggested by writers on Senegal. My research particularly calls into question both interpretations that would rely too heavily on Islam and those which consider it too lightly. Much of the recent literature on the role of Islam in politics has sought an explanation in Muslim theology. In the Senegalese case, inherent attributes of the black African Sufi version of that theology have been proposed as central to its political role. For some scholars this theology has been the source of a hegemonic ideology, a religious opiate or false consciousness through which the Senegalese masses consent to their own domination. Although seductive, the model ultimately fails to account for the empirical realities of Senegalese social life. At the same time models of elite politics, which would necessitate no consideration of Islam *per se*, while also tantalizing in the Senegalese case, prove to be deficient because they ignore such crucial issues as why religious leaders become "elites" and how and why they persist as such. Building on a grass-roots examination of what religious affiliation and interactions with the state actually entail in the lives and relationships of Senegalese Muslims, this work proposes an alternative means of understanding the effect of religion on politics in the country.

There is an ongoing debate about the nature of the Sufi orders with which most Senegalese are affiliated: stated most simplistically the question is to know whether they are instruments of exploitation or vehicles for transmitting popular sentiments. My fieldwork in Fatick has led me, contrary to my initial prejudices, to a qualified adherence to the latter camp. This benevolent view of the orders has been put forward most notably by Donal Cruise O'Brien, who has argued for their "democratic" aspects at various times in his later work, perhaps most explicitly in a short article entitled "Wails and Whispers: the People's Voice in West African Muslim Politics."[7] This book builds on such an understanding of the orders to explore the interrelationship of the two dimensions of Senegal's exceptionalism. More specifically, it develops an analysis which specifies the *process* and examines the *institutions* through which "the people's voice" is expressed and heard, and places this discussion in the context of current debates about state and society in Africa.

Sources and contribution of the study

Recent developments in the field of comparative political studies, and of African politics in particular, have emphasized a new theoretical concern with explaining the variations across political systems in terms of relations between state and society. "The nature of state-society linkages," one long-time scholar of Africa has suggested, "is ripe for reconsideration."[8] And the past several years have witnessed the emergence of a broad consensus among a wide array of scholars about the particularly acute need for studies of the specific contours of African societies. Jean-François Bayart, the French political scientist who has been at the forefront of this endeavor, has argued that "the shape of African societies, which is scarcely considered by political analysts, has much to do with the way power is exercised."[9] And Michael Bratton has issued a call for further work that could fill the gap noted by Bayart: "political scientists should devote more research attention to the associational life that occurs in the political space beyond the state's purview."[10] Although several noteworthy studies have begun to fill this gap, the process of accumulation is slow due to the inherent difficulties and limitations of the required research. One goal of this work is to make a contribution to this broader research agenda.

This study is thus devoted to the effort to detail and examine the specific "shape" of Senegalese society, with particular attention to what is undoubtedly its most salient feature: the forms of its religious organization. Throughout the discussion I attempt to relate the examination of societal structures to the way power is exercised by the Senegalese state. Although my concern is with the broader processes that distinguish the Senegalese case, by its very nature such an understanding requires a firm basis in a local-level understanding, a close portrayal of the view "from the bottom up" in a specific locale. There is a difficulty in such an endeavor, however, in that the intensive study of the narrow details of a particular case which it requires may blind one to the broader issues; the local tree may obstruct our view of the national forest. A study such as this, therefore, can only be built on the solid foundations constructed by the work of many scholars.

The analysis offered here is built on the substantial accomplishments of large and varied bodies of literature in three domains: in addition to that on African state-society relations I am indebted to numerous writings on Islam and politics, as well as to studies of Senegal itself. Often directly and at other times implicitly, I rely heavily on each of these literatures in approaching the examination of the case study, and it is my hope that the empirical information from this case will in turn prove of interest to scholars working in each of those domains. Moreover, a major goal of this effort has been to attempt an integration of these islands of research as a means of contributing to the development of theoretical propositions in each. Such intellectual hybridization, I hope, will expand our understanding of social processes by posing new questions or suggesting alternative explanations.

There exist several excellent studies of Senegalese Islam. The early works of the French colonial official Paul Marty provided the foundation for subsequent research.[11] Although Marty's motivation was at least in part that of prescribing colonial policy, and his writings are consequently shaped by this perspective, his empirical research is nevertheless an exceptional source for other scholars. Among those who have followed Marty, the works of Lucy Behrman, and especially those of Christian Coulon and Donal Cruise O'Brien merit particular attention.[12] Religious issues in the country have also been examined by Senegalese academics. In addition to several important historical and theological studies – among which the doctoral thesis by El Hadji Ravane Mbaye deserves particular note – the Senegalese sociologist Cheikh Tidiane Sy (not to be confused with the marabout of the same name who appears periodically in this work) has devoted a book to the Mouride order.[13] The foundation laid by Marty has been built upon and expanded by subsequent researchers, and the merits of any contemporary studies of Senegalese Islam must be evaluated in light of their contribution to this edifice.

This book aims to contribute to the literature on Senegalese Islam in various ways. Research for virtually all of the existing work, first of all, was carried out before the advent of the much discussed worldwide Islamic "revival," which has captured the imagination of both scholars and Muslim activists in the wake of the dramatic events of 1979 in Iran. There was a need, therefore, to update and reconsider the existing studies in terms of this important development. Scholarly activity, in addition, has been characterized by two major traits: a concentration of research on one particular Sufi order, the Mourides, and, secondly, a focus at the elite level. In addition to Cruise O'Brien's now-classic works and that of Sy, the French scholar Jean Copans has contributed a radical critique of Mouride economic organization.[14] No comparable degree of attention has been given to the other orders in the country, including the majority Tijaniyya.[15] Moreover, given the obvious importance of the topic and the relative accessibility of information, Behrman and other scholars have tended to focus their attention on the elite level, in particular on the relationship between the religious leaders of the Sufi orders, the marabouts, and the political elite. The Senegalese population in its dual role as citizens and disciples has received substantially less scholarly attention. By contrast, this work offers a *comparative* look at the membership, structures, functioning, and interrelations of the different orders at the *local* level.[16] Additionally, those scholars interested primarily in Senegal may find the focus on the town of Fatick and its hinterland, a relatively unstudied area of the country, of inherent interest.

Most importantly, however, this books aims to make a contribution to a more theoretical understanding of both African political processes and of the role of Islam in politics. Because of the paucity of data on African societies, the work of the first generation of scholars in the post-independence period was largely devoted to the description of socio-political structures and systems; the questions asked were of necessity more fre-

quently "what?" rather than "why?" As knowledge of sub-Saharan societies has accumulated, however, it has become possible to shift the discussion to a more theoretical and comparative level.

The relations that characterize the interaction of states and societies can
be conceptualized in many ways. Indeed, many of the major themes of
modern political science (clientelism, corporatism, pluralism, authoritaria-
nism, totalitarianism, class-rule, and much more) might be understood
precisely in these terms. Given the particular attributes of independent
African states and societies, however, recent Africanist scholarship has
been especially concerned with studying the variations in societal responses
to state actions, and various models of these variations have been proposed.
The most important of these, which I shall examine in the following
chapter, have focused on societal efforts to either flee or challenge state
authority. Departing from a detailed empirical consideration of the ways in
which the exercise of state power in Senegal is shaped by the structures of
Senegalese society, I propose an alternative typology of patterns of
interaction between African states and societies and explore the requirements of a stable pattern of relations as suggested by the Senegalese case.

Considering this theme in the specific context of Muslim societies, we
find certain parallels with the long intellectual tradition in Muslim discourse and scholarship about the appropriate nature of the relationship
between rulers and people. While frequently encouraging acquiescence and
cooperation with just leaders, Islamic scholars have also elaborated
theories based on the life of the Prophet to justify the options of either
fleeing or fighting (*hijra* or *jihad*) when faced with unjust rulers. Considering
this tradition in the light of the theoretical concerns, the conceptualization
of state-society relations that I propose lies on a continuum characterized
by three modal responses ranging from "contestation" to "cooperation" to
"isolation." The discussion of religious structures in Senegal is thus placed
within the broader context of societal organization as it relates to the state,
and the analysis of the Senegalese political system which I offer is built on
an examination of societal capabilities for varying responses to state
actions.

The political role of Islam, I will argue below, can only be usefully
discussed in terms of specific contexts – the confrontation of state and
society in Africa providing one such context for study. The model of
responses I propose, therefore, while derived from and influenced by
aspects of Islam, is not inherent to it. Rather this is a theoretical construct
suggested by the literature on state-society relations and built on the
understanding that the specific role which Islam will play is largely
determined by the broader context. This approach departs from most
recent considerations of Islam and politics. Assuming an essential core

element of religion which shapes behavior in Islamic societies, the focus in recent studies has usually been on how an existing religious belief or affiliation affects political action. In this study, however, I am equally interested in the reverse process: how has a specific political context affected religious organization and affiliation? The relationship between religion and politics, I believe, is dialectical and interactive; each shapes and influences the other.

This understanding of the relationship between religion and politics also guides my approach to the broader question of culture – of which religion is but one part. The perennial but unsatisfying debate in political science concerning the utility of cultural explanations for variations in political outcomes is ultimately plagued by an unsolvable "chicken and egg" paradox: do cultures shape politics or do politics shape cultures?[17] Again, I believe, the question is unanswerable, because it is misstated. Rather than a one-way causality, the relationship must also be understood as dialectical: culture and behavior both shape and are shaped by each other. As Piscatori argues in the specific context of Islamic theory and practice: "dogma interacts with ritual, the past with the present, to define one's faith. There is a complex dynamic by which practice that has evolved modifies theory, and the believer's perception of theory begins to change accordingly."[18] It is with this conceptualization in mind that I thus speak periodically in the discussion that follows of cultural practices (such as the ritual celebrations of the Sufi orders examined in chapter 5) which *both* reflect *and* reinforce political attitudes and behavior.

A conception of politics

This approach to the study of the political impact of cultural variables might be elucidated by an explanation of the conception of political science which underlies this study. In attempting to explain the functioning of the Senegalese political system – or more precisely the patterns of Senegalese state-society relations – I refer frequently to the incentives which motivate individuals, whether state functionaries, marabouts, or ordinary citizens, to act in particular ways. Such an approach necessitates an assumption that people will act rationally in response to those incentives. But what, in fact, is entailed in this assumption? In what sense might the much-disputed "rationality" of individuals be understood?

In its broadest sense, rationality implies nothing more than that individuals have a set of preferences and use whatever knowledge they might have at their disposal to choose courses of action that are most likely to lead to outcomes consistent with those preferences. People try to get what they want. To explain what people do, therefore, we must also specify what they want (their preferences), as well as what they "know" (their knowledge, regardless of whether it proves to be empirically right or wrong). In many ways, the most difficult tasks for students of comparative politics involve the attempt to develop an understanding of the set of preferences and the knowledge on which people act in any given society. We should not, of course, simply assume any particular preferences or knowledge; rather the determination of both of these domains requires careful empirical research. Both of these factors are shaped by a multitude of forces; history, culture, ideology, psychology, societal structures and political institutions all play a role in shaping both the preferences and the understanding/knowledge which individuals have about their social world. All of these, therefore, are directly relevant to a study which assumes the rationality of individuals.

Knowledge, which is a function of both available information and the way this information is used, is at least in part culturally transmitted and determined. An individual's preferences, in addition, are clearly in large part a function of prevailing cultural norms in his or her society. Religion, as a central component of culture, plays a crucial role in both. Senegalese Muslims, for example, make choices about how to act in particular circumstances by considering the knowledge they have derived from religion concerning such things as the existence of an afterlife and the method of achieving it, or the value of a religious intermediary in solving problems of various types. Their preferences, in addition, are shaped by an understanding of issues within the context of religiously derived values. It is precisely this fact that makes religion an exceptionally powerful agenda-setting agent in many societies. The way religion influences both knowledge and preferences, therefore, must be understood and considered if we are to explain why people undertake particular courses of action.

In part, of course, both an individual's knowledge and preferences are constantly modified in accordance with the well-known propensity of people to adjust "their ideas to circumstances, which is easier than adjusting circumstances to one's ideas."[19] The need to take account of the psychological processes involved in these adjustments further complicates the specification of the parameters of rationality. Social scientific explanation presuming rationality, therefore, might at times also require an examination of such phenomena as the way individuals process information in such a way as to ensure cognitive consistency. At all times, as a result, an adequate explanation requires taking into account the nature of the "circumstances" to which people adapt their "ideas." The most central of these circumstances must be understood in terms of historically evolved institutions, structures, and social processes. Socio-political outcomes are never reducible to the preferences of individuals currently affected by them, because choices are always made in the context of circumstances over which the individual has had little or no control. These, therefore, must also be specified in order to explain the choices of individuals in any given society. The discussion of "the state" in this work, for example, is guided by an understanding that its existence and parameters are among the central circumstances to which people adjust their ideas. Location in relation to the institutions of the state – which exist independently of the choices of most individuals who deal with it – influences both the knowledge that individuals receive concerning the state and the formulation of their preference ordering of possible outcomes.

Although I believe it may ultimately enrich a "rational actor" paradigm, this approach also complicates the study of political action. In this work, nevertheless, I assume that people make rational calculations about their actions *within the framework of local knowledge, preferences, and "circumstances" or institutions*. I attempt to avoid, therefore, the use of terms which imply extra-rational choices: "religious fanaticism," "blind obedience," or even "exploitation." But I also avoid simple assumptions about the preferences or knowledge that shape rational action. Rather, the emphasis is on examining the local historical and cultural factors within which choices are made. Such an approach necessitates intensive anthropological fieldwork and research in order to gather the qualitative data that can allow one to examine what it is that people "know" and how they formulate what they "prefer."

Fieldwork methods

"Theory," John Lonsdale has written, "multiplies by spontaneous generation, data are added to only in travail."[20] I agree, at least about the travail. The difficulties of data gathering would appear to be especially acute when the theoretical concerns one wishes to address are inherently slippery and nebulous. Forrest Colburn has pointed to a number of difficulties of studying state-society relations beyond the definitional problems posed by the concepts themselves. The relationship between state and society is, first of all, "interactive" and "dialectical," making it "virtually impossible to isolate causal relationships." A second difficulty arises due to the nature of civil society. "Society is differentiated in countless ways: class, race, ethnicity, religion, ideology, ubiety, and economic activity, to name the most obvious." And this "fragmentation of civil society" can complicate generalization by leading to variable behavior; not all of "society" may react in the same way to a state action. Moreover, another problem in studying state-society interaction arises from the fact that "opposition to state behavior rarely takes the form of collective outright defiance, a form of resistance which is easily studied. Instead, resistance is more tacit: foot dragging, false compliance, feigned ignorance, and sometimes even more violent forms of sabotage."[21]

Yet precisely such "popular modes of political action"[22] are central to the analysis of how state and society interact, and the difficulties of studying them may be partially responsible for the still-limited understanding of such processes in Africa. The recent interest in these theoretical concerns, however, has led to a renewed interest in more appropriate fieldwork techniques. Michael Schatzberg, whose own "travail" has added significantly to the understanding of African political processes, has argued for the need for more intensive local-level research in Africa if we are to formulate "a view of the state as it appears in the countryside from the vantage point of those who must endure it as part of their daily routine; a picture not of what the state should do according to the dictates of an abstract, elegant theoretical edifice, but of what it does do."[23] And David Laitin has suggested that social science should address general propositions and confront the "big questions" armed with broad concepts. "But," he notes, "the way it collects data to support any proposition must be sensitive to, and suggested by, the particular environment in which the research is carried out ... More technically: our variables should be universal; our indicators particularistic."[24] It was with these concerns in mind that I settled on an intensive local-level fieldwork technique for this study.

Although of course no one site can capture the full complexity of an entire country, a detailed empirical study of social structures in a carefully chosen small town seemed to be an appropriate prism through which to examine the theoretical issue of how Islam affected relations between state and society in Senegal. Having considered several possibilities and visited various potential sites, the dusty town of Fatick emerged as a particularly propitious site for fieldwork for various reasons. As a small urban center with close rural ties, the town straddles the rural-urban dichotomy. It is, in addition, ethnically and religiously mixed, with all of the major Senegalese ethnic groups and Sufi orders represented there. At the same time, the town is in no way noteworthy as a center of religious learning or practice. It is thus more representative of religious practice in Senegal as a whole than are any of the centers of the various Sufi orders. Most importantly, Fatick in 1989 was still in the process of accommodating an increased state presence following its elevation to capital of a new region in 1984. For all of these reasons the town provided an appropriate and interesting "laboratory" in which to examine state-society relations.

I arrived in Fatick after a six-month period of intensive Wolof language study and background research in the Senegalese capital of Dakar. In addition to local marabouts, I also made the rounds to introduce myself to numerous state officials in the town as well as to various other people who had been identified as individuals of some importance. My planned initial period of participant observation and informal interviews was almost immediately facilitated by a series of invitations to ceremonies and events, many of which were extended as a result of my introductory visits. In the months that followed, I found myself more and more integrated into many aspects of life in the town, and developed friendly working relationships with several locally important religious leaders as well as with people active in the local organizations of the Sufi orders (the *daairas*). I thus had the opportunity to regularly attend meetings and ceremonies organized by the different Sufi orders, participate in numerous other community activities, and most importantly carry out regular informal interviews, in both Wolof and French, with individuals from all levels of society and representing all of the major ethnic and religious groups in the town. I occasionally asked someone with whom I had a good relationship, and who had a connection to the individual in question, to accompany me when calling on more important people for the first time. I did not, however, rely on any regular assistant. Notes from these interviews were written up as soon afterwards as possible in a field log, which serves as my documentary source for the interviews cited in the chapters that follow.[25]

As I developed a better understanding of local issues I began in the second half of my year in Fatick to carry out more formal interviews, involving prepared questions on various issues, with members of the town's religious and state elite. These were generally conducted without any assistance, invariably in Wolof with religious figures and predominantly in French with state officials. Having established a personal relationship with many of these individuals, the interviews were generally characterized by a high degree of candor and openness. The choice of whom to interview was made with purely local considerations in mind; I kept a list, which I amended when appropriate, of significant people who might be capable of giving me information on issues which emerged as significant during the course of fieldwork. With only one exception, all of those I approached proved not only willing but generous in sharing their knowledge with me.

Through this method of research I learned a great deal about social life in Fatick, much of which does not appear directly in this work, but all of which is significant to my arguments and my conclusions. Innumerable "trivial" details about relations among individuals – whose child is named after whom, which old men sit with certain others, where children are sent for Qur'anic study, who patronizes certain vendors in the marketplace – all provided important insights into the workings of Fatick society and contributed to whatever understanding of local knowledge and preferences I was able to achieve.

While the flexibility of my method was thus a strength in many ways, its inherent ambiguity was also a difficulty, requiring a constant capability for improvisation to take advantage of opportunities or to find alternatives to things which proved impossible. This ambiguity also led to various dilemmas which must be recognized. The immersion in society required by a technique of intensive participant observation leads seemingly inevitably to at least a partial enmeshing of the researcher in the local "economy of affection," the network of ties which we shall explore in chapter 3. There is, in addition, a constant difficulty for the Western social scientist to explain his or her peculiar questions and interests without misrepresentation, but also without alienating his interlocutors. Many in Fatick, for example, assumed that my interest in religion was motivated by personal piety or a desire to convert. Attempting to correct misperceptions without insult is a delicate and precarious undertaking. I have tried to be conscious of these issues in writing about Fatick, and at times have pointed them out explicitly. The reader, however, should also be sensitive to the inevitable subjectivities involved in field research.

In 1993 I had the opportunity to return to Fatick, first in February during the period of the campaign and the presidential elections of that year, and then again in July/August. These visits allowed me to catch up on developments since my initial fieldwork, and thus to update and make a few corrections of fact in the material presented in this book. Most importantly, however, they underlined the point that the dynamics I have described in what follows continue unchanged in all significant respects.

The structure of the argument

Drawing on the results of fieldwork, this work attempts to build a framework for understanding the Senegalese case in terms of the role Islam has played in shaping state-society interactions. The dynamic model that I construct could be characterized as follows: A particular version of Islamic social structures – which was given what is perhaps its most distinctively Senegalese expression with the rise early in the colonial period of the Mouride Sufi order in the central Wolof zone of the country – serves to constitute what might be described as a religiously based "civil society" in Senegal. Certain elements of these structures – most notably their organiza- tion around the figures of the marabouts – along with justifications based on Islamic political thought, allow them to function effectively as viable channels for three modal types of political activity which I postulate in state-society interactions. Senegalese society, that is, can vary along a "contest – cooperate – flee" continuum in its response to state actions, and from the state perspective these responses are credible yet not overly threatening challenges. Senegalese society, therefore, is given some leverage over the state, while at the same time avoiding the excessive insecurity that, as Schatzberg has convincingly argued, feeds state oppression in such countries as Zaire.[26]

This system is made possible by the contingent nature of relations among three sets of actors: the state elite, the marabouts, and the ordinary people of Senegal in their dual role of citizen-disciples. The patterns of interaction between any two of these actors can only be understood in the context of their respective relations with the third. The core of this study is organized around the examination of these interactions. Thus after an overview of theoretical issues (chapter 1) and an exposition of the relevant background information in the local context (chapter 2), I turn to a sequential discussion of the relations of each of these pairs of actors (chapters 3 to 6). A case study of a recent maraboutic movement illustrates this discussion and serves as a springboard for drawing conclusions about the functions of Islam in Senegalese state-society relations (chapter 7). The model which emerges from these considerations depicts a set of interactions which has tended to produce an equilibrium that results in a relative "balance of power" between state and society. And while this balance is certainly "precarious" (to echo the title of one of the more important books on the topic)[27], it is nevertheless much less so than in most of sub-Saharan Africa.

This analysis has potentially significant implications both for Senegal and for the field of Comparative Politics. To the extent that my argument is valid, the relative stability that has marked Senegalese politics is not assured simply by the continued collaboration of state and religious elites. It should be possible, in fact, to specify conditions under which the dynamics of the three-sided model might shift and upset the equilibrium (the continued growth of an urban population only weakly tied to the maraboutic system, for example). Yet the analysis also suggests the resilience of the system, and thus the reasonably good prospects for its survival. To the rapidly growing literature on Islam in politics, the Senegalese case contributes an example of a politicized Islam that deviates from the pattern of strict contestation and "non-conformism" portrayed in most recent case studies. More importantly, it underlines the need for a contextual analysis of Islam's political role and offers a theoretical framework for such an analysis. The study also points to an alternative explanation to the simple patron-client or "spoils system" model of Senegalese stability. Such systems, after all, figure prominently across the African political landscape without any concomitant frequency of stable state-society relations.

Most importantly, for scholars interested in questions of state and society in Africa this study underlines what various theoretical discussions have suggested: that the existence of social structures capable of flexibly channeling societal responses to state actions is a prerequisite condition if a stable and less precarious balance is to be achieved. Although built on an empirical case study, my hope is that this book will ultimately be read as a statement about the conditions shaping the exercise of state power in Africa. As a growing number of scholars have come to argue, diverging patterns of politics in Africa must be understood in terms of variations in the specifics of societal structures and in the capabilities of those structures to effectively organize and transmit societal concerns. Politics in Africa are largely shaped and conditioned by the evolving fortunes of the continent's still-fragile civil societies. It is from this perspective that I approach the analysis of the political impact of Senegal's Sufi orders.

1　Islam in the politics of state-society relations

Stated most boldly, the central argument of this book is that religion has been at the source of Senegal's political exceptionalism because, in the Sufi version of Islam which has developed in the country, religious structures and ideology have facilitated and encouraged a system of social organization outside the state and a range of possible responses to the actions of that state which have served as an effective counterbalance to its weight. Islamic social structures have proven to be effective conduits for mediating the processes of state-society relations in Senegal, redressing the mismatch that has usually characterized African "state-society struggles."[1] The analysis presented here, therefore, draws directly on and has implications for a theoretical perspective that posits the possibility of distinguishing analytically between state and society and approaches the nature of their interaction as a phenomenon to be explained.

The argument also has implications for a theoretical understanding of the relationship between Islam and political action. The dramatic success of the 1979 revolution in Iran directed the attention of scholars, journalists, statesmen – and Muslim activists – to the potential political import of a force that many, influenced by theories of social and political "modernization," had assumed to be receding into the domain of personal conviction.[2] In the wake of that revolution, with its militant and explicitly Islamic façade, much energy has been devoted to the analysis of Islam as a political force. The result has been a voluminous body of literature devoted to this issue, a literature rich in descriptions of a wide range of political conflicts and frequently insightful into the relationship between religious theory and social practice. Yet despite these strengths, it is also a literature marked by scholarly dissension about the role of Islam in politics. In large part the debate has fed on the dual assumptions that religion is a cohesive and unitary force and that it independently shapes politics, and it has been fueled by the consequent efforts to specify *the* (implicitly unique) political role of Islam.

In fact, as James Piscatori has commented, "religion is probably more often dependent on politics than politics is dependent on religion."[3] I suggest, in this vein, that any effort to make sense of the political impact of Islam must: (1) maintain a clear analytic distinction between different facets of Islam; conceived variously as theology, ideology, or organizational basis of a social order, Islam might be attributed with different roles, and (2) consider the relationship between religion and politics as an interactive one in which each shapes and influences the other. The application of these considerations, in addition, will vary according to the context and the political dynamic in question. Before one can address the question of what role Islam has played in politics, therefore, there is a need to first ask, "the politics of what?" and then secondly, "Islam in what sense?" No single political function can be attributed to Islam, rather its multifaceted potential political roles can only be fruitfully analyzed within the context of specific political conflicts, and taking into account the cultural, historical, economic, and institutional parameters of that context. And the context may well, in turn, influence the nature of Islamic political discourse or shape the articulation of religiously based social movements and structures.

The numerous and varied countries that comprise the "Muslim world" share traits other than religion, and these traits are held in common with other, non-Muslim, countries. Thus the Muslim world, William Roff notes, is "not only, or always, the Muslim World, but part of the 'capitalist periphery,' of the 'Third World,' of 'post-colonial state systems,' and much else, depending on the lens one chooses."[4] It is in one or more of these contexts that much of the politics of the Muslim world must be understood; many of the political patterns that characterize Muslim countries are those which similarly mark other countries in the Third World. Thus such phenomena as nationalist movements, class-based demands for redistribution, and social conflict along the lines of politicized social cleavages are as common to Muslim countries as to their non-Muslim Third World counterparts. And yet in the Muslim world these political patterns frequently, indeed almost always, take on a religious coloration.

In considering questions of Islam in politics the central questions that arise concern the extent to which Islamic structures and ideology are significant in giving socio-political movements a distinctive shape or in influencing their outcome. While it is true that Islam is important throughout political struggles in the Muslim world, it does not follow that Islam is the cause of those struggles or that it determines their outcome. Islam *does* matter in that it both shapes behavior and influences the capacity for collective action in Muslim societies, but it does not *determine* those actions. This approach to Islam necessitates a departure from the tendency in recent studies of Islamic societies to begin with considerations of Islamic theology, and then explore the application of theologically derived principles within a given context. In this work, by contrast, I begin with a consideration of the political context, and then proceed to an examination of how Islam in various forms has shaped political outcomes. Because the politics of relations between state and society provide the primary context within which Senegalese Islam has played a political role, they are the central focus of this book. Senegal is part not only of the "Capitalist periphery" and the "Third World," but of the African subspecies of these categories, and thus Senegalese state and society – and their relations – must be considered in the context of post-colonial Africa. It is thus to a discussion of African states and societies that I now turn.

State and society in Africa

The state as a conceptual variable was never completely taken out of studies of African politics.[5] Nevertheless, the recent theoretical vigor that has resulted from the renewed focus on the state by social scientists has been particularly fruitful for the field of African Studies.[6] In contrast to earlier society-centered explanations of politics, proponents of the state-centric approach have regarded states as relatively autonomous actors and institutional structures capable to varying degrees of shaping society. Pluralist and structural-functional models had previously conceptualized the state primarily as a political arena within which competing social groups pursued their respective interests. Marxist analyses, on the other hand, tended to regard states as instruments of class domination, shaped by the forces of class struggles. State structures, in these views, were thus fundamentally epiphenomena of society-based political interactions.[7]

If, on the contrary, states are to be depicted as actors, then they must enjoy a degree of "autonomy." That is, in Theda Skocpol's definition, they must have the capacity to "formulate and pursue goals that are not simply reflective of the demands or interests of social groups, classes, or society."[8] Seen as autonomous actors, states then become an object of theoretical interest not simply in themselves, but rather in terms of their interactions with other political actors, namely the societies within which they exist. Forrest Colburn has emphasized this point: "an adequate appreciation of the state can emerge only from an understanding of the interaction between state and society. The state does not act in a vacuum. It may be the single most consequential actor in most polities, but what it does is conditional upon civil society."[9] The interesting questions for political analysis are thus those which concern the *interactions* between these actors. The state-centric approach does not provide a "theory of the state," but rather it furnishes a conceptualization of the state that can allow for the formulation of theoretical propositions to explain different patterns of interaction between states and societies.[10]

African states: the weakness of power

The point of departure for such an explanation lies in an understanding of the attributes of the state and society to be considered. The first step, therefore, is to define the key terms. Most definitions of the state are based on Max Weber's classic formulation: "a compulsory political association with continuous organization [is] called a 'state' if and in so far as its administrative staff successfully upholds a claim to the *monopoly* of the *legitimate* use of physical force in the enforcement of its order ... within a given *territorial* area."[11] Weber's definition has enjoyed widespread currency, but conceptual problems resulted when scholars attempted to apply the definition to the independent countries that replaced the European empires in Africa and Asia. Many of these countries, though consecrated as legitimate actors in the new international state system of the post-war world by their inclusion in the United Nations, could not satisfy one or more of the essential elements of the definition. Faced with this anomaly, one type of analytic response has been to maintain the definition and re-examine the applicability of the concept on a case-by-case basis. "[T]he existence of a state in any given political unit is an empirical question," argues Lisa Anderson, and therefore "[t]he extent to which today's countries – or any other political units – meet the definitional standards of statehood ... must be determined empirically."[12] We may need to conclude that such varied countries as Lebanon, Sudan, Zaire, or Chad, at particular periods of their histories, did not comprise "states" at all.

Perhaps a more frequent response to this difficulty has been to attempt to redefine the term in a manner that more closely approximates the empirical conditions of what we commonly call "states." The attempt to capture the peculiarities of African states in their various manifestations has led to some rather complex formulations. Michael Schatzberg, in a penetrating analysis of Zaire, defines the state as "a congeries of organized repositories of administrative, coercive, and ideological power subject to, and engaged in, an ongoing process of power accumulation characterized by uneven ascension and uneven decline." In addition, he notes, the state is, "at least in some ways, a fluid, contextual, and protean phenomenon."[13] Other scholars have foregone a restrictive definition, preferring instead to discuss characteristic attributes of African states as a means of grappling with their complexity.[14]

The insights offered by these efforts have contributed significantly to our understanding of the nature of African states, but many of the resulting formulations have proven to be too unwieldy for comparative analysis of state-society relations. A more concise definition focusing on the state in the context of society is required for my purposes here and (resisting the temptation to innovate out of sympathetic agreement with Colburn's critique of the excessive "product differentiation" which has characterized the field of Comparative Politics)[15] I thus follow Michael Bratton in adopting in its essence a definition proposed by Victor Azarya.[16] In this book *the state is conceptualized as an interrelated – but not always cohesive – set of legal, coercive, and administrative organizations within a society which coexist and interact with other organizations, but is distinguished from them in that it claims predominance over them and aims to institute binding rules regarding their activities.* While states tend to be, as Lonsdale describes them, "the most inclusive and powerful of social structures,"[17] the definition does not necessarily require that states meet this standard empirically – a test that not all African states could pass. Rather, I believe, the strength of the definition is that it captures the sense of the state as actor *attempting* to assert its hegemony over other actors in society. The empirical questions for research are thus those of the extent to which a given state is successful in this endeavor, and why.

The overwhelming consensus among Africanist scholars, indeed the obvious conclusion for anyone who has considered the fate of Africa since independence, is that as a category African states have been widely, at times dramatically, unsuccessful in this effort. "Soft" is undoubtedly the most frequently used adjective to describe the African state in the recent literature.[18] The context in which it is used varies, but the term typically refers to the weakness of the state *vis-à-vis* the society in which it is located. That is, the state is "soft" because it is largely incapable of achieving the goals posited in its definition; the soft states of Africa have failed either to establish their predominance over other organizations in society or to institute binding rules to regulate their activities, or both.

Joshua Forrest has explored four dimensions of the "quest for state hardness" in Africa which usefully elaborate the sense of the term "soft state."[19] In an effort to achieve "hardness," he argues, states seek four things: (1) a measure of structural autonomy from social forces, (2) the political penetration of society in the sense of control over local-level structures, (3) the extraction of resources from society, and (4) a degree of ideological legitimation sufficient to facilitate the achievement of the first three goals without resort to coercion. In the first, and to varying degrees the third, of these efforts some African states have made partial advances. Significant control over local-level structures, however, has largely eluded these states, and only among very restricted portions of their population, if at all, have most of them been able to impose a legitimating ideology for state power – that is, achieve "hegemony" in the particular Gramscian sense of that term.[20] On all of these dimensions, then, African states remain relatively weak and ineffectual.

The "soft state" is rooted in its colonial origins. The imposition of colonial rule in Africa resulted, as Jean-François Bayart notes, in states that were "deliberately set up *against* civil society rather than evolved in continual conflict with it."[21] Colonial rulers, of course, were required to adapt the structures of rule to the sociological realities over which they ruled – the numerous pragmatic variations in the implementation of the official British and French colonial policies of "indirect rule" and "assimilation," respectively, present the most obvious examples of this imperative. Nevertheless, the organizing principles of the colonial state were formulated primarily in accordance with metropolitan, rather than indigenous, interests and constraints. Given this origin, there has been a tendency to see post-colonial African states as alien institutions, almost totally unrelated to their societies. Goran Hyden speaks of African countries as "societies without a state" in which "[t]he latter sits suspended in 'mid-air' over society and is not an integral mechanism of the day-to-day productive activities of society."[22] Although there is clearly an important element of validity to this description, others have more recently begun to insist on the need to consider the historical evolution of the African state, arguing that while there are important continuities between the colonial and the independent state, these have been modified by the logic of evolving political goals and shifts in the balance of power among social forces.[23]

In a masterly synthesis of Africanist literature on the state, Jean-François Bayart has recently called for a rejection of the "paradigm of the yoke" (*le paradigme du joug*) which depicts African countries as saddled with states which rest above, but are not of, their societies.[24] He argues instead for an approach that recognizes the "historicity" of African societies in the study of the state. Thus pre-colonial, colonial, and post-colonial factors must all be considered in the interaction of forces that have shaped the contemporary state. By focusing on the historical evolution of patterns of interaction, this approach, which guides my analysis of the Senegalese state, can help to elucidate the dimensions of relative state "softness" or "hardness."

One other issue requires discussion to complete this characterization of the African state. It may appear paradoxical that states described as "soft" could inflict as much terror on their societies as African states have frequently done. Robert Fatton, in fact, has argued in a stinging critique of the "soft state" concept that "the thesis of the 'soft state' is mistaken because it denies the reality of an authoritarian, interventionist, and class-based state." Because it is "the organ of public coercive force that organizes the political domination of the ruling class, and disarticulates the unity of subordinate classes," the state "constitutes an apparatus of repressive dominance" and thus for Fatton is most accurately characterized as "hard."[25] African states, he notes, regularly pursue coercive, repressive, and authoritarian policies *vis-à-vis* the "subaltern classes" that constitute the vast majority of their population.

Fatton is certainly correct in pointing to the authoritarian policies pursued by most African states, but his critique of the model of the "soft state" based on this fact appears ultimately to be a terminological quibble. While many scholars have described the state as "soft" in reference to its limited capacity to secure compliance *without resorting to coercion*, Fatton prefers to label it "hard" *because* it is frequently coercive. The two points are not only reconcilable, but actually complementary. In fact, many scholars have argued that the "hard" policies of African states are the direct result of their "softness." Bratton has noted the "authoritarian behavior born of profound political insecurity" that has characterized African political elites.[26] And Schatzberg's analysis of the "dialectics of oppression" hinges on the interplay between pervasive insecurity and coercion on the part of the Zairian state.[27] Anderson has expressed succinctly how a state that pursues harsh policies could be labeled weak or "soft": "This is not to say that states with limited administrative penetration or widespread patronage cannot be brutally repressive. The use of these terms ... is analogous to that of psychology: just as it requires a 'strong' ego to adjust appropriately to the demands of life in society, and a 'weak' ego often produces aggressive or defensive behavior, strong states are those which can accommodate and respond to popular demands while weak states attempt to ignore or suppress such demands."[28] African states, therefore, are "soft" in that their capacity to elicit societal acquiescence to their actions is severely limited. And while "softness" leads at times to harsh policies *vis-à-vis* their societies, this harshness is best seen as a product, rather than a repudiation, of that "softness."

Having concluded that the states of sub-Saharan Africa are marked primarily by the weakness of their institutional capacities, we are left with another apparent paradox: how to account for the survival, indeed the remarkable resilience, of these "soft states"? The phoenix-like Chadian state, which has managed more than once in the years since independence to re-emerge from the scattered remnants of its own ashes, presents perhaps the best example of this resilience. Despite its "weakness" and its "softness," and although it is of alien origin with only tenuous ties to the society in which it is located, the African state remains "the most prominent landmark on the African institutional landscape, ... project[ing] upwards from its surroundings like a veritable Kilimanjaro."[29]

A highly persuasive explanation for this apparent paradox has been elaborated by Robert Jackson and Carl Rosberg.[30] Their analysis is founded on a distinction between two aspects of statehood, which they label the "empirical" and the "juridical." Few African states, they note, can meet the requirements of an empirical definition of statehood such as the Weberian one. Since, in their view, the elements of such definitions are the required conditions for statehood to be sustained *internally*, these two authors look elsewhere to explain the persistence of African states. They thus posit the centrality of the "juridical" aspect of statehood, which is predicated on membership in the international state system. Territory and independence are the required attributes for juridical statehood and, as Jackson and Rosberg demonstrate, these are also sufficient attributes; "Even the most profound socioeconomic inadequacies of some countries are not considered to be a barrier to their membership" in the international system which recognizes their statehood.[31] African states, in their view, have been able to persist and survive primarily as a result of the juridical aspect of their statehood, that is, of their external relations.

In light of this consideration, there is a need to add a qualification to the definition of the state proposed above. The persistence of the state – that is of the interrelated set of organizations attempting to assert its hegemony over other societal actors – is in the extreme case simply a function of its ability to successfully lay claim to juridical statehood in terms of international recognition as the legitimate representative organ of an independent territorial unit. For the former colonies of sub-Saharan Africa juridical statehood has been assured from independence by entry into the joint systems of the United Nations and the Organization of African Unity. Empirical statehood, in the sense of meeting the definitional criteria proposed by Weber and others, may or may not accompany it.

This situation is a unique phenomenon of the modern state system, and its departure from the model followed by the European states which created that system must be emphasized. As Jackson and Rosberg note, empirical statehood in Europe generally preceded or was concurrent with juridical statehood.[32] The former was, in fact, most often a necessary prerequisite for the latter. By contrast, in the post-Second World War period in which the African states came into existence, the situation was reversed. Colonies were granted independence, and hence achieved juridical statehood, without the prior establishment of the requisite basis for dominance over their societies. The politics of "nation-building" in Africa, however one chooses to define that controversial term, are clearly not analogous to the historical processes by which European nation-states came into existence.[33] Indeed, the process is largely reversed; the independent countries of sub-Saharan Africa face the prospect of creating viable "nations," however defined, within the context of a statehood – in the sense of independent territorial integrity – guaranteed a priori by the international system. While African states have clearly been modified and influenced by the history of interactions with the rapidly changing societies which they have in turn helped to transform, they do not depend for survival on foundations anchored in society. States may of course collapse, as the tragic examples of Liberia and Somalia have recently shown. But the important fact is that they do not consequently disappear; the re-emergence of these states as juridical entities is virtually assured by the international system, regardless of their empirical status. African states thus present prototypical examples of what Jackson has more recently termed "quasi-states."[34]

The disjuncture between juridical and empirical statehood leaves a "gap," an open political space that lies between the state in its juridical reality and a society which can only be incorporated into the state through the construction of the structures that define empirical statehood. It is within this space that the "quest for state hardness" and the "hegemonic search" of African states must be understood; the "autocratic and hegemonical impulses which were the more enduring legacy of the colonial state"[35] are nothing less than the attempt by the state to close that gap. African states, that is, have been engaged at least since independence in an ongoing attempt to forge an empirical reality commensurate with the juridical one. In this effort, the state attempts to fill the gap by occupying all "political space," an endeavor which brings it into direct confrontation with societal institutions.

The paradigm of "state-society struggle," to borrow Thomas Callaghy's phrase, thus provides a useful point of departure from which to approach the politics of sub-Saharan Africa in the post-independence period.[36] If at times the analytic distinction between state and society seems an artificially created dichotomy in the context of those countries whose existence had been well established by the time of the Second World War, it is a useful, and indeed necessary, distinction in the context of the colonial entities that achieved the status of independent states in the post-war world.[37] Although (as we shall see in chapter 3) there are important ambiguities in defining boundaries in any specific case, state and society in Africa *do* stand in opposition to each other. The state as "ruling organization" attempts to dominate society and ensure its compliance, and societal groups struggle to resist that domination or shape it to their own advantage.[38]

African societies: the power of weakness

The attempts by African states to achieve "domination," "hardness," or "hegemony" – broadly comparable to what earlier authors had referred to as "state-building efforts" – have received the bulk of scholarly attention in the study of African politics. More recently, however, the state-society paradigm has focused attention on the societal side of the equation. The result has been a new understanding of the ways in which African societies have attempted to deal with the state's hegemonic drive. Despite the apparent weaknesses of those societies, sources of strength have been identified in the power to thwart state actions and derail state initiatives.

African societies are generally weak and poor, frequently miserably so.

Bratton has suggested that they are weak *because* they are poor. The organization of "associational life," he argues, "is likely to be most developed in economies that have undergone the greatest degree of indigenous capitalist industrialization." This is so because it is in such contexts that one finds "the highest rates of domestic capital accumulation outside of the state."[39] An independent economic base is central in defining the capacity for effective societal organization. The problems presented to the articulation of effective organizations by endemic societal poverty are further compounded by the multiple cleavages and centrifugal forces that fracture the populations of African countries. The multiplicity of ethnic groupings within the arbitrarily defined boundaries of African states and the pervasiveness of ethnically based conflict in many countries are too well known to require elaboration here. In many cases religious differences have exacerbated those conflicts. In addition, the predominance of patronage networks, known as "clans" in Senegal, has tended to create vertical social cleavages that hinder the organization of groups sharing common class interests. Faced with these difficulties, strong societal organizations capable of constituting effective African civil societies have failed to emerge in most countries.

The term "civil society," found all too frequently in current usage as a simple synonym for "society," requires a more precise definition if it is to be of analytical utility in discussing state-society relations. At its broadest, "civil society" might be understood as "a bevy of institutions for protecting collective interests,"[40] thus implying some degree of societal organization. A more precise definition, however, must also include a statement of its relation to the state. This has been stressed by scholars who define civil society as "society in its relations with the state ... in so far as it is in confrontation with the state."[41] In light of these considerations, I adopt here the definition proposed by Patrick Chabal: *"Civil society is a vast ensemble of constantly changing groups and individuals whose only common ground is their being outside the state and who have ... acquired some consciousness of their externality and opposition to the state."*[42] Understood in this way, African societies have tended to be ineffectual counterbalances to African states due to the weakness of their *civil* societies; the failure or inability of social groups to organize in such a way as to defend and promote their interests has often crippled their ability to counter the state's hegemonic drives.

Ironically, however, this very fragmentation has often also protected society from the state. The lack of organization which has made societies relatively weak also makes it difficult for states to enforce the rules for social and economic interactions. As a result not only peasants, but also the swelling urban populations of Africa, have remained "uncaptured" by state initiatives.[43] Notably in the economic realm African populations have increasingly managed to escape state efforts at control; parallel ("black") markets are widespread throughout the continent and sometimes far more vibrant and active than official markets.[44] In this context of fragmentation states might be tempted to attempt the creation of corporatist structures as a means of asserting control over society.[45] Almost without exception, however, such efforts have failed, at least in part subverted by societal responses.

While African societies are weak and fragmented, this weakness is not translated into total passivity; faced with state actions, social groups react. The myriad of subtle techniques, brilliantly described by James Scott, which Malaysian peasants have used to evade and resist the actions of the state are available in various forms to peasant societies everywhere.[46] In a similar vein, Nathan Brown's depiction of the Egyptian peasantry's history of resistance to the state also provides a model for sub-Saharan societies.[47] Jean-François Bayart has rightly insisted on the need to consider the "popular modes of political action" through which African societies exact their "revenge" on the state. "There is a long list," he writes, "of popular practices that limit and relativize the state's domain, thus also assuring society a degree of revenge over it and contributing to its economic failure."[48] The state's hegemonic search – its attempts to bridge the gap between its juridical and empirical statehood – meets with society-based efforts to influence the dimensions of those bridges, undermine their foundations, or even at times use them to their own advantage. It is important to note, therefore, that in contrast to the view that might be suggested by the metaphors of "struggle" or "balance" between state and society, the weakness of one side does not always imply the strength of the other; state-society relations are not necessarily a zero-sum game. Weak civil societies, in fact, are likely to coexist with weak states. Where social groups are amorphous and ill-formed, states are unlikely to be able to institute binding rules for their interaction.

Noting the "dialectic of attraction and repulsion"[49] which characterizes African societies in their confrontation with the state, most attempts to model state-society relations from the societal perspective have been dichotomous. Societies are depicted as attempting either to flee the state or to challenge it.[50] The most fully developed of these models of societal responses to the state is that proposed by Naomi Chazan and Victor Azarya. These scholars have suggested a variety of activities which social groups undertake in response to the state, and which they group into two modal types under the rubrics of "disengagement" and "incorporation." Social groups can choose to either "disengage" by "exiting" from the state arena – parallel market activities or even emigration being the most obvious examples of such options – or they can choose to "incorporate," that is to "associate with the state and take part in its activities in order to share its resources."[51]

This bivariate typology has provided a useful point of departure for the analysis of the societal side of state-society relations. The model, however, also has some significant shortcomings. While "disengagement" is rather easily identified as a discrete pattern of societal response to the state, the notion of "incorporation" appears overly inclusive and consequently of limited utility as an analytic category. Bratton has also critiqued the term "incorporation" for its semantic connotations, and has suggested that it be replaced with the term "engagement."[52] Even with this modification, however, the Azarya and Chazan model offers no distinction between complementary engagement, and engagement characterized by societal "struggle" with the state, in the sense of attempting to shape the state or directly challenge state-sponsored initiatives. It does not distinguish, that is, between cooperation and contestation in societal responses to the state.

In light of these considerations, in this work I propose to use a framework that allows us to distinguish analytically between *three* modal types of societal responses to state actions. These three types of reactions by social groups to the initiatives undertaken by the African state in its hegemonic search can be labeled (1) isolation, (2) engagement, and (3) contestation. "Isolation" covers that range of activities which society can undertake in order to distance itself from the state; it thus overlaps broadly with Azarya and Chazan's concept of "disengagement." In choosing isolation, social groups are refusing to acknowledge the "rules of the game" concerning societal interactions which the state attempts to impose. It may, in fact, signal a refusal to play the game at all. "Engagement" refers to those types of state-society interactions which might be considered complementary. It signals the willingness of social groups to deal with the state in playing within the established rules of the game. Finally, "contestation" includes the confrontational elements of society-based struggle with the state. Social groups contest the state when they challenge the rules of the game which it attempts to impose and endeavor to change or invalidate those rules. While it may at times be difficult to empirically categorize particular societal activities in this schema – social groups may simultaneously play a game and attempt to change the rules – the analytic distinction among these ideal types allows for a more nuanced consideration of state-society relations that can be of use in the comparative analysis of variations in such relations among states.

In the study of a particular case, therefore, a series of questions arise: How capable are social groups of pursuing a given pattern of relations? Which pattern of societal reaction is most important or dominant in a given country? That is, how effective is a particular "mode of political action" in allowing society as a whole or a single social group to either isolate itself from, engage with, or contest the initiatives of the state? What is the degree and type of social organization – that is, the nature of civil society – in a given country and how does this contribute to the establishment of a given mode of state-society interactions? And under what conditions can a stable pattern of engagement emerge and be maintained?

On the basis of the analysis of the Senegalese case, I suggest that a stable political system requires, by definition, the predominance of engagement as the principal mode of state-society interaction. Maintaining engagement requires, however, both an effective civil society and a relative balance of power between state and society. While the potential for state power is inherent in the guarantee of survival derived from the juridical aspect of statehood, societal power *vis-à-vis* the state can only result from a credible potential for opting to pursue alternative responses to state initiatives by either challenging them or shielding itself from them. Long-term "engagement," that is, can only be maintained if significant social actors can demonstrate their capability to either "isolate" themselves from the state or "contest" its activities, or both. This potential, in turn, lies in the relative strength of civil society – in the degree of organization and the resources available to social groups that stand outside the state and in opposition to it. The state, for its part, draws strength from the potential to directly engage social groups politically; strong societies can produce strong states, and the engagement of the two provides the necessary conditions for the establishment of a stable political order. The central question in this work, therefore, is the extent to which Senegalese society has been able to counteract state initiatives by the threat of choosing one of these types of response.

As in any political system, the potential for all three types of societal responses to state activities exists in Muslim countries. My concern is with exploring the role that Islam has played in the articulation of such responses in the Senegalese case. This role is rooted in the multifaceted potential political impact of religion in its various aspects. While much of the political impact of Islam in Senegal is a function of the specific local manifestations of religion, these draw on, intersect, and at times contradict broader political themes derived from religious considerations across the Muslim world. An adequate explanation must therefore distinguish theoretically between each of these various aspects of religion.

Islam between state and society

Nearly four hundred pages into a book devoted to a discussion of "the politics of Islam," Edward Mortimer turns to his conclusion under the surprising title, "What is Islam?"[53] The question is not simply rhetorical; its seemingly belated position is in fact intentionally provocative. Indeed, it mirrors the development of the recent literature on Islam, in which the attempt to define the object of study has only followed a bewildering array of works devoted to it. To speak of "Islam and politics," and to attempt to uncover "the political role of Islam," is to imply that there exists a uniform and consistent set of beliefs which is common to all (or at least most) Muslim societies and that guides the actions of individuals in those societies. Yet it is far from clear that this assumption is valid, and as scholars have attempted to distill the essence of Islam from the analysis of different Muslim societies its validity has increasingly been questioned.

The range of positions in the resulting debate might perhaps best be conceived of as a continuum. At one extreme lies the argument that there does indeed exist a historic Islamic "essence," a core set of beliefs and practices shared by all Muslims everywhere, and thus that it is possible to isolate and identify characteristically "Islamic" modes of behavior. At the other end of the spectrum lie scholars who stress the diversity and randomness of cultures and of forms of social and political behavior found among societies labeled "Muslim." "Islam" for these scholars thus becomes virtually meaningless as a category for social analysis, and some have preferred instead to speak of "islams," thus denoting semantically the diversity of Muslim practices and the pre-eminence of none.[54] In theological and theoretical terms any Muslim society will share traits with others that can be identified as "Islamic." These traits are rooted in the shared symbols and texts of all Muslim societies, and reinforced by the existence of a broader Muslim community engaged in a dialogue, a discourse that is uniquely Muslim.[55] At the same time each Muslim society is distinct from all others in terms of which Islamic traits it embodies, how these have been modified in the adaptation to local situations, and the extent to which they are salient in the local context. And because local structures are an important part of the determinants of the political role of religion in the Muslim world, the "islams" approach has been proposed as a corrective to the excessive abstraction of earlier "essentialist" studies. While there is, of course, some validity to each of these perspectives – there are both similarities and differences among Muslim societies – the inconclusive debate has been driven in large part by the overly inclusive use of the term "Islam" to connote both the shared traits and the unique ones.

The complexity of defining Islam as a conceptual category for political analysis might best be dealt with by distinguishing between three aspects of Islam. Islam presents, first of all, a theology – a system for explaining man's relationship to the metaphysical and for assigning meaning to human lives. While it is this aspect of Islam that is no doubt most frequently central to individual Muslims, its political importance is limited to its influence on the second aspect, and I consequently devote relatively little attention to theology in this work. Secondly, Islam incorporates the fundamentals of an ideology, Islam draws most significantly on the set of commonalities that are shared by all Muslim societies – the notion of an Islamic socio-political ideology, Islam draws most significantly on the set of commonalties that are shared by all Muslim societies – the notion of an Islamic socio-political "blueprint" and the scriptural sources for defining it, sometimes referred to collectively as the "great tradition." Finally, Islam can be understood as a framework for social organization; it provides a basis for the establishment of the institutions which structure societies. These, however, vary widely across the Muslim world as they have been adapted to local histories, traditions, and economies. It is the numerous local manifestations of this aspect of Islam, representing the "little tradition" of individual communities, that some have suggested might best be described by the term "islams." Both of these facets of Islam – the ideological dimension and the framework for societal organization – play a role in the politics of state-society relations.

Ideology and the "great tradition"

Taking their cue, perhaps, from the normative writings of Muslim thinkers who have been concerned throughout the centuries with the formulation of the appropriately Islamic approach to political and social issues – and with critiquing deviations from it – contemporary students of Islam and politics have tended to cluster at the "essentialist" end of the spectrum.[56] In the most extreme form of the argument even the differences among sects and legal schools are ignored. Thus Daniel Pipes writes: "Mainstream Muslims (that is, Muslims whose faith is acknowledged as valid by a majority of other Muslims) follow legal tenets so similar to each other that their differences can be ignored." In addition, he notes, there is a specifically Muslim "script for political action" that is "so detailed, so nuanced, it requires a lifetime of study to master." Consequently, "the mere fact of adherence to Islam has profound political consequences."[57] In this view, therefore, the key to an understanding of the role of Islam in politics, presumably across the Muslim world, lies in an analysis of the content of the essential Islamic "script."

Few analysts adopt such a thoroughly essentialist posture, no doubt due to the fact that even a cursory empirical overview of the Muslim world contradicts its central tenet. Still, an essentialist streak characterizes much discussion of Islam. This is tellingly reflected in the amount of attention devoted in many studies to early Islamic history – most frequently in the highly idealized form that has served as the central referent for much of

Islamic political thought – and which is intended to serve as a springboard for analyzing contemporary Islamic political movements.[58] The argument is that the essential core of Islam, including its political role, was formed during this period and that this core has come down to the present largely intact. Thus, for example, John Esposito notes that Islamic jurisprudence had "by the end of the ninth century produced a detailed, systematic body of law that provided the established blueprint for Islamic state and society throughout subsequent centuries."[59]

Such scholars are certainly correct in acknowledging the weight of history and in pointing to the existence of a blueprint – or more accurately to the widespread consensus among Muslims that there exists an Islamic blueprint – and to its relevance to contemporary Islamic political movements. Muslim political discourse is replete with references to the ideal past, and there can be said to exist an Islamic "essence" at least in the sense that Muslims regularly refer to it in the formulation of political rhetoric. Within Muslim discourse we find constant reference to such concepts as "Islamic government," "Islamic economics," or "Islamic social order." And while there is virtually no agreement on the specific practical shape of any of these concepts, there is nonetheless widespread agreement on their relevance. Consequently, much of Islamic political thought has been characterized by attempts to define these concepts in terms of an ideal and describe a system for their implementation.[60] The ideological powers of Islam are built on the premise of an essential Islamic core.

The cornerstone of this essential core lies in the shared belief in the fundamental unity of the Muslim world. This perception is rooted in the concept of the *umma*, the community of believers within the *dar al-Islam* (the land of Islam) who together stand in opposition to the outside *dar al-harb* (the land of war). No even marginally alert observer, of course, whether within or outside the Muslim world, can accept this myth of community at face value. Muslims, historically and in the contemporary world, have been no kinder to each other than any other human groupings. Yet this does not belie the deep sense of belonging to a larger community felt by many Muslims, as indicated by the manner in which events in one part of that community reverberate throughout the whole. No political activity carried out in the name of Islam occurs in isolation; rather the entire Muslim world is implicated in such action. Thus even in far-away Senegal, for example, one occasionally finds portraits of the Ayatollah Khomeini interspersed with the omnipresent ones of local marabouts. Yet when asked, the owners of such portraits rarely (if ever) display any knowledge of – much less any sympathy for – either Shi'ism or Khomeini's political agenda. He is simply recognized as a "great man of Islam" and his portrait thus serves as a symbolic reminder of membership in the *umma*.[61]

This sense of belonging is reinforced by the common use of Arabic as the language of prayer and religious learning, as well as by the shared texts of Islam, the Qur'an and the *hadiths* – the collections of traditions concerning the prophet's life – which together provide the basis for the legal code known as the *shari'a*. In addition the *hajj*, the pilgrimage to Mecca that constitutes one of the fundamental duties ("pillars") of those who can afford it, brings together Muslims from all over the world in a shared ritual that helps to reinforce the sense of community. Radical transformations in the technologies of communication and transportation in the last several decades have gone even further to expand and deepen contacts within the Muslim world. Air travel has greatly increased the numbers of pilgrims on the *hajj*, and the masses for whom this is still well out of reach are provided with images of the pilgrimage on television, or at least hear accounts of it on the radio. In a poor country like Senegal, far from the holy cities, only a small percentage of the population ever completes the pilgrimage. But the diffusion effect is nevertheless quite significant given the coverage of the event in the national media. The frequently mythical nature of the idealized *umma* does not negate participation in its concrete manifestations.

Concurrent with this sense of belonging to a larger world community, and inherent in the very status of being Muslim, is a conviction that there exists an identifiable Islamic essence with relevance to the organization of individual and social life. This premise of direct relevance to social and political life is a (perhaps *the*) central component of the ideological powers of Islam. The standard observation, made by virtually every student of Muslim societies, concerning the lack of theoretical (or theological) distinction between the religious and the political in Islam bears emphasizing. To the outside observer the Prophet was the founder of both a religion and a state, but from within there is no distinction between the two. Thus we find no injunction to segregate what is Caesar's and what is God's; everything belongs to God, and Caesar is the executor of his will. As I have suggested above, it is the wide *agreement* that this is an essential component of Islam, rather than any particular aspect of Islam *per se*, which is a crucially important factor for the analysis of Islam as an ideological force in politics. Because of this shared belief, and independently of any inherent characteristics of Islam itself, religion becomes central to the political life of Muslim societies.

Difficulties arise, however, when analysts of Muslim societies attempt to develop a method for deciphering the essence and isolating and identifying its impact on the social and political behavior of Muslims. As I have argued, the crucial variable is not the essence itself – which proves on close inspection to be rather amorphous, even mythic – but rather the fact of a widespread consensus among Muslims about the existence of an essence.

Failure to recognize this distinction has led to a notable dearth of theoretical frameworks with which to approach the question of Islam as an ideological force. Since an analysis of even a few cases frustrates any attempt to identify a single Islamic pattern of politics, scholars have tended to define a "true" or "valid" Islamic political role, look for elements of it in various different cases, and then explain deviations from the "legitimately" Islamic pattern as the product of non-Islamic factors. The implication, therefore, is that Islam has a specific political role to play, but that other factors sometimes (perhaps frequently) distort it.

This approach has not only proven ineffectual, but it is dangerously misleading because it has the potential for involving the analyst in unanswerable normative debates. John Esposito, in the preface to a book rich in the presentation of case studies but lacking a substantive theoretical framework, grapples with the question: "How does one distinguish between genuine Islamic practice and the calculated manipulation or misguided use of religion in politics to achieve questionable political goals?"[62] The answer, it seems to me, (and assuming that one is functioning as a social scientist and not as a Muslim theoretician) is that one does not. This is not to say, of course, that one can ignore either the fact that sincere Muslim thinkers do strive constantly to distinguish the genuine from the misguided, or that conflict frequently arises from competing claims to the authority to define the truly Islamic. But from the perspective of the social scientist surely "calculated manipulation," to the extent that it is coherent and potentially effective, is as interesting to consider as "genuine practice" in the analysis of the political importance of Islam. In the effort to understand the political role of Islam we must attempt to delineate not the "true" or "valid" place of religion, but rather how its ideological potential is used in practice. As with any ideology, Islam's political powers are rooted in such characteristics as the potential for setting agendas, providing the structures that shape collective action and the vocabulary that legitimizes it, and serving to mobilize people for such action.

Because Islamic theology is held to be central to Islamic social life, and because certain aspects of that social life are given pre-eminence in the theology, the agenda-setting function is one of the fundamental political powers of Islam as ideology. In addition, because Islam is held to offer an entire social blueprint, there is an implicit possibility for establishing an appropriately Islamic preference ordering for the implementation of the political agenda. This is most strikingly apparent in explicitly Islamic social movements. Emmanuel Sivan, for example, in discussing "radical" twentieth century Muslim activists, notes that "the radicals set the issues and the terms with which they are discussed. All other social forces have to react to them."[63]

But the agenda-setting power of Islam is no less significant in less "radical" settings. Thus a comparative look at various Muslim countries reveals a variety of issues that tend to become politicized and debated largely in Muslim terms within those societies. Prime among these are aspects of family law (questions of polygamous marriage, rights of divorce, birth control and reproduction, and inheritance), a domain which, as we shall see in chapter 6, has been important in defining the relations between the religious and the political elite in Senegal. Significant debates also tend to arise on issues concerning criminal law (the nature of punishments, trial systems, and questions of acceptability of witnesses and evidence) and the economic system, notably related to banking practices (given the Qur'anic injunction against charging interest) and to state taxation and its relation to the obligatory duty cf the tithe or alms tax called the *zakat*.

In addition to setting political agendas and serving to politicize particular aspects of social life, the agreement on the existence of a theologically prescribed social "blueprint" renders Islam a monistic ideology of impressive mobilizational potential. Ali Merad, in exploring the "ideologisation" of Islam, argues that this strength is rooted directly in the concept of Islam as both religion and state: "Such a concept leads naturally to the formulation of doctrines of power in modern Muslim societies whose primary frame of reference is Islam. Here the meaning of Islam as a fundamental ideological frame of reference must be explicitly explained. By 'Islam' it is essentially understood that it is not only a system of religious beliefs, but also a set of principles which should guide the general organization of the community."[64] Following this argument, therefore, Islam is uniquely poised to lend itself to transformation from a theology to an ideology capable of serving the mobilizational interests of political activists. It is thus Islam *qua* ideology, rather than theology, that lies most often at the heart of Islamic political movements. Discussing Muslim fundamentalists, whom he characterizes as "activists with scriptural shibboleths," Lawrence argues that "[t]hey espouse an ideology but not a theology."[65] Yet because Islam as ideology is most frequently presented wrapped in the mantle of theology, it not only presents a set of political and social ideas to direct action, but it links them to the transcendental. As such it is a singularly powerful mobilizational instrument.

Islam, then, sets agendas, provides the rhetoric for the formulation of ideological movements, and serves as a force for mobilizing people in the pursuit of goals defined by those movements. This is facilitated – indeed it is made possible – by the broad consensus within Muslim societies on the existence of an Islamic blueprint for social and political life. But, as I have suggested above, this sword has another edge. While there is agreement on the *existence* of a blueprint, the specific outlines of that blueprint are far from clear and thus there is no broad agreement on its implementation. Islam, therefore, can also be a significant divisive force in that it politicizes many aspects of society for which it ultimately provides no uncontested resolution. Competing claims to the authority to interpret the "reality" of Islam are the very stuff of much political debate within the Muslim world. "Whose Islam?" asks Esposito, and indeed that is the question with which Muslims must contend. "Who is to interpret the role of Islam and its place in state and society – rulers such as Sadat, Khomeini, or Qaddafi, religious leaders, or Islamic organizations?"[66] The study of the ideological dimension of Islam in politics, therefore, must be focused not on the question of what political role is inherent in Islam, but rather on how Muslims have attempted to implement political choices derived from Islam or justified by recourse to it, and debated them in Islamic terms.

Most centrally to the concerns of this work, in what ways might the "great tradition" of Islam influence the politics of relations between states and societies? As an ideology, Islam provides a vocabulary that can serve the goals of both state and society in their interactions with each other. States have frequently attempted to legitimate their rule, and justify particular actions, by appeals to Islam. Social groups, for their part, have often been mobilized in opposition to the state by appeals made in the name of Islam. Islam, as Jean-Claude Vatin notes in the case of Algeria, is "the language of both power and resistance to power."[67] The issues of legitimacy and political accountability have been intensely scrutinized through the prism of Muslim political theories concerning the appropriate qualities of an Islamic ruler and the nature of the desirable relations between ruler and people. In practical terms these often translate into debates about the need for, or the role of, a consultative body or legislature and about the relationship of the ruler with the ʿulama, the class of religious scholars.

Debates about legitimacy and accountability have consequently been central to political life in Muslim countries; some have argued that they are, in fact, "the themes of contemporary Islamic political activism."[68] In the terminology proposed above these can be described as ideological debates about the parameters of "engagement" between state and society. Most importantly, the consensus among Muslim thinkers has endorsed the need for engagement – within the appropriate limits; there exists an important body of Islamic literature about the duties and responsibilities of cooperation between just leaders and good Muslims. Islam has also, however, provided a basis for the articulation of an ideology to support the "isolationist" and "contestatory" patterns of societal responses to the state.

Emulating the example of the Prophet when he fled his native city of Mecca to settle in Medina, where his message fell on more fertile ground, one pattern of Muslim response to intolerable state demands has been to retreat from that state. This action, known as *hijra*, has been central to the political thought of Muslim intellectuals throughout Islamic history.[69] As articulated in Islamic theology, *hijra* can refer to the literal emigration from one jurisdiction to that of a more amenable sovereign, or it can involve a figurative flight by seeking isolation and non-involvement with state initiatives. *Hijra*, therefore, can lend Islamic legitimacy and hence mobilize people for undertaking the political response of "isolation" from the state.

More well known as an Islamic mode of political action – though probably no more frequent than *hijra* – has been the choice of *jihad*. Frequently translated as "holy war," the verbal root of the Arabic word means more literally "to struggle." As another central concept in Islamic political thought, the precise meaning of *jihad* – notably the extent to which it refers to physical struggle or war – has been much debated among Muslim scholars. But in the ideological domain of Islam social groups regularly resort to the term as an inducement and a legitimation for challenging political authority. *Jihad* can, and frequently does, serve to legitimate the actions of social groups who seek to "contest" the state.

In choosing isolation or contestation in their reactions to states deemed undesirable, Muslim societies have regularly had recourse to options expressed in these Islamic terms. In nineteenth-century India, for example, Muslim groups depicted the alternatives for resisting British rule as a choice between *jihad* and *hijra*, in either the literal or the figurative sense. And Muslim responses reflected the perception of these options: "some Muslims emigrated to Muslim territories, a greater number joined *jihad* movements ... [and] the majority of traditionalists advocated a policy of cultural isolation: withdrawal and non-cooperation."[70] Closer to the geographic focus of this book, Muslim responses to the nineteenth-century imperial expansion of the French into the area between the Senegal and Niger rivers were also at times cast as a choice between these two responses. Threatened by the French incursion at a time when he was still attempting to consolidate the gains of the religious reformist campaign and wars of conquest he had waged in the area, the Muslim leader El Hajj Umar Tall responded by "adding the weapon of *hijra* to the arsenal of *jihad*."[71] The debate about which of these options should be pursued was to continue with El Hajj Umar's successor, and played a crucial role in shaping the subsequent history of the region. Building on these concepts, Islam as ideology provides a basis for the articulation of both isolation and contestation as societal responses to the state across the Muslim world.

The opposition between state and society has frequently provided a basis for politicizing Islam across the Muslim world and throughout Islamic history. I have noted above the argument that political legitimacy and political accountability are themes that run through Islamic political thought. "These themes," the same scholars argue, "are manifested on two levels: in the efforts of various regimes to legitimate their rule officially through Islam; and in the efforts of various popular activist groups to challenge the legitimacy of existing regimes on the grounds of accountability to Islamic codes."[72] Others have noted the same duality: "Islam has been used by various rulers to acquire and sustain legitimacy, or to mobilize masses, in support of particular policy options ... But Islam has also emerged ... as an expression of political opposition and social discontent."[73] Islam as an ideology that is, is used both by states attempting to elicit societal approval and by Muslim societies attempting to shape and limit the character of state actions. Ideology, however, is clearly insufficient to determine political outcomes; the relationship between states and societies in the Muslim world will depend largely on the relative strengths of individual states and of social structures, most notably those specific Islamic social organizations that have developed in a given context and that can be mobilized for collective action. The third aspect of Islam is thus the primary focus of this book.

Social structures and the "little tradition"

The failure of students of Muslim societies to explain the diversity of Islamic political action by recourse to an Islamic essence has led others, as one scholar explains his approach, "to challenge this essentialism, and to argue that the Islamic phenomenon in politics is the product of particular political and socio-economic conjunctures."[74] The Sunni-Shiʿa split, the numerous other sects and splinter groups, as well as differences among legal schools and among Sufi orders, all further complicate the search for a "true" Islam. There are thus significant analytic limits to focusing primarily on the impact of the "great tradition" in explaining any given political outcome, leading some scholars to conclude, as Mortimer has phrased it, that "it is more useful, in politics at any rate, to think about Muslims than to think about Islam."[75] Such scholars tend instead to depart from the empirical analysis of local manifestations of Islam, rather than any theoretical or abstract notions of Islam based on Muslim theology or political thought. Such an approach has highlighted the need to consider the specific Islamic social structures in a given local context in the analysis of Islam and politics.

The "little tradition" of religion in any given community is the result of the historical evolution of social structures borrowed from or rooted in the shared great tradition of Islam, but modified and adapted according to the imperatives of political, economic, and non-religious social factors within the local context. And the contours of a religious society are both shaped by these factors and in turn play a role in shaping them. The relationship is thus both dynamic and dialectical, and the examination of Islam in this sense must be focused on the specific manifestations of religion in a given case.

This third aspect of Islam, its role as a basis for social organization, becomes central to an analysis of state-society relations when we consider how the particular configuration of religious structures in a given country contribute to the patterns of state-society interactions. Here the crucial questions concern how Islamic organizations in their local manifestations affect the incentives for, and the relative effectiveness of, patterns of societal responses to the state. Most significant in this respect are the ways in which indigenous religious structures affect the articulation of a viable civil society, of organized social groups that can represent and protect societal interests vis-à-vis the state by facilitating a range of societal responses to state actions. The most significant variables to consider are thus the relative cohesiveness of religious organizations, the extent to which they aggregate interests and facilitate collective action, and the nature of the resources available to them. There is a need, therefore, to examine closely the internal structure of such organizations, the nature of the relationships both between leaders and followers and among the followers themselves, and the patterns of interaction between religious structures and other societal organizations.

In the case of Senegal the examination of the internal dynamics of the Sufi orders, particularly such aspects as the role of the religious elite known as marabouts and the organization of disciples into local "cells" known as daairas, is the central component of this aspect of the analysis. Much of the discussion in this work will therefore focus on Islam as a system of social organization within the specific context of independent Senegal. And the important questions to be addressed concern the extent to which this system has shaped and influenced societal capabilities to respond to the state along the lines of the three modal types we have discussed.

At the heart of the debate about the political role of Islam is the question of what weight should be given to religion as an autonomous factor in political outcomes. I have argued that there is no single Islamic essence that can serve as an independent variable to explain the outcome of political debates in Muslim societies. My consideration of Islam and politics in Senegal, therefore, proceeds in the opposite direction of many previous analyses.[76] Politics, rather than Islam, is the point of departure; I first identify the nature of the political conflict, then ask how Islam – whether in the broad sense of what is shared by all Muslims or in the narrow sense of specific local history, tradition, and structures – influences political encounters. As the discussion of the Senegalese case will make clear, the role of local Islamic social structures, the nature of leadership and the relations between leaders and followers, the nature and sources of power and authority, and the limits and constraints of the economy are all factors which mediate and direct the impact of Islam on politics.

In addition to a theology, Islam offers the basis for a monistic, and hence powerful, ideology. It is this face of Islam which is emphasized by scholars who attempt to define its essence. Islam is also a basis for social organization. Yet the particular forms of that organization – the local "islam" – have varied widely from one Muslim society to another in accordance with local histories, economies, geography and political structures – including most centrally in the modern world the state itself.[77] An analysis of Islam in politics in any given context, therefore, must consider both the relevance of Islam as ideology found in the "great tradition," and examine the impact of Islam as a basis for social organization reflected in the "little tradition" of that context. We need to ask, therefore, two types of questions: How have universal Islamic themes or concerns of political importance been manifested or submerged in the specific local context? Secondly, how has this context served to transform Islamic social structures or, indeed, to create new ones? And how have those structures interacted with the broader political system in which they are found?

Departing from these theoretical considerations, then, this book seeks to explain the nature of the relationship between state and society in Senegal. In Senegal the central opposition between state and society which characterizes post-colonial African regimes is mediated and negotiated in Islamic terms – and via Islamic structures. In considering the political role of Islam, I focus my attention on how religion both as ideology and, most importantly, as a basis for social organization, serves to influence that relationship. I seek to explore the role of Senegalese Islam in shaping patterns of isolation, engagement, or contestation in the face of state power. The discussion of these patterns thus provides an example of the determinants of state-society relations in an important African case. In addition, for scholars of Islam, the Senegalese case proves especially interesting for exploring how the context of the specific political interaction in question shapes the political role played by Islam. The implications of the case for both of these theoretical concerns are thus central to this work.

2　The structure of society: Fatick in the Senegalese context

Poverty and a legacy of economic decline

Much of the physical presence of the state in Fatick is housed in the remnants of colonial-era optimism and ambition. The *tribunal*, the *préfecture*, and other essential components of local government now occupy the buildings that were once the commercial outposts of French *maisons de commerce* and the more successful of the Lebanese traders and middlemen. This transition in the occupants of the more durable – if today somewhat decrepit – architectural structures in the town reflects symbolically the historical development of its significance. While the original impetus for Fatick's transformation from a Serer village to a small but heterogeneous urban center was provided by the logic of colonial commercial expansion, the town's brief prosperity evaporated with the demise of the colonial economy. Today it is only the presence of the state that justifies Fatick's appearance on maps of Senegalese cities and towns.

Its proximity to the areas of expanding peanut cultivation and its location on the Sine river near the opening into the Saloum estuary placed Fatick in a good position to capitalize on the emerging colonial economy of the second half of the nineteenth century. References to the town in Martin Klein's seminal history of Sine-Saloum during the period of implantation and consolidation of French colonial rule document this rise in its importance. When a French gunboat first dropped anchor at Fatick in March 1849 in pursuit of a trade agreement with the *Buur-Siin,* or King of Sine, it was a simple "village on the Sine river that was becoming commercially important." Ten years later, dissatisfied with the state of trading relations and wary of British expansionism from the Gambia, governor Louis Faidherbe undertook to exert French hegemony over the region and, after a battle there against the forces of the Buur-Siin, the French burned Fatick. The village was rebuilt and continued to develop as a commercial center, in spite of the disruptions caused by the religious wars waged by Ma Ba Diakhou, a Tukulor Tijan marabout whose armies dominated the region from the early 1860s until his death in battle in 1867.

By 1871, Klein reports, Fatick had surpassed the important coastal town of Joal in the volume of trade handled. Despite the fragility of the French protectorate, commerce expanded over the next two decades. "Factories", or trading posts, were maintained in Fatick by four of the most important French commercial houses operating in West Africa: Maurel et Prom, Maurel Frères, Buhan et Teisseire, and the Compagnie du Sénégal et de la Côte Occidentale d'Afrique (precursor to the famous CFAO, the Compagnie Française de l'Afrique Occidentale).[1]

This relative prosperity was built, improbably enough, on peanuts. Senegal's poor sandy soils and short rainy season limit the possibilities for much commercial agriculture, but are particularly well suited to peanut production. The French encouraged this production, particularly after 1857 when a functional industrial system for extracting the edible oil was developed in Bordeaux – a city that was to remain the metropolitan center of colonial trade with West Africa. The imposition of head taxes as populations came under direct colonial rule made peanut cultivation virtually compulsory, no other source being available for procuring the required cash. In the regions of Sine and Saloum production grew swiftly, and ports like Fatick rose up to handle the resulting trade. French trading companies worked with Lebanese middlemen to organize the export of peanuts for processing in Bordeaux or Marseille, and in return provided consumer items – textiles, perfumes, soap and other household goods – for sale to the newly capitalized peasantry.[2] Around these exchanges villages were transformed into towns.

In the 1880s the French completed the construction of a railroad across the state of Cayor, linking Dakar with the city of St. Louis at the mouth of the Senegal river. Encouraged by the expansion of peanut cultivation that resulted from the increased facility of exporting the crop from the region, a more ambitious project to link the coast with Bamako in the Soudan (today's Mali) was launched after the turn of the century. Construction began in 1906, and by 1915 the railroad reached as far as the town of Tambacounda, at the eastern limit of Senegal's peanut basin. Again the project resulted in a dramatic expansion in the volume of peanut exports. While in 1895 only 8,000 tons had been exported from the region, that amount jumped to 40,000 in 1909 and more than doubled again by 1914 to reach 100,000 tons. From there it continued to expand so that by the 1930s Sine-Saloum exported an average of 250,000 tons of peanuts a year.[3] The railroad, however, also shifted the geographic patterns of trade, thus initiating the decline of Fatick as a commercial center. Bypassed by the railroad, which served instead the rival town of Kaolack on the Saloum river some forty kilometers to the east, Fatick found itself unable to compete. As Kaolack expanded to become a busy commercial center and Senegal's second largest city, Fatick entered a period of slow decline.[4] The trend accelerated at independence, when the reorganization of the peanut marketing trade to consolidate control in the hands of the state eliminated the final vestiges of this commerce which remained in Fatick.[5]

Today only some decaying pilings arranged across the sand flats and shallow water mark the location of the wharves that once managed Fatick's trade. Years of periodic drought have resulted in the virtual disappearance of the small source that fed the Sine river; what remains today at Fatick is in fact a false river, an ocean inlet whose brackish water is subject to tidal fluctuations. And because efforts to dredge it have long been abandoned, only the occasional small pirogue can navigate as far as Fatick. An old Serer fisherman who uses one such pirogue to bring clam shells from nearby coastal islands for use in local construction represents virtually the only economic activity taking place today on the sandy stretches between the ruined wharves and the handful of abandoned buildings and non-functioning factories that line the river.

Fatick, however, is not dead. Moving away from the river to the main paved street that runs through the center of town, the level of activity increases significantly. Particularly on Sundays, when people on foot or in carts drawn by horses and donkeys stream in from surrounding villages for the *marché hebdomadaire*, the central market carries on an active trade. Few luxuries are available, and most of the commerce is simply in small quantities of the basic necessities of life, but its role as a marketing center for the surrounding region plays an important part in Fatick's economic survival. A new bakery opened in late 1989 by a Lebanese businessman from Kaolack competes with the two other established bakeries, and together they comprise virtually the only secondary sector economic activity a step above the artisanal level of the various small shops run by carpenters, smiths and jewelers. Most of these are located in the central area whose French name, "Escale," recalls its origins as a trade depot. Moving away from Escale toward the road to Kaolack a gas station and a few small shops and food sellers circle the large lot known as the *gare routière* where a fleet of diverse vehicles wait to fill up with passengers before departing. Some small-scale vendors mingle with beggars to hawk their wares: fried dough, roasted peanuts, cola nuts, and other items for the traveler. Its role as a transportation hub for the immediate region is also an important element in Fatick's economic survival.

Stretching to the west along the river's edge is Ndiaye-Ndiaye, the largest and oldest of Fatick's neighborhoods. Populated almost exclusively by the Serer, Ndiaye-Ndiaye persists as the legacy of the town's village origins. It is only in this neighborhood that agriculture still remains a significant part of Fatick's economic base. In fields on the outskirts of town millet is cultivated by Serer men, and in the low areas near the river that become swampy during the rainy season women from Ndiaye-Ndiaye grow small plots of rice. Both of these crops today are almost exclusively kept for domestic consumption, and most compounds in Ndiaye-Ndiaye include one or more of the small granaries that resemble miniature versions of the thatched Serer huts. In addition some plots of peanuts are grown, generally by young and otherwise unemployed men in the hopes of generating some cash income.

Petty trade, transportation, and agriculture sustain Fatick at a level just marginally above subsistence, if that. Lacking industry or productive capabilities, anything beyond subsistence can only be the product of economic connections beyond the town's immediate hinterland to the larger centers of the Senegalese economy. The hopes raised by Fatick's elevation to capital of a new region in 1984 hinge on the prospect that the state might be the vehicle through which such connections could be developed. This post-colonial orientation has led Fatick to turn its back on the river and develop instead along the two paved streets that lead from Escale to join the main Dakar-Kaolack road on the northern edge of town.

In the older neighborhood of Ndouk, through which one of these streets passes, most of the houses are constructed in relatively expensive cinder-block and tin. And along the other the presence of the state is slowly making itself more clearly felt. A large *lycée* that draws students from the surrounding areas and brings in salaried teachers to teach them has made Fatick a regional center for secondary education.[6] Nearby construction on a large new *gendarmerie* (police station) and administrative building was begun in late 1989 and completed some three years later, though it still stood empty in 1993. Somewhat further down the road, away from the town center, a new HLM housing complex provides lodgings for many of the teachers as well as other state functionaries who can afford to live there.[7] There are some tentative signs that the salaries paid by the state to these new arrivals are beginning to trickle down through the town's economy. But the effects are still slight, and many are skeptical. The responses of three of the more visible local marabouts to the question of the impact of the new region on Fatick represent the full range of sentiment in the town: one with the closest ties to the state elite insists on the great benefits that becoming a new capital has brought Fatick; another dismisses it as totally insignificant, even disruptive, to date; the third is openly nostalgic for the colonial period, "when things were really good."[8]

These inherent tensions are an important part of the interest of focusing on Fatick in a consideration of issues of state and society in Senegal. No one locale, of course, can be tagged as "typical" of an entire country, perhaps especially so in Africa where societies and economies are marked by such sharp dichotomies as the rural-urban disjuncture. Nevertheless, Fatick captures many of the difficulties and contradictions that mark Senegal in its fourth decade of independence. Linked to both the rural and the urban sectors of the country, Fatick continues to feel the difficulties of the decline of the peanut economy and persistent economic stagnation. The arrival of the state in the form of the administrative apparatus of the new regional government has intensified the ambivalent feelings that everywhere mark Senegalese, indeed African, sentiments about the wielders of political power. Because the state in Africa has consistently served as the locus for capital accumulation, there are on the one hand expectations that access to the state may provide the means to improve one's economic standing. At the same time there coexists a skepticism about the possibilities for securing that access, the formally stated channels being clearly little more than a façade that disguises the real network of relations which determine an individual's chances for success in this endeavor. And for those who find themselves without access, there is always the fear that *they* may serve as the productive source of the capital that is accumulated via the state, or at least that it might have otherwise been disbursed more equitably. With its newly augmented strength in a context of scarcity and decline, the state in Fatick clearly shows both of these faces, determining the ambivalent relations with its society which we will explore in more depth in the next chapter.

The demographic characteristics of that society in Fatick also account for part of its interest. The majority of the population is still Serer, an ethnic group that has been little studied in terms of the issues considered in this work.[9] But like virtually all (even small) urban centers in Senegal, Fatick is an ethnically plural town in which the Wolof influences in particular continue to expand. In the religious domain the town is also varied, in proportions that roughly parallel the composition of Senegal as a whole. This variety is particularly important because, as we shall see in discussing the nature of relations within the Sufi orders, a focus on only one order may prove misleading in generalizing about the functions of Islam in Senegal.

The remainder of this chapter will explore more fully the nature of society and religion in Fatick in the broader context of contemporary Senegal. In providing background information for the subsequent discussion, I also make an effort to provide the reader with the means of evaluating the ways in which Fatick is representative of other areas of the country, as well as how it differs.

Cultural cleavages and their relevance

Like virtually all African countries, cultural pluralism in the form of a diversity of ethnic and linguistic groups is one of the more noteworthy and readily apparent characteristics of Senegalese society. In Senegal, however, these divisions have been far less likely to become politically significant than elsewhere on the continent. Although never absent from socio-political considerations, ethnicity in Senegal has never become the primary mode of political organization at the popular level, and Senegalese elites have not found appeals to ethnic solidarity a productive means of building a mass following.[10]

Social scientists concerned with questions of ethnicity have posited various competing explanations for why ethnic cleavages may emerge as politically salient in certain contexts but not in others. A brief consideration of three possible types of explanations for variations in patterns of ethnic politicization may be a useful point of departure for a discussion of the relative quiescence of these cleavages in Senegal. Early analysts of the newly independent states of Africa and Asia tended to see the patterns of politics in these countries as the result of "primordial sentiments" that arose from "given" attributes of individuals.[11] Politics in such states were thus determined primarily by the nature of those sentiments and their interactions. From this analysis arose the concern about the importance of "nation-building" in the new states; there was a need, that is, to find ways to surpass these primordial sentiments and forge instead a larger, national, sentiment. During the move towards independence, the hope was that nationalist movements and the mass parties which they organized would be the means for achieving this synthesis. But the failure of these movements to maintain their cohesion and effect the transformation of diverse groups into a single national identity after achieving independence rather quickly called into question the assumptions of this model.

In addition, as anthropological and ethnographic studies accumulated, the evident complexity of the determinants of identity challenged the notion of the primacy of any one element. Depending on the situation, individuals can call on different "layers" of identity – linguistic, ethnic, regional, clan, caste or familial, for example – and any one of these can emerge as "primordial" in a given political interaction. Moreover, the fluidity and contextuality of any one of these aspects of identity clearly provides the potential for manipulation, either at the level of the individual or by elites in search of a following.[12] Noting these facts, proponents of a second school of analysis argued that the politicization of ethnic (or other) cleavages must be seen as the product of choices made by individuals attempting to maximize their utility in the pursuit of their individual preferences.[13] In cases where an appeal to ethnicity is the most efficient means for rational individuals to organize so as to maximize their benefits – as, they argue, it is in the context of much of independent Black Africa – such cleavages will become politically central. Should this not be the case, ethnic divisions will remain politically latent.

The importance of historical and institutional forces in determining the parameters of ethnic conflict, in conjunction with the renewed interest in the state as an independent actor in political systems, has recently inspired a third type of explanation for this phenomenon. Finding neither "primordial sentiments" nor "rational action" models convincing as explanations for why ancestral city rather than religion has become the primary political cleavage in Nigerian Yorubaland, David Laitin has recently argued that such cleavages can only be understood in the context of state action. He proposes a model of hegemonic control which he defines as follows: "When a central administration has the motivation and power to structure the pattern of political group formation in society, that administration can be considered to be *hegemonic*."[14] The focus in his approach is thus on the external forces which shape the contexts that give rise to particular patterns of cleavage politicization.

A careful consideration of these three arguments reveals that they need not be seen as mutually exclusive, and can in fact be complementary. Individuals are clearly born into systems within which the range of possible identities is restricted, and socialization serves to imbue them with a sense that certain aspects of their identity are inherent and immutable. People, however, also make choices about the grounds on which they can appeal to others for help, solidarity, or patronage, and such choices serve to determine which aspects of identity become politically salient. At the same time, those choices are made in the context of historically determined structures and institutions that do not depend exclusively on the contemporary actors involved In the consideration of any given case, therefore, as well as for comparative analysis, the crucial consideration is the extent to which these factors are weighted relative to each other, or whether indeed one of them is in itself determinative.

Although it is beyond the scope of this study to attempt a detailed evaluation of the relative importance of these competing models in explaining the Senegalese case, what is most important to note is that factors that mitigate against *all three* proposed reasons for ethnicity to become politicized are clearly present in this case. Numerous cross-cutting cleavages and particularly fluid ethnic boundaries make it difficult to identify "primordial" aspects of identity in Senegal. In addition the French colonial regime, and to a large degree its post-independence heirs, have carefully avoided structuring institutions and policies in such a way as to make ethnic mobilization profitable. For both of these reasons there have been few incentives for rational individuals to organize their political activity around ethnicity.

A fuller exploration of the dimensions of these mitigating factors will emerge from the discussion below, and indeed throughout this study. Given its centrality, however, the issue of the influence of religion in ethnic relations merits a brief consideration here. Because it includes the vast majority of all significant ethnic groups and encompasses well over ninety percent of the total population, it might be argued that Islam is a primary factor in the relative non-politicization of social cleavages in Senegal.[15] Such an argument could be built on a recognition of the importance of the concept of the *umma*, the community of believers, in Islam. Clearly, to varying degrees and depending largely on the individual, common religious affiliation will play a role in defusing the potential for tensions that arise from other social cleavages. For various reasons, however, it is doubtful whether this factor alone can be credited with Senegal's relatively harmonious ethnic relations.

If Islam were to serve as the most fundamental, "primordial," identification of the majority of individuals in Senegal, and hence as the basis for good relations, it should follow as a corollary that cleavages will develop between this group and others who do *not* share this identity. Yet the division between Muslims and the Christian minority in Senegal has never been the basis for political action, despite the fact that the five percent of the population who are Christians are in fact over-represented both in the state and in the modern sectors of the economy. Likewise in social relations caste, or particularly among certain groups ethnicity, are more likely to be seen as impediments to marriage than religious differences. Secondly, focus on the *umma* ignores the very real potential for divisive conflict based on competing interpretations of Islam. In fact, however, possibilities for political divisions exist *within* Senegalese Islam. In addition to the latent potential for mobilization along the lines of affiliation with Sufi orders, which, though rare, occasionally surfaces in particular local contexts, the animosity between the various small and mostly urban groups of reformist Muslims and the religious elite of the Sufi orders attests to these intra-Islamic divisions.

Finally, further dramatic evidence of the insufficiency of Islam to avoid the politicization of ethnic cleavages is provided by the tragic events of April and May 1989 in which the Moorish population of Senegal became the victims of widespread violence against both their property and their persons. The Moors are all Muslims, their role in the Islamization of other Senegalese ethnic groups is widely acknowledged, and several Moorish maraboutic families claim a large following in Senegal. Yet these facts were insufficient to mitigate the animosity that had built up against them and which exploded, ironically enough, during the holy month of Ramadan. An effort to specify the sources of this violence is complicated by various factors, namely the issues of race and citizenship. Many – but by no means all – Moors are light-skinned, and in fact refer to themselves as *beydane*, or "white," in Hassaniya, the Moorish language. In addition the violence in

Senegal took place in the context of similar violent outbursts in its northern neighbor, Mauritania, which has been controlled since independence by its majority Moorish population, frequently to the disadvantage of the black populations of the Senegal river valley, most of whom have kinship connections on the Senegalese side of the river. Although the factors of race and nationality cannot be ignored, the violence must nevertheless be understood primarily as an *ethnic* phenomenon – the most significant exception to Senegal's history of ethnic harmony. Both light and dark-skinned Moors were targeted in the attacks, but no other "white" population was affected – not even the Lebanese community, which is also resented by many Senegalese and which goes by the same name in Wolof (*naar*) as the Moors. Additionally, Moors were attacked regardless of citizenship, while no non-Moorish Mauritanians suffered in the violence on the Senegalese side of these events.

This incidence of ethnic violence remains a rare anomaly, and one that seems highly unlikely to be re-enacted among other ethnic groups in the country. The case nevertheless points to the fact that although ethnic cleavages historically have not been the primary modes of socio-political organization in Senegal, there is still a potential for them to become tragically relevant. And despite the high degree of fluidity in ethnic boundaries, ethnicity regularly plays an important role in many varieties of socio-political interaction. This fluidity is further complicated by another social cleavage, that of caste, which despite its theoretical incompatibility with Islam and with the Westernized "modern" sector has demonstrated a surprising tenacity in remaining central to much of social life. While Senegalese socio-political organization cannot be reduced to the politics of caste or ethnicity, neither of these issues can be ignored in any full account of the Senegalese political system.

Ethnicity: categorization and its difficulties

Depending on how one counts there may be well over twenty indigenous ethnic groups represented in Senegal. The 1988 census questionnaire specified twenty possible responses, but in the reporting of the results related groups have been combined to collapse this diversity into a more manageable seven categories, as shown in Table 2.1.[16]

Of these, three main groups – the Wolof, Serer, and Haalpulaaren, or Pulaar speakers – together comprise over 80 percent of the total population. Of the minor groups only the Diola – who make up 5.5 percent of Senegalese and who are concentrated in the lower Casamance in the southwestern corner of the country – represent over five percent of the total population. Because they tend to be geographically concentrated in specific

Table 2.1. *Senegalese ethnic groups by census categories*

Census reports	Possible responses
Wolof:	Wolof
	Lébou
Haalpulaaren:	Tukulor
	Peul
	Fula
	Laobé
Serer:	Serer
Diola:	Diola
Manding:	Malinké
	Manding
	Socé
Others-Eastern:[a]	Bambara
	Saraxolé/Soninké
	Khassonké
Others:	Balant
	Bassari
	Coniagui
	Mancagne
	Manjaag
	Moor and others

Note:
[a] Refers to ethnic groups concentrated in the eastern parts of Senegal, in particular near the border with The Republic of Mali.

Table 2.2. *Ethnic composition of Senegal and Fatick*

(in percentages)

	Senegal	Fatick
Wolof	43.7	20.4
Haalpulaaren	23.2	12.6
Serer	14.8	58.1
Diola	5.5	1.2
Manding	4.6	1.8
Others-Eastern[a]	3.5	2.3
Others[b]	4.7	3.5
Total	100.0	100.0

Notes:
[a] In Fatick, Bambara and Saraxolé.
[b] In Fatick, includes non-Senegalese (mostly Guineans and Mauritanians).

Table 2.3. *Speakers of principal
Senegalese languages as either a
first or second language*[a]

(in percentages)

	Senegal	Fatick
Wolof	70.9	84.2
Serer	13.7	56.9
Pulaar	24.1	9.4
Other	n.a.	3.9

Note:
[a] The percentages of actual speakers of
these languages are almost certainly
somewhat higher. particularly for Wolof,
since they may be spoken as a third or
even a fourth language.

areas, the smaller ethnic groups are frequently significant in local contexts. But the three main groups, along with the Diola, dominate discussions of ethnicity at the national level. These three groups taken together also include virtually the entirety (91 percent) of Fatick's population, which in 1988 numbered 19,595, including 9,305 (or 47.5 percent) under the age of fifteen. Table 2.2 compares the ethnic breakdown of Fatick with Senegal as a whole.

The Wolof are by far the single largest ethnic group in Senegal – almost 44 percent in 1988 – and one that has been at the same time dominant both culturally and economically and highly amorphous in terms of the delineation of its boundaries.[17] From the perspective of many of Senegal's neighbors (as well as for many people within Senegal), to the extent that a "Senegalese national character" may be said to exist, it is seen first and foremost as a *Wolof* character. Within Senegal, however, answers to the question of who is a Wolof are complicated and highly nebulous.

Historically the Wolof constituted the bulk of the population of a series of states between the Senegal and Gambia rivers, notably Walo, Jolof, Cayor, and Baol, while in neighboring Saloum, and to a much lesser extent in Sine, the Wolof represented significant minorities. Their dominance in the region facilitated the emergence of the Wolof language as a widespread *lingua franca*, and as immigrants and others adopted their language a process of absorbing such groups into Wolof society began. These processes continue today, most strikingly in urban areas. Some 71 percent of Senegalese spoke Wolof as either a first or a second language in 1988, and in many urban areas – even in relatively small towns like Fatick – virtually the entire economically active population can speak and understand Wolof;

Table 2.4. *Language spoken as first language, by ethnic group in Fatick*

(in percentages)

	Wolof	Serer	Haalpulaaren	Diola	Manding	Other-East	Others	All Groups
Wolof	99.3	16.5	33.6	31.1	62.0	70.5	36.5	38.4
Serer	0.6	83.4	2.7	4.1	7.6	3.5	2.3	50.2
Pulaar	0.0	0.1	63.6	1.2	0.6	1.6	8.4	8.4
Other	0.0	0.0	0.0	63.5	29.9	24.4	52.8	3.0
Total	100.0	100.0	100.0	100.0	100.0	100.0	100.0	100.0

Table 2.5. *Languages spoken as either first or second language, by ethnic group in Fatick*

(in percentages)

	Wolof	Serer	Haalpulaaren	Diola	Manding	Other-East	Others
Wolof	100.0	78.3	84.7	75.6	87.7	91.6	80.8
Serer	8.0	90.4	7.5	5.3	16.3	10.8	7.9
Pulaar	0.6	0.2	69.6	1.6	2.3	2.3	8.9
Other	0.5	0.3	0.5	77.0	34.2	37.0	60.1

the only significant exceptions are those non-Wolof with few contacts outside the family compound, namely small children and some elderly women. (See Table 2.3) For many children born in such settings Wolof emerges as the primary ethnic identification, regardless of parentage, particularly if the parents are themselves of different ethnic groups. The process of "Wolofization" is thus slowly but persistently transforming the patterns of cultural identity in Senegal, although it is a trend that triggers its own counter-forces, and thus whose ultimate trajectory remains unclear.[18]

The phenomenon of Wolofization and the virtual monopoly of Wolof as *the* Senegalese *lingua franca* has numerous social and political ramifications in Senegal. To be Senegalese, for many, implies automatically to speak Wolof. At a seminar on legal matters organized at the Fatick Chamber of Commerce the young speaker, himself a Serer from Fatick, was asked to make a statement in "a national language" (that is, not in French) for broadcast on the radio. "As a good Senegalese," he responded, "I would certainly be pleased to speak in Wolof. But given that we are in Fatick, I will take the liberty of speaking Serer." The implicit equation is clear; Wolof is the language of Senegal, Serer that of local use in Sine.[19] Tables 2.4 and 2.5 may be useful to indicate the dimensions of Wolof use as applied to Fatick.

As these tables indicate, all individuals of Wolof ethnicity speak Wolof, and in fact very few speak any other Senegalese language – the vast majority of them (90.9 percent) speak *only* Wolof. By contrast, members of other ethnic groups tend to speak Wolof in addition to their own language. For many of them Wolof is actually a first language, and particularly among the smaller ethnic groups in Fatick frequently the only one. Few non-Wolofs speak a language other than Wolof and their own, although given the demographic predominance of the Serer in Fatick some members of each other ethnic group in the town have learned the Serer language. In linguistic terms, these general patterns found in Fatick are quite typical of Senegalese urban centers, though there are of course regional variations in how these trends are reflected locally.

The second most widely spoken language in Senegal is Pulaar,[20] and together the speakers of this language, the Haalpulaaren, constitute the second most important ethnic grouping. A linguistic appellation more than a true ethnicity, the Haalpulaaren include various peoples frequently identified as distinct groups. The most significant of these are the Peul or Fulbe, pastoral nomadic cattle herders by tradition, and the Tukulor, settled agriculturalists who are probably the descendants of the original inhabitants of the Senegal river valley. Despite their common language and much shared history, most notably in the participation in the *jihad* and subsequent state created by El Hajj Umar Tall in the Futa Toro in the mid-nineteenth century, the Peul and the Tukulor have generally tended to maintain their distinct identity. The continued sedentarization of Peuls and an increased migration to urban areas in search of employment, however, has begun to blur this distinction. Most importantly, for ideological reasons that appear to be at least partly a response to the threat posed by Wolofization, a movement has arisen in recent years among Pulaar speakers who refuse to make the distinction between the two, preferring instead the Haalpulaaren label. Their political mobilization seems destined to further the pace of the emergence of Haalpulaaren as a single ethnic identity.

A contrasting problem surrounds the identification of the Serer ethnic group; the label "Serer" has long been applied to several different groups, some of which speak unrelated languages. The "true" Serer, who make up over 90 percent of the population identified by that name, are comprised of the speakers of Serer-Siin and the closely related Serer-Niominka, fishermen who inhabit the coastal islands north of the Gambia river and who are consequently known as the *seereer-u-ndox*, or "water Serer" in Wolof. The most significant of the distinct small groups also called Serer are the Non, Ndut, and Safène peoples who inhabit a series of villages around the region of Thiès.[21] Because their numbers are quite small, however, and given their proximity to the major urban centers, these groups seem to be especially affected by the phenomenon of Wolofization. In a strict sense, therefore, the term Serer refers to the people who constituted the majority of the population of the traditional states of Sine and Saloum, as well as a significant minority in Baol. Today the Serer comprise the third largest ethnic group in Senegal, and the majority of the population of Fatick.

Contextual ethnicity: Serer identity in Fatick

Given not only its ethnic composition, but also its location in the heart of pre-colonial Sine, Fatick must in many senses still be considered a Serer town. But such a description is only partially true; like all Senegalese urban centers Fatick is increasingly characterized by an ambiguous diversity of ethnic relations. Moreover, if the Serer dominate the town numerically, they certainly do not control it economically or politically. They manage, nevertheless, to maintain a stronger sense of ethnic distinctiveness than the other groups found in Fatick.

Patterns of residential settlement in Fatick are indicative of the ethnic situation. Although it is a very small town, distinct neighborhoods can be identified, but only the Serer neighborhood of Ndiaye-Ndiaye retains a virtually absolute ethnic homogeneity. Not all Serer, however, reside in this neighborhood; many have settled elsewhere in the town. Among these latter families Wolof is more widely spoken in the compound, younger people are more likely to marry out of ethnicity, and ethnic identity is otherwise less likely to be central to social relations. On the north side of town the neighborhood of Peulgha, as its name indicates, contains a high density of Pulaar speakers, in particular members of a Tukulor community which has long resided in the town. Peulgha, however, is far from homogeneous, and many Pulaar speakers are interspersed throughout Fatick's other neighborhoods. These others are all ethnically diverse, containing many Wolof in addition to the other groups, and the Wolof influences – most notably linguistic – are dominant throughout. This is true even in the central neighborhood of Escale, where the handful of remaining Lebanese and the few members of the small ethnic groups in Fatick are concentrated. Only Ndiaye-Ndiaye stands as a bastion of resistance to Wolof cultural influences – though small cracks are beginning to show even there. Table 2.6 provides an indication of the patterns of ethnic settlement in Fatick.

Serer identity in Fatick is linked to the history of the pre-colonial kingdom of Sine. One of three Serer kingdoms to emerge between the fourteenth and the sixteenth centuries, Sine survived as an independent state in various permutations until the colonial conquest.[22] Although by 1887 the kingdom was fully under French control, in contrast to other pre-

Table 2.6. *Ethnic composition of Fatick's neighborhoods*

(in percentages)

	Escale	Logandème	Ndiaye-Ndiaye	Ndouk	Peulgha
Wolof	28.C	26.1	2.7	36.1	14.6
Serer	41.8	54.3	90.7	38.2	58.0
Haalpulaaren	13.4	9.2	2.7	18.2	17.9
Others[a]	12.1	9.4	2.9	6.6	8.3
Non-Senegalese[b]	4.7	1.0	1.0	0.9	1.2
Total	100.0	100.0	100.0	100.0	100.0

Notes:
Certain characteristics of neighborhoods noted in the text (e.g. the virtually total homogeneity of Ndiaye-Ndiaye as Serer, or the concentration of Haalpulaaren in Peulgha) are somewhat diluted here due to the imperfect overlap of administrative divisions and sociological reality.
[a] No one group over 2% of total.
[b] Mostly Guineans and Mauritanians.

colonial states (notably the Wolof kingdoms) the conquest did not result in the complete collapse of the political system. The *buurs* (kings) of Sine and Saloum, unlike their counterparts elsewhere, were allowed to retain their titles throughout the colonial period and into independence; the throne of Sine only disappeared with the death of the last *Buur*, Mahecor Diouf, in 1969. During the colonial period the *buurs* became, in effect, French civil servants. Although the result was that their traditional authority was gradually undermined as they became more closely identified with the colonial and then the Senegalese state than with their historical subjects, this arrangement also had the effect of allowing for the maintenance of the distinct identity and traditions of the *Siin-Siin*, the people of Sine. Thus in Fatick today the Serer of Ndiaye-Ndiaye still identify strongly with the history of Sine and preserve numerous practices and celebrations associated with the pre-Islamic religion of that kingdom. But at the same time there are virtually no ties remaining between the descendants of the *buurs* and those of their former subjects. Among those in Fatick, El Hajj Farba Diouf, an old son of penultimate *Buur-Siin* Coumba Ndoffène Diouf, *fa ndepp* (i.e., the younger), has had an important political career spanning most of modern Senegalese history. He played various roles in the colonial administration as well as in independent Senegal, and in retirement he retains sufficient status to permit him to gain audiences with President Abdou Diouf. Yet he carries no noticeable authority or prestige among the

Serer population of Fatick, and is in fact virtually unknown to the residents of Ndiaye-Ndiaye.[23]

The strongly traditional nature of Serer society explains in part the relations between the Serer and other ethnic groups in Fatick. Serer oral tradition recounts the group's origins in the Senegal River valley, where it was part of, or closely related to, the same group as the ancestors to today's Tukulor. Having emigrated toward the southwest in several waves – perhaps largely in resistance to Islamization – these people intermarried with indigenous populations and others to the south and eventually coalesced as a distinct Serer ethnicity.[24] A significant legacy of this history is that today the Serer enjoy a ritualized teasing relationship with both the Tukulor and the Diola people further south, both of whom they regard as ethnic "cousins."

Known in Wolof as *kaal* (*massir* in Serer), teasing relationships are an important aspect of many Sahelian cultures. The *kaal* relationship can exist within kinship networks (cross cousins are united by these ties) and between patronyms (e.g., the names Diop and Ndiaye are *kaals* in Senegal, regardless of ethnicity), as well as between ethnic groups. The relationship involves the good-natured exchange of usually ritualized insults. Even two strangers whose names or ethnicity make them *kaals* can immediately upon meeting pronounce the other their "slave," or accuse each other of an excessive taste for rice (i.e., of gluttony). The *kaal* is sociologically very important because it preempts potential tensions, given that it is virtually inconceivable for an individual to take offense at a *kaal's* insults. On the contrary, the relationship tends to produce amicable feelings.

Kaal ties help to define the generally good relations between Serer and Tukulor in Fatick, and Tukulor administrators who choose to play on these ties find that they have an advantage over their Wolof colleagues in their interactions with the Serer population. The Tukulor administrator of the Fatick Chamber of Commerce, for example, enjoyed much better relations with the local population than did most of his fellow state functionaries, at least in part due to his regular (and boisterous) use of the *kaal* in addressing all Serer as his "slaves." Such behavior may also have direct political impact. As far back as the 1950s a Tukulor teacher in Fatick named Oumar Sy successfully used the technique to build a Serer electoral constituency.[25] Moreover, the Tukulor are credited locally with having taught Islam to the Serer, and some important local marabouts, namely El Hajj Montaga Diallo, who died in 1966, as well as many of the imams of the central mosque in Fatick, have been Tukulor.[26] Along with these good ties, however, there coexists some ambivalence arising from a resentment of the somewhat better economic situation enjoyed by the Tukulor in Fatick. Many of the merchants in the market, including virtually all of the more successful sellers of fabric, shoes, and household utensils, are Tukulor. Their relative success is apparent, and even state officials are quick to contrast it to the "backwardness" of the Serer.[27]

Even more ambiguous relations exist between the Serer and the Wolof. Paradoxically, while ties with Tukulor or other Pulaar speakers may be closer, it is far easier for a Serer to "become" Wolof, particularly in an urban context. And to the extent that links are developed with the main centers of Senegalese Sufi Islam, religious interactions are almost certain to be conducted in Wolof.[28] Yet perhaps precisely because of the threat posed by Wolofization, anti-Wolof sentiment tends to run fairly strong among the Serer population of Fatick. Several older Serer men regularly warned me not to accept what Wolof individuals told me as valid for the Serer. And it is frequently said that until a few years ago no Wolof – and particularly no young Wolof male interested in courtship – would have dared enter Ndiaye-Ndiaye. Even today few would feel comfortable doing so.

These various factors result in a significant ambiguity in Senegalese ethnic relations. Interactions between the Wolof and other groups in particular are marked by two contrasting tendencies. While the Wolof continue to absorb members of other ethnic groups and the common use of the Wolof language facilitates social interactions, anti-Wolof sentiments can frequently emerge, whether in regional resistance to Wolof influences, as among the Diola and the Serer, or in the Haalpulaaren politico-linguistic movement. Two anecdotes may help to illustrate this complex and contextual nature of ethnic identity in contemporary Senegal.

Travelling from Dakar to Fatick I once listened as the occupants of the *car rapide* ("bush taxis" – which belie their French name), who happened to be mostly Serer and Diola – and hence joined by a *kaal* relationship – spent the three hour ride engaged in non-stop teasing rivalry about the relative merits of the two ethnic groups, their agricultural production, livestock, and their major cities of Kaolack and Ziguinchor. Tellingly enough, however, the entire good-natured exchange among previous strangers was – of necessity – carried out in Wolof. While neither the Serer nor the Diola would have any basis for engaging in such an exchange with Wolof individuals, it is their common use of the Wolof language that allows them to build and maintain amicable ties by participating in such social rituals. Yet the adoption of Wolof in itself also signifies the potential for actually losing their ethnic identity and becoming Wolof, certainly within their children's generation. Learning Wolof is thus a two-edged sword.

On another occasion I turned a young Dakar soda seller's query about my ethnicity around to ask about hers. "My father is a Tukulor" was her response after a brief hesitation. And her mother? "She too is a Tukulor?" Well then what about herself? "Well ... I'm Wolof, because that's what I speak best ." Teased about in fact being no more than a "boy Dakar" (the Senegalese equivalent of a young "city slicker"), she retrenched defensively, protesting that she was in fact Tukulor, and insisting on her desire to travel to the Futa Toro and to improve her Pulaar language skills. Clearly ethnic identity was dependent on the contextual situation. While Wolof provided her with an appropriate ethnic identity in a more casual context, her Tukulor identity provided a more appropriate fall-back in the context of distancing herself from the jokingly derogatory urbanized label.

Unifying forces: common Sahelian traits

Further complicating questions of ethnicity in Senegal are several shared characteristics found throughout the cultures of the Sahel region, including those of all of the most important ethnic groups in the country.[29] The most significant of these are the system of social stratification and the shared set of cultural norms that permeate Senegalese political culture.

While there are some minor variations in the specific forms of social stratification among the different groups, all three of the main ethnic groups in Senegal are characterized by parallel systems of caste relationships that determine an individual's placing within the group. Abdoulaye-Bara Diop's research has established the original existence of two separate systems of social stratification among the Wolof.[30] One was a political distinction between what he labels "orders," and which served to distinguish free men from slaves (géer and jaam in Wolof), while the other was a socio-economic distinction which separated the non-casted peoples from the casted (géer vs. ñeeño). Interestingly enough, the first of these distinctions has virtually disappeared in contemporary Senegalese society, perhaps as a consequence of the demise of pre-colonial political structures. The second, however, remains very much alive.

Remnants of an original hierarchical stratification remain, but the caste system today has largely collapsed into a two-tier distinction between casted and non-casted people. One of the interesting consequences of this is that the descendents of former slaves, who were originally external to this system, enjoy a rather ambivalent status, and can even be absorbed into the higher status, non-casted, group. While all non-casted individuals tend to be referred to as géer (sometimes erroneously translated as "noble"), casted people are subdivided into several occupationally linked groups, the most important of which are the leatherworkers (wuude in Wolof), blacksmiths and jewelers (tëgg), weavers (ràbb), and praise-singers (géwél), known most frequently by their French name, "griot."[31] Caste status is hereditary and does not depend on an individual's actually practicing the traditional occupation of that caste. Thus caste status cannot easily be shed by abandoning the traditional economy and entering the modern one. Castes are also endogamous, and this aspect of the system endures as its most significant social legacy; caste status still remains a far more significant barrier to marriage than either religion or ethnicity. Because caste cuts across ethnicity among most Senegalese groups, and since cross-ethnic marriages are widely tolerated as long as they do not cross caste lines, the salience of ethnicity is further undercut.

The caste system, in fact, at times blurs with ethnicity. No word exists in Wolof for either caste or ethnic group *per se*, and instead the single word *xeet*, meaning "group," "kind," or "type" is commonly used for both. The question *"Ban xeet nga?"* (What group/type are you?) can thus be answered with either an ethnic or a caste identification.[32] A good example of the fusion of caste and ethnic identity is provided by the Laobé, speakers of a Pulaar dialect who live among different societies in the Senegambia region where they fulfill a particular socio-economic function by serving as woodworkers, thus demonstrating characteristics of both a caste and an ethnicity.

The caste system finds no justifying rationale in either the Westernized "modern" system or in Islamic theology which, on the contrary, tends to be hostile to any distinction that is incompatible with the notion of the fundamental equality of all men before God. As a result, occasional challenges to the system arise and some individuals feel justified in defying social convention by, for example, marrying out of caste. Such cases, however, are quite rare, and caste distinctions are noteworthy for the tenacity of their persistence in social relations. They regularly, in fact, manage to permeate the other presumably incompatible social systems. Thus, for example, a large percentage of employees of Senegalese national radio and television, even at the administrative levels, are individuals from the traditional griot caste. And, in a local example, the relatively wealthy proprietor of a welding and metalworking shop in Fatick who also served as the president of the Chambre d'Industrie in Fatick is of blacksmith caste. Such cases of continuity, in fact, are the norm rather than the exception in much of Senegal. The contradictions that arise from the persistence of the traditional system in the context of the modern one are vividly exemplified in *Borom Saret*, a film by Senegalese filmmaker Sembène Ousmane in which the impoverished but "noble" (*géer*) protagonist is obliged to turn over his miserably meager day's earnings to an obviously wealthy griot traditionally attached to his family when he encounters him on a Dakar street and the latter proceeds to publicly recite the ancient glory of the family. Caste status even plays a role in Islamic structures. It is far less likely for a casted individual to be chosen as imam of a mosque (although as we shall see there are some important cases of casted marabouts). And in Fatick most of the muezzins at the local mosques were of griot origin, a fact that one imam found "normal" given what he saw as the innate attributes of that caste.[33]

The complexity of the ethnic and caste systems in Senegal obviously functions as a barrier to having any one such social category be seen as "primordial" and hence provide a likely basis for political action. In addition the country's political elite has been careful not to create any opportunity for action that could have the result of politicizing these cleavages. The formation of any political party on the basis of ethnicity or region is forbidden by the Senegalese constitution, and no efforts to mobilize politically on these grounds have ever been tolerated by the state. Former president Léopold Senghor admitted to intentionally challenging caste prejudices in making presidential appointments, once protesting: "There used to be caste prejudices, but they are in the process of being reabsorbed. In [making] nominations, I always try to take them into account. I take them into account, I never speak of them and I think that, now, we have surpassed these prejudices of caste."[34] Senghor's ambiguity in simultaneously declaring them a thing of the past while acknowledging their continued relevance tellingly points to the fact that caste structures, like ethnic ones, are still very much alive as systems of social diversity, yet are also in flux. Both remain potential influences on political behavior, but both are mostly latent and neither represents a primary mode of political organization *vis-à-vis* the state.[35]

More amorphous shared characteristics of all of the major Senegalese ethnic groups – but equally central – are a series of cultural presuppositions that together form the core of a distinctive political culture. More broadly, Thomas Hale and Paul Stoller have argued that important commonalities underlie ethnic diversity throughout the Sahel, noting that "the ethnic groups which make up this mosaic share a common ecosystem, a great deal of history, and a variety of common cultural behavior reflected in both Islamic and pre-Islamic traditions."[36] They posit, therefore, the existence of a "deep Sahelian culture" that unites the region. In Senegal certain distinctive traits of that culture can be identified as particularly important for both religious and political organization.

The major ethnic groups all share similar notions about the distribution of authority in society. All of these are highly stratified societies – by caste, but also by age, sex, and other non-ascriptive attributes – in which the ranking of individuals relative to each other on a social hierarchy is accepted as the appropriate, indeed necessary, order and in which authority is inherent in the higher categories. The structures of hierarchy are accompanied by suppositions about the dependent status of individuals in the lower positions. Slaves, griots, younger family members, and any other individuals in an inferior position are judged not only to have less authority but to be dependent on others.[37] Most importantly, however, this dependence involves not only degrees of authority but also obligations on the part of the holder of the superior position. More than once in response to my question of what it meant if someone were one's slave (a status, I should note, no longer openly applied to individuals, but one which people nevertheless still understand as theoretically possible), interviewees responded in terms of obligations: "It means you have to give them money" or "you have to feed them." And the obligations of individuals toward griots from dependent lineages are frequently so strong as to permit the exploitation of the relationship even when the economic corollaries of hierarchy no longer apply, as in the example from Sembène Ousmane's film.

This dependence creates a larger system of interdependence which shapes Sahelian attitudes about wealth and its distribution. Rather than being perceived as inequitable and therefore unjust, concentrations of wealth are actually desirable for everyone concerned – as long as the holder of wealth recognizes and acts on his (rarely her) obligations to those in dependent positions. The surest guarantee against hunger for many people is that their patron be well supplied. This concern therefore means that generosity is enshrined as a pre-eminent individual virtue. The extravagant expenses frequently associated with public events of various sorts answer to this cultural imperative. In this vein the anthropologist Abdoulaye Bara Diop has noted that the "generosity [of a noble] towards the members of a lower caste is a source of prestige and honor.... It is inconceivable in Wolof society for a *géer* to receive a gift from a *ñeeño* without giving more in return."[38] Senegalese state officials have attempted at various times since independence to legislate limits to the "wasteful" excesses of family rituals like marriages or naming ceremonies – always unsuccessfully. Hale and Stoller similarly note the Bambara notion of *fadenya* that leads individuals returning from periods of labor abroad to "waste" their earnings in extravagant gestures that frustrate development planners (and no doubt scholars of various persuasions) mystified by the seeming economic "irrationality" of these acts.[39]

The need to ensure the "generosity" of individuals has undoubtedly also been an important contributory factor in the importance given in Sahelian cultures to the public persona. No act of generosity or other virtuous deed is allowed to pass unlauded, and individuals are always praised publicly for such deeds. One of the most important functions of griots is to serve as the propagators of this type of information, and at ceremonial occasions griots frequently announce publicly and loudly the various contributions made by individuals, in cash or kind. As we shall see, these cultural patterns are centrally important in shaping both the style and substance of religious and political structures.

Religion: the shape of local Islam

If neither ethnicity nor caste have proven to be particularly important in Senegal as a basis for social organization in interactions with the state, the same cannot be said of religion. On the contrary, the structures of religious organization have consistently been the primary mediators of relations between state and society in Senegal. Indicative of the recognition by state officials of the pre-eminence of religious ties over other forms of identity is the fact that while the 1988 census collected data on both ethnicity and religious affiliation by Sufi order, only information on the former has been made available by the government. The exact relative demographic strength of the orders is withheld both because it is sure to be a source of contention and because this information is too valuable to political aspirants to be easily relinquished by government officials.[40] Because some ninety-four percent of the population declares itself Muslim, the structures of Islam have naturally been overwhelmingly predominant, although the religious organization of the small Catholic minority has found itself – not entirely willingly – filling many of the same political functions.[41] Yet what are these structures of Islam in the specific context of Senegal? Why have they emerged as the primary mode of religious organization? And to what extent are they determined or influenced by the broader ideology of Islam held in common with the rest of the Muslim world?

The local manifestations of Islam in the form of the Senegalese variant of the institutions of the Sufi orders have been and continue to be far and away the most significant aspect of religious organization in the country, and the primary focus of this work is consequently on this form of Islam as lived in Senegal. Increasingly, however, a part of the experience of religion in Senegal involves the perception of tensions between local practices and those of other areas of the Muslim world, most notably the Arab heartlands. As we shall see, challenges to the Sufi system have consequently made themselves felt. But outside a small urban minority the logic of continuity still prevails over the forces of change; the Sufi orders remain as the primary form of religious affiliation and the most significant mediators of political loyalties in Senegal. This section, therefore, provides a brief introductory sketch to the historical background and institutional parameters of the social structures of local Islam, which will then be explored in depth throughout the balance of this work.

Senegambian Islam: origins and evolution

The history of Islam in the Sudanic belt of West Africa is a chronicle of advances and retreats in which the long-term trend has nevertheless been one of expansion and consolidation.[42] From the eleventh century historical records note the presence of Muslims in the state of Tekrur in the Senegal river valley, which subsequently became involved in the Almoravid reform movement that extended northward into Morocco and Spain. From there the religion spread south and east through migrations and conversions, in a process that continued slowly into the eighteenth century. Throughout this period Muslims were present in virtually every state of the region, and the advantages of literacy in Arabic meant that Muslim scholar-clerics were maintained in royal courts throughout these states, regardless of the religion of the ruler himself. In very few cases, however, could Islam in this period be described as the religion of the majority of the population.

The impetus for that transformation, from minority religion to dominant faith, was provided by two forces that shook the region after the mid-eighteenth century: (1) a series of reformist *jihads* launched against pagan rulers or nominal Muslims whose commitment to Islam came under question, and (2) the imperatives of reconstructing social orders in the context of the upheaval which resulted from the collapse of the existing states following the colonial conquest. To varying degrees in different areas, these forces sparked an initial wave of widespread conversion to Islam, which in the period since then has been characterized by a continued peaceful expansion in the number of adherents and a slow process of consolidation in the sense of absorbing or eliminating local pre-Islamic beliefs and practices.

In the region that is now Senegal the influence of Islam was expanded by all of these means, although with unequal impact among different ethnic groups. The *jihad* launched by the Tukulor cleric El Hajj Umar Tall in the 1850s against the rulers of the various states in the upper Senegal and Niger river areas did much to establish the preeminence of the Tijaniyya order in the region and particularly among the Haalpulaaren. El Hajj Umar's influence continues to be strongly felt throughout the Senegambia, and he still serves as both a referent and a legitimating link in the spiritual genealogies that link the Tijaniyya in the region to its North African roots.

In the Wolof states of Cayor, Jolof, and Baol, the impetus for widespread conversion to Islam among the majority of the population (whose adherence remained either nominal or non-existent despite the centuries-long presence of important Muslim minorities) was provided by the collapse of the traditional order which followed the colonial conquest. The Sufi orders, and notably the indigenous Mouride order which arose in this period, were able to provide an alternative means of social reorganization, to include in particular the numerous nobles, slaves, *ceddo* (a class of powerful military slaves of the crown), and other displaced persons whose positions had been linked to the old order.[43]

In the Serer areas, especially in Sine, these influences were also felt. But what is most noteworthy about the Islamization of the *Siin-Siin* is how little was achieved either by *jihad* or as a direct result of colonial occupation. In his thesis on Senegalese Islam El Hajj Ravane Mbaye reflects the wide-spread belief in the strong attachment of the Serer of Sine to their own religion until the twentieth century, and their resulting "hostility" to Islam that led to a rejection of all forms of proselytizing: "Neither the material well-being of the Dioula [traders], nor the charm of the Moors, nor the almost bellicose mysticism of the Tukulor were able to have any effect on their belief."[44] Both *jihad* and the establishment of the colonial system, however, were no doubt of some importance in preparing the ground for the subsequent spread of Islam in the region.

The most important of the efforts to spread Islam among the Serer by the sword was the *jihad* launched by Ma Ba Diakhou in about 1861 from his home base in the small state of Rip on the northern bank of the Gambia river.[45] Ma Ba was a cleric of Tukulor origin who joined the Tijaniyya and met El Hajj Umar personally sometime around 1850. A reformist who wanted both to overthrow the traditional (impious or worse) elite and to resist the advances of the Christian colonizers, Ma Ba found himself embroiled in a series of campaigns involving numerous allies (most famously the claimant to the position of *Damel* of Cayor, Lat Dior Diop) against different enemies. Although he succeeded in overthrowing the ruling dynasty in Saloum, he was never successful against the largely pagan kingdom of Sine, and he was ultimately killed in battle against the forces of the *Buur-Siin* in 1867. Ma Ba was never able to consolidate control over his empire, which proved to be short lived, but his military exploits dominated the history of much of the region during the 1860s.

The fact that he was unsuccessful in removing the pagan rulers of Sine obviously served as an impediment to the proselytizing mission of Ma Ba in that kingdom. But the general lack of success of his *jihad* may also be related to the fact that the propagation of the faith was not the only motivating force behind the wars. Given that Ma Ba allied himself with ambitious rulers whose commitment to Islam was questionable (notably the only nominally converted Lat Dior himself), and that in fact not all of Ma Ba's soldiers were themselves Muslims, one student of this period has suggested that Ma Ba's motivations may have been three-fold; Ma Ba was at once a propagator of the Muslim faith, a conqueror with political ambitions, and a "nationalist" in that he opposed the French.[46] Leaving aside this final possible motive – one attributed retroactively to many a pre-colonial warrior in the building of a national mythology by latter-day nationalist leaders – it still seems clear that from the perspective of Sine the secular and the religious were not clearly distinguished in the two sides of the fighting. The story of how a Tukulor marabout named Amadou Thierno Ba made a protective amulet for the pagan *Buur-Siin*, thus securing his victory in battle and the demise of Ma Ba, was recounted to me with no sense of irony both by an old griot in Fatick, widely reputed to be the most knowledgeable source of local history, and by one of the more important local marabouts.[47] Not only was resistance to Ma Ba possible without a rejection of Islam, but the powers of Islam could actually be pressed into service in what was fundamentally a struggle to maintain the independence of Sine.

Sine, of course, did not remain independent for long. But as already noted, the protectorate status which the French devised for the kingdom nevertheless preserved the formal political structures around the figure of the *buur*. And the fact that no wide-scale conversions to Islam followed directly on the French conquest lends support to the hypothesis noted above which links the Islamization of the Wolof regions to the collapse of those states. Sine in this sense also contrasts sharply with Saloum, which Klein labels "the most striking victory for Islam" in the period between the French conquest and the eve of the First World War, a victory which he argues was "closely related to the decline of the traditional political system."[48] Paul Marty, the French colonial official whose writings on Islam in Senegal provided the basis for most subsequent studies of the topic, estimated that in 1912–13 only some fifteen percent of the population of Sine was Muslim.[49]

The process of Islamization in Sine has thus been somewhat slower than elsewhere in Senegal, but the long-term trend has nevertheless been toward conversion. Today, aside from the existence of some important Catholic minorities – particularly in coastal towns of the "Petite Côte" like Joal and the neighboring island village of Fadiouth – the vast majority of the *Siin-Siin* are at least nominally Muslim. The depth of commitment varies, as all local religious leaders are quick to admit, but nevertheless the trend is clearly toward the consolidation of Islam particularly among the younger generations born and raised in a predominantly Muslim culture. This eventual "triumph of Islam," Klein notes, was achieved by "a small army of humble and unarmed marabouts [who] won the final victory that had eluded Ma Ba's proud warriors."[50] The slow but steady spread of Islam which began under the colonial regime continues today under the aegis of the Senegalese state. This seemingly incongruous "victory" must be explained in terms of the role religion has come to play in Senegal today. It is a major part of the argument of this work that the expansion of Islam can best be understood as a result of the fact that religion in Senegal has regularly provided the most effective basis of social organization in interactions with the state.

The orders and their propagators

As the discussion so far has only implied, Islamization throughout the Senegambian region took place via the Sufi orders, known in Arabic as *turuq* (sing. *tariqa*), and Wolofized as *tarixa*. With their virtual monopoly over the organization of Senegalese Islam, the orders are subject to intense scrutiny throughout this work, and they are here introduced only as a means of setting the stage for this examination.

The organizational genius of the orders which is clearly responsible in large part for their preponderant role in the spread of Islam in the region lies in their capacity to simultaneously localize Islam – that is to allow for the formulation of structures adapted to existing cultural values and institutions – and provide a basis for the maintenance of ties to the broader Muslim world. In Cruise O'Brien's words, the "limited, circumscribed, popular adherence to the Islamic community" which the orders permitted also allowed them to fill a shielding function in distancing black African populations from the perceived racism of Arab Islam.[51] Yet all of the orders also provide a link – though of varying directness – to the world of Arab, and especially North African, Islam.

Adherence to a Sufi order involves, in theory, an initiation into the more or less "mystical" rituals that characterize it, most particularly through the learning and recitation of the litany of prayers known as the *wird* that distinguishes each order. The *wird* is transmitted to a follower by a marabout, known most frequently in Arabic as a *shaykh*, a religious scholar learned in the mystical secrets of the order.[52] The act of transmission establishes a theoretical relationship of subordination between the master and his disciple. In its Senegalese manifestation, however, this latter aspect is the pre-eminent one; adherence to a Sufi order in Senegal involves first and foremost declaring oneself a follower, a disciple, of a marabout. The relationship may or may not involve the actual transmission of the *wird*.[53]

The exact nature of the ties that bind followers to marabouts is an absolutely crucial factor in determining the political role played by the orders, and chapters 4 and 5 will be dedicated to an exploration of this relationship. It bears noting here, however, that this form of organization also serves to render the orders particularly effective vehicles for Islamization. Because the orders provide in effect the potential for an "apprenticeship" under a marabout, they require only the most rudimentary understanding of Islam for conversion, and are thus particularly effective among largely illiterate populations with little previous exposure to the religious sciences.[54] This characteristic of the orders is one that is not only pointed to by social scientists, but also at times acknowledged explicitly by those that are actively involved in proselytizing. The Moorish founder and the Wolof Arabic teacher of a small Franco-Arabic school in Fatick, each of whom had ties to different orders but who also argued that distinctions among orders should not be given much importance, both emphasized that the orders were especially useful for the illiterate, who were restricted from direct access to the Qur'an, and for whom they could thus serve as an efficient means of learning about and practicing religion.[55]

Most discussions of Islam in Senegal identify three main Sufi orders of importance in the country, to which is appended the Layène order, dominant among the Wolof-speaking Lebou people of the Dakar region. The Layènes have a distinctive belief system, marked primarily by the identification of their founder, Mouhamadou Seydina Limamou Laye, as the Mahdi, the spiritual renewer who, it is popularly believed throughout much of the Muslim world, will appear in preparation for the judgment day.[56] The order is, however, of little importance at the national level, and quite insignificant in Fatick, and it is consequently not discussed further here. Of the three "main" orders, two in fact incorporate the vast majority of Senegalese Muslims; the Qadiriyya, despite claiming the longest presence in the region, is today far smaller than either the Tijaniyya or the Mourides.[57]

The Qadiriyya owes its name and its origin to the Arab *Shaykh* Abd al-Qadir al-Jilani who lived and taught in Baghdad until his death in the year 1166 AD. The practices adopted by early adepts of the Qadiriyya, probably the first mystical order to emerge in Sunni Islam, served as a basis for much of what became classical Sufi patterns. In the Western Sudan region the order was disseminated by members of the Kunta lineage, an extended and widely dispersed Arabo-Berber clan. Three maraboutic families associated with this clan have survived as important in Senegal: (1) that mentioned above with which the *Buur-Siin* maintained ties, the family of *Shaykh* Sidiyya al-Kabir (d. 1869) of Boutilimit in Mauritania; (2) that of *Shaykh* Saad Bou Aïdara (d. 1917) based in Nimzatt, also in Mauritania; and (3) the lineage founded by *Shaykh* Bou Kunta (d. 1914) in the Senegalese village of Ndiassane near Tivaouane.[58]

Each of these three families has followers throughout Senegal, including Fatick. The connections of Coumba Ndoffène Diouf's descendants with the family of *Shaykh* Sidiyya have already been noted, while the heirs of Saad Bou enjoy equally important ties in Fatick in part via their relationship with the widowed daughter-in-law of the last *Buur-Siin*, Mahecor Diouf. A highly respected public figure in the town, in addition to organizing the annual reception for the visit of Saad Bou's *xalifa*, or successor, to the late *buur's* house where she lives, she serves as the president of the women's section of the ruling Parti Socialiste (PS). Other members of the Saad Bou family have settled in Senegal, including a grandson in Thiès and another in the town of Diofior in Sine, whose proximity to Fatick (where he has a wife) has meant a fair amount of influence there. Until the break in relations with Mauritania, disciples of the Saad Bou family made an annual pilgrimage to Nimzatt at the time of the feast of *Korite*, marking the end of the fast of Ramadan.[59]

There are two faces to the Qadiriyya in Senegal which are reflected in the relations of adherents of the order in Fatick. Primarily among the disciples of the families cited above the order demonstrates the traits which Cruise O'Brien points to in referring to it as "the venerable Qadiriyya," an institution which "may in a sense be seen as already reformed" (i.e., practicing an Islam less tainted by anthropolatry than that of the other orders).[60] But another less "sophisticated" side coexists, most significantly among disciples whose allegiance lies with Ndiassane. Bou Kunta himself was reportedly illiterate, and his family has never particularly distinguished itself for its religious learning. It is this side of the order that an unsympathetic Tijan informant criticized when he pointed to the decidedly secular nature of much of the singing and dancing that occurs at many Qadir ceremonies, and a more sympathetic one identified as the strength of the order because it made it "easy" to be a Qadir.[61] A loose and somewhat uneasy alliance joins these two groups, which maintain politely cordial relations but function rather autonomously.

In addition to this disunity the Qadiriyya has long been in decline *vis-à-vis* the competing orders, at least partly due to the fact that all of these maraboutic families are of Moorish, rather than indigenous black African, ethnic origin. The fact that many Qadir marabouts are Mauritanian and frequently resident in Mauritania has provided a further handicap for the order in Senegal in that it limits their influence with the Senegalese state – a major source of maraboutic appeal to disciples. The explosion of the long-submerged animosity against Moors in Senegal in the Spring of 1989 further tarnished the image of the order among many Senegalese. The order suffered a serious setback in Senegal as a result of those events, not least because travel was hindered and hence the crucial contacts and attendance at ceremonies which maintain the relationship between a marabout and his disciples were minimized. Although it has survived and seems indeed to be making a comeback following the gradual and cautious rebuilding of Senegalo-Mauritanian social and political ties, it remains a distant third place to its two main competitors.

Like the Qadiriyya, the Tijaniyya order takes its name from its founder. *Shaykh* Ahmed al-Ti ani, a cleric of southern Algerian origin, gathered a wide following in his adopted city of Fez, in Morocco, with teachings which he claimed were revealed to him directly by God and the Prophet.[62] After his death in 1815 his tomb in Fez became a popular pilgrimage site and the spiritual center of the order. In West Africa the order was spread largely by the efforts of El Hajj Umar Tall, who had received the Tijan *wird* from Moorish clerics in his native Futa Toro. Returning from years of travel in North Africa and a pilgrimage to Mecca and Medina, El Hajj Umar settled for some time in the Islamic state of Sokoto (in modern northern Nigeria), whose sultan, Muhammad Bello, he reportedly initiated into the Tijaniyya, thus establishing the order in that region.[63] Leaving Sokoto after Bello's death in 1837, El Hajj Umar spent another decade or so in Futa Jalon (today in the Guinean highlands), before beginning in the 1850s the military campaigns for which he became famous – a series of *jihads* against states in the Senegal and Niger rivers area and resistance struggles against French attempts to occupy the region. Although El Hajj Umar was killed in battle in 1864, his influence continued through a series of other Tijan-led efforts at reform and resistance in neighboring states, including the campaigns of Ma Ba.[64]

All Tijan marabouts in Senegal today claim links to El Hajj Umar in tracing their spiritual genealogies. Several of his direct descendants have played important roles in twentieth-century Senegal, the most famous of whom was his grandson El Hajj Saidou Nourou Tall, who served as "grand marabout of the AOF" (French West Africa) during the colonial period. In addition, numerous less important Tijan maraboutic families, particularly among the Haalpulaaren, claim links of varying directness with El Hajj Umar.[65] Two families in particular, however, have established themselves as the primary representatives of the Tijaniyya in Senegal today: The Sy family based in Tivaouane, and the Niasse family of Kaolack.

El Hajj Malik Sy (*c.* 1855–1922), the founder of the dynasty at Tivaouane, was an assimilated Wolof from a Tukulor clerical family. His link to El Hajj Umar came from a maternal uncle who had been initiated into the order by El Hajj Umar himself and who in turn initiated his nephew. Sy maintained close ties with the Tall family, eventually giving his daughter in marriage to Saidou Nourou Tall, who had himself been confided to Sy's care as a child. The French were firmly in control of the Wolof states by the time Sy began his teaching career, and rather than attempt what he recognized would be futile resistance, he concentrated his attention on piety and learning, preaching peaceful cohabitation with the French and a purely spiritual version of *jihad*. He won numerous followers among the Wolof, particularly in the new towns that were emerging along the railroad lines. Since his death in 1922 his sons and grandsons have maintained the influence of the Tijan *zawiya* (center) at Tivaouane,[66] and the family continues to be one of the two most important maraboutic families in Senegal today.

Almost exactly at the same time that Malik Sy was building his reputation and his following, a rival branch of the Tijaniyya was being established in Saloum, in the town of Kaolack, by a Wolof cleric named El Hajj Abdoulaye Niasse (*c.* 1850–1922). His son Ibrahima, known as "Baye" Niasse, developed an even larger following in the years following his father's death, eventually surpassing him in fame and importance. The family developed a reputation for erudition in Islamic sciences and a mastery of Arabic, but the ambivalent attitude displayed by both father and son toward the colonial regime and later the independent state deprived them of a degree of official patronage comparable to that enjoyed by the Sy marabouts. In addition, Abdoulaye Niasse was of blacksmith origin, and despite several generations of clerical careers the taint of caste seems to continue to play a role in limiting the family's capacity to draw followers from non-casted people. Perhaps partly as a result, the Niasse have been especially successful in developing a following outside Senegal, most notably in northern Nigeria where their "Reformed Tijaniyya" represents a powerful religious and political force.[67] Disciples and students from all over West Africa join numerous Senegalese in pious pilgrimages to the Kaolack *zawiya*, in particular at the occasion of the *Mawlud*, or Prophet's birthday celebrations.

Far more than either the Qadiriyya or the Tijaniyya, the Mouride order has achieved a certain degree of fame – indeed at times of notoriety – among both Africanists and Islamicists. The order's reputation must be seen as the combined product of its unique, frequently colorful, characteristics and the fact that it has been the subject of more and better studies than most any other African religious movement.[68] So influential have these studies been that critiques have recently been made about the excessive *"mouridocentrisme"* of the study of African Sufism.[69] There is an element of truth to this critique, particularly within the narrower field of studies of *Senegalese* Islam. But various characteristics of the order nevertheless mean that its importance does surpass its second-place position in purely demographic terms. Its cohesion and *élan* have led to a Mouride *esprit de corps* that leads many disciples to believe (wrongly) in their numerical superiority and (perhaps less wrongly) in the inevitable further spread of the order.

The Mourides are a uniquely Senegalese order, founded over the course of his lifetime by *Shaykh* Amadou Bamba Mbacké (1850–1927), himself originally a Qadir and a disciple of *Shaykh* Sidiyya at whose compound in Boutilimit he spent some four years in French-imposed exile.[70] Although it has developed a highly distinct and far more cohesive identity than the parent order, the Mourides nevertheless retain the link to the Qadirs and the two are still occasionally identified as one, particularly by older disciples. With their heartland in Baol around the towns of Touba, Mbacké, and Diourbel, the Mourides are more closely linked to one ethnic group (Wolof) than any other order. Among the distinctive aspects of Amadou Bamba's teachings were an emphasis on the spiritual value of work and an especially strong version of the Sufi ideology of submission to a marabout (see chapter 4). This dual emphasis was translated into a concentration of Mouride disciples in agricultural work, particularly in the production of peanuts, and the organization of this production around the figures of Mouride marabouts – a link so strong that the latter have been dubbed *"les marabouts de l'arachide."*[71] Among one sub-branch of the order, the highly unorthodox Baye Fall, work and submission have actually replaced the observance of even the rudiments of Islam, including prayer and fasting. Although the Baye Fall have held an important place in the order from its inception, its more extreme practices are increasingly seen as a source of embarrassment for some members eager to improve the order's image in the broader world of Islam.

As peanuts have declined in importance in Senegal's economy, the Mourides appear to be successfully achieving the adaptation of the order to an urban setting and establishing themselves in trade and commerce.[72] In Dakar, most trade in imported goods in the sprawling and chaotic Sandaga market is dominated by Mourides, as it is in many other cities and towns even outside the central Mouride zone, notably the busy Kaolack market. Senegalese traders throughout West Africa are most frequently Mourides, as are the majority of those who have managed to establish communities in various European cities. And in New York this group has expanded to the point that there now exists an organization calling itself "The Senegalese Murid Community of Khadimul Rasul Society" (*Khadimul Rasul*, roughly "friend of the Prophet," is a nickname for Amadou Bamba). In 1989 this group sent out invitations for a celebration "in commemoration of the proclamation proclaiming July 28, 1988, as Cheik Ahmado Bamba Mbacke Day, in Harlem." The American Embassy in Dakar was swamped with requests for visas from Mourides wanting to attend the event – and take the opportunity to engage in some lucrative business on the side.[73] Such Mouride dynamism has been at the root of the high profile which the order has maintained both within Senegal and among international observers.

Sufism as practiced in Senegal has developed some unique theological and ideological variants on Islam as found elsewhere in the Muslim world. Its most significant innovation, however, has been in the third aspect of Islam, that is, in the formulation of the religious bases of social organization. It is in their production of a distinctive "islam" that structures the impact of religion on Senegalese political life that the orders are most centrally important to the concerns of this work. In what follows, therefore, a consideration of Islam as system of social organization takes pre-eminence over that of Islam as ideology or theology. The sources of cohesion and the systems of allegiances within orders, the structures and rituals that reinforce and maintain their cohesion, and the relations of orders to each other and to the state are thus the central issues to be explored in what follows.

It is important to note, however, that while the orders are absolutely central to Senegalese religious organization, they do not enjoy a strict monopoly. In a religiously mixed town like Fatick the orders overlap and interpenetrate other local Islamic institutions – mosques, Qur'anic schools, and such – but they are not coterminous with these. It is possible for an individual who is so disposed to attend prayers at the mosque and otherwise practice Islam without an intermediary affiliation with an order.

This possibility has given rise to two types of challenges to the supremacy of the orders in Senegalese religious organization. Much has been made of the amorphous group known as *"arabisants,"* who will be discussed in some detail in chapter 6. More accurately they might be described as a social category, since they have never organized into a single cohesive group. These people are generally young men who have pursued an Arabic language education, usually abroad in one of the states of the Maghreb, but occasionally as far away as the Arabian peninsula. Fluent in Arabic, well-versed in Islam as theology, and imbued with various versions of Islam as ideology, these individuals are frequently highly critical of what they see as the corruption of Sufi Islam. With limited chances for success in the modern sector – which requires a Western-style, French-language, education – they present a pool of likely recruits for movements aimed at challenging the system.

The odd bedfellows to the *arabisants* in the critique of the Sufi system are Westernized intellectuals disenchanted with the central role of the orders in the maintenance of the ruling party and, as they see it, in its resulting conservatism. While both groups are critical of the role that the Sufi orders have tended to play in politics, the prescription of the *arabisants* calls for a different and more systematic (in their view "purer") application of Islam in the political system. The Westernized dissenters, on the other hand, advocate a further *distancing*, indeed at times the total extrication, of religion from the world of politics. Because this intellectual position is spreading among urban populations, especially among youth who are increasingly likely to regard their marabout's pronouncements as irrelevant

Table 2.7. *Religious composition
of Senegal,* c. *1960*

(in percentages)

Qadir	13.4
Mouride	18.7
Tijan	45.6
Other Muslim	1.0
Non-Muslim	21.3

to their political activities, it is this second trend that appears to be more potentially threatening to the stability of the Senegalese system. The various reformist efforts that arise from these two intellectual tendencies and their intersection remain relatively small, but they nevertheless have important implications for the future evolution of the Sufi system described in the chapters that follow.

The ethno-religious mosaic in Fatick

Like Senegal as a whole, Fatick is divided not only along ethnic lines, but also on religious ones. No recent statistics are available for all of Senegal on the exact relative demographic strength of the various orders. At the time of independence in 1960, however, one estimate listed some 80 percent of the population as Muslim, in the percentages in Table 2.7.

Some 40 years earlier, in 1917, only 60 percent of the population had been estimated to be Muslim. This rapid expansion of Islam under colonial rule was the fruit of the labor of the great popularizers of Senegalese Islam discussed above, and consequently the growth of Islam benefited primarily the Mouride order and the Sy and Niasse versions of the Tijaniyya. These trends continued in the post-colonial period. As a result, it is generally accepted that both the Mourides and the Tijans must constitute somewhat higher percentages of the population today than they did in 1960, with the Mourides making up the lion's share of that growth, although remaining in second place. The Qadiriyya has almost certainly declined in importance relative to its two main competitors. While the bulk of non-Muslims in colonial Senegal were followers of traditional indigenous religions, with only a small number of Christians among them, today this group has largely disappeared; exactly eight individuals in the total population of Fatick claimed to be neither Christian nor Muslim in 1988, and only 1.1 percent of Senegal was identified as "animist" in the 1988 census. The

Table 2.8. *Religious composition of Fatick, 1988*

(in percentages)

Qadir	7.8
Mouride	24.6
Tijan	57.7
Other Muslim	4.2
Catholic	5.8

Catholic minority in Senegal is well implanted, but remains small (4.9%) and restricted almost entirely to two ethnic groups which were in early contact with French missionaries, the Serer and the Diola. In terms of religious affiliation, therefore, the demographic profile of Fatick, given in Table 2.8, must roughly parallel that of contemporary Senegal as a whole, though the proportion of Mourides in Senegal may be somewhat higher.

The ethno-religious composition of Fatick today is a product of its history. In much of rural Saloum and in parts of Sine conversion to Islam was tied to the transition to the production of peanuts as a cash crop via the model provided by the Mouride order, which consequently gained adherents among Serer in the area. In Fatick, however, as in most towns of the region, conversion was organized primarily by Tukulor marabouts, thus establishing many links with the Tijaniyya. In 1885 a cleric named Makhary Diattara settled in Fatick and became "the first religious chief to Islamize in part the Serer community in Fatick."[75] And in the neighborhood of Ndiaye-Ndiaye almost all of the early teachers of Islam were Tukulor. A certain Samba Ba, who had the advantage of also speaking Serer, was chosen as imam of the first small mosque (*jàkka*) in the neighborhood.[76] The early importance of Fatick as a commercial center helped to diversify the population. The ties which the *Buur-Siin* maintained with Qadir marabouts were no doubt reinforced by the presence of Moorish traders, who as recently as the early 1970s still occasionally arrived by camel caravan to engage in trade in the region of Fatick. Like elsewhere in the Serer area, French Catholic missionaries operated from their long-established bases on the Petite Côte to build churches and win converts in the region. In Fatick a church larger than the main mosque of the town was built in the colonial period, and though their numbers are insufficient to fill it the small Catholic congregation remains quite active. Continued rural migration to Fatick has brought many Mouride Serers, while other Mourides who have come have been Wolof traders and craftsmen.

Table 2.9. *Religious affiliation by ethnic group in Fatick*

(in percentages)

	Wolof	Serer	Haalpulaaren	Diola	Manding	Other East	Other[a]	All Groups
Qadir	5.7	6.2	7.8	6.6	28.7	27.6	34.5	7.8
Mouride	33.8	25.1	14.3	7.0	12.4	12.4	17.3	24.6
Tijan	57.3	56.5	73.7	32.0	46.5	51.8	27.4	57.6
Other								
Muslim[b]	3.0	3.8	4.2	14.7	12.1	8.0	9.1	4.2
Catholic	0.2	8.5	0.0	39.7	0.3	0.2	11.7	5.8
Total	100.0	100.0	100.0	100.0	100.0	100.0	100.0	100.0

Table 2.10. *Ethnic identification by religious group in Fatick*

(in percentages)

	Wolof	Serer	Haalpulaaren	Diola	Manding	Other East	Other[a]	Total
Qadir	15.0	47.2	12.8	1.1	6.9	7.9	9.1	100.0
Mouride	28.2	60.5	7.4	0.4	0.9	1.1	1.5	100.0
Tijan	20.4	58.1	16.3	0.7	1.5	2.0	1.0	100.0
Other Muslim[b]	15.1	53.4	12.8	4.5	5.4	4.3	4.5	100.0
Catholic	0.6	86.2	0.2	8.7	0.1	0.1	4.1	100.0
All Groups	20.5	59.3	12.8	1.3	1.8	2.2	2.1	100.0

Notes:

[a] At the time of the census 66% of this group in Fatick were Moors, thus accounting for the high association with the Qadiriyya.

[b] Includes a small number of Layènes, who make up less than 6% of this group.

The sum product of these diverse forces and relations is a cross-cutting cultural heterogeneity on both religious and ethnic lines. While neither the religious nor the ethnic distribution of the town is spread uniformly across the other system of cultural cleavages, the two nevertheless intersect broadly. No one order is concentrated predominantly in one ethnic group, nor is any one ethnic group homogeneous in its religious affiliation. Tables 2.9 and 2.10 give the precise dimensions of their intersection. These tables paint the broad outlines of Fatick's cultural mosaic, but they do not tell the whole story, and various correlations may thus require some explanation.

Because of their numerical preponderance in the town the Serer make up the majority of all religious groups in Fatick (with the single exception of the Qadiriyya of which they comprise just under half). But in terms of their proportion of the total population a moderate correlation between Mouride affiliation and Wolof ethnicity shows up; while Serers are Mouride almost exactly on a par with their demographic weight (60.5% compared to 59.3%), Mourides are more likely to be Wolof than a random distribution would allot (28.2% compared to 20.5%). This correlation is by no means absolute – only one-third of the Wolof in Fatick are Mourides – and other figures indicate that in fact the most significant correlation of being Mouride in Fatick is to *both* Wolof and Serer ethnicity. Together these two groups make up 88.7 percent of all Mourides. And if we consider linguistic identification the figures are even more telling; nearly half (45.5%) of Mourides speak Wolof as their *first* language, while an even greater percentage (48.9) speak Serer. Almost 95 percent of this religious group, therefore, speak either Wolof or Serer as their first language. Wolof, however, takes precedence over Serer in all Mouride religious interactions; the principal Mouride marabout and representative of the order in Fatick is himself a Wolof from Baol, and Mouride meetings and ceremonies are always conducted exclusively in Wolof.

By far the strongest correlation between ethnicity and Sufi affiliation is that of the Haalpulaaren to the Tijaniyya. As discussed above, this is a legacy of El Hajj Umar's *jihad* in the Senegal River Valley, where virtually all of Fatick's Tukulor population has its origins. This link was carried to the Serer by the proselytizing of Tukulor marabouts. Among the Serer of Ndiaye-Ndiaye, where ethnic identification is the strongest, the vast majority eventually came to declare themselves Tijans. Thus in 1980 when the ten-year project of constructing a Friday mosque for the neighborhood was finally completed (on a site of great symbolic importance: the ancient location of the arena for traditional wrestling matches – an activity of quasi-religious importance among the Serer) the Tijan marabout Abdoul Aziz Sy Junior was invited to preside over the inauguration. Although most of these early ties were to the Sy family, they proved relatively weak.[77] For reasons that will emerge in further discussions of the orders, the marabouts of that family were unable to maintain their appeal to the majority of the Serer of Ndiaye-Ndiaye. In a case that is highly revealing about how the Sufi orders have been able to address other societal concerns, including ethnic ones, a massive ethnically based switch in religious affiliation occurred among the Tijan Serer of Ndiaye-Ndiaye over the course of the 1980s. While the majority still identify themselves as Tijan, they have declared their allegiance to a Serer marabout who himself refuses any identification with a Sufi order.

This case will be discussed in some detail in chapter 7, but it is significant here because it points to the ambiguous meaning of calling oneself a disciple of a Sufi order in Senegal. Allegiances, in fact, are more frequently personal than organizational. And yet this also varies; as an order the Mourides exhibit a far greater organizational coherence than any of the others. The result is a social tapestry that interweaves various aspects of identity, most significantly ethnicity and religious affiliation, but in which different strands may emerge as salient in different circumstances. Depending on the situation, sometimes religion, sometimes ethnicity may prove to be the determining factor in an individual's identity and behavior. The organizational versatility of the orders that has made them the primary modes of organization *vis-à-vis* the state lies in their capacity to adapt to this ambiguity, and even capitalize on it.

3 The state–citizen relationship: struggle over bridges

Introduction: a story

On January 27, 1989, the Senegalese Minister of Youth and Sports came to visit Fatick. In recognition of the honor, and in order to greet him properly, the important men of Fatick went out early in the morning to the Kaolack road to meet the motorcade. All of the most important administrators were there – the governor of the region, the *préfet* of the department, the municipal administrator – along with dozens of minor bureaucrats and functionaries from Fatick and other towns in the region and such elected figures as the local deputy to the Senegalese parliament and the town's mayor. In addition, the representatives of innumerable organizations from throughout the region, as well as various local notables – including the Tijan marabout who represents the Sy family in Fatick and the pastor of the Catholic church – joined the reception line on the side of the road. On his arrival the minister stopped to shake hands with all of those present, before everybody climbed back into their vehicles and headed into town. At the turnoff to Fatick a group of young joggers, most of whom wore matching outfits, fell into place alongside the minister's car and escorted him into town.

After a tour of the soccer field, the local offices of the ministry, and several other sites relevant to the occasion, the entire convoy ended up at the *Gouvernance* and filed into the meeting hall of that building. The minister's visit had been arranged to coincide with a meeting of the Comité Régional de Développement (CRD), expanded for the occasion from the usual membership of regional officials to include all of those directly interested in the minister's visit. Some seventy-five people were in attendance. After a welcoming speech by the governor, another by the *Inspecteur* of Youth and Sports – the local representative of the ministry – and then one by the minister himself, the floor was opened. In a touch of Gallic influence, a list was first made of all those wanting to address the meeting, and this order then followed as one after the other was called upon to speak.

For the next three hours the thirty-odd speakers each followed a similar script in directing their comments to the minister. After enthusiastic praise for the minister and the president who had the vision to select him, and a description of the dynamism of the particular group represented by the speaker, each turned to a catalogue of highly specific requests and pleas for governmental assistance. *Monsieur* the president of the handball federation of Fatick emphasized the need for cement to repair a wall on the local court; *monsieur* the mayor of Sokone insisted on the urgent need for balls and nets for the town's basketball team; and *monsieur* the president of the football federation of Foundiougne begged the minister to provide ten T-shirts and ten pairs of shoes in the following sizes; and so it went.[1] Each locale presented a wish list, hoping to receive some handout from the limited inventory of goods which the ministry was said to have stockpiled in Dakar, much of it received as gifts from the People's Republic of China.

The minister listened patiently, then answered cautiously, walking a thin line between the twin dangers of raising expectations and of leaving no room for hope. He praised the local organizations for their good work in the service of youth and development, made some general promises about his great interest in helping out, and offered a symbolic initial contribution of some equipment to Fatick's sports teams. Careful lest expectations outstrip possibilities, he intermixed throughout his response a heavy dose of realism about the limited capabilities of the state given the scarce resources at its disposal. And in a concession to World Bank-sponsored pressures toward decentralization and privatization, he encouraged initiatives to find alternative ways to meet needs locally. Given the almost total lack of local capital, the concession was purely symbolic, and thus was not taken to undercut another aspect of the minister's message – encouraging the continuity of the existing pattern. In response to a request for state help for karate in Fatick, the minister answered emphatically: there he could do *nothing*, because there was no recognized karate organization or federation in Fatick. He gave the example of chess; there might be some in the audience who liked to play chess, but that gave them no right to request or receive any help from the state. If such groups wished to have standing to request state help like the others, an organization recognized by the local *inspecteur* would need to be founded. The message was clear: state patronage is reserved for those social groups that organize in accordance with state-sponsored patterns.

The extended recounting of this story is not meant to reflect any intrinsic importance of the event itself – the meeting eventually ended, the minister went on his way, and no significant noticeable transformations occurred in the region's sport or youth. Rather the story of this interaction is of interest because it is indicative of the underlying dynamics of the predominant patterns of interaction between the state in Senegal and local populations. Several key elements of these dynamics are readily apparent.

In a very real and concrete sense, state and society in Senegal confront and interact with each other, each attempting to exert a direct influence over the other. By its very nature, of course, the state is a rather amorphous phenomenon whose precise boundaries are difficult to discern. The ambiguous status of many of those who made requests of the minister points to the difficulties of drawing precise lines of demarcation between the two; many of these people might be simultaneously described as agents of the state and of society. This ambiguity, however, need not negate the analytic distinctiveness of the two concepts, but rather should itself be explored as an aspect of the state-society relationship.

Poverty and scarcity in Senegal provide the primary determining features of the context in which state and society interact. The need to approach the state to request the basic commodities for organizing a societal activity such as sports points to the non-independence of civil society under conditions of poverty. Lack of resources makes social groups dependent on the state which controls such resources. Herein lies an important source of leverage for the state in attempting to shape the society over which it presides. Scarcity allows the state to dictate the need to organize elements of society in ways subject to state control and supervision. That is, the state can attempt to determine the structures of civil society by allowing access to scarce resources only to those groups that conform to state-sponsored patterns of organization – hence the potential for instigating the formation of a karate club in Fatick. Such groups, then, come into existence in relation to the state and only for the purpose of mediating the interactions between Fatick's karate kids and the state. This origin, however, also allows the state to prescribe the binding rules of interaction *among* such groups, thus moving towards the accomplishment of goals attributed to the state in its very definition.

The state's control over resources is an important part of its attraction to social groups, of the reasons for opting for "incorporation" or "engagement" rather than "exit" as a strategy of interaction. The enthusiastic turnout to the minister's visit illustrates this clearly. But in the realm of local sports organization the risks and costs of engaging with the state are low, the potential payoffs worthwhile, and the alternatives virtually nonexistent. When conditions vary, the enthusiasm for engagement may wane. The basic relationship, however, remains the same; the state attempts to shape and control a society which is simultaneously attracted to the state and wary of its attempts at control. The current chapter explores the factors that influence this dynamic in Senegal, as reflected locally in Fatick.

The parameters of the state

The "elusiveness of the state-society boundary," Timothy Mitchell argues in a critique of the literature on the issue, should be approached "not as a problem of conceptual precision but as a clue to the nature of the phenomenon."[2] As Mitchell rightly insists, the state is a human construct, the product of a set of relations of power and authority. But at least in its local manifestations in a provincial town like Fatick – as, I suspect, in villages and towns throughout the world and certainly in sub-Saharan Africa – the state cannot be reduced to an "effect" produced internally. As experienced by the population of Fatick the state *does* exist as an empirical reality, external and distinct from the society in which it functions. There are not only a set of institutions and organizations, but also of practices, behavioral and linguistic patterns, and even beliefs, that belong unambiguously to the domain of the state. And as Mitchell recognizes, "[t]he cultural forms of the state *are* an empirical phenomenon, as solid and discernible as a legal structure or a party system."[3] Much of the fuzziness that renders state boundaries elusive at the local level is, instead, a product of the duality lived by the individuals who staff the state. Although agents of the state, they are also simultaneously part of the societal web that includes ties of ethnicity, kinship, and religion. The state as a concept therefore cannot be reduced to the collectivity of individuals that staff it, nor to the relations of power and authority that unite those individuals with others. While it is a human construct, the state also has a *historical* reality that transcends, indeed helps to structure, the relations of the contemporary human actors involved in its perpetuation. The historical parameters of the Senegalese state are therefore reviewed below, before turning to the more elusive issue of the state-society relation as reflected locally in Fatick.

Historical and ideological foundations

The historical legacy weighs particularly heavily in Senegal where (to date) a rupture with the colonially erected structures has been avoided – though these have, of course, been modified and manipulated by post-colonial forces. Several general features of the colonial state are still readily discernible in the Senegalese state some three decades after independence: relations of authority within the structures of the state are characterized by an exceptionally high degree of centralization; the state bureaucracy remains comparatively "heavy" both in terms of its size in relation to the population and in terms of its influence on the economy; there is a marked emphasis on adherence to procedural rules in the bureaucratic functioning of the administration; and, finally, the task of applying these procedures is seen as the legitimate job of a bureaucratic elite trained especially in the technical skills of administration. Quite clearly such features owe a great debt directly to the Senegalese state's French parent, itself the prototype of the modern bureaucratic state. But their exceptional continuity – particularly in contrast to many other failed graftings of the French model in Africa – is also largely attributable to the unique history of the colonial state in Senegal.

For a brief historical period early in the development of a colonial policy, the French attempted to apply in Senegal what later remained as the official – but elsewhere purely theoretical – policy known as *assimilation*. As Michael Crowder has pointed out, the policy was erected on seemingly contradictory twin principles: the "revolutionary doctrine of the equality of man" on the one hand and the "assumption of the superiority of European, and in particular French, civilization" on the other.[4] Given these beliefs, the early logic of French colonial rule was an attempt to effect the transformation of French subjects into cultural Frenchmen, a goal that became known as *"la mission civilisatrice."* From the revolutionary period of 1848, when France began organizing local elections, the colony of Senegal – then little more than the coastal city of Saint Louis and the island of Gorée – elected a deputy to the French Assembly. Although the early deputies were all either of metropolitan French birth (and hence white) or *métis* (mixed race), indigenous black residents of these cities enjoyed equal rights to vote as French citizens. These liberal policies, however, came increasingly under attack by the turn of the century when France's African and Asian empire was firmly in place and it became readily apparent that, if such a policy were maintained, *white* Frenchmen could soon form a minority of the electorate.

In the "four communes" of Senegal – Dakar and Rufisque, in addition to Saint Louis and Gorée – there resulted a historically unprecedented political struggle as black citizens of these cities organized in the fight to preserve their rights as French citizens – a struggle that led to such paradoxical positions as the insistence by African citizens that they, like all citizens, be obliged to perform French military service.[5] The movement led to the election of Senegal's first black representative to the French Assembly, the *goréen* civil servant Blaise Diagne, in 1914 on the eve of the outbreak of the First World War. Seizing on the issue of military service at a time when French concerns about a shortage of manpower was acute, Diagne won the confirmation of full French citizenship rights for the *originaires*, the residents of the four communes, with the passage of the 1917 laws that bore his name. The result, however, was the establishment of a dual system in Senegal that distinguished the *citoyens* who comprised a small urban minority from the vast majority of the population who held the status of *sujet*.

The distinction between French citizens and subjects was preserved until 1946, when the rapid changes in the international consensus on colonialism and in the domestic political situation in Senegal following the war made it untenable. Although after that date all Senegalese shared the same legal status as "citizens of the French Union" (not of France), the distinct historical experience left a legacy of a dual political culture, one involving a Westernized Francophone minority with a long experience in electoral politics in the major urban areas, and another marked principally by a system of indirect administration of the rural masses via the intermediaries of local notables of various sorts – including, most significantly, marabouts of the major orders – which effectively shielded much of the population from French cultural influences.

The dichotomy continues to be felt in the rural-urban distinction in Senegalese politics, but the inherent potential for divisive conflict along these lines was largely muted through the actions of the man who was to become Senegal's first president, Léopold Sédar Senghor. The comparatively great weight of single individuals in shaping the character of sub-Saharan African states in the post-independence period has been explored in studies focused on the concept of "personal rule" on the continent.[6] In relatively small countries such as Senegal that potential is magnified, and Senghor proved himself determined and capable of leaving a distinct personal imprint on the Senegalese state.

Born a subject, Senghor managed via a French Catholic education to become one of the extraordinarily rare few of his generation to achieve the status of naturalized French citizen. His varied and illustrious accomplishments ranged from famous poet, linguistic scholar, and teacher to politician and minister in French governments, president of Senegal, and back to a literary career crowned in 1984 by his election as the first black member of that most exclusive of European institutions, the French Academy.[7] These experiences left Senghor deeply steeped in French culture, the very model of the "assimilated" African. Maintaining close ties with France was central to his political goals, and in the period between the Second World War and independence many of his energies were in fact devoted to maintaining the unity of the French Empire – although under conditions that would recognize the equal status of African citizens.[8] Yet in one of the many paradoxes that mark his career Senghor built his political base on close ties with the former "subjects" of rural Senegal, those least touched by the influence of French culture.

The Bloc Démocratique Sénégalais (BDS), the political party which

Senghor founded in 1948 as a vehicle for organizing the rural vote, has survived in various permutations and name changes to remain the ruling Parti Socialiste (PS) of today.[9] The alliances which Senghor formed with rural notables, notably the marabouts of the central peanut basin, provided the electoral base for the BDS's 1951 victory to take both of Senegal's seats to the French Assembly, and eventually carried him to the presidency at independence in 1960. The only significant challenge to Senghor's near-total domination of the party and the structures of the state (a distinction not always visible at the local level) was the 1962 crisis provoked by the alleged *coup d'état* attempt led by Prime Minister Mamadou Dia, Senghor's long-time collaborator from the early days of the BDS. For the rest of that decade Senghor systematically concentrated control of the state in his own hands, before beginning a gradual relaxation of the political system which nevertheless maintained the dominant position of Senghor and his party. On 31 December 1981 Senghor became the first African head of state to turn over power voluntarily to a successor, his vice president and long-time protégé Abdou Diouf.

The constitutional and legal structures which established the Senegalese state at independence were transplanted in all essential respects from the French system: a constitutional republican form of government, a civil code of law, and administrative, educational, and judicial organizations all patterned on the French model. Although any decisive rupture with the system has been avoided, these have not always been preserved in their original form; throughout Senghor's tenure modifications were made as the president himself saw the need for adaptations. Yet the role of Senghor in shaping the Senegalese state is not limited to structural adaptations, but also to a set of intangible but no less real attributes of the contemporary state. As Gerti Hesseling has noted, the influence of Senghor today is felt not only in the "modifications of the constitutional regime," but also in "the imprint which he has affixed on the ideological frame within which this regime saw the light of day."[10]

Among the characteristics which Senghor bequeathed to the state in Senegal is the continued reliance on a theoretically elaborate ideology of "African Socialism" which, though rather amorphous in practical terms and systematically jettisoned for pragmatic reasons, nevertheless envisages the *transformation* of society.[11] The deviation from the colonial situation which this represents must be stressed. While the colonial state sought to dominate and control society, the independent state's goals are expanded to attempt to incorporate and transform society. As we shall see this not only affects its relations with social groups, but was responsible for provoking an important shift from the colonial model in terms of state relations with the marabouts.

Officials of the state at all levels have also demonstrated a regular commitment to a *de jure* constitutional order which, among other things, assures the secular nature of the state. Although the appropriateness of the secular state (*l'état laïc*) has occasionally been questioned, most seriously by reformist Muslim groups, the commitment of the state to the concept has never wavered. Finally, Senghor preserved and reinforced the predominance of distinctly French cultural traits and attitudes in the organization and functioning of the bureaucratic apparatus of the state. It bears emphasizing that these are not merely cosmetic, but form a very real part of the ideological machinery which keeps the state distinct from the society in which it functions. The most significant of these is language, a realm particularly dear to the poet-president's heart. An emphasis on literacy and the use of the French language in a country where only a small percentage of the population has such skills serves not only to symbolically demarcate the domain of the state, but more concretely as an exclusionary barrier that precludes much societal intrusion into the state's domain.[12] Carol Myers-Scotton has explored this phenomenon in Africa, and suggested the use of the term "elite closure" to describe it. Her definition applies directly to the Senegalese case:

Elite closure is a strategy by which those persons in power maintain their powers and privileges via language choices ... Thus elite closure is a tactic of boundary maintenance: It involves institutionalizing the linguistic patterns of the elite, either through official policy or informally established usage norms in order to limit access to socioeconomic mobility and political power to people who possess the requisite linguistic patterns.[13]

As is true virtually everywhere in Africa, in a quite literal sense the language of the state and those of society are not the same in Senegal.

Structures

On the more pragmatic level of organizational structures, the debt of the contemporary Senegalese state to its colonial parent is no less strongly felt. From 1902, when the Government General was transferred from Saint Louis, Dakar had served as the administrative capital of the entire territory of French West Africa (the AOF, Afrique Occidentale Française). At independence in 1960, after the aborted effort to retain at least some of the unity of the AOF in the short-lived Mali Federation, Senegal inherited the lion's share of the administrative structures and of the functionaries that had staffed the territory. Of the eight countries to emerge from the "balkanization" that Senghor had so long fought, Senegal had by far the largest and most developed state apparatus. These structures were, in addition, centered overwhelmingly in Dakar. In a study of state functionaries carried out in the Senegalese capital a decade after independence, a full fifty percent of those questioned themselves believed that the state bureaucracy suffered from a "plethora of functionaries" and that this situation was the product of the colonial heritage.[14] In the years since then these two trends – an overstaffed bureaucracy and its concentration in the capital – have continued unabated, leading one Senegalese intellectual to describe postcolonial Senegal as "an enormous and artificial superstructure centered on Dakar."[15]

Away from the center, in the majority of the country, the structures of the state are organized in a hierarchical pyramidal fashion, with all lines of authority passing upwards through a series of links to end in Dakar. Since 1984, when the regions of Casamance and Sine-Saloum were each divided in two – thus resulting in the creation of the new regions of Fatick and Kolda – the country has been divided into ten regions, each bearing the name of its capital city. Each region is in turn divided into three departments, which are themselves divided into various *arrondissements* (districts). At the base of the pyramid are the *communautés rurales* (rural communities), comprising either a single large village or a set of villages. Parallel to this structure are the urban municipalities (*communautés urbaines*), which in the case of regional capitals have a special administrative status. Given its unique characteristics as an overwhelmingly urban region, Dakar alone has a special status with structures that differ from those of other regions.

These structures of the state are staffed by a bureaucracy comprised of civil servants appointed to their positions by the president in consultation with the Ministry of the Interior. At the head of each region is a governor, under which *préfets* (prefects) serve as the state representative at the departmental level, followed by *sous-préfets* (sub-prefects) in the *arrondissements*. Officials are frequently rotated from one region to another, the more successful among them gradually moving up the administrative ladder and even occasionally into the top echelons of government. President Abdou Diouf himself served briefly as governor of the old region of Sine-Saloum, from which he was promoted to various positions in the office of the president.

Diouf, who returned to Senegal after studies in France at the time of independence in 1960, was among the last generation of Senegalese officials to be trained in the metropole, at the Ecole Nationale de la France d'Outre Mer (the National School of Overseas France). Following independence Senghor launched on a program of developing institutes in Senegal for the training of cadres specifically for purposes of staffing the state bureaucracy. In addition to various technical training schools, the Centre de Formation et de Perfectionnement Administratif (CFPA) was established in 1965 to train mid-level administrators.[16] This institute is administratively linked directly to the office of the president, and functions in conjunction with the more prestigious Ecole Nationale d'Administration et Magistrature (ENAM), patterned after the famous French Ecole Nationale d'Administration (ENA) and responsible for the training of the personnel which staffs the highest echelons of the state structures. In the regions the majority of prefects, governors, and other important officials are graduates of ENAM, as are most of the officials who hold important posts in the ministries in Dakar, as well as in the Senegalese diplomatic service.

One effect of this system of staffing the state is the formation of a bureaucratic elite that views administration as a technical skill for which it is uniquely suited. Their common training, dependence for appointments on the office of the presidency, and regular rotation among positions all serve to imbue this staff with certain unifying characteristics. The result of the shared period of socialization in the urban, secular, and westernized political culture is an administrative solidarity among functionaries which, although it is not necessarily determinative of political behavior, nevertheless provides an important measure of cohesion to the state as an institution distinct from its predominantly rural and religious African society. Moreover, as direct representatives of the executive branch of the central government, regional state officials are tied directly to a centralized pyramidal structure in which all significant administrative decisions are made at the apex in Dakar.

The centralized and hierarchical system of administration has posed difficulties for independent Senegal both in terms of barriers to administrative efficiency and in local responses to state initiatives. Senegalese politics have consequently been marked by periodic demands for both "deconcentration" and "decentralization" of power, and by subsequent state efforts to accommodate such demands without sacrificing the hegemony of state structures or the power of the presidency which the established system ensures. The most recent policy shifts in the direction of promising greater local autonomy were provoked by the social and political unrest which followed the February 1988 elections. Following those elections, and then with renewed urgency when the PS attempted to rebuild its popular support as the 1993 elections approached, several initiatives were undertaken in the name of a renewed commitment to the decentralization of state administration. Though these initiatives will no doubt lead to some changes, the promise of any radical restructuring must be treated with caution.

The ambivalence within the state itself about the degree of concentration of state power is reflected in the periodic changes in the structure of the executive branch of government which has marked Senegal's independent political history. The frequently extreme concentration of decision-making powers in the highest levels of government which, as in most of the countries of the continent, has marked independent Senegal produces a pervasive tendency to "pass the buck" up the administrative ladder. This "Pontius Pilate-ism," as Senghor referred to the practice, has the effect of diverting top officials from the broad formulation of policy goals by occupying much of their time in dealing with relatively trivial issues.[17] This tendency was further exacerbated by the strong presidential system provided for in the 1963 constitution as a corrective measure to the tensions that sprung from the bicephalous character of executive power in the first post-independence constitution. By 1970, the situation was so acute that the proposed bill to modify the constitution to restore the office of prime minister referred directly to the president's analysis of the problem: "The concentration of executive power has had too often the result of providing all agents of the state with a convenient pretext to unload their responsibilities on the president of the republic. This situation had ultimately given rise to a general spirit of 'pontius pilate-ism' harmful to the proper functioning of public services."[18]

The approval of the constitutional reform and the subsequent naming of the young technocrat Abdou Diouf to the restored office of prime minister – where he was to remain for a decade before succeeding Senghor in the presidency – temporarily defused the crisis of administrative concentration. But the tension that is inherent in the tendency of the president and his ministers to simultaneously attempt to oversee all aspects of the functioning of the state bureaucracies while delegating responsibilities to ensure greater efficiency in the execution of administrative tasks has remained a central feature of Senegalese political life, though one felt primarily *within* the state rather than between state and society. In 1983, in response to the crisis provoked by the opposition's contestation of the results of the February election, the constitution was again revised to re-abolish the post of prime minister and re-concentrate power in presidential hands – a move provoked, Abdou Diouf announced, by the need for "greater efficiency, speed, and simplicity" in government operations.[19] Then in February 1991, Diouf announced that once again the prime ministership would be restored, and in April appointed his long-time friend and political ally, Habib Thiam, to the post.[20] The swinging of the pendulum reflects the tension between the desire for hegemonic control and the demands of efficiency at the very highest levels of the Senegalese state.

In addition to the question of the *concentration* of power, Senegalese politics have also been marked by debates about its *centralization*. While pressures for deconcentration arise from the need for "increasing the powers of the local representatives of the central authorities in order to relieve the congestion" of the central institutions, decentralization, by contrast, "suggests the idea of a degree of local autonomy."[21] While the former addresses concerns about where power should be concentrated within the structures of the state, the latter challenges the very right of the state to claim certain powers. Demands for greater democracy in the sense of local control over decision-making to counter the hegemonic tendency of the state has been the central source of tension faced by Senegalese administrators in their local-level dealings. Calls for decentralization, therefore, have consistently marked the history of relations between state and society in independent Senegal.[22]

Throughout this history there have been various initiatives and administrative reforms periodically proposed in the name of decentralization, but these have regularly foundered on the unwillingness of state officials to actually relinquish control and risk uncertain outcomes likely to escape state tutelage. Thus locally elected representative institutions have been established at various points, but their power then systematically curtailed to maintain centralized control. The case of the Regional Assemblies illustrates this point. Established in 1960 as part of the first administrative reforms of the independent government, the Assemblies were intended to democratize politics at the level of each region. Because they quickly became a locus for political struggles that escaped central government control, however, Senghor promptly moved to limit the scope of this experiment in local democracy. By establishing strict controls over the budgets and available resources for the Assemblies, and by increasing the powers of governors and other regional administrators, the Regional Assemblies were eventually reduced to being "little more than rubber stamps for approving government-initiated programs."[23] In 1972 they were finally abolished outright. Then in 1992, on the occasion of the president's Independence Day speech on April 4, a broad series of new regional reforms were proposed. Among other things, the Regional Assemblies would be re-established and given a significant degree of autonomy over local affairs and finances. As Richard Vengroff has noted, this was clearly a politically motivated and timed initative, and one whose promise cannot be taken at face value. To the extent that the announcement represents merely "another attempt by the regime to use the promise of decentralization . . . to shore up its sagging popular support" it may be little more than a reflection of a shift in the balance of power in the struggle between state and society over defining control over local issues.[24]

A similar case of particular importance in Fatick involved the debate over control of the administration of the municipality. At independence in 1960, Fatick was named a *commune de plein exercice*, a nominally self-governing urban "commune" or municipality. In towns with this status, municipal councils were popularly elected by universal suffrage, and the council in turn elected a mayor. Because elections are by party list with a "winner-takes-all" system, the ruling party is assured control of mayoral positions in virtually all towns with that status. In addition, the local prefect plays an important role in executing many of the functions of the council and, in cases where the Ministry of the Interior determines that council activities are not in the "population's best interests," municipal councils could be suspended by decree – something that in fact has been rather common.[25] In Fatick this occurred in May 1963, following accusations that the council had been compromised by its ties to the government of Mamadou Dia, author of the alleged 1962 attempt at a *coup d'état*.[26] In 1964, however, new elections were held in Fatick to re-establish the system of municipal government which, though subject to this tutelage, nevertheless granted some leverage to local populations.

A 1974 administrative reform modified the status of urban communes. For the majority of the smaller communes, like Fatick, the modification entailed principally the addition of several non-elected councilors to the municipal council, who would be appointed at the ministerial level but nominated by local corporate groups, namely youth groups, trade unions, or professional associations. But for those communes that were also regional capitals the changes were more significant. The new post of municipal administrator (*administrateur municipal*) was created to preside over the administration of such communes. The effect was to reduce the powers of the elected mayor even further, leaving him with little more than ceremonial functions. Like prefects and governors, the municipal administrators were to be functionaries appointed to their positions by the Ministry of the Interior and hence to serve as direct representatives of the state. In the regional capitals, therefore, even the modest decentralization of the municipal councils was effectively neutralized by this reform.

The system was highly unpopular in the regional capitals and quickly became the focus of heightened demands for decentralization and greater local-level democracy. In 1989 even the municipal administrator in Fatick acknowledged what he labeled the "nearly unanimous" demands by local municipal councils and officials to abolish outright the position which he held.[27] In Fatick the transition from the system of *commune de plein exercice* to the "special status" of regional capital that followed the creation of the new region in 1984 fed local grievances against the state and became the focus of protests against the administration. One local-born former administrator, retired to Fatick, vocalized the complaint explicitly in a speech commemorating the 70th anniversary of the naming of the commune of Fatick:

The new status introduced in July 1984 is a clear retreat from the status of 1960 which was the normal outcome of the commune's progress from its inception. In effect, under the regime of the 1984 reforms, elected authorities have no administrative power over the commune. This situation is a profound and frustrating restriction on the democratization of the management of local collectivities.

And alluding to the recent World Bank and IMF-sponsored initiatives toward decentralization in the domain of economics, he continued:

The direction taken by the new options of the state in its policy of making economic agents totally responsible in the economic domain may leave room for hope that, in the political domain, there will be a complete decentralization of the 'special status communes' [i.e., regional capitals] in a not-too-distant future, thus permitting citizens to fully manage and administer their own communes.[28]

The reforms of October 1990 were indeed to return the "special status" municipalities to the position of *communes de droit commun*, and the municipal administrator was henceforth to be placed under the elected mayor's authority.

There were, however, also a series of new limitations placed on municipal councils and the power of mayors. And the maintenance of a party-list and "winner-takes-all" system for local elections ensured a continued central role for state officials as long as the PS maintained its dominant position in Senegalese politics. Even more tellingly, all of these reforms have been implemented by decree, and ironically the fact that local state officials have frequently been caught off guard by their promulgation indicates the degree to which even decisions about decentralization have been centralized in Senegal. In any case, to the extent that the history of the debate concerning decentralization in the country is reflective of a more fundamental opposition between state attempts to dominate local structures and societal efforts to keep the state at bay, or at least reduce its local control, it appears likely that despite the 1990 announcement of some state concessions on these issues, the underlying dynamics that give rise to such tensions will remain.[29]

An integral part of the reality of the state, therefore, is the tension inherent in the political debates surrounding the extent of concentration and centralization of power. And the logic of asserting state control over a society in which it has only shallow and fragile roots ensures the continuation of a state preference for the hierarchical concentration of centralized power. The experience of the government and the state in Fatick, therefore, is almost exclusively the experience of interactions with the representatives of the state center, officials who have been socialized in the model of the Western state system, who justify policies in accordance with the logic of national imperatives and who execute their functions in the language of the former colonial power. In addition to the governor, the prefect, and the municipal administrator, each of the relevant ministries appoints an official, generally known as the *inspecteur* (inspector), to serve as its representative in each of the regional capitals. Some eight years after its elevation to capital status most of these regional offices were functioning in Fatick, although a few state services were still in the process of being established. The inspectors are direct representatives of the centralized state, responsible for carrying out the initiatives of each ministry, overseeing projects or policies under its jurisdiction, and providing the relevant goods and services to the public – all under the supervision of the more important local functionaries. The interactions of individuals with the state, therefore, are frequently channeled through these officials. In addition to the Inspector of Youth and Sports, whose position was noted in the introduction to this chapter, examples of inspectors through whom local citizens frequently approach the state are the representatives of the Ministries of Education and of Urban Affairs and Housing. Like various others, the monopolistic control of these officials over certain resources makes them poles of attraction and provides the leverage by which the state exerts control over local populations and social groups.

The state agency: dynamics of local level functioning

In July 1959, a year before Senegalese independence, the future president of the country addressed a congress of one of the short-lived interterritorial parties that had been formed in a last-minute effort to save at least some of the unity of French West Africa. "The state," he argued, "is the expression of the nation; it is above all the means of realizing the nation."[30] Both the state and the nation to which he referred were much larger entities than independent Senegal proved to be, but Senghor's theoretical exposition of this relationship was intended to serve broadly as a guiding principle for independent African states.

The internal contradiction is readily apparent – the "state" is simultaneously defined as the *creation of* and the *instrument for creating* the "nation" – but the statement serves nevertheless to indicate some of the ambiguous duality at the very core of the state which is a source of the tension inherent in its existence. As part of the ideology by which it justifies itself the state in Senegal is regularly said to be a reflection of its society: "The state, like civil society of which it is the legitimate emanation ..." intones an article in the official government newspaper.[31] Yet the agents of the state also readily recognize the fact that they are engaged most clearly in an effort to reshape sociological reality. Both rationales coexist – sometimes rather uneasily – in the structures of the state. Senghor's comment thus indirectly suggests two sets of issues to consider in examining the relations between state and society at the local level, in the concrete patterns of interaction between agents of the state and individuals in society. (1) How implicated is the state in its society; that is, what distinguishes state officials from the broader society, what ties them into it, and how is this relationship maintained? And (2) what is entailed in the efforts of the state to "realize" the nation by transforming social structures; what vision and ideas guide relations with local groups and individuals? As we shall see, and as Schatzberg has demonstrated so convincingly in his exploration of the "triple helix" of state, class, and ethnicity in Zaire, the phenomenon of the state at the local level can only be fully explored in the context of other economic and social variables.[32]

"The economy of affection" versus "la solidarité administrative"

Two contrasting codes of behavior make demands on the allegiances of state functionaries at the local level and, indeed, at every level of the state bureaucracy. Individuals in their capacity as agents of the state find themselves simultaneously faced with the need to compete with society to secure the gains that come from a measure of control over the state and at the same time obliged in varying degrees to respond to demands arising from their ties to society. The tensions inherent in these contrasting demands are a primary source of the "fuzziness" which makes it difficult to identify the boundaries of the state at the local level. It is, nevertheless, an integral part of its reality, relevant to a consideration of its relations with society.

The individuals who staff the independent state in Senegal, like elsewhere on the continent, are themselves part of broader social systems which include ties of family, ethnicity, and religion. In this respect the independent state contrasts sharply with the colonial one, and it is in this context that the prevalence of "corruption" throughout Africa following the accession to independence must be understood. These societal ties involve the functionaries of the state in a web of relations that give rise to what Goran Hyden has called "the economy of affection." The term "denotes a network of support, communications and interaction among structurally defined groups connected by blood, kin, community or such other affinities as religion. It links together in a systematic fashion a variety of discrete economic and social units which in other regards may be autonomous."[33] These ties, Hyden argues persuasively, result in individuals making economic decisions that may seem "irrational" from the perspective of much of classical economic theory and "counterproductive" from the position of development administrators, but which must be taken into account in an explanation of patterns of governance in African societies.

The African bureaucrat, like the peasant, stands "with one foot in the economy of affection and the other in the wider national economy."[34] This strategic location makes him a link between society and the resources of the state. The most direct and concrete indication of this position in the economy of affection is the need of virtually all state officials to house, feed, and otherwise support an array of relatives or other dependants. In a 1972 study of Senegalese state functionaries, Fatou Sow found that even in Dakar among the bureaucrats she interviewed, all but an "infinitely small percentage" regularly provided aid to dependants *other than* wives or children. A full 85 percent acknowledged supporting at least one other person fully, and almost 70 percent actually had dependants in addition to wives and children living with them. For many these obligations are extensive: half claimed three or more dependants, and 22 percent supported six or more. In terms of resources this aid also represents a "relatively important charge in relation to total monthly income"; 43 percent of those willing to answer the question admitted to giving 20 percent or more of their income to people not living with them in order to fulfill social obligations.[35] In addition to these regular expenses, salaried bureaucrats can count on being frequently requested to contribute to the expenses of life-cycle ceremonies such as naming celebrations, circumcisions, and funerals; asked to help out individuals who can establish a claim to a social connection in times of crisis or difficulty; and required to feed or house temporarily such kin, fellow villagers, or others who have a basis for making such requests.

The potential for extreme social mobility that results from the overlay of the Western state system and the capitalist economy on traditional systems further complicates the patterns of economic relations and confounds the attempt to locate class-based modes of behavior by bringing the economy of affection to the fore. Differential access to education in particular results in many cases of families in which members span the full range of socio-economic statuses, as in the case of a well-placed bureaucrat, a graduate of ENAM in a position of some importance in the office of the president whose siblings, among them a peasant farmer, range from totally illiterate to his own educational level. The demands of the economy of affection make this man responsible for meeting the needs of a broad array of members of the extended family, and his placement within the state thus serves as one of the innumerable links to wider social networks.

The location of state bureaucrats at the center of such social networks arises from the confluence of two factors: the mosaic of social relations within the political culture of hierarchy and dependence and the fact of state control over scarce economic resources. While similar networks of dependency form around any individual with the economic resources to support them – marabouts in the peanut basin being the most striking example – in a town like Fatick, with few sources of revenue beyond the level of simple subsistence, the state provides the most significant locus of access to goods or services. The array of state functionaries ranging from the governor to lower level employees of ministerial offices and teachers make up virtually all of the salaried workers in Fatick. The rhythm of the local economy, the size of the weekly market and the volume of trade that takes place, is closely linked to the pay cycle for state officials.

There is a virtually limitless number of examples of variations in the ways in which the economy of affection may impose obligations on individuals. The case of a high school teacher who found it necessary to constantly maneuver to limit the number of nieces and nephews which his twenty-odd siblings – only one of whom also had a salaried job – regularly tried to place in his care is an extreme but not isolated case demonstrating the pressure resulting from the need to support relatives of various sorts. In addition, officials are regularly called on in their private capacity to aid other kin or individuals with whom they have a religious tie or to contribute to the functions of a religious group such as a *daaira*. Ethnic or even caste ties can likewise be called on in making similar demands. Most importantly, the demands which the economy of affection makes on state agents are directed not only toward their personal resources, but more significantly on their potential for helping to secure preferential access to state goods and services. Thus, for example, when it was announced that the state was to establish a system that would allow individuals with few resources to invest in small shops as a means of replacing those maintained by Moors before the April 1989 events, state officials in Fatick were swamped with requests outside the officially established channels for help in securing a priority position on the list of applicants.[36] Such examples of "corruption" must be distinguished from acts of embezzlement or outright stealing, and the fact that they are integral to the economy of affection renders them a persistent aspect of the "clan politics" which have attracted so much attention in writing about Senegal.[37]

Proximity to the state is crucial to the emergence and maintenance of patronage networks of this sort. But in situations of scarcity there is a strong incentive for state officials to *limit* access to state resources in order to ensure their own positions. This situation, therefore, gives rise to a contrasting code of behavior, an emphasis on solidarity among state administrators which leads to an ethic of giving preference to fellow bureaucrats in facilitating access to goods and services. This reaction, of course, is not unique to Senegal. The authors of one of the more thorough studies of the Zairian state, for example, argue that the "units of the state are committed to securing from their subjects a living for the state itself." The state thus sees "first to its own preservation and nurture."[38] Faced with scarce resources and overwhelming societal demands on them, administrators draw ranks to secure their own positions.

The conscious application of a notion of *solidarité administrative* was acknowledged, indeed insisted on, by an official at the local office of the Ministry of Urban Affairs and Housing (Ministère de l'Urbanisme et de l'Habitat), and a description of how that particular bureaucracy operates may serve as a useful method for illustrating the scope and limits of this feature of Senegalese administration within the context of the functioning of the state in Fatick.[39] The local office of the ministry is primarily occupied in implementing regulations made in Dakar concerning the application within Fatick of laws dealing with the complex issue of land tenure, a pervasive difficulty in Senegal resulting from the coexistence of traditional, colonial, and post-independence legal systems.[40]

In Fatick, as in all urban areas with a population of approximately 10,000 or more, the most significant function of the office concerns the executing of "*lotissements*" (establishing the division into lots) and the subsequent distribution of residential lots. *Lotissements* are done within the framework of a long-term plan carried out by the local office, in conjunction with urban planners from the ministry in Dakar, when a town's growth reaches a point where planning is required. Although the old neighborhood of Escale and some of the surrounding area had already been regularized in Fatick during the colonial period, much of the more recent growth of the town was in the form of unplanned settlement in the peripheral neighborhoods, and in 1978 a plan for the long-term urbanization of the town was undertaken. Before being implemented, such plans are reviewed by a "Regional Committee on Urbanism," composed of representatives of other interested state services, such as the offices of education and of health, who study the plan and are allowed input in light of their particular interests.

The approval of the plan tends to be relatively non-controversial in cases like Fatick where there are few, if any, opportunities for land speculation. Far more difficult, however, is the question of how lots are to be distributed once the *lotissement* is complete. Applications for lots on which to settle and build are reviewed by a commission established especially for that purpose, and composed of the prefect, the municipal administrator, representatives from the local offices of the appropriate services (Urbanisme, Cadastres, and Domaines), and two municipal councilors chosen from that body. Much potential for tension is pre-emptively defused by important conservative aspects of the system: all existing legal statuses, of titles, deeds, or leases, are respected, even when they originated in the colonial period and even when they would no longer be legally possible to establish under the post-independence system – the titles held by the old commercial houses and Lebanese merchants on water property are the most significant of these in Fatick. Secondly, priority in establishing legal occupation of a lot is always given to the *de facto* occupants of that lot, and again this principle is well respected. One indicative case in Fatick involves an area of predominantly Fulbe (Peul) settlement near the principal entrance to the town. A previous governor of the region had strongly insisted on attempting to put up "nice" buildings near the entrance in order to improve the town's appearance, and regretted the (to him) rather unsightly huts there. Yet despite the fact, as the official bemoaned, that "everyone knows that Peuls don't buy bricks" – and thus that they would probably never build more "modern" structures on that site – nothing could be done about the governor's wish because of the existing *de facto* occupation of that site by the Fulbe settlers.[41]

The delicate task of deciding on applications, which as Fatick has grown in size far outstrip lots made available by the periodic *lotissements*, presents the commission with more overtly political pressures, and reveals the codes under which these state officials function. Two official criteria are established for the commission to consider in reviewing applications: (1) the solvency of the applicant, and (2) his or her "social status." Such criteria clearly allow a great deal of leeway for other considerations, prime among which is the notion of "administrative solidarity." By common understanding among the members of the commission, the administrative personnel of the state are given preference in awarding lots. The ultimate decisions of the commission must all, in fact, ultimately be based on such unwritten understandings. There is no established rule about how decisions are reached; the cases are simply discussed and a consensus achieved. In reality, by the time the commission meets to discuss applications, all serious applicants are already known to the individual members. The process, therefore, is highly personalized. The necessity for compromise, reflected in the official's insistence that conflicts within the commission are extremely rare as long as everyone remembers that "one must be reasonable," limits the potential for excessive abuse.

Moreover, because of the flexibility available to the commission, a façade of procedural legitimacy is always maintained. Administrative solidarity consists not only in giving preference to fellow bureaucrats but also in facilitating procedures and bending regulations so as to grant them favors *without* abandoning the procedural requirements of administration. Thus, for example, one young official in the office of the municipal administrator was able to have an inspector in the office of Urbanisme re-evaluate a lot that had not previously been assigned because of concerns about drainage patterns during the rainy season, thus clearing the way for him to get title to it. A friendly perfunctory visit to the site was all that was required for its "re-evaluation."[42] Another functionary achieved similar ends via different means by simply occupying and beginning construction on an unassigned lot, then using his administrative ties to legalize his status by having a declaration of previous occupation made.[43]

The state in this case has established its monopoly over a particular good, namely lots for new construction, and thus controls access to this good. And the procedures established for granting access are structured so as to allow room for an administrative solidarity which ensures first of all the position of those within the state, while also providing a means for those officials to answer to the demands of the economy of affection by distributing patronage on the basis of personalized claims. An evaluation of this system presents some difficulty. Clearly the lack of a transparently objective method of distribution contains an element of injustice which can fuel dissatisfaction and protests against the state. Yet there is also an element of stability introduced by the fact that the system is inherently conservative and answers to prevailing notions of entitlements based on "social status." Perhaps more significantly, the relative security which agents of the state in Senegal derive at least in part from the ethic of administrative solidarity is a crucial component of the comparative non-repressiveness of the Senegalese state in the African context. In contrast to cases like Zaire, where administrative insecurity feeds cycles of oppression as officials struggle to get as much as they can as fast as possible, never knowing when their turn will end,[44] the Senegalese state at the local level exhibits a far more benign face.

Agents of incorporation and transformation

If one determinant of the behavior of state officials at the local level is the effort to influence the distribution of benefits from the state in accordance with the twin desires of securing their own positions and diverting benefits towards those to whom they have obligations, there is nevertheless another guiding aspect of state action in Senegal. As occupants of positions created and defined by the state and which, in light of its historical evolution, are sufficiently institutionalized to transcend the individuals who occupy those positions, state agents in Fatick also carry out functions intended to execute the broader goals of the state. At their most general level these goals involve the effort to incorporate, shape, and indeed transform society in accordance with a vision of "modernity" which owes its most direct intellectual debt to the model elaborated by Senghor.

A belief in the potential for transforming the social order is firmly embedded in the Senegalese state and reflected by its agents. In the same survey of state officials noted above, an astounding 68 percent claimed to believe that within thirty years Africans would live "in a completely new manner which will resemble neither the old manner nor the European manner." Only 15 percent believed that the future would bring greater Europeanization, and an even smaller percentage foresaw the continuity of existing cultural patterns. While the prevalence of this vision was certainly in large part a product of the historical moment – the euphoria of independence had yet to be indelibly tarnished by political events on the continent – the beliefs of the officials nevertheless contrasted sharply with those of other salaried workers in Dakar, a group of roughly comparable socio-economic status and education. In a separate study which posed the same question, only 25 percent of this latter group agreed with the majority of state agents. Somewhat over half, by contrast, expected the expansion of Europeanization. While a large majority of both groups thus anticipated significant social change, officials of the state were far more likely to hold a visionary belief in social transformation, an attitude, the author of the study noted, which reflected their "will to historical creation."[45]

No obvious *methods* are available for achieving such an abstract goal, but following the convictions of Senegal's "founding father," the notion that the state must serve as the *instrument* for "realizing the nation" remains virtually unquestioned within Senegalese administration. A degree of leverage or control, however, must precede efforts at transformation; people must be involved in state actions, integrated into state structures, or otherwise incorporated into the state if they are to be remolded into citizens of Senegal. As with the case of sports organizations, control over scarce resources under conditions of poverty provide what is perhaps the most important source of leverage for the state. Yet scarcity also applies to the state, and the constraints on its ability to deliver places significant limits on this source of influence. State officials thus find that the most persistent barrier to their efforts at transformation is not outright hostility or resistance, but rather an indifference to those state initiatives which are not obviously related to the more immediate need to survive which preoccupies much, indeed most, of the population in Fatick.

The need to respond to this difficulty and attempt to overcome this barrier is reflected in the importance assigned to various seemingly symbolic activities and efforts organized by the local officials of the state. At any given moment throughout the year in Fatick, state officials are occupied in preparations for some ritual event intended to attract a segment of the population. Thus the "youth week," the "women's fortnight," "culture week," and other such events each involve drumming sessions, parades, speeches, and conferences designed to attract as much attention as possible. Although much of the population is frequently oblivious to these events, for those with political ambitions they offer an opportunity to gain access to the state by presenting themselves as the spokesperson for a group over which the state seeks leverage. A young man who had managed to establish himself as a "youth leader" in the eyes of state officials in Fatick – with various direct benefits – openly acknowledged that his influence was due to the anxious search by state officials for some bridge to the country's urban youth, a group which has clearly demonstrated its capacity to challenge the state in recent years.[46] Telling in its implications for state-society relations is the fact that this same young man enjoyed very limited popularity among the town's youth, who saw him as a clear opportunist for his involvement in state activities. Yet the access to official channels which this granted him nevertheless helped him maintain his position.

Other characteristics of state administration at the local level also reflect the imperative of incorporation. The marked proliferation of titles and symbolic offices created by the state can only be explained as an effort to involve potentially important local actors in the state. Without this rationale these positions would at times appear highly improbable, indeed ludicrous. An illustration: one older man whose retailing business had completely collapsed was named president of a council of economic actors, a position which, an official of the Chamber of Commerce acknowledged, carries no functions or responsibilities, but is rather simply a title.[47] The fact that this man was joined daily by a group of older men who gathered to sit and chat in front of his failed business was certainly not lost on officials who recognized his potential as an opinion leader. Such cases are virtually innumerable, and as we shall see this method of incorporation has also been adapted to serve the parallel needs of the structures of local religious organizations.

In addition to these indirect methods, of course, considerable energy is invested by the state in purer, more direct, efforts to shape a citizenry via education and persuasion. Again, an example may serve as the best exposition of this aspect of state administration. Since its passage in 1964 (over the objections of various elements of Senegalese society, notably many marabouts, as we shall see in chapter 6) the set of laws known as the *Code de la Famille* (Family Code) which regulates questions of marriage and inheritance has encountered resistance from many social groups, and is still quite widely ignored. Modeled on the French system, with some concessions to Muslim (Maliki) law,[48] the code was passed at Senghor's absolute insistence and its application has consistently been sought by the state as an integral aspect of "modernization."

In this effort, a state-sponsored group from the "Association of Young Lawyers of Senegal" came to Fatick in the summer of 1989 as part of a tour of several provincial towns. The prefect, the governor's adjunct, and several other state officials presided over a program organized in the meeting hall of the local Chamber of Commerce. Seventy or so people were in attendance, no doubt attracted by the opportunity to get the free legal advice which the group offered, as well as by the relevance of the topic to be discussed. The centerpiece of the program was a presentation on the question of inheritance in the Family Code, with special attention to its application in the

"Serer milieu."[49] The rather scholarly talk, in French legal language, was followed by a question and answer period which made the issue more accessible to most of the audience. The emphasis throughout was on attempting to convince the audience of the need to abandon legal tradition in order to accept the prescriptions of the Family Code.

The transformational goals of the state thus served as the guiding rationale behind the program. The association itself was introduced by its president as a group which existed for the purpose of "participating in national construction." And throughout the program the focus was on the need to accept the state's authority in this domain in the name of "modernity," which was contrasted explicitly with "tradition." If Senegal is to become a modern state, it was emphasized, it must adhere to a code of law in conformity to "international standards." "We are therefore obliged," concluded the president, "to bow to the necessities of modern law." Such pleas, of course, are not likely in themselves to result in significant changes in the attitudes of Fatick's citizens, but they nevertheless indicate the conviction of the state to seek social transformation in accordance with an idealized vision of modernity and via the tools of persuasion and education.

For many of the agents of the state the notion of transformation takes on the more concrete formulation of an ideal of economic development. And there exists a prevailing belief that the problems of development are administrative problems. "As a general rule, under-development is a corollary to under-administration, in that it is true that economic growth and administrative modernization are interdependent," writes one observer of Senegalese administration. She notes, however, that a disjuncture can occur: as in parts of Latin America the administrative structures can lag behind the economic ones, or as in the recently colonized countries like Senegal, "endowed with a modern administration without a common link to the economic and social apparati," they can precede economic development, leading to a "severe structural disequilibrium."[50] In the spirit of this analysis, much of the effort of state officials at the local level is directed at attempting to use the administration as a means of fostering development.

In light of the general disillusionment in both scholarly and policy circles with the capacity of state agents in Africa – and the Third World in general – to pursue broader societal goals, it must be emphasized that many, perhaps most, local officials take this task quite seriously. Clearly numerous factors work against the accomplishment of many programs of development, most seriously the intense demands imposed by both the ethic of administrative solidarity and the economy of affection under conditions of extreme scarcity. But the goal of fostering development is still an important determining factor guiding state action, and is perhaps most clearly visible in the technical services of the state such as those involved in the medical and agricultural fields. While individuals may at times, perhaps frequently, be distracted from their efforts by outside pressures, the underlying logic of state action in the execution of vaccination campaigns, hygiene education and literacy programs, or tree-planting initiatives remains one of transforming society via and for economic development.

Such initiatives, of course, can have only a circumscribed, gradual, and long-term impact. The quest by most administrators for a more elusive rapid development has frequently tended on the contrary to have a negative impact on relations between the state and local societies. In a manner that, although perhaps not generalizable, is certainly not unique to Fatick, the ways in which the administrators in Fatick who oversee the broader policies of the state envision development leads to frustration with the slow pace of change and hence to the relative marginalization of one social group, namely the indigenous Serer. Improvements in human capital via health and education programs, while essential in the proverbial "long run," bring little in terms of measurable economic growth to a region within the tenure of any given administrator. Productive enterprises, by contrast, represent a crucial engine for economic growth. In rural areas, therefore, most of the attention of the state is devoted to the attempt to increase – or at least maintain – agricultural production. In an urban area, however, manufacturing or processing of some sort present the only plausible sectors for productive development.

But lacking local raw materials in the form of natural resources of any significance, and without the infrastructure or other comparable advantage to attract any of the sharply limited investment in such enterprises in Senegal, Fatick exhibits virtually no potential for developing a productive economic sector. As a result administrators in the town have resorted to placing a large degree of emphasis on the expansion of *commerce* in their development goals, seeing in the spread of an epiphenomenal *result* of development the signs of the process itself. The Regional Development Plan drawn up in 1987 for the Fatick region reflects this emphasis. Noting the difficulties for Fatick of competing with the nearby city of Kaolack, the portion of the plan devoted to the development of the regional capital calls only for the continued implantation of state institutions and the expansion of commerce.[51] The single largest public state celebration of "economic development" in Fatick in all of 1989 centered around the opening of a retail outlet for Senegalese-produced SOTIBA textiles in March of that year.[52] In an hours-long ceremony that included speeches by the governor, the prefect, the mayor, the secretary general of the Chamber of Commerce, and another dozen or so local personalities, the contribution of this shop –

which differed in style but not in merchandise from many stalls in the marketplace – to the development of the region was lauded. Two local young women were hired to sell (at a monthly salary equivalent to fewer than ten meters of a moderately priced fabric) and a nephew of the owner's was brought from Dakar to manage the shop. The contribution of the shop to the "development" of Fatick was thus virtually nil and, in fact, may have been negative in that it undercut established merchants in the town. But the expansion of "modern" commerce provided administrators with a symbolic but tangible indicator of "development."

In interviews with state officials, development in Fatick was regularly discussed in terms of commerce. In this respect, the Tukulor population is frequently singled out for some praise because of the fact that they include many of the merchants in consumer items in the Fatick market. The Serer, by contrast, are invariably the butt of administrative complaints about their lack of contribution to local development because of their limited involvement in the market. This variable participation by ethnic group in the commercial sector is, of course, the product of the town's history and not, as administrators tend to indicate, of differing cultural proclivities. As we have seen in the preceding chapter, an early period of commercial expansion in the colonial period attracted social groups which became directly involved in this commerce, leaving the then still important realm of agriculture to the Serer.

These patterns continue today largely because of the severely limited potential for new entry into the commercial sector. And because administrators have focused on commerce as the crucial sector in the pursuit of economic development, there is a marked frustration among officials with the Serer, who are assigned much of the blame for the lack of development. In a particularly acrimonious mood one high level official remarked that even the Serer "mode of consumption" did not contribute to development. "Others," he said " at least try to buy a little bread and butter for breakfast, and prepare a decent rice dish for lunch. But the Serer are unwilling to make an effort, content instead just to eat their millet couscous day after day."[53] Tellingly, the practices the official decried are actually the sounder ones in economic terms; flour, butter, and rice must all be imported in Senegal, while millet is produced locally, much of the supply in Fatick actually being produced by its Serer residents. At the national level, in fact, the state has engaged in campaigns to encourage the substitution of millet for rice in the urban diet. The focus on commerce, therefore, reflects no coherent policy choices, but rather answers to the desire of local officials of the state to attempt to foster some transformation of the local economy as a means of "development." And this activist element in state functioning, like the distributive one, presents local populations with constraints and opportunities to which they must respond in their dealing with the local agents of the state.

Citizen reactions/societal responses

Reviewing the current state-of-the-art in the study of relations between African societies and their states, Michael Bratton finds some "undue emphasis" on the "exit" option. "As I see it," he argues,

citizens in Africa have an ambivalent attitude toward the state; they are simultaneously attracted to it and wary of it. True, they resent the intrusion of the state into family life, especially when there are costs in time, money, or property. The history of rural political protest in Africa can be written in terms of the resistance of autonomous agricultural producers to the regulations and requirements of an extractive state. On the other hand, ordinary people remain drawn to the state because, even in diminished circumstances, it remains a major source of spoils and one of the only available channels for getting what little there is to get.[54]

The relative degree to which this generalization is valid certainly varies from country to country; the prevalence of any given pattern of societal response to the state might, as I suggested in chapter 1, best be considered a domain for comparative research. In the Senegalese case, however, Bratton's characterization is indeed highly relevant; despite its limitations, the state in Fatick continues to exert an appeal – though an inconsistent and limited one – to its citizens.

The appeal of the state: poverty and the uses of affection

As has been suggested throughout the discussion so far, and as Bratton notes, the attraction of the state for its citizens springs ultimately from its situation as the locus of otherwise unavailable goods and services. We have already noted the ways in which local populations approach the state to request sports equipment or lots of land. In a similar manner individuals might, and do, seek access to those other local offices of the state which control goods of various sorts – medicine and medical care present one crucial example in Fatick. But it is an integral component of the state in Senegal that many, perhaps most, of the needs which it is uniquely placed to fulfill are in fact needs of its own creation. To an extent far greater than many of its neighbors on the continent, the state in Senegal has been able to both regulate societal activities and prescribe the degree of access to its own resources. This relative hegemony thus creates for the state a realm of services which become essential, but which only it can provide. Access to these services, moreover, is only in theory open equitably to all interested citizens. In a situation of severe scarcity the Senegalese state thus manages to maintain its appeal in large part by its monopoly over the satisfaction of needs which would not themselves exist without the state.

The potential services of this sort which individuals can request of the state range from the essential to the trivial, and include most notably the state-determined prerequisites for engaging in various activities or acceding to other state-controlled goods. These might include such things as the following:[55]

- In order to reserve a place in school for a child for whom, as is most frequent, the parent has no birth certificate, state-issued papers are required in the form of either a certification that the birth was indeed registered in the civil register or a declaration of non-registration of birth that will then allow one to request a court date at which a judge can have the birth retroactively registered, thus allowing a birth certificate to be issued.

- In order for a young man to be eligible to apply for the highly desirable possibility of entry into the army, a certificate of residence is necessary since recruitment can only take place in the locale of primary residence. In a town this requires certification by the local *chef de quartier* (neighborhood chief) to the appropriate office of the municipality in order for the certificate to be issued. Since the rate of acceptance is higher in a small town like Fatick than in a larger urban center, at recruitment time there is always a large influx of young men with some link to a household in the town who require such "proof" of residence.

- In order to engage in most any type of commercial activity, whether a stall in the marketplace or even a small street-side table to retail at the lowest level – sugar by the cube, single cigarettes, and such – various permits are required. For any retail business involving weighing, for example, a certificate is required from the local office of the *Service des Mines* of the Ministry of Industrial and Artisanal Development attesting to the accuracy of the scales involved.

- To allow an evening drumming session – in celebration of a circumcision, for example – during the rainy season when drumming is otherwise prohibited,[56] one can apply to the office of the prefect for a permit granting an exception.

Like these, there is a virtually unlimited number of reasons for citizens in Fatick to approach the state in attempting to improve their life chances or the quality of life for themselves or their children. But how is this to be understood in comparative perspective? That is, in what ways do these activities differ from those of states elsewhere?

In Senegal, the high level of acquiescence in the regulation of societal activities reflects the achievement of a measure of state hegemony over its society that is far more significant than that of most of its African counterparts. The central position of the state in the social and economic life of Senegalese society is thus enshrined. In the legal framework that surrounds this position – the rules and regulations that determine the need for citizens to approach the state – the legacy of the European state model, and particularly its French version, is readily apparent. Unlike the French state, however, the procedures that have been established for granting access have not been in themselves legitimated. This is instead the domain of the contrasting code of social interactions derived from the economy of affection. At times the two are actually fused into the functioning of the state itself, as in the consideration of "social status" or the reliance on the agents being "reasonable" as a means of determining the distribution of state benefits.

At the popular level the ties of the economy of affection in fact represent the *normal and automatic* means by which individuals approach the state. To attempt to approach it otherwise is virtually unthinkable, because it would be almost certainly useless. Thus someone in Fatick who requires any type of permit or certificate, as in the examples discussed above, proceeds first and foremost to attempt to determine if there is a basis for a *personalized* appeal to an agent of the state to request help in the matter. A direct connection is of course frequently not available to many individuals, in which case the entire network of possible relations is explored for potential chains of relations that might bear fruit. A youth with no direct links to the *chef de quartier* in an area where he would like to claim residence would, for example, automatically attempt to locate someone of whom he might make requests to act as his intermediary, and who might himself pass through another intermediary in soliciting the help. Even in cases where the individual and the state agent are known to each other, passing through an influential intermediary strengthens the likelihood of access to the desired good. Personalized distributive networks of this sort throughout the world are familiar to students of political anthropology, but what is particularly interesting about the Senegalese case is the extent to which these networks coexist with a legal framework prescribing objective and depersonalized rules for access to the state. Seen from the local perspective in Fatick, therefore, the state in Senegal represents a type of hegemonic institution, but one in which the bases of its influence rest not on the legitimacy of its prescribed operating procedures, but rather on its continued monopoly of the means for improving one's life chances.

I have referred throughout to the poverty of Fatick and the leverage which the state derives from the unavailability of other options for individuals to improve their life chances. A full statement of these circumstances within which people make choices must, I believe, include some accounting of the human dimensions of this scarcity. The existence of social networks of dependency ensure a distribution of the essentials of life sufficient to make sure that no one starves in Fatick. Most people in the town, however, are faced daily with the challenge of securing the means of survival. Most non-salaried heads of households – virtually all of those not on the state payroll – concern themselves on a day-to-day basis with being able to provide for the day's expenses in food.[57] Primary food items are in fact frequently discussed as a measure of wealth; an individual's purchase of rice by the sack or oil by the bottle, rather than in the smaller single-meal portions which are the norm, are pointed to as indicators of success. Children are almost invariably clothed in the assorted pieces of used clothing known in Wolof as fëgg-jaay ("shake and sell"), which are discarded in Europe and the United States and imported to Senegal in bails which are then sorted and resold. For most adults such items are also a portion of day-to-day clothing. Illness among one of the members of a family regularly places the head of household in the position of needing to tap his network of relations to attempt to purchase some medication at Fatick's single pharmacy, though perhaps more frequently prescriptions go unfilled for lack of money to pay for them. Beyond the basic necessities of food and clothing, consumer goods – whether a radio, wristwatch, book, sunglasses or other such items – represent luxuries which could only be afforded by most people in exceptional circumstances.

The extreme limitations on possible routes for improving one's life chances are perhaps felt most strongly by the youth of Fatick, in particular young men, who must establish some basis for supporting themselves before they can marry. The reserve pool of unemployed youth in large urban centers like Dakar or Kaolack – the two poles of attraction for Fatick – has limited the appeal of emigrating to such locales for Fatick's youth. But the almost total lack of local employment opportunities means that many remain dependent on their families for extended periods of time. At best, some serve as apprentices to local artisans for years, hoping to eventually establish themselves independently. The workshop of a local metalworker, whose connections provided him with state contracts for various aspects of the new construction associated with Fatick's rise to regional capital, is a good example of this process. Some twenty-odd boys and young men whom he has accepted as apprentices work daily in this man's modest shop, frequently for many years, at no pay. The only benefits are the connection to this relatively influential man which, in times of need, might be exploited to secure some aid,[58] and the hope that in some unspecified long run the experience might result in a more lucrative employment opportunity. It is in this context that the prospect of the army which, at least for a few years, offers food, clothing, shelter, prestige, and some regular income, appears highly attractive to many young men. The prospect is so attractive, in fact, that re-enlistment is only allowed for a very select few, and many young men who have been discharged bemoan the fact that they did not have the personal connections necessary to help them secure their own selection.

The lack of opportunities outside the state is particularly acute in Fatick, and it is noteworthy that in fact the situation is at least partly caused by state decisions. As we have seen in the preceding chapter, Fatick's growth to an urban center was the product of the emergence of the colonial peanut trade, and its decline was the result of external decisions concerning the organization of that trade. With independence the state moved to limit the existence of independent economic bases in society by establishing a complete monopoly on all aspects of the peanut economy. Already in decline from the restructuring of the trade, Fatick's last remaining economic potential in the form of peanut processing became a casualty of these policies. Two processing plants in Fatick constructed by the influential Lebanese Khoury family are non-functional for lack of access to the raw materials. One, a peanut shelling plant, would actually produce as a by-product the essential raw material – the shells themselves – to be used by the other in the production of animal feed pellets. The constraints on their operation, as an official of the Chamber of Commerce stressed quite critically, are purely political and not economic ones; just the quantity of peanuts wasted due to rotting because of the inefficient state monopoly would be sufficient to keep the Fatick plants operating, he insisted.[59] The goal of promoting development sometimes conflicts with the imperative of maintaining the state's hegemony over the means of advancement, thus resulting in tensions within the state itself. To date, however, and certainly in the case of Fatick, the ideals of the former goal have been subordinated to the more immediate political concerns.

The state in Fatick, therefore, while perhaps not quite a "veritable Kilimanjaro," nevertheless figures prominently on the flat landscape of the Senegalese economy.[60] Located at the center of criss-crossing networks of social relations, it has managed to monopolize control over what little there is to get, and distributes this largely via the ties of affection. But because so little is actually available, citizens in fact receive relatively little from the state. Ironically, the constraints which this places on officials contributes to the stability of the system; scarcity and the need to distribute via patronage networks means that while agents of the state manage better than most individuals, their position is in no way a passport to great wealth. Likewise for citizens, while the ties of the economy of affection provide – unequally – the *possibility* for receiving from the state, the limited number of goods available means that only occasional requests can be granted.

With so little to distribute, then, how does the state sustain the interest which provides it with leverage over society? The answer lies at least in part in the relative scarcity of economic resources over which the state has no control, that is, in the relative lack of alternatives. In contrast to a country like Zaire, where a thriving parallel economy located in the abundant sources of wealth which escape state control has allowed for the growth of indigenous capitalism, there are few bases for independent economic entrepreneurship in Senegal.[61] At a much reduced level, the relationship of poverty to state influence over society varies even within Senegal; in the cities of Dakar or Ziguinchor, or a religious center like the city of Touba, the relatively greater level of independent economic activity results directly in reduced state leverage over societal activities. In Fatick, however, where so little is otherwise available, even a simple possibility of receiving is thus sufficient to focus attention on the state. "It's like a lottery," explained one citizen of Fatick in predicting the decline of a state official who was notoriously tight in distributing patronage. "Even if he can't help them all, a political figure must help *some* of the people that make requests of him. That way he at least keeps hope alive because there is always the possibility that you might 'win' something, so you keep on playing."[62] Because most officials of the state are at least intuitively aware of this popular perception, the state in Fatick continues to exert an appeal over its sometimes reluctant citizens.

The limits of the appeal: exclusionary solidarity and resistance to transformation

As the above discussion suggests, there are limits inherent in the very basis of the appeal of the state. Societal failure to conform to state demands is at least as likely to be the result of a perceived irrelevance in terms of potential benefits as from outright hostility – though as we shall see that also exists. Efforts at transformation like those related to the organization of private and family life along the lines prescribed by the Family Code find their greatest obstacle in passive non-compliance with the state. Only when the state is able to establish clear benefits, or when the gradual disintegration of the traditional system results in otherwise unresolvable tensions, is the "modern" system applied. Even securing the demographic information related to the effort of transformation presents difficulties for the state, relevant regulations being simply ignored by most people. A civil registry has been kept regularly in Fatick since 1963, and the information is available, notes a state-sponsored study of the town, "to the extent that the population makes the declarations." A simple look at the registry is sufficient to determine that the extent is limited indeed. While by no means universal, a large number of births *are* consistently registered, as would be expected given the incentive provided by the need for a birth certificate to enroll a child in school. As for deaths, however, the study estimates that no more than one in two is declared, and concerning marriages it only notes obliquely that "certainly not all" are registered with the state.[63] While the efforts of the state to gather such information do not usually bring it into direct conflict with society, its lack of demonstrable benefits result simply in a practice of non-compliance.

Other aspects of local state functioning, however, are more likely to elicit societal resistance. The ethic of administrative solidarity and the priority given by state agents to securing their own position brings the state at times into direct competition with society. This is particularly apparent with the emergence of new sources of goods for which the distribution has not been already established. Such cases are quite rare in Fatick, but the process by which the rather modest benefits from one such incident were claimed is nevertheless illustrative of this source of conflict between state and society.

The installation of a new modern bakery in Fatick by a family of Lebanese origin from Kaolack presented a rare possibility for new employment in the town. Working within the paradigm of the economy of affection, unemployed men in the town immediately began to maneuver to find a connection that might lead to preferential treatment for hiring, many approaching the widow of a Fatick-born Lebanese who had once run a bakery in the town. This ultimately came to naught, however, when the owners decided to simplify matters by bringing in workers from their other business in Kaolack. The most significant benefit which then remained to be distributed in Fatick were the concessions for kiosks to sell the bread. Typically the benefits from such a concession are of some 10 CFA francs[64] per loaf sold plus a free loaf of bread daily – a modest sum, but a windfall for a household with few other sources of income, or of bread. Two hundred applications were made for the ten kiosks to be distributed throughout the town. The applications had not been considered, however, when it became known that the kiosks had already been allotted to state officials and their families, three high-level officials together taking seven of the ten. Presumably an understanding had been reached during the negotiations concerning the baker's applications for the required permits for the business and the kiosks, and the benefits had been distributed among state agents in accordance with the ethic of administrative solidarity. Other state officials likewise used their position to profit from the new source. One technical agent responsible for inspecting elements of the installation, though he was critical of the method of distributing kiosks, nevertheless found it "normal" that *he* should, literally, receive his daily bread free because of the "good relations" he had established with the owners in the process of inspection, insisting nonetheless that this did not influence his technical decisions.[65]

This event triggered a strong resentment among many in Fatick, particularly those with fewer opportunities for access to the state. Most significantly, it brought the line which separates state and society into focus, and pitted one against the other in local perception. Solidarity among administrators caused them to draw ranks in this circumstance, and Fatick society was left out. Virtually all local residents who discussed the case expressed their displeasure in terms of the state ("them," or "the functionaries") appropriating what should instead have gone to local society, the *doom-i-Fatick* (children of Fatick). Resentment, however, while it draws the lines between the two, does not provide in itself a basis for challenging the state directly. Because the benefits are so scarce, the potential for social organization to challenge the state tends on the contrary to be defused by the greater possible benefits of attempting an *individual* challenge. One young man angered by the episode said he intended to directly confront one official with whom he had some ties, but his demand was personal and not general: that his own mother be given one of the several kiosks claimed by this man. Should the young man in fact secure such an outcome, the lines would be once again blurred. But the demonstrated ability to claim resources and then redistribute them via the ties of the economy of affection could actually reinforce, rather than weaken, the position of the official, and by extension the state.

Like conflict over claims to resources, the transformational aspect of local state functioning also leads to tensions with society, and it is in this endeavor that the state most clearly encounters the limits to its own power. By its very nature the effort at transformation requires the intrusion of the state into traditional domains that have previously been considered part of the realm of society and not the state. Particularly when there are no obvious benefits, there is a clear reluctance on the part of social groups to accept the intrusion. In Fatick tension is felt most strongly between the state and the Serer population, notably the more conservative community of Ndiaye-Ndiaye. As we have seen, the Serer are regularly the focus of administrative criticism due to frustration with their relative distance from state-sponsored plans for "development." The Serer, for their part, mark their distance from the state in various ways, most notably during the period of elections by demonstrating strong support for the only viable opposition party in Senegal, the Parti Démocratique Sénégalais (PDS), a distinctly anti-state gesture given the sociological – if not institutional – fusion of the state apparatus with the Parti Socialiste.

Given the Serer's relative lack of involvement in the commercial sector, the state's efforts at incorporation leads to a search for other sources of leverage over them. One particularly significant such effort in Fatick was

the construction, under the authority of the Ministry of Plan and Cooperation and with the aid of international donors, of an Experimental Center
for Traditional Medicine on the outskirts of the town. As an official in the
regional medical service in Fatick emphasized, the state's motivation in
undertaking this project was predominantly political and not in fact
technical or scientific; nothing more than the incorporation of traditional
Serer practitioners into a state-sponsored organization with such broad
goals as "combating charlatanism" and "contributing to the development
of the region and the country" was programmed.[66]

Traditional medical practice is a domain which almost totally escapes
state control, and which involves the vast majority of the population,
including the urban sector, to an extraordinarily high degree. Research by
Maghan Keita into the relationship between traditional and modern
medicine in Senegal has led him to conclude that the "widespread acceptance and usage of traditional health care practices by the overwhelming
majority of the Senegalese population has been a phenomenon which the
modern medical sector can neither stop nor reverse."[67] Among the Serer
the continued strength, indeed flourishing, of these practices is particularly
significant because of the incorporation brought on by Islamization of
elements of the powers attributed to marabouts into the role of the
traditional Serer healers known as *saltigis*, with the concomitant reinforcement of the social power of this occupation. Given this situation, then, the
motivation behind state interest in penetrating and incorporating this
aspect of societal activity is clear. As Keita expresses it, state control over
traditional health care "is one of the keys to making the 'marginalized'
segments of the population more responsive to the monied economy.
Traditional health care has provided one more vehicle for the incorporation
of people and areas which have rested beyond the pale of market forces."[68]
Such an understanding underlay the decision to construct the center in
Fatick.

Given the conflicting interests of the state and Serer *saltigis*, it is not
surprising that the construction of the center was plagued by controversy
from its inception.[69] Various *saltigis* in the region actually attempted to
prevent its construction, but were unsuccessful at least in part because
others saw the project as an opportunity to gain access to state resources.
Yet the disagreements about control of the center which has marked its
existence emerged from the moment of its inauguration. The ceremony was
due to have been presided over by the Minister of Plan and Cooperation
himself, but at the last minute he sent a representative instead. All other
important regional state officials were present, however, along with Serer
healers and *saltigis* from throughout the region.

The struggle for control of the center was reflected symbolically in the struggle for control of the ceremony itself, and this was most strikingly evident in the sociolinguistics of the event. As is common in such situations, state officials gave their speeches in French, while representatives of the social groups concerned – in this case the Serer healers – spoke in Wolof, with *elected* local officials, most importantly the local deputy to the Senegalese parliament, speaking a mixture of both. Although a list of speakers had been prepared in advance, numerous representatives from the *saltigis* inserted themselves into this list, to the obvious impatience of state officials. As tensions mounted, many began to speak in Serer, thus effectively excluding virtually all of the state officials. Asked to speak in Wolof, they refused, forcing the governmental delegation to find a translator instead. Having won this symbolic victory, the Serer speakers in fact regularly reverted to Wolof, the better to have their angry discourse understood by state officials. When the governor's delegation attempted to rush the speeches, protesting other engagements, the *saltigis* stalled, insisting that the importance of the event was such that the governor and others should sit and listen. The ceremony eventually ended rather abruptly, with a hurried departure by state officials who retired to the governor's residence for a lunch prepared for the benefit of the governmental delegation and the foreign guests in attendance. The *saltigis* and local population stayed on at the center for an all-day celebration which, in local style, lasted well into the night. The efforts of the state to further the incorporation of the Serer population by exerting control over a traditional domain thus proved, at the very least, inconclusive in the face of local resistance.

The marked preference of the Serer population of Fatick to avoid the state, therefore, has two sources. First, the relative lack of involvement in the commercial sector has meant that they are the least likely to benefit from the state's sponsorship of this domain. Secondly, there is a strong local resentment of the attempts at incorporation which involve the state's intrusion into areas of traditional importance. And the ability to actually translate this preference into a limited involvement with state-sponsored activities, in Fatick, arises from their relatively lesser need for access to the state in the struggle to survive. The president of the local section of the opposition PDS in Fatick recognized this factor as the source of PDS strength in Ndiaye-Ndiaye. Noting certain cultural characteristics and the relevance of "simple disagreement" with government policy, he nevertheless emphasized that the most important basis of Serer opposition was their independent means of survival due to continued ties to agriculture, and thus a reduced need to "ask favors of the state, like others do."[70] In this context then, the Serer preference for millet over commercialized grains which provoked the prefect's critique might be seen to be more significant than a simple question of taste, and more reasoned than an inherent lack of initiative.

In accordance with this imperative other groups, indeed even individuals, vary in the extent to which they approach the state depending on their needs and the relative potential benefits to be gained from the encounter. The state's efforts at incorporation, therefore, must focus on creating needs for things only it can provide. The limited resources at its disposal, however, and the actions by local state agents to secure their own position first, hinder its potential for creating such needs and thus define the limits of the state's appeal to local populations.

Conclusion

The state structure in Senegal is a highly centralized one, with power concentrated towards the top of the hierarchy. Its historical inheritance is an institutional structure patterned on an imported model which remains alien to much of the society over which it presides. Yet seen from the bottom up, at the local level, it blurs more readily with that society. This effect is the result of the status of the individuals who staff the state. The ebb and flow in the appearance and fading of the line that separates state and society is a product of the responses of state agents to the dual imperatives of securing their own positions and of answering to the obligations demanded by the economy of affection. This vacillation feeds the "dialectic of attraction and repulsion" toward the state displayed by local populations.[71]

A clearer distinction between state and society persists in a different aspect of state functioning, that of attempting to exert a degree of hegemony that will permit the transformation from a "traditional" to a "modern" social order. To the extent to which rules concerning the organization of society are instituted, needs are also created which only the state can fulfill. A method for permitting access to the means to satisfy those needs must be provided, however, in a situation where the rules established are alien to the prevailing norms of the political culture. One manner by which the resulting gap between state and society is bridged is with the appearance of legal fictions in a process by which the state makes concessions in response to, and as a means of encouraging, societal willingness to play by its rules. The process allows, quite literally, for the reconciliation of the disjuncture between the juridical and the empirical aspects of the state-society relation.

The issue of the establishment of documents pertaining to age is one area which, if not particularly controversial, is nevertheless highly indicative of the workings of this process. The requirements of age established by the state for access to certain benefits – examinations at various levels of the school system, or entry into the army or state training institutions, for example – places serious demands on a population where age is frequently unknown, or where social development in the traditional system is at odds with these requirements. The process by which the state has reconciled these needs, therefore, has resulted in a pervasive practice of establishing fictional ages; a practice so widespread that it could be described as the norm. As alluded to above, by a process that involves declaring that a birth was never registered (even when it was), a birth certificate can be issued retroactively, thus allowing for the establishment of a required legal age. The joke told by a one-time judge, whose duties involved hearing such cases, is indicative of the attitude of both state and society to this issue: asked by the judge what brought him there, a "hefty young man" who had presented himself at court responded, "I want to have been born *today*." The official's amusement at this story reflected his recognition of the essentially fictive nature of many of his duties in this regard, at the same time that it indicates the willingness – and need – of individuals to play the state's game.[72]

A somewhat more significant area in which this pattern emerges is in the case of establishing residency for applying for admission into the army. Describing the officially stated rules, the functionary in the Fatick municipality in charge of maintaining the civil registry insisted that it was "absolutely essential" that applicants be residents in the town. Asked whether in fact they all *were* residents, he simply laughed and said "well, of course many 'arrange' things with a *chef de quartier*."[73] Again the fictive nature of compliance with state demands is readily recognized, but the insistence on the appearance of compliance with the rules disguises the limits of the state's hegemony. At the popular level it is widely recognized that the state concern is with the administrative need to maintain the existence of a logical and consistent juridical order, regardless of its relation to empirical reality.

The willingness of local populations to play by the rules of the game reflects the relatively low costs and the potential benefits of doing so. As we have seen most notably in the case of the Serer in Fatick, however, when the benefits to be gained are less evident, the leverage of the state is diminished accordingly. In such circumstances social groups attempt instead to pursue a strategy of isolation by maintaining their distance from the state. Yet this strategy is fragile, and for various reasons appears to be becoming increasingly more difficult for local populations. Poverty and the vagaries of agriculture in the Sahel continue to erode the potential for self-reliant autonomy based on that activity. The spread of the capitalized economy also results in an increase in relative needs which require entry into the modern sector to secure. And in the case of the town of Fatick, the greatly increased weight of the state following the declaration of the new region has raised the relative costs of isolation, while increasing the potential benefits from engagement. With few societal bases for contestation, and a diminished potential for isolation resulting from a weak economic base, the balance between state and society in Fatick would appear to be a particularly precarious one. One other important factor, however, serves to reinforce the position of civil society, thus introducing a stabilizing measure into the equation. This is the weight of Islam, in the form of the organizational structures of the Sufi orders. These centrally important institutions are thus the focus of the two chapters that follow.

4 The marabout–disciple relationship I: foundations of recruiting and following

Central to an understanding of the organization of the Sufi orders, and hence to the political impact of Islam in Senegal, is the question of the nature of the ties that bind Sufi religious leaders, the marabouts, and their disciples, or *taalibes*. As I noted briefly in chapter 2, the preeminent aspect of the orders in their Senegalese manifestation involves a relationship of dependence between marabouts and their disciples. There exists, therefore, an evident potential for the marabouts, and particularly the most important ones who command large followings, to play a leading role in the Senegalese political system. Relations between the state and the marabouts have consequently attracted the attention of virtually every student of Senegal. While such attention is certainly warranted, a full explanation of the patterns of interaction between state and religious elites hinges ultimately on the extent of control or leverage which the marabouts can, in fact, exercise over their followers. Yet despite its importance this issue has received relatively little attention in research on Senegal – with the important exception of the case of the Mouride order in its rural agricultural setting. This chapter and the one that follows, therefore, examine comparatively the nature of those ties across Sufi orders at the grassroots level.

Discussing the relationship first from the popular perspective, I find that the high degree of stability in the attachment of individuals to specific marabouts or to an order has not been translated into any significant degree of rigidity in these relationships. Declaring allegiance to a marabout, that is, does not preclude an interest in – or a potential relationship with – other marabouts. And neither have the varying degrees of recognition of the differences among orders resulted in the development of fixed sociopolitical cleavages along religious lines. Because the cohesion of an order is not a function of "primordial sentiments," to use Geertz's celebrated term,[1] the social costs associated with a realignment of religious affiliation are not so high as to absolutely preclude such a move. Thus, though realignments are rare – at least in part because they are costly – they do at times occur, and the potential for realignment is clearly central in shaping a marabout's attitude toward his followers.

On the maraboutic side of the relationship the most noteworthy characteristic is the competition among marabouts which obliges them to regularly seek to legitimate and reinforce the appeal on which their following depends, what might be called their "charisma." Drawing to varying degrees from three sources – their own earned reputation, inheritance, and the association with figures of greater charismatic authority – marabouts must exert a broad popular appeal in order to maintain their positions. Ideological formulations – whether based on classic Sufi thought or on its local modifications – serve to reinforce these relations. But it is my premise here that such formulations are not in and of themselves sufficient to explain the stability of relations between marabouts and their *taalibes*. I also, therefore, examine the incentives for both sides to maintain long-term ties. The following chapter then explores the rituals and social structures through which those ties are maintained and reinforced, as well as their limits. The resulting analysis has important implications for our understanding of Senegalese politics because it suggests a greater relativity of maraboutic authority than has frequently been assumed by students of Senegal.

The assumption of strict control

Most contemporary analyses of Senegalese politics are constructed on an assumption of strict maraboutic control over disciples. "Believers are bound to demonstrate absolute obedience toward their spiritual chiefs," writes one observer in a thorough exposition of Senegalese political history and legal institutions.[2] This assumption of strict control, I believe, is an artifact of two aspects of the literature on Senegalese Islam: (1) a frequent reliance on Sufi ideology, rather than fieldwork-based empirical research, in portraying the nature of marabout-*taalibe* ties, and (2) the concentration of much of what empirical research has been done on the economically crucial – but nevertheless quite exceptional – case of the Mouride order in its rural forms. Islam in Senegal cannot be reduced to Sufi theology or to Mouride agricultural *daaras*, proto-villages of young men in the service of a marabout. Both of these aspects, however, are important components influencing the shape of Senegalese religious structures. I thus build and expand on the contributions of various scholars in examining the nature of the ties between marabouts and their followers.

Behrman's pioneering study of the political role of the *tarixas* in Senegal focused primarily on the relations between the marabouts, in particular the most important national figures within the Sufi orders, and the political elite.[3] Her description of these relations concentrates on the relative powers of each and on the resulting historical patterns of collaboration and

conflict. By contrast, her characterization of the relations between marabouts and their followers, on which the argument of maraboutic power is
constructed, is grounded almost exclusively in a consideration of Sufism in
its "classical" form. Noting the oft-cited injunction attributed to the
founder of the Qadiriyya order, "You should be in the hands of your
shaykh like a corpse in the hands of the mortician," she paints a picture of
submission and obedience based on Sufi theology:

The *major reason* for the dependence of the followers on their leaders stems from the
emphasis in later sufism on the ability of the leaders of a brotherhood [order] to act
as intermediary between Allah and man. . . . It became characteristic of a *tarixa* for
the followers to *blindly obey the commands of their leaders* in religious matters and in
most secular matters as well.[4]

Behrman notes variations in this pattern in Senegal; the Mouride order, for
example, is clearly characterized by a greater degree of maraboutic control
over disciples than the rival Tijaniyya.[5] Yet she argues that these differences
should not be overstated, and she joins other scholars of Sufi Islam in
attributing the centrality of the political role of the orders to the cohesion
that results from the submission of disciples: "The blind obedience of the
disciples to their leaders, and the members' loyalty to the brotherhood as a
whole, [is] the major source of strength of the Muslim orders."[6]

   A more nuanced view of the marabout-*taalibe* relationship is to be found
in Coulon's study of Islam and power in Senegal.[7] Like Behrman, Coulon
concentrates on the relations between the religious and the political elites
("*le marabout*" and "*le prince*" of his title), and in particular on the
exchange of services that has characterized that relationship. Coulon notes
that the potential for the marabouts to perform such services for the state is
rooted in the influence they wield over their disciples, and that this is the
result of the fact that "the marabout-*taalibe* relationship in Senegal is
essentially a relationship of personal dependence."[8] Then in examining the
sources of that dependency relationship, Coulon identifies two distinct
aspects which define it: the "charismatic" and the "clientelistic."[9] He
discusses the first motivation for submission to a marabout in terms of the
Weberian notion of charisma and situates that charisma in the context of
Sufi theology: "Demonstrations of devotion and abnegation towards the
marabouts can only be explained because their *taalibes* see them as
intercessors or even intermediaries with God."[10] This is reinforced in the
Senegalese context by the widespread faith in the magical and supernatural
powers marabouts derive from their *baraka* (grace, sanctity).

   The relationship of personal dependence inspired by maraboutic charisma, Coulon argues, is reinforced and complemented by a parallel
clientelistic relationship between marabout and follower. Making the

distinction between "pure" charisma – that of the founding fathers of the Sufi orders – and "functional" or "hereditary" charisma, Coulon argues that the first provides a sufficient explanation for dependence in and of itself, while the latter is more tenuous, because it is more "rational." The result is that marabouts are expected to provide certain *material* benefits to their followers in addition to the spiritual ones. "The marabout," writes Coulon, "should not only see to it that his *taalibe* attain paradise, but also that they benefit from a measure of well-being."[11] This patronage function of marabouts, he notes, has been particularly important in the distribution of land, notably in the periods and areas of expanding peanut cultivation. The relative importance of these two aspects of dependency may vary not only across orders, but also in relation to such factors as caste status, geographic location, and "modern" contacts.[12] The "clientelistic" aspect, as we shall see, is crucially important for an understanding of the functions of the orders in mediating relations between state and society in Senegal. Yet later analysts of Senegalese politics have tended to rely most frequently on the aspect of the relationship which Coulon labels "charismatic," that based on Sufi theology, which in his vision remains universally central to the maintenance of ties between marabouts and followers, and hence to the political power of the marabouts in Senegal.[13]

The concentration of scholarly attention on the Mouride order, and particularly on its rural innovations, has been a second source of the assumption of strict control which pervades analyses of Senegal. As discussed in chapter 2, it is a uniquely Senegalese order, in contrast to its main rivals which were brought from North Africa, and of relatively recent vintage – the founder only died in 1927. Because the order arose following the collapse precipitated by the French conquest of the pre-colonial Wolof states in the area that was to become the major source of peanuts, the linkage of the Mourides with the cultivation of this cash crop brought the order a degree of economic clout disproportionate to its demographic importance.[14] Mouride social organization was developed in the context of the expanding peanut economy, and its unique formulation was adapted to the economic imperatives of this context. This, along with its interaction with the highly stratified Wolof social structure, resulted in a Sufi order characterized most distinctively by the organization of agricultural production around the figure of the marabout.[15]

The most distinctive institutional expression of Mouride agro-religious innovation is the *daara*.[16] These collective farms worked by groups of boys and young men in the service of a marabout were largely responsible for the expansion of peanut cultivation into previously unfarmed regions in what is now the heart of the Senegalese peanut basin. Frequently committed by their parents at a very young age, the *taalibe*-farmers in a *daara* typically devote many years to their marabout, working without remuneration under harsh physical conditions before being released from their servitude. Upon their release they are usually granted a field by the marabout, and at times even provided with a wife. *Daaras*, therefore, were gradually transformed into villages – the many villages in the central Mouride zone whose names begin with "Darou" all being transformations of original *daaras*. The eventual prospect of his own field and a wife was (and still can be) an attractive proposition for a young man in rural Senegal, and there are thus various indications that service in a *daara* reflects, as Cruise O'Brien puts it, "the *talibé's* expectation of some reciprocity in this world as in the next."[17] The seeming inequality and exploitation of years of unremunerated work for a religious leader, however, have drawn the attention of most observers of Senegalese religious structures.

Most significantly in the context of this discussion, the reorganization of Wolof society along the lines of the production of a cash crop for export to the world market was accompanied by a vigorous emphasis on the Sufi notion of submission which both facilitated and justified the particular forms of that reorganization. The result was the development of a distinctly Mouride ideology which enshrined the act of submission to a marabout as a central defining feature of the order. This ideology is given its concrete expression in the ritual of the *njébbal*, whereby an individual declares allegiance to a marabout.[18] The *njébbal* involves the pronunciation of a vow of obedience, generally along these lines: "I place my soul and my life in your hands. Whatever you order I will do; Whatever you forbid I will refrain from." The act binds disciple to marabout in a relationship which, under normal circumstances, lasts as long as both are alive, and which is usually expressed in the rhetoric of obedience, submission, and even slavery. The submissive aspect of Mouridism has figured prominently in all analyses of the order and is explored most richly in Cruise O'Brien's definitive monograph on Mouride organization.[19]

There is no doubt that the Mourides go much further than most Sufi orders, whether in Senegal or elsewhere, in their ideological emphasis on submission to one's marabout. Yet the extent and impact of this ideology has been magnified and exaggerated in discussions of the order by two factors. First, because most studies have been carried out in the agricultural heartland of the order – the central peanut-producing zone of the country – there has been a tendency to attribute behavioral patterns that may well be linked to specific local socio-economic imperatives to Mouride ideology. This would seem to be the case given the modifications – and the weakening – in the practice of submission that follows a migration out of this region, particularly to an urban area.[20] Thus a Mouride peasant may submit to a marabout's organization of agricultural work because it is the best option available to him, independently of the ideology which supports it. Secondly, as Cruise O'Brien noted in a later reconsideration of his original fieldwork, the ideology of submission as articulated by both disciples and marabouts has been perhaps too readily accepted at face value by outside observers.[21] As in most every case of human activity, practice may deviate significantly from the declared norm even as expressed by the participants.

Drawing on this literature, other analysts of Senegalese politics have frequently reflected its emphasis on Sufi theology, particularly on its Mouride ideological version. This has led, I believe, to a tendency to overstate the extent of control which marabouts exert over their followers in many analyses of Senegalese politics. Markowitz, for example, seems to have accepted Sufi ideology at face value in arguing that:

Adherents of the marabouts are supposed to be like "a cadaver in the hands of the washers of the dead." This means – and this fact should be emphasized – that a large proportion of the population of Senegal is highly committed and tightly organized on the basis of personal, charismatic relationships built on irrational emotional appeals.[22]

Discussing the electoral system, Hesseling states that the population "follows *to the letter* the voting instructions given by the marabouts."[23] Similarly, Zuccarelli describes the "perfect cohesion" of the orders which he attributes to the fact that disciples are "psychologically dependent" on their marabouts.[24] And in an otherwise insightful analysis of Senegalese democracy cast in Gramscian terms, Fatton's description of the "systematic hold over their mass peasant followings" enjoyed by marabouts in Senegal is clearly evocative of a somewhat caricatured version of rural Mouride organization as discussed above.[25] In contrast to other patron-client relationships in the country, he argues, the marabout-*taalibe* relationship is not characterized by clients' calculations of which patrons are most effective, or by patrons' struggles to maintain and expand a following. Because this relationship is "profoundly imbued with Islamic fervor," he writes, "it possesses a spiritual and religious dimension that imparts to it a relative stability and resistance to change."[26]

The analysis offered here lends nuance to these assessments, with important implications for our view of Senegalese politics. In contrast to a vision of masses blindly manipulated by a religious elite, the ties of *taalibes* to their marabouts are frequently far more contingent and tenuous than assumed. As a result, marabouts confront the problem of recruiting and retaining followers – a problem not unrelated to their relations with the state. And the corollary to this is that people, at times and to varying degrees, confront a choice of which marabout to follow, the level of attachment to that marabout, and the domains or situations in which to follow him. I find that while there is a widespread, in fact virtually universal, belief in the validity of the maraboutic system in Senegal, and consequently a strong commitment to it, this is not necessarily accompanied by an absolute attachment to any one living marabout. Marabouts' fortunes can, and do, wax and wane as their following fluctuates.

The issue here is clearly one of degree and not an absolute. There is no denying that, taken as a whole, marabouts in Senegal exert a great deal of influence over their followers and that this is at least partially founded on Sufi ideology. Yet the extent of that influence varies significantly from one context to another and, indeed, from one individual to another. And for the purposes of examining the politics of state-society relations in Senegal, the important question is itself one of the degree to which Senegalese society controls some space for autonomous action *vis-à-vis* the state. By positing some significant role for disciple-clients in determining the relative power of marabout-patrons – a power which hinges on their following – I suggest that the degree of societal influence is great enough that an elite analysis which fails to take it seriously into account must ultimately be deficient for an understanding of Senegalese politics.

Popular perceptions of marabouts and the orders

Most people in Senegal are born into a connection to a marabout and his *tarixa*. While these ties are, as we shall see, fluid and manipulable, they are also absolutely central to people's lives. The need for such ties is accepted as commonsensical by virtually all Senegalese, and it thus plays a central role in their actions and decisions. This section lays out the "knowledge" that individuals have about marabouts and the orders in terms of their culturally based understanding of these institutions and their significance. It is intended, therefore, to describe the basic parameters within which people function in their interactions with marabouts.

Marabouts in the networks of affection

"*Sa sëriñ baax na*," people commonly say in Wolof, "You've got a good marabout," when some one encounters a bit of good luck. Although frequently a casual remark, often partially in jest, the statement nevertheless reveals a central core of popular belief in Senegal: an individual's fate is in many ways tied to the efficacy of the marabout(s) with whom he or she associates. Consequently, relationships with marabouts are crucial components of people's strategies for advancement or, indeed, at times survival. And while all marabouts are good in popular opinion, all are certainly not equal. The search for a particularly efficacious marabout to aid in some difficult situation is a familiar aspect of Senegalese life, one in fact whose very familiarity has made it a stock element of popular stories and literature. Thus, for example, in Aminata Sow Fall's novel *La Grève des Bàttu*, the protagonist-politician regularly makes the long trek to a remote village to consult a marabout reputed to be able to help him achieve (via supernatural, not political, clout) his goal of being named minister.[27] For a real life – and more tragic – example: a former important state official in Fatick whose seriously ill daughter was not responding to medical treatment consulted locals on the reputation of marabouts in the region. He learned of and sent for a Moorish marabout in the town of Diofior alleged to be especially powerful in the treatment of illness. The marabout was paid well for his services, but the child ultimately died.

Few people, of course, are either as ambitious as the politician or able to afford the expenses associated with searching out marabouts in other locales. Yet in the normal course of everyday life almost everyone has occasion to require the services which a marabout can provide. In cases of illness or accident, wanted or unwanted pregnancies, or to deal with interpersonal difficulties with spouses or neighbors, as well as in such routine things as weaning a child or the making of the protective amulets known as "gris-gris" (*téere* in Wolof) that are worn by the vast majority of people, marabouts are regularly consulted. Although there is frequently a degree of skepticism about the efficacy of particular marabouts in accomplishing these tasks, very few Senegalese – certainly outside the small Westernized sector, but even within it – reject the notion of maraboutic power *per se*. Marabouts, therefore, are central to the personal domain.

There is, of course, also an important spiritual dimension to a relationship with a marabout. To the extent to which the relationship follows the classic Sufi pattern, the marabout serves as the principal spiritual guide for his disciples, as well as a source of grace (*baraka*) which adds to the efficacy of prayer. In all cases marabouts perform, to varying degrees, such services as instruction in religious matters and officiating at religious events. As in the case of spiritual leaders in all societies, the theological knowledge of marabouts is sought by individuals in need of guidance or solace in times of difficulty. It merits emphasizing here that it is in fact their role in the spiritual domain that both marabouts and disciples most often identify as the fundamental bases for the existence of the social category of marabout. The very real centrality of the metaphysical is all too often ignored in secular discussions of Senegalese Islamic organization. Descriptions of marabouts focused on the fact that they *do* have significant social and economic powers read at times almost as if the spiritual aspects of the maraboutic position were only an elaborate ruse by which the population is tricked into acquiescing to its own exploitation. This, it seems to me, does justice neither to the marabouts themselves nor to their disciples. Ultimately, the evaluation of the relationship of the metaphysical to the political hinges on the answer one provides to the fundamental psychological and philosophical question of how and why people come to believe that what is in their interest is also right, an issue that clearly cannot be resolved here. Lacking evidence to the contrary, however, there is no basis for calling into question the sincerity of individuals.

In any case, the powers of marabouts in Senegal are not in fact restricted to the spiritual and the magical. The very real social and political powers that are derived from their central positions within networks of affection, from their status as leaders to whom people have declared their allegiance or to whom they look for guidance, have been the focus of most discussions of the marabouts. The social powers of a marabout in, say, such matters as mediating disputes depend primarily on the authority which he derives from the degree of respect he commands in the community. The more explicitly political powers – facilitating access to goods, services and jobs, or protecting a *taalibe* in legal trouble, for example – are a function of the marabout's relations with the state. But these relations depend in turn on the size and importance of a marabout's following, his power *vis-à-vis* the population; the relationship, therefore, is a dialectical one.

Given the reputational bases of marabouts' social importance, there is a wide range of variation in their standing. While there are thus marabouts at different "levels" of society, there exists no pre-established hierarchy or chain of command within the orders. The Mourides do indeed display a higher degree of organizational cohesion around the figure of the founder's *xalifa*, but even within that order there is no basis for a description of strictly hierarchical authority. Rather, in all cases, what exists is a network of individuals of greater or lesser importance, with varying degrees of ties among themselves, but all of whom must constantly negotiate their relative personal influence within the network. The distinction between "local" and "national" marabouts made below, therefore, is meant only as a rough analytical means of distinguishing between those whose zone of influence is geographically limited to a locale – in this case Fatick and its hinterland – and the restricted number who can claim a following, and hence influence, throughout the country.

As with all relationships within the economy of affection, the opportunities open to individuals are a function of the ties on which they can draw. Wealthier people, or those better placed within the social network for some reason such as inherited status, can more easily gain the access that will allow them to develop personal ties with religious figures of greater importance. Likewise, when faced with the task of dealing with matters of

exceptional importance people are more likely to seek the help of intermediaries in an effort to gain access to figures of greater power. The position of
many local marabouts – as we shall see below – is in fact partially dependent
on this characteristic of the affective network; one benefit which a local
marabout can offer a disciple is to facilitate access to a more important
marabout of the order. The fluid and personalized aspects of marabout-
disciple relations, therefore, do not preclude – on the contrary they
encourage – the cultivation of a multiplicity of such ties on the part of
citizen-disciples.

There is no gainsaying the importance of the socio-political powers which
the religious elite in Senegal derive from their placement at the center of
networks of relations within the economy of affection. What is most
important to note here, however, is that these powers, unlike the magical
and spiritual ones, are not unique to marabouts. Disputes can be mediated
by non-religious authorities in the community, and access to state-
controlled goods and services may be better secured via the patronage of a
well-placed bureaucrat, politician or businessman. The extent to which
drawing on a position as the client of a marabout rather than of another
patron presents the optimal strategy for an individual will depend on the
local context, the benefit sought, and an individual's personal network of
relationships.

In Fatick, as in most towns outside the religious "capitals" of Senegal,
marabouts are recognized as important individuals who, in addition to
their magical and spiritual powers, can facilitate the acquisition of essential
goods and services. In dealing with religious leaders, individual citizens
may vary in the degree to which they are willing to submit to their
recommendations in either the spiritual or the temporal domain, but there
is no widely established pattern of "blind obedience" to a marabout. And
the fact that no local marabouts have a monopoly on desired goods
weakens the incentives for constructing close relationships on the basis of
Sufi ideology. Rather than as figures of unquestionable authority, marabouts are simply recognized as important individuals whose good position
in the network of affective ties grants them a greater degree of leverage over
the state than is otherwise available to individuals in society. Maraboutic
power, therefore, is not absolute but relative; cultivating a marabout's
patronage is one possible strategy a person can adopt in the daily struggle to
secure some benefits, get ahead, or at times simply survive. The importance
of marabouts in Senegal is at least in part a function of the fact that this is
frequently (but not always) the best available strategy. When it is not
perceived as such, affiliation with a marabout and his *tarixa* may well have
only a nominal reality.

The orders

At the local level marabouts, like Serer *saltigis* and others with specialized skills, can be consulted or requested to perform routine services without a previous *taalibe* relationship – although usually with the payment of a fee. But the need for patronage, both material and spiritual, usually requires a long-term relationship, and therefore means that most people identify a specific marabout, whom they follow as a *taalibe*, and thereby claim affiliation with a particular Sufi order. In theory, as discussed above, an individual's initiation into a Sufi order comes via the establishment of a relationship with a *shaykh* of that order. During the period of widespread expansion of the orders in Senegal, and still occasionally today in cases of conversion, this has indeed been the pattern. In current practice, however, people tend to be born into a nominal affiliation with an order; children are normally said to have the same religious allegiance as their fathers. As a rule people maintain this affiliation, with the occasional exception of women who, should they marry someone of a different order, frequently declare a change of allegiance, adopting their husband's affiliation. These tendencies, however, vary depending on circumstances.

While a nominal adherence to an order may facilitate certain social interactions, effective exploitation of the advantages of clientelism can only come by developing personal ties to the marabouts of that order. In a town like Fatick, removed from the main centers of maraboutic authority, such ties are likely to be developed first with local marabouts, themselves *taalibes* of the most important marabouts of the order and who serve as their representatives in the locale. Depending on a person's preferences, however, and most importantly on the resources available to him, he may become more active and influential in the local structures of that order, and thus be more capable of gaining access to the benefits of the patronage of the more important marabouts of the *tarixa*. While virtually all Senegalese Muslims are affiliated to an order, this does not directly translate into the ability to secure a marabout's patronage.

What then does affiliation to an order mean at the local level? My suspicion, before beginning fieldwork, was that religious affiliation would provide the basis for group solidarity and hence for the formation of socio-political cleavages along religious lines. This seemed particularly likely given the relative non-politicization of ethnic cleavages in Senegal. Yet rather quickly after arriving in Fatick I began to see evidence to the contrary. While social differences were identifiable between orders, particularly between the Mourides and the more numerous Tijans, this was not accompanied by any politicization of this cleavage at the popular level. My initial sense of both of these facts – the existence of clear distinctions among orders and the lack of politicization of these differences – was confirmed when I learned that the members of a Mouride *daaira* (the local associations of the orders to be discussed in the next chapter) were putting up a tent for a religious ceremony being planned by a Tijan *daaira*. To the question of why the Tijans were not doing the work themselves, the Mouride *taalibe* I was interviewing responded, "Tijans can't, they don't know how to do that kind of work." Why not? "Tijans are much too *civilisés*."[28]

I was to hear this myth of greater Tijan "civilization" (always referred to with the French term, even in a Wolof conversation) various times again, from both Mourides and Tijans. From Tijans it occasionally carried the critical connotation of Mouride "backwardness." But nevertheless, the primary significance of the term was clearly to distinguish the cultural styles of the two orders. "*Civilisé*" in effect meant more Westernized, more urbane, and having adopted more French cultural traits. Clothing, perfume, and speech were pointed to as evidence. By contrast, Mourides are occasionally said to be more adept at manual labor, more willing to undertake hard work. This is in keeping with the much-observed emphasis of the Mouride order, from the time of the founder, on the value of work. It also follows from the observation that the Mourides, at least in the early years of the order, drew disproportionately from the lower, artisanal, castes in the highly stratified Wolof society because those groups were more willing to make the declaration of submission required in the *njébbal* to a marabout.[29] But while there is thus some concrete sociological basis for the occasional recognition of cultural differences among orders, this should not be overstated. Variations do exist among them, but there are no absolute distinctions in style, caste status, occupation, attitude towards work, or political orientation among Sufi orders.

This is not of course to imply that affiliation with an order is socially insignificant. In specific local contexts, the orders have indeed at times provided a basis for at least a temporary political cleavage. There are moreover organizational differences among the orders, some of which will be discussed in the following chapter. Most important to note in terms of its impact on popular religious affiliation is the higher degree of institutional cohesion currently exhibited by the Mouride order, and which appears to be a development of the past twenty years or so. While Mouride *taalibes* have usually been pointed to as the prototypical examples of Sufi submissiveness in Senegal, it is interesting to note that in fact the greater institutionalization of that order which now appears to strengthen its cohesion also has the effect of weakening the leverage of any given marabout, even the *xalifa-général*, over individual disciples. For some Mourides, particularly in urban areas, affiliation with the order actually appears to be replacing the relationship with a marabout as the central fact of religious identity. By contrast, Tijans have always exhibited less cohesion as a group, at least in part due to fact that there are various independent Tijan maraboutic branches which compete for the allegiance of *taalibes*. In terms of the potential for collective action, therefore, as well as in the interactive possibilities based on networks of ties available to individuals, there are some increasingly significant implications of affiliation with one of these two Sufi orders.

Despite these differences, however, the evidence is overwhelming in pointing to a lack of socio-political cleavages based on religious affiliation at the local level.[30] Socializing, commercial transactions, and marriage regularly occur without regard to *tarixa* membership.[31] It is not uncommon to find in houses and shops the portrait of a marabout from another order among the omnipresent portraits of the marabouts of an individual's own order. Invariably the explanation goes something like the following: "No, he's not my marabout, but I managed to get the picture so I put it up anyway. After all, *ali* marabouts are good."[32] The distinction between the Mourides and the less numerous Qadir order (of which it is an offshoot) is even further blurred. There are actually cases in Fatick of double membership in both Mouride and Qadir *daairas*, and on at least one occasion a Qadir religious ceremony was cancelled because another event scheduled on the same day by the local Mouride *daaira* would draw from the same clientele and hence reduce attendance.[33]

Most significantly, even various local Islamic structures are kept distinct from *tarixa* membership. Children are frequently sent to study the Qur'an with a local Qur'anic teacher or marabout without regard to order. The various privately run "Arabic schools" (*écoles arabes*), which teach a mixture of Arabic and religious studies as an alternative to the French-based school system, likewise are not directly affiliated to an order. The daughter of the imam of one of the two main mosques in Fatick runs one such school. The imam is a Tijan, *taalibe* of the Malik Sy family of Tivaouane. His daughter studied with the Niasse family branch of the Tijans, in the nearby town of Kaolack. When asked, however, the imam resisted forcefully the implication that the school was in any way "Tijan." "*Tarixas*," he said, "have nothing to do with schools."[34]

The central "Friday mosque" (*jumaa*) in Fatick tends to be dominated by Tijans, and it is highly unlikely that a Mouride could be chosen imam – at least partly because the Mourides, following the *xalifa-général* of the order, frequently celebrate the most important religious holidays of the year a day later than other Senegalese Muslims.[35] In the neighborhood mosques (*jàkkas*), however, *tarixa* membership is not in itself a relevant criterion for the post of imam. An example is provided by a case in which, in trying to recruit someone to fill the vacant post of imam (a responsibility many are reluctant to accept), the members alternately offered it to both Mourides and Tijans.[36]

Considering these various aspects of the maraboutic and *tarixa* system at the popular level, fluidity and relativity emerge as its most noteworthy characteristics. There are exceptions to be found for most any generalization concerning membership in an order or relationships with marabouts. Still, the general context explored above can be broadly summarized as follows. The need for affective ties that can be called on to provide patronage – in both the metaphysical and the temporal domains – means that most everyone declares an allegiance to a marabout and that there is a general concern with the efficacy of specific marabouts in those domains. The relationship of most individuals with a marabout is derived from the association with a Sufi order which they received from their parents, but developed through a history of personal encounters and exchanges. Women may declare a change of affiliation at marriage, but otherwise such changes are relatively uncommon – though as we shall see certainly not unheard of. And while certain sociological differences distinguish the styles of the orders, and symbolic choices such as the regular celebration of holidays on different dates reinforce their distinctiveness, these have not been translated into fixed social cleavages.

As a result, membership in an order is not rigid, and absolute loyalty to the marabouts of that order is not ensured. And given the widespread faith in the powers of all marabouts, there is consequently always a latent interest in other marabouts, regardless of order. Moreover, as we shall see below, the diversity of marabouts available even within orders provides alternative options for the realignment of clientelism. The fact that an effective patronage relationship with a marabout can only be developed over considerable time makes such realignments infrequent and also provides incentives for the acceptance of the notion of inherited charisma. But to the extent to which the personal history of a relationship is weak the incentives for maintaining it are diminished, and thus the option of simply allowing it to lapse into a purely nominal affiliation is more likely to be exercised. This may, in turn, be followed by the establishment of an alternative clientelistic relationship, should there exist sufficient incentives to do so.

The maraboutic situation

There are many marabouts in Senegal. "More than one hundred thousand," bemoans one of the most powerful of them in an obvious bit of hyperbole that nevertheless reflects maraboutic perception of the competition.[37] All, of course, are not of equal stature; only the direct descendants of the founding fathers of the main maraboutic lineages have been able to systematically maintain a broad national following in Senegal. Nevertheless, particularly for the Tijaniyya, divisions even within important maraboutic families have meant that no one descendant claiming to be heir to the founder's *baraka* can grow complacent about his following. And while the Mourides have been able to achieve a greater degree of institutionalization, the accompanying weakening in the personal ties that bind *taalibe* to marabout appear to presage the weakening of the authority of individual marabouts within the order – if perhaps the strengthening of the order as an organization. Marabouts, therefore, face the need to distinguish themselves from others and to demonstrate the characteristics that will merit the maintenance and/or expansion of their followings, but without undermining the legitimacy of the maraboutic system *per se*. As we will see in the next chapter, addressing this double imperative is a crucial aspect of the numerous ritual celebrations organized by marabouts. This section explores the diverse bases on which maraboutic legitimacy can be built in the search for a following.

The sources of maraboutic appeal

There is no fixed system for acceding to the status of marabout. A marabout is simply one if people say he is, and if some are willing to declare themselves his students or disciples. Reputation, therefore, is crucial to a marabout's standing. In theory a reputation is earned via an individual's learning, wisdom, reputed sanctity, or the magical or miraculous powers which draw people to him. As such, the reputational basis of maraboutic appeal bears a strong resemblance to Weber's notion of charismatic leadership, a comparison which has been fruitfully explored in recent scholarship.[38] In practice however, more often than not, maraboutic status – or more correctly the potential for maraboutic status – is inherited. Most (if not all) of the most significant marabouts in Senegal today are the direct descendants – sons or grandsons – of the great figures of Senegalese Islam from the late-nineteenth and early-twentieth century Islamic flourish that accompanied the colonial conquest. What has been achieved, in effect, is a degree of "routinization of charisma" along the lines of Weber's formulation; to varying degrees all of the more successful maraboutic families in Senegal today owe their positions to their success in managing the transition to a "charisma of office," or a "lineage charisma" via popular acceptance of the inheritability of the founder's original charisma.

Yet this inheritance is not automatic; the heir to sanctity must also demonstrate that he embodies the most important of his ancestor's qualities if he is to benefit from the transfer of allegiances. And the more numerous the descendants, the more difficult this process for any one individual. Ideological formulations have consequently been provided to legitimate the notion of inheritance. In one rather disingenuous manifestation a grandson of El Hajj Malik Sy, speaking during the course of a massive religious celebration, cited the (presumably rhetorical) question posed by one of his sisters: If God had not wanted her to have the position of importance and responsibility which she held, why then had he made Ababacar Sy her father, and why El Hajj Malik Sy her grandfather?[39]

While the interest of the descendants of marabouts in legitimating the notion of inherited sanctity is obvious, the willingness to accept it on the part of the *taalibes* is less so. But *taalibes*, in fact, can be quite anxious to declare their allegiance to their marabout's *xalifa* (successor). An intriguing case is posed by a local Tijan marabout in Fatick who had had many *taalibes* in a large nearby village. Although the marabout had been dead many years, his *taalibes* continued to perform services for the marabout's family in Fatick (I witnessed the rethatching of a roof that had been damaged by rains, for example). Most significantly, they insisted on attempting to declare their allegiance to the marabout's son, though he emphatically and explicitly rejected the idea of establishing himself as a marabout, at times resorting to symbolically flouting social convention to make his point (e.g., joining a group of young men at playing cards – a singularly impious activity – during a celebration in the village). Particularly telling for the argument of this chapter is the reason which the son – a devout, practicing Tijan with an extremely solid Arabic and Qur'anic education but no formal Western schooling – gave for his refusal: he values his freedom too much, and marabouts are not "free" because they must always worry about conforming to disciples' expectations.[40]

The reluctance of the villagers to abandon the *taalibe* relationship is not due to any perception of "saintliness" on the part of the son; he was, indeed, not very well known to most, having spent years pursuing his studies elsewhere. Rather it must be understood as the product of their reluctance to lose the "investment" they had made in the relationship. A son succeeding his father is bound by the obligations his father has incurred. Should the villagers be obliged to seek out a new and unrelated maraboutic patron, the new relationship must be built "from scratch." *Taalibes*, therefore, also have incentives to accept the notion of the potential inheritability of a marabout's *baraka*, and this is an important source of stability in the relationship. As discussed below, however, it is also a source of potential difficulties for the most important maraboutic lineages of each order.

In addition to the earned and potential hereditary sources of their legitimacy, the position of less important marabouts, especially at the local level, can be further enhanced – but as we shall see also complicated – by their association with the most important maraboutic lineages of the order, of which they are themselves *taalibes*. An attribute of this sort, what might be called the appeal of "reflected" charisma, is a function of the degree of proximity a local marabout enjoys to a more important one, and it is most often expressed in terms of the special relationship established by initiation into an order via the transmission of the *wird*. The greater prestige and status associated with a direct chain of transmission of the *wird* from one of the acknowledged great marabouts of the region, notably a historical figure like El Hajj Umar Tall, mean that rivalries among maraboutic families frequently take the form of debates about *silsila*, spiritual genealogies of initiation.

Marabouts, therefore, can draw on three types of sources in justifying their status and thus appealing to potential disciples: (1) the reputation developed as a result of their own demonstrated powers and personal qualities; (2) claims to special access to the founder's *baraka* via their inherited status; and (3) the "reflected" charisma gleaned from an association with more influential marabouts. In general terms, these three sources decline in importance in the order in which they are listed here. Yet most individuals who aspire to maraboutic status in Senegal must draw on a combination of these factors in order to attract a following. The ability to do so successfully is the primary factor in determining the relative solidity or precariousness of a marabout's situation.

Local marabouts: drawing on diverse sources

Drawing to various degrees from each of these sources, marabouts must seek to maintain ties with their clientele. While occasionally new figures of personal charisma have been able to attract a following in the years since the founding of the most important Senegalese *zawiyas*, in fact the majority of important Senegalese marabouts today owe their position to inheritance. For local marabouts, the need to rely on reflected sources of legitimation is complicated by the fact that their followers frequently also declare allegiance to the most important marabouts of the order. A brief description of the cases of the four most significant local marabouts in Fatick, each with some association with a different major maraboutic lineage, may be useful to illustrate the variety of ways in which such marabouts can draw on each of these sources to maintain their positions. These descriptions will serve in addition to introduce the four men, whom we will see again throughout the remainder of this work. One of these men is a Mouride, one a Tijan associated with the Niasse family branch of the order centered in the town of Kaolack, and two are *taalibes* of the Malik Sy branch of the Tijaniyya, each associated with one of the two currently rival branches of that family.[41]

1 Of the four, "*Sërin* Alpha"[42] is the one whose position is most dependent on an earned reputation for learning, piety, and integrity. A native of a town in the Saloum region of Senegal, he came to Fatick in 1969 at the personal invitation of some local state officials, who were looking for someone to replace a Qur'anic teacher who had been forced to quit teaching due to illness. Unlike the other three below, Alpha's father was not a marabout, but Alpha had distinguished himself as a young man by his mastery of Arabic and the Qur'an. As a teacher at a neighborhood mosque in Fatick, he quickly established a reputation for his pedagogy and piety. Thus, with the help of state officials, he was able to establish his own household and his own school within a few years.

   Five years after his arrival in Fatick, he also founded a *daaira* (a local association of *taalibes* of a marabout or order) comprised of *taalibes* of the Tijan *xalifa* at Tivaouane, El Hajj Abdoul Aziz Sy. This *daaira* has been the most active of the three in Fatick dedicated to this marabout. As a result, Alpha has become the local representative-spokesman for the *xalifa* in Fatick. Like the *xalifa*, he espouses a separation of religion from the state, recognizing the necessity for each to exist, but arguing that the role of religious leaders is to maintain themselves above the dirtiness of politics, concentrating instead simply on the spiritual. This position has determined his relations with state officials, which remain polite but somewhat tense due to his reluctance to collaborate systematically in state initiatives. It has also influenced the composition of his following, which is drawn primarily from those Tijans attracted to Abdoul Aziz Sy's emphasis on piety and religious purity. Alpha's maraboutic position, therefore, is built on and sustained by a combination of his personal qualities and his association with the *xalifa* at Tivaouane.

2 "*Sërin* Baldé" is also a Tijan, also affiliated with the Sy family, but with a different branch of that family. He was born in a village near Fatick, the son of a local marabout of Peul origin. He studied first with this father, and then as a boy of ten or twelve was sent to Tivaouane to study there. During his years in Tivaouane he became a *taalibe* of the then-*xalifa* Ababacar Sy, son of the original charismatic founder of the maraboutic lineage, El Hajj Malik Sy, and eventually received the *wird* from him. He subsequently spent several years studying in Saint Louis, and then for a brief period went to Mauritania, to the town of Boutilimit, to study with members of an important Moorish maraboutic family there.[43]

Upon his return to Senegal he founded Qur'anic schools and taught in two different towns before returning to his birthplace to join a brother (also a marabout) in continuing the work left by his father. For fifteen years he ran a school (*daara*) in the village, apparently drawing many students from surrounding areas to study Arabic and the Qur'an, as well as to learn a trade. The students practiced their skills by building a house and a large mosque for the marabout. Then, in 1972, he made a break and moved to establish himself in Fatick. Although he is reticent to elaborate, the move seems to have been at least partially motivated by the desire to strike out on his own and distinguish himself from his brother. He established another school in Fatick and again was able to build a house and a mosque with the labor of his students.

In the last several years, however, he has quit teaching and has devoted himself instead to working full-time with the sons of Ababacar Sy in their various endeavors and serving as their representative in the town. Ababacar Sy's sons had contested the succession upon their father's death in 1957, but it nevertheless eventually passed to Ababacar's younger brother, the current *xalifa* Abdoul Aziz Sy. As discussed below, however, several of the sons have maintained a very high profile in Senegal and are clearly positioning themselves in anticipation of their uncle's death and the passing of the *xalifa* position to the third generation. Most notably, Ababacar's sons have involved themselves very directly in politics. The most famous of the sons, Cheikh Tidiane Sy, founded a "Committee in Solidarity for the Re-election of President Abdou Diouf" to campaign actively at the time of the February 1988 elections.[44]

Baldé served as chairman for the local chapter of this committee in the region of Fatick. He heads, in addition, the most active of the three *daairas* in Fatick dedicated to Ababacar Sy and his descendents. Like his patrons, Baldé believes the role of the religious elite should be to work closely with the state, ostensibly in the pursuit of the goals of "national development." As a result he is clearly the "favorite" marabout of state officials in Fatick and frequently described in glowing terms by them. This has brought him a certain measure of success; he is the only marabout (and one of the few non-state officials) to own a car in Fatick.

While Baldé, therefore, is able to draw on both heredity and learning in legitimating his maraboutic position, he has clearly chosen to define his status primarily in terms of his cooperation with the Ababacar Sy branch of the Tijans in Tivaouane. His following in Fatick, therefore, draws heavily from local state officials and others who feel comfortable with a direct involvement in party politics, notably those more educated in the Western school system.

3 "*Sërin* Cissé," the Mouride marabout in Fatick, is less visible locally than either of the two Tijans discussed above, though certainly no less influential. He is the son of an early follower of Amadou Bamba, the founder of the Mouride order. Cissé's father traveled to the town of Boutilimit in Mauritania during the period when Bamba was exiled there by the French.[45] He made the vow of allegiance (the *njébbal*) to Bamba there, and after six months returned to Senegal. Cissé was educated in the order by his father, and then sometime in the early 1950s he was sent to Fatick by Bamba's son, Falilou Mbacké, then *xalifa-général* of the order, to serve as his representative in the town. He has been in Fatick since then, and does no travelling except to go back and forth to the Mouride "capital city" of Touba.

Cissé is nominally responsible for the two Mouride *daairas* in Fatick, and both maintain close contact with him, but he plays no direct part in their organization or functioning. In keeping with the dominant ideology of the order, Cissé emphasizes that he simply serves to follow the commands (*ndigal*) of the *xalifa* in Touba, of whom he is a *taalibe*. He shows no direct interest in state affairs and protests ignorance of politics, thus exemplifying the Wolof phrase which he has painted on the door to his room: "Only commands [read: of the *xalifa*] are certain."[46] Yet despite his lack of direct political involvement, Cissé clearly wields significant clout in that he can report local needs, difficulties, or conflicts to the most important marabouts of the order, who can in turn deal directly with the higher levels of government to exert pressure in local issues.

An example may illustrate how this can occur. It was reported in Fatick that at the time of the last *lotissement* – the granting of lots by the state on which houses can be constructed in the town – a list of sixty people whose applications were to receive preferential treatment was sent to the local office of the Ministry of Urbanism and Habitat by the Minister's office in Dakar. Of these, thirty were Mouride *taalibes* whose names had been submitted by the *xalifa-général* of the order. The list of these Mouride names could only have been drawn up locally, then transmitted by *Sërin* Cissé, as the local representative, to the *xalifa* or his assistants in Touba, who could then relay it to the Ministry in Dakar. The local office dutifully follows the instructions from the capital.[47]

More than any of the other local marabouts, then, Cissé makes no claim to owe his status to anything other than his (inherited) ties to the major marabouts of the order, and this status in fact depends on the role he plays in serving as a representative of the order. The quite significant influence he has over the Mouride community in Fatick thus reflects the greater institutionalization of the order.

4 *"Sëriñ* Diakhaté" is the most enigmatic of local marabouts in Fatick. He comes from a long line of marabouts which he can name back for forty or so generations, the earlier ones being "Arabs." Although his name is of Saraxole origin, he like his father was born to a Serer mother, and he thus speaks Serer as a first language. Diakhaté is also of casted origin, a fact that has some influence on his position. The family's affiliation to the Tijaniyya comes from a visit to the tomb of the founder of the order in Fez (Morocco) which Diakhaté's grandfather made in the company of the Tijan marabout Abdoulaye Niasse, founder of the Niasse lineage in Kaolack. At that time Diakhaté's grandfather received the Tijan *wird*, and declared himself a *taalibe* of Niasse, since it was he who had brought him to the order. The relationship was maintained into the next generation, and in 1954 Diakhaté's father, who had settled in Fatick, was visited by Ibrahima "Baye" Niasse, son of Abdoulaye and the most famous of the Niasse marabouts. Via Ibrahima Niasse's intercession with Farba Diouf, a local notable and son of Coumba N'Doffène Diouf, the second-to-last *buur* (king) of Sine, the elder Diakhaté received a lot of land on which to establish himself. There, with the help of a large number of *taalibes* that had come to perform the *tarbiya* (an apprenticeship, which can last for years, undertaken in the expectation of receiving some mystical secrets from the marabout) he constructed a house and began a mosque that Diakhaté was later to finish.

Diakhaté studied first with his father, then for four years in Kaolack with Ibrahima Niasse, and one more year in Dakar at a school run by the Niasse family, before returning to Fatick to help his father who had grown rather feeble. Since his father's death in 1980, Diakhaté has inherited his position, and he calls himself his father's successor (*xalifa*). He has a decidedly mystical bent, and claims to have visited the moon during the course of a *khalwa* retreat, a rigorous forty-day fast which he performed alone, out in the bush.[48] He also once devised an original writing system for Serer, inventing the alphabet himself. For several years he taught Serer children at his father's school to write in this alphabet, and a sign with his father's name and profession written in Diakhaté's alphabet hung for years at the entrance to the house. He was motivated to do this, he says, because everyone needs to have a "secret" – and thus it would not do to write Serer in either the Roman or the Arabic alphabet.[49]

Diakhaté's maraboutic legitimacy is derived in part from his stature as his father's *xalifa* but also largely from his own mysticism. He is thus concerned to maintain the personal allegiance of his followers, and consequently his ties to the Niasse family are ambiguous. Although he acknowledges being a *taalibe* of the Niasse, he neither emphasizes this point nor serves as their representative in Fatick – this task being performed instead by a *taalibe* of some importance in the town.

Diakhaté's concern for his following also influences his relations with the state. In early 1989 he was visited by a delegation of local officials, including the governor of the region, who requested during the course of the visit that he join the ruling Parti Socialiste (PS). Diakhaté agreed, and his "adherence" was announced in an article in *Le Soleil*, the official government newspaper. But he dismisses his agreement as being simply the requirements of hospitality; how could he refuse when the officials were his guests? On the contrary, he states that he should neither belong to a party nor vote, those not being appropriate activities for a religious leader ("Does the pope vote? Or belong to a political party?" he asks rhetorically). He sees his role instead as that of an intermediary with local officials for his disciples, should one of them be in trouble. And since he has *taalibes* from all political parties, it would be impolitic of him to affiliate with any. This position, therefore, arises out of a concern to maintain his ties to his *taalibes*.

As these sketches indicate, the position of local marabouts is an ambiguous one. To the extent that they wish to cultivate a personal clientele, they must downplay the importance of their connections to the more visible "national" marabouts. At the same time, their limited resources, particularly in a town like Fatick, mean that the courting of such connections may be the most effective means for them to legitimate their position. They frequently become, as a result, first and foremost intermediaries between local *taalibes* and national marabouts. This, however, poses a double danger for the local marabout and for the national one. To the extent to which their status is derived from the association with a national marabout, local marabouts can find themselves circumvented in cases where local *taalibes* either find a more appealing intermediary or become sufficiently prominent themselves to be able to dispense with an intermediary altogether. For national marabouts, the channeling of their charisma through local intermediaries poses different dangers. On the one hand, should the relationship between local *taalibes* and the intermediary-marabout weaken, the connection to the national marabouts may lapse into a purely nominal affiliation. More rarely, but more dangerously, a local marabout can at times achieve sufficient renown to be able to establish his legitimacy and maintain a following independently of his ties to a more important one.

A prominent example of this latter case is that of the Tijan marabout El Hajj Madior Cissé in the city of Saint Louis in northern Senegal. Cissé was a *taalibe* of the Tijan *xalifa* Ababacar Sy and served as his representative in Saint Louis. By the time of Ababacar Sy's death in 1957, however, Cissé had developed a large and devoted local following due at least in part to the importance he wielded as an official in the colonial administration. At his marabout's death, then, Cissé did not transfer his allegiance to the new *xalifa*, Ababacar's brother, or to his sons. He maintains, instead, a nominal allegiance to the dead *xalifa* and his father, but he is clearly a competitor of the Sy family for Tijan *taalibes* in the Saint Louis region. Each year at the occasion of the *Mawlud* (the feast of the prophet's birthday), he holds a large religious celebration (a *gàmmu*) which rivals the one held in Tivaouane by the Sy family at the same occasion.

"National" marabouts: the dilemmas of inherited charisma

The most important marabouts in Senegal, therefore, those located at the main centers of each Sufi order, face certain difficulties in maintaining ties to their disciples in areas outside their immediate domain – that is, in most of the country. Even more significantly, these marabouts each face the thorny problem of legitimating their inheritance and maintaining the cohesion of the saintly lineages in the face of a large and ever-growing number of heirs. All of the most significant Senegalese marabouts owe their positions first and foremost to their heredity, and they seek to legitimate it through regular claims to be continuing the vision of the charismatic founder. In the first generation, that of the founder's sons, it has frequently been possible to achieve such legitimation. Every indication, however, points to the potential for fragmentation in the next generation.

The Mouride order has managed to achieve a higher degree of cohesion and institutionalization than any of its rivals. Paradoxically, this seems to have been the result of its original fragmented leadership. Each of the brothers of the founder, Amadou Bamba, as well as many of his more important *taalibes*, were established as great *shaykhs* of the order during Bamba's lifetime.[50] Each, as a result, was succeeded by a *xalifa*, usually the eldest son, who inherited the father's position. At each succession, however, problems arose due to the tensions inherent in the system of succession. Faced with multiple claimants to their loyalty in such situations some marabout-members of each lineage, along with their *taalibes,* preferred instead to declare their allegiance directly to the *xalifa* of the founder himself, the *xalifa*-general of the order. Cruise O'Brien noted shortly after the death of the second *xalifa*, Falilou Mbacké, that this trend seemed to have developed during his tenure (1945–1968).[51] Under the tenure of the third *xalifa*-general, Abdou Lahatte, the pattern appears to have continued, leading to an even greater centralization of allegiances in the office of the *xalifa*-general.

The position of *xalifa*-general has yet to make the crucial transition to the third generation, that of the founder's grandsons. The system of succession which was developed over the course of the first two succession crises (1927 and 1945), and which appears to have been agreed to by all of the major marabouts in a secret pact which dates from about 1952, involves the succession to the position of *xalifa* by the founder's eldest son at the founder's death, and the subsequent inheritance of the position laterally from brother to brother through all of the founder's sons.[52] Only at the death of the youngest is the position due to pass to the next generation, to the sons of the founder's eldest son.[53]

The death in July 1989 of Abdou Lahatte Mbacké, who had become the third *xalifa*-general in 1968, was followed by a peaceful and uncontested transition of the position to the next brother, Abdoul Qadir. He, however, lived less than a year after his inheritance, and the succession in June 1990 to the next brother, Saliou Mbacké, again passed without incident.[54] Only one other son of Amadou Bamba, Mamadou Mortalla, remains alive today. And given both his advanced age and that of the current *xalifa*-general, the transition to the third generation is likely to occur within the next few years.

Amadou Bamba had twelve sons who survived to adulthood. To my knowledge there exists no enumeration of the grandsons, but a reasonable (perhaps conservative) estimate might assign a number of offspring equal to their father's to each of the sons, thus yielding a number on the order of 144 grandsons.[55] In addition, Cruise O'Brien estimated the number of important marabouts, the *shaykhs*, of the order at three to four hundred at the time of his research in the late 1960s.[56] That number is likely to have at least doubled today. There are, as a result, a multitude of potential rivals for positions of leadership within the order.

In addition, there is some evidence that there are political divisions among the leaders of the order. At the time of the February 1988 elections in Senegal, the *xalifa*-general pronounced an *ndigal* (order) directing all Mourides to vote for the re-election of President Abdou Diouf, saying that anything else would be a betrayal of the founder, Amadou Bamba. Despite those instructions, however, a well-known nephew of the *xalifa's* named Khadim Mbacké (one of the many grandsons), made a public pronouncement in favor of the opposition candidate, Abdoulaye Wade. Although he was apparently eventually "persuaded" (by senior marabouts of the order?) to revoke his endorsement in a dramatic public apology on Senegalese radio for his "mistake", other important marabouts – most significantly the *xalifa* of one of Amadou Bamba's brothers – continued to call for the election of Abdoulaye Wade.[57] In 1993, under the leadership of a new and less political *xalifa* and in a particularly tense and uncertain political atmosphere, the major marabouts of the order refrained from pronouncing on the elections. Among the various minor marabouts in the family to publicly take partisan positions, however, were supporters of both the government and the opposition.

It is quite conceivable that a mutually satisfactory solution to the problem of succession in the third generation will be found, particularly given the incentives for cohesion provided by the institutional clout of the order. At the same time, it seems highly likely that there will be at least some defections from any solution, and there is even the potential for a significant schism in the order over this issue. Nevertheless, as discussed below in the case of the electoral *ndigal*, even when the marabouts of the order do not find themselves faced with the problem of competing among themselves for *taalibes*, they are confronted with the equally difficult issue of maintaining effective leverage over *taalibes* whose allegiance lies with a large organization united primarily by the shared symbol of the founder rather than the charismatic authority of a living leader.

The Tijaniyya order, with which more than half of Senegalese Muslims declare affiliation, has never exhibited the centralized cohesion of the Mourides. Nevertheless various charismatic Tijan figures were able to establish themselves as "great marabouts" and founders of saintly lineages not dissimilar to the Mouride model.[58] As discussed in chapter 2, the most noteworthy of these is that founded by El Hajj Malik Sy (*c.* 1855–1922) in the town of Tivaouane, followed by the Niasse family branch of the order established in the town of Kaolack. In addition to competition among different Tijan lineages, however, both of these maraboutic families have experienced internal divisions and rivalries for the inheritance of the founder's charisma – and his *taalibes*.

Upon Malik Sy's death in 1922 his eldest living son, Ababacar, inherited the position of *xalifa*.[59] Ababacar's inheritance, however, was challenged by his younger brothers Mansour (the founder's personal favorite) and Abdoul Aziz (the current *xalifa*), and the rivalry between the two brothers occasionally became public, as in their support of rival political factions in the early 1950s.[60] Ababacar's death in 1957 was followed four days later by Mansour's, and resulted in a succession crisis that pitted Ababacar's dynamic son, Cheikh Tidiane Sy, against his uncle Abdoul Aziz. With the support of Léopold Senghor, Abdoul Aziz emerged as the new *xalifa*, thus establishing the same pattern of inheritance as that practiced by the Mourides.

Once again, however, rivalries have persisted long after the succession had been decided. In opposition to his uncle the *xalifa*, Cheikh Tidiane Sy has maintained a high profile in Senegalese politics, initially working against Léopold Senghor and his party, but beginning in the late 1960s as a close ally of the party, most notably in his active public support for Abdou

Diouf's 1988 re-election. With two of his brothers, confusingly named Mansour and Abdoul Aziz "Junior,"[61] he has been aggressive in the attempt to recruit and maintain *taalibes* dedicated to the memory of his father, thus establishing a basis for a claim to the position of *xalifa* after his uncle Abdoul Aziz's death. This will no doubt be complicated by the existence of one last son of the founder, Habib Sy, who should inherit the *xalifa* position in accordance with the lateral rules of succession. But while Habib can lay claim to an inherited legitimacy, he has developed none of the personal charisma necessary to maintain a following, preferring instead to establish himself as a very successful businessman in Gambia.

A significant cause, perhaps the most significant cause, of rivalry among these members of the family has been the political positions they have each adopted, particularly at various crucial moments in Senegalese history. And as the cases of the two local marabouts in Fatick dedicated to the two branches of this family demonstrate, these positions have been an important part of the appeal of these marabouts to local *taalibes*.

In the 1980s another family member launched the first major effort by a member of the fourth generation to secure a national following for himself by founding an innovative religious movement with overtly political connotations. This is the "Dahiratoul Moustarchidina wal Moustarchidaty" founded by Moustapha Sy, son of Cheikh Tidiane Sy, and directed primarily to the widely disaffected Senegalese youth. The movement has attracted a broad national following, although its fortunes have fluctuated at the local level as Moustapha Sy has engaged in various controversial interactions with the Senegalese government. In February 1989 he hosted a widely publicized conference on Islamic youth in Dakar with the odd bedfellows of the Libyan Islamic Call Society and the Senegalese government as patrons, and during which he declared his allegiance to Diouf and the ruling party. With the difficulties of the organization in maintaining grass-roots support, by 1993 Moustapha Sy had become highly critical of the government, launching a scathing personal attack on Diouf just days before the February elections. More than any other, the Sy family demonstrates that the rivalry for *taalibes* is based not only on the personal patronage resources of a marabout, but also on the affinity of the disciples to the spiritual and especially the political positions adopted by their marabouts.

The maraboutic lineage founded in Kaolack by Abdoulaye Niasse, a contemporary of both Malik Sy and Amadou Bamba, has also experienced divisive rivalries. At Niasse's death in 1922 he was succeeded by his eldest son, Khalifa Niasse. But the dynamic charisma of a much younger son, Ibrahima "Baye" Niasse, rather quickly allowed him to develop a larger following than that of his older brother. Ibrahima Niasse eventually separated from his older brother to establish himself in what was to become the Medina neighborhood of Kaolack. He soon surpassed even his father in fame, developing a large and highly international following throughout West Africa – most significantly in northern Nigeria. Following Niasse's death in 1975, the division of the family has continued into the next generation. The eldest sons (both named Abdoulaye) of each of the brothers continue as marabouts in their respective neighborhoods.

The descendants of Ibrahima Niasse have benefited from the hereditary transmission of his greater charisma, and that branch of the family continues to attract the greatest number of *taalibes*. The status of the individual marabouts of this family, however, was further complicated by Baye Niasse's intentional efforts to break the pattern of direct inheritance. In his will Baye Niasse made the surprise request that rather than his eldest son, his *taalibe*, son-in-law, and imam of the Medina-Kaolack mosque, El Hajj Alioune Cissé, should be named his *xalifa*. This in fact occurred, but the power of inheritance in maraboutic positions is demonstrated not only by the fact that Baye Niasse's eldest son continues to play a role as an important marabout, but that Alioune Cissé's son, Hassan, inherited *his* father's position after the elder Cissé's death, and now rivals Niasse's sons in maraboutic status.[62]

At the same time, various members of the other branch of the family (heirs to Baye Niasse's older brother) have attempted to create other sources of influence for themselves. One, Ahmed Khalifa Niasse, made a dramatic call for an Islamic revolution in Senegal at a Paris news conference in 1980 at which he announced the formation of an Islamic political party to be called "Hizbollah" (Party of God). The appeal found no supporters, at least in part due to Ahmed Khalifa's reputation as a flamboyant opportunist.[63] Yet he continues periodically to play a role in Senegalese politics; following the hotly contested 1988 elections he was recruited as a go-between in efforts to arrange a compromise between Abdou Diouf and Abdoulaye Wade, and early in the campaign for the February 1993 elections he began to campaign publicly for Abdou Diouf's re-election.[64] Ahmed Khalifa's brother, Sidy Lamine Niasse, is the founding editor of the Islamic weekly *Wal Fadjri*, which has moved from a "radical" pro-Iranian orientation to a more moderate and widely respected position as among the best of the Senegalese opposition press.

In addition to the rivalries within families, the Sy and Niasse marabouts compete not only with each other, but also with other Tijan maraboutic families established in Senegal. One common aspect of this competition is the recourse to sources of "reflected" charisma. Most Tijan marabouts in

Senegal base their legitimacy at least in part on a spiritual connection to the famous Tijan marabout El Hajj Umar Tall, leader of the nineteenth-century *jihads* that did much to spread the order throughout the region.[65] The key to such legitimation involves claims concerning the chain of transmission of the *wird*, with the greater prestige attached to the more direct connections to the most important figures of the order. Thus rivalry among Tijan marabouts frequently involves disputes about the chain of transmission of the *wird*.

One case of some importance in Fatick involves the maraboutic lineage established by Thierno Alioune Dème near the town of Sokone. The current *xalifa*, Cheikh Tidiane Dème, is a grandson of the founder. His substantial local following in the region, including some *taalibes* in Fatick, is nevertheless significantly less numerous than the Niasse family following. According to the Dème family, however, it was Thierno Alioune Dème himself who gave the *wird* to Abdoulaye Niasse. Moreover, the story is told, when the latter was a young man with no significant following, Dème visited him and his new wife. Because of their relative poverty, the wife was forced to request help from neighbors, who provided her with a chicken in order to receive the marabout properly. Recognizing the hardship he had caused, Dème thanked Niasse for his hospitality and predicted that he would have a son who, should he be named after the prophet Ibrahima (Abraham), would become a great man. The Dème family thus takes a degree of credit for Ibrahima Niasse's greatness, implicitly laying claim to some of his *baraka*.

The Niasse family, not surprisingly, denies this story, claiming instead that Abdoulaye Niasse received the *wird* directly from a companion of El Hajj Umar Tall's. These contrasting accounts of the relationship of the two families is a reflection of what a descendant of Dème's describes as the "intense competition" among Senegalese marabouts today. Each, he says, must claim to be "the biggest and the best" in order to establish a basis for attracting disciples.[66] Although the relative historical accuracy of the two accounts cannot readily be evaluated, the interest of the story clearly lies not in its veracity but in its illustration of maraboutic competition for establishing claims to a more direct link with a source of "reflected" *baraka*.

The competition of new charisma

In addition to the competition among individual marabouts within families in laying claims to inherited charisma, and the competition within orders – particularly the Tijaniyya – for establishing claims to the pre-eminence of a particular lineage, marabouts in Senegal also find themselves occasionally faced with competition for *taalibes* from entirely new sources of "original" charisma. Like the earlier social movements around such figures as Amadou Bamba or El Hajj Malik Sy that resulted in the establishment of new maraboutic lineages, these movements revolve around a marabout who has emerged as a charismatic figure in his own right. Also like the earlier movements, the most significant of these seem to emerge more from a society-based imperative for restructuring than from the personality of the charismatic figure himself.[67] It is not surprising, therefore, that they should frequently incorporate or reflect the concerns of certain marginalized social groups, most significantly ethnic groups.

One such movement in the Casamance region of Senegal revolved around *Shaykh* Sountou Badji, the first ethnic Diola marabout to emerge as a significant figure in Senegalese Islam. Badji's movement, centered in the village of Sindian north of the town of Bignona, drew its support almost exclusively from the Diola population of this region that has long felt itself dominated by the northern part of the country. Badji's movement flourished in the late 1970s and early 1980s, attracting large numbers of *taalibes* and thus permitting him to undertake the construction of a large mosque and an "Islamic Institute" in Sindian. Yet for reasons that remain unclear but that are no doubt related to Badji's personal ambitions and public over-eagerness to parlay his large number of disciples into political clout, his following evaporated dramatically in the space of a brief period, leaving him by the mid-1980s with virtually no following and half-completed buildings. There is not much hard evidence on which to base an interpretation of this phenomenon, but what does exist is at least compatible with the hypothesis that the movement arose because Diola society was "ripe" for the emergence of a charismatic figure to provide a basis for social restructuring that would serve as a shield from northern domination. Badji's evident willingness to collaborate too closely with the state, however, cost him his credibility as the center of such a restructuring and aborted the movement before it could coalesce. It is significant in this regard that since late 1989 the Casamance has entered what may be the most serious ethnically based rebellion in Senegal's history.[68]

Most significant for Fatick has been the rise to prominence over the course of the last decade of a Serer marabout in the village of Sirmang only a few miles from the Gambian border. El Hajj Ousmane Mama Ansou Niang, known popularly as Ma Ansou Niang, has attracted a broad following among the Serer in Fatick, particularly from the large majority who previously claimed an affiliation with the Sy family in Tivaouane. This very important movement will be explored in depth in chapter 7, but it merits mentioning here as an indication of the extent to which existing maraboutic ties can be challenged by entirely new movements. As we shall see, by the late 1980s, the institutional structures of allegiance to the Sy family had been almost totally replaced by those of Ma Ansou Niang among the Serer of Ndiaye-Ndiaye.

In addition to ethnically linked movements, occasional others based on sources of "original" charisma compete with the established maraboutic lineages for followers. The most interesting of these manage to combine elements of "reformist" (anti-*tarixa*) Islamic movements with aspects of popular maraboutic Islam. Once such movement is headed from the historically important town of Rufisque by El Hajj Mouhamadou Moustapha Ngom. Ngom describes his movement, which he calls "Dalailoul Khairate," as "a friend of the Prophet's association" (*Une association amie du Prophète*). Know popularly as the "Mouhamadiyya," it incorporates an element of preparation for the imminent apparition of the *mahdi*, who will reside in Dakar.[69] Ngom nevertheless claims that his movement is one of "orthodox" Islam, and he rejects much of the Arabo-Wolof terminology of Senegalese maraboutic Islam. He thus refuses to use the term *tarixa* for his "association" and insists that he be referred to by the French term "chef religieux," rather than as "marabout" or *sëriñ*. He also refuses to accept any *addiya* (financial offerings) from his followers, earning a living instead by his various business dealings. These, of course, are no doubt enhanced – particularly if they involve the state – by the fact that he commands a large following.

Yet despite these distinctions, Ngom is said to have the magical and mystical powers normally associated with marabouts in Senegal. Thus his followers recount fantastic stories of his childhood – the resuscitation of dead and mutilated birds and mice, for example, or his ability as a child to harvest his quota of peanuts without ever entering the field. As for all important marabouts, there are numerous *daairas* of Ngom's followers organized around the country. The Fatick *daaira* claims a membership of some seventy-five men and forty women. As opposed to most *daairas* which meet on Thursday evenings – eve of the Muslim holy day – Ngom's *daairas* gather every Sunday for religious chanting. Ngom is said to personally attend a different religious ceremony (a *gàmmu*) organized by one of his *daairas* in a different town in Senegal every Sunday of the year, except for that following the *Korite* (end of Ramadan) feastday.

Ngom's movement is peculiar even by Senegalese standards.[70] It is criticized by "reformist" Muslims for its bizarre and innovative aspects, and by the Sufi majority for his audacity in daring to criticize marabouts. Many of his followers are from the smaller or more marginalized Senegalese ethnic groups; in addition to Serer there are numerous Diola, Bassari, Socé (Manding) and Manjaag members. The leaders of the *daaira* in Fatick explicitly point out that many of these people have very little previous education in Islam. Thus, like the ethnically linked movements, Ngom competes most directly with the established marabouts in Senegal among those groups that are most accessible for the expansion of a following.

Ngom's reliance on many of the trappings and organizational methods of the established Sufi centers in Senegal, like the rapid, wholesale, and seemingly unquestioned adoption of these forms by other "new" marabouts such as Badji or Ma Ansou Niang, is also indicative of another fact of particular importance. The institutionalization of charisma in the major *zawiyas* as demonstrated by the importance of inheritance for maraboutic status has resulted in the legitimation of the entire maraboutic *system* in Senegal. In a very real sense, it is not only specific instances of original charisma that have been "routinized," but in fact the very notion of maraboutic charisma and the accompanying forms of social organization have benefited from this status. The potential for new religious leaders to gain a following seems to lie primarily in the successful adoption of the existing model for recruitment of a clientele. As we shall see, the potential for the organization of social groups and the articulation of societal interests which is inherent in this model has important implications for the analysis of state-society relations in Senegal.

Conclusion: the ambiguity of maraboutic power

A marabout's position, the political power and the influence he wields within Senegalese society, is a direct function of the size of his following. This following, in turn, is attracted by the marabout's charisma – his reputation for efficacious use of magical, spiritual, and socio-political powers. While there are some differences of style among the different orders that can make them more or less appealing to some individuals, adherence to an order *per se* is still of very limited socio-political consequence in Senegal. It is, rather, the nature and extent of the personal relationship with a marabout which has a direct impact on an individual's opportunities, and on his or her behavior.

I have identified three sources of the reputational component of a marabout's appeal, that is, of his "charisma." As we have seen, all three sources – original, inherited, and reflected – pose certain difficulties. Sufficient "original" charisma to attract a large following is rare, and its emergence seems to be linked more clearly to changing social circumstances than to the qualities of an individual. As a result, most of the major marabouts in Senegal today depend heavily on legitimation via recourse to an inherited or reflected charismatic source. Each, however, encounters numerous competitors in such an endeavor. The competition that results from the need to distinguish, legitimate, and reinforce a marabout's charisma as founded in any of the three sources of *baraka* means that marabouts face a constant need to safeguard their appeal in order to attract, maintain, or expand their followings.

The most successful cases of a marabout's being able to distinguish himself from others are those that resulted in the establishment of an entirely new maraboutic lineage, or even of a distinct order. The potential for such an outcome presents a strong incentive for a marabout to strike out on his own. Farba Diouf, a son of *Buur-Siin* Coumba N'Doffène Diouf, recalls that when he first met Amadou Bamba in 1924, the new Mouride movement was just a small branch of the Qadiriyya order. But Bamba, he says, did not want to remain just a "little marabout," so he started his own movement. "And he was right to do so," Diouf notes, "because he is now famous and *un grand homme*."[71]

Such success, of course, is not within the reach of most marabouts. Nevertheless, each must make efforts to distinguish himself from the competition. It is in this context that the efforts of Ababacar Sy's sons to promote their father as a source of original and powerful *baraka*, distinct from his own father's appeal, must be understood. In the absence of such a move, the number of potential heirs to the founder's original charisma increases dramatically. Similarly, the innovative *siyaare* (Arabic *ziaara*) to Tivaouane at the feast of *Tamxarit* which Moustapha Sy has instituted as the major celebration for the Dahiratoul Moustarchidina wal Moustarchidaty answers to this imperative to "create something new to get followers for himself," as one skeptical Tijan *taalibe* put it.[72]

To the extent to which they base their legitimacy on their own charismatic sources, rather than simply on reflected *baraka*, local marabouts are similarly faced with the need to distinguish themselves. In addition to the stock of extraordinary stories of magical powers which are told about all marabouts in Senegal, various other postures can serve this goal. *Sëriñ* Baldé's peculiar choice of location for constructing his house (rather distant from the town, on the main road) was characterized by one state official as a result of the need for marabouts to "do something a little bizarre" to add to their mystique, and therefore to their local appeal. Stories of angels descending to this site at night, he pointed out, circulated in the town.[73] *Sëriñ* Diakhaté's various non-traditional undertakings, notably his invention of a Serer alphabet, can also be seen as a response to this need.

The resulting drive of marabouts to distinguish themselves feeds the frequent complaints about the exaggerated claims of some marabouts concerning their own strengths. Like the Dème family complaint that the Niasse marabouts refuse to acknowledge their version of the spiritual genealogy of transmission of the *wird* because of their claim to be "the biggest and the best," Abdoul Aziz Sy Junior, criticizes the "hundred thousand marabouts" of Senegal for their presumption each to proclaim, "I am the champion; I am the best; I am the only one."[74]

In pursuit of the goal of distinguishing themselves, marabouts seeking to recruit and maintain a following also face a parallel need to develop a keen sense of popular opinion and reflect it in their public statements and in the image they choose to portray. Tellingly, even in religious matters a marabout must be careful to give people what they want to hear or risk alienating them. Asked about the popular amulets (*gris-gris*) worn by almost all Senegalese, Abdoul Aziz Sy Junior acknowledges that they are not acceptable in "orthodox" Islam and says that El Hajj Malik was much against them. "But," he notes, "they are a deeply rooted tradition in the Senegalese population and people believe in them profoundly. And whoever forbids them becomes their enemy. Someone who forbids that to them ceases to be credible."[75]

Because marabouts are largely seen as intermediaries with the state (and since they regularly describe themselves that way), the positions that they adopt *vis-à-vis* political issues and the political elite are especially important in the maintenance of their popular appeal. As we will see, some, like *Sëriñ* Baldé and the sons of Ababacar Sy whom he follows, have opted for a close involvement with the state and electoral politics as an important component of their appeal to followers. Most, however, are far more ambivalent about their relations with the political elite, and this ambivalence arises clearly from their concern to avoid conflict with popular sentiment. Both *Sëriñ* Alpha and *Sëriñ* Diakhaté explicitly attributed their careful distance from political involvement as a choice taken deliberately to avoid causing difficulties for their followers. Alpha poses the problem in the form of a question: what if he told his disciples to vote for Diouf, and it turned out that one of them was a relative of Abdoulaye Wade's? This would put that person in a difficult position, and a marabout should not do such a thing. Diakhaté's argument is virtually identical; if he were to join a political party, and one of his follows were for some reason a member of a different party, this could cause pain.[76] This also, of course, could cause a certain amount of cognitive dissonance on the part of the *taalibe*. And because marabouts cannot be certain that this dissonance will be reconciled in their favor, the careful decision to avoid placing a *taalibe* in a position of having to choose is a very rational one.

A highly revealing statement of this need for caution, indeed this fear, on the part of marabouts is found in the interview with Abdoul Aziz Sy Junior cited above. "Currently in Senegal," he says, "there is a rivalry among the assemblies [of *taalibes*], a rivalry for the procession [*sic* possession?] of the biggest assembly. And this rivalry means that sincerity itself no longer exists. *The marabout who is attached to spiritual values no longer dares speak the truth, precisely for fear of losing his followers.*"[77]

This statement turns the common assumption of near-total maraboutic control over disciples on its head. Not only can marabouts not count on the blind obedience of their followers, but they must be careful of their stated positions – to the point of ignoring "the truth" – in order to avoid losing them. While the situation is clearly not as extreme as the marabout depicts it – followings do not usually disappear at the utterance of an ill-advised opinion – his statement nevertheless points to the existence of important constraints on maraboutic authority. And the ultimate result is that there is a significant amount of leverage for Senegalese society over the religious, and consequently over the political, elite of the country. Neither can afford to grow complacent over their sources of authority and control.

5   The marabout–disciple relationship II: the structures of allegiance

On Thursday nights in Fatick, as in any city or town in Senegal today, groups of local disciples of a particular marabout gather in the compound of one of their number for an evening of religious chanting, planning, and socializing. Usually several such groups can be heard at once; the Qadirs are distinguished by the rhythmic beating of their large Moorish drums, the Mourides with their preference for electronic amplification are inevitably the loudest, and groups of Tijans tend to sing the devotional poetry of El Hajj Malik Sy. The proliferation of such local groups, known as *daairas*,[1] has been noted by many observers of Senegalese society. Along with the creation of religious study groups, the founding of new Arabic-language schools, the growing frequency of religious ceremonies, and the seemingly ever-increasing numbers of pilgrims at the annual commemorations in the holy cities of Touba and Tivaouane, the phenomenon has usually been interpreted as an indicator of religious fervor, another incidence of the much discussed "Islamic revival."

No doubt there is some truth to this perspective – although in fact much of the motivation behind this new attention appears to follow the increased scholarly (and not-so-scholarly) concern with "resurgent Islam" in the wake of the success of the Islamic revolution in Iran, rather than any demonstrated importance of such developments in Senegal. The declaration from a Paris hotel room by a marginalized member of the Niasse maraboutic family, Ahmed Khalifa Niasse, concerning his intention to found an Islamic party in Senegal is a case in point; the event seemed to attract more attention from outside observers of Senegal than from potential voters in the country.[2] The most notable result of that effort, in fact, was its unqualified failure.

It is nevertheless undeniable that, in addition to the universal rituals and celebrations of Islam, there are indeed a great number of religious ceremonies organized in contemporary Senegal by the various Sufi orders. Moreover, the institution of the *daaira* gives every indication of having become a permanent part, indeed the essential distinguishing feature, of the country's socio-religious landscape. Rather than simply interpreting them

149

as signs of a new-found religious fervor, however, it may be more useful to examine these phenomena in terms of the reasons for their centrality to Senegal today. I thus prefer to discuss the structures and rituals that shape and define the relationship between marabouts and their followers in terms of their relevance to the needs of both of these sets of actors. The crucial questions concern the roles these structures play and the functions they fill which have made them attractive to both marabouts and disciples, leading to practices which produce the apparent effervescence of Islam.

The analysis offered here points to the incentives present for both marabouts and their disciples to adhere to the structures and participate in the rituals which serve to maintain and reinforce the bonds that tie these two sets of individuals. The convergence of two factors – the need for marabouts to constantly recruit disciples as well as maintain ties to existing ones, and the imperative for individuals to establish a position in a network of affective relations – results in a system with an important degree of inherent stability, but one which also includes a latent potential for defection. This chapter, therefore, examines the structures and rituals of allegiance, evaluates the relative benefits to each side in this system, and then concludes with an evaluation of the limits of these affective ties.

Daairas: the structures of collective allegiance

One important distinction between the groups of dependants or clients that form around non-religious elites in Senegal and the network of affective ties centered on a maraboutic figure concerns the relative degree of organiza-tion and social contact exhibited by these groups. In contrast to the generally amorphous organization of "clans," in which ties are most significantly established vertically from leader to follower with few or only random lateral ties, the followers of a marabout in any given locale are more likely to display a greater degree of cohesion as a group. Particularly in urban areas – today including small urban centers like Fatick – this cohesion is structured and maintained primarily through the institution of the *daaira*. The organizational adaptation of the *daaira* must therefore be seen as a basic component of the continued strength of the orders in the era of increasing urbanization. As a key unit in the articulation of Senegal's religiously based civil society, the structure and distribution of *daairas*, as well as their functioning, merit our attention here.

A Senegalese institution

Both the name and the specific institutional form of the *daaira* are original to Senegal. Those *daairas* which have occasionally been established in other countries, notably Mali or other neighboring states, tend to owe allegiance to Senegalese marabouts and are composed most frequently of Senegalese residents in those countries and their dependents.[3] If Sufism can be called "the Senegalese mode of Islamic devotion,"[4] the *daaira* is the Senegalese mode of urban Sufism.

Information on the history of the institution is rather scarce, and its precise origins remain ambiguous. The first *daairas* seem to have arisen during the inter-war period, a time of increased urbanization in Senegal. Ibrahima Marone has described the organization of a group of some ten Tijan disciples into an association which took the name "Dahiratul Kirame Tidjaniyu" in Dakar in the 1920s. He describes this as "the first official channel for relations with Tivaouane," although he gives no indication of the inspiration for either the institutional form or the term "dahira."[5] One knowledgeable marabout in Fatick attributed the "invention" of the institution to Ababacar Sy, son and first *xalifa* of El Hajj Malik, whose tenure as head of the family *zawiya* (1922–1957) coincides with the period of their emergence indicated by Marone. *Sëriñ* Ababacar, it seems, was criticized in Senegal for this, presumably because the institution represented an "innovation" in Islam. In his defense, Ababacar is said to have written a tract defending the concept of *daairas*, which was successful in winning wide acceptance for the institution not only among the family's disciples, but within all Senegalese *tarixas*.[6]

Cruise O'Brien is certainly correct in pointing to the difficulties which the urban setting poses for maintaining both the cohesion of the orders and the ties between marabouts and followers as the motivating impetuses behind their emergence – a particularly acute problem, of course, for the predominantly rural Mourides.[7] By his account, while the first Mouride association to be called a *daaira* (following the example of existing Tijan and Qadir groupings) was only formed in Dakar in 1946–1947, various earlier efforts had been made, both by marabouts and by their followers, to form associations of disciples adapted to the new conditions of urban life.[8] The much higher degree of urbanization of the Tijaniyya during the colonial period would thus explain the fact that the first *daairas* were of this order. It is important to note, however, that the contemporary institution of the *daaira* carries no connotations whatsoever of being linked to any one particular order. On the contrary, it is today the accepted and virtually unquestioned unit of religious allegiance for groups of a marabout's disciples in a given locale, regardless of *tarixa* affiliation.

Evidence of the acceptance of the *daaira* as the "normal" means of organizing a marabout's clientele is provided by the fact that even if they are unaffiliated to any existing order, "new" marabouts who manage to gain a popular following, such as Ma Ansou Niang (who will be discussed in more depth in chapter 7), quickly see their disciples organized into *daairas*. This is true even of such movements as that of Mouhamadou Moustapha Ngom in Rufisque, who is openly critical of much of Sufi Islam; Ngom's followers in Fatick and around the country are organized into *daairas* along exactly the same lines as other groups of co-disciples. Sufi organization in Senegal has been codified into a pattern that enjoys wide legitimacy in the country and which provides a ready-made model for the organization of varying societal concerns, with important implications for relations between Senegalese society and the state.

The ambivalence noted in the previous chapter concerning the nature of the primary allegiance for Senegalese Muslims is reflected in a parallel situation concerning the *daairas*. While an individual's primary attachment is most frequently to an individual marabout, and then through that marabout to the entire order of which he is a part, there is at times a basis for identification along the lines of order. *Daairas*, therefore, while originally created to unite the disciples of one particular marabout – sometimes in opposition to or direct competition with other marabouts of the same order – are often today organized simply along *tarixa* lines. This varies, however, and the variation reflects the degree of integration or dissent found within the *zawiya* itself.

As both Cruise O'Brien and Coulon noted, Mouride *daairas* as well as *daairas* to the Sy family in Tivaouane were long divided by marabout along the lines of the succession struggles which each of those families had experienced after the death of the first *xalifa*.[9] The rivalries among members of the family were reflected in parallel rivalries among *daairas*. However the currently greater degree of institutionalization of the Mouride order, resulting perhaps primarily from the agreement within the family at Touba concerning the succession through the line of Amadou Bamba's sons, has meant that today Mouride *daairas* are more likely to unite all *taalibe* of the family in a given locale, even if those individuals might declare themselves disciples of marabouts other than the *xalifa* himself. In a situation that seems to parallel the state of the order throughout the country, therefore, the two Mouride *daairas* in Fatick both declare allegiance to the *xalifa-général* himself, and through him to the entire order. Evidence of the general agreement on this affiliation is provided by the fact that the death of the long-reigning *xalifa* Cheikh Abdou Lahatte Mbacké in June 1989, and the succession by his younger brother Abdoul Qadir (who was himself to die less than a year later), created no disruption in the membership or the organization of the *daairas* in Fatick. This occurred despite the fact that some members had previously declared themselves *taalibe* of the deceased *xalifa*, while others had long claimed allegiance to the new *xalifa*.[10]

Not all Mouride *daairas* in contemporary Senegal are devoted to the *xalifa* himself, however; many of the more important marabouts of the order as well as local marabouts with a concentration of disciples in one area may have *daairas* which are organized in their name. This thus introduces an element of competition for the allegiance of disciples inside the order itself, but not one that is necessarily disruptive of its stability. It is possible, and occurs, that an individual declares himself a disciple of one marabout within the order, but belongs to a *daaira* organized for the benefit of the *xalifa*. In addition, individuals may belong to more than one *daaira*, including some to the order as a whole and others comprised of followers of a local or less central marabout. One Mouride marabout of the sub-sect known as the Baye Fall in the nearby town of Gaindiaye, for example, counted *taalibe* in Fatick where only *daairas* to the order as a whole exist, as well as among the membership of three other daairas – one that "belonged" to him, another to his late predecessor, and a third from Kaolack dedicated to the Baye Fall *xalifa* in Diourbel. And one fervent Mouride *taalibe* in Fatick insisted that she belonged to a total of *seventeen* Mouride *daairas* in her hometown of Kaolack, including some to the *xalifa* and others to other marabouts of the order.[11] Mouride *daairas*, therefore, parallel the situation within the order in which there are a multiplicity of claimants to maraboutic authority, but where – for the moment – unity prevails over centrifugal forces.

In a similar vein, the tensions which remain unresolved within the Sy family marabouts at Tivaouane are reflected at the local level in the organization of disciples into *daairas* that follow different branches of this family. In Fatick Tijan *daairas* to the Sy family are thus more or less evenly divided between those that follow the current *xalifa*, Abdoul Aziz Sy, and those that profess allegiance to the sons of the previous *xalifa*, Ababacar Sy. The split is not absolute, and there are occasional efforts to coordinate activities in the name of the unity of the family and more broadly of the order, but they tend to be unsuccessful. The followers of the current *xalifa* in particular reproach the others for what they consider their lack of respect for his authority.[12]

The combined effect of these forces of both unity and disunity is a degree of variation in the number and type of *daairas* found in any one locale. In most urban centers *daairas* are organized by neighborhood or other basis of proximity, such as workplace. In Dakar or other large urban areas, *daairas* are frequently organized in factories or other similar enterprises, and even within government agencies. There exists, for example, a Mouride *daaira* composed of employees of the government's "Service de la Statistique." Student *daairas* also exist at the University of Dakar, as well as in many *lycées*. Depending on the number of disciples, however, in a small town like

Fatick all of a marabout's disciples may be combined into one *daaira*. Conversely, divisions such as age may form the basis for separate *daairas*, or local conflicts may provoke disciples to form independent *daairas* to the same marabout. As Table 5.1 shows, all of these factors combine with the legacy of religious pluralism to result in a variety of active *daairas* in Fatick. As the table reflects, there is a propensity for one of the *daairas* to each marabout or family to be more active than the others in Fatick, usually by drawing on the more committed or capable disciples of that marabout. The fate of other *daairas*, in terms of their degree of activity, thus fluctuates over time, and only those which were to some extent active at the time of research, excluding some with only a nominal existence, are included in Table 5.1. Also not included is the intriguing case of an all-women's *daaira* with no single maraboutic or order affiliation, which will be discussed below.

The fact that the institution of the *daaira* arose during the colonial period, and as a response to the social transformations which accompanied that experience, has meant that their organizational structures owe more to political than religious logic; this local transformation of Islam answers directly to a non-religious imperative. The internal organization of *daairas* is normally based on a model that reflects most significantly the French colonial experience. Not only do the divisions of official responsibilities and the proliferation of titles parallel the structure of numerous state-sponsored associations, but the vocabulary and terminology which refer to those offices are all French, rather than Arabic or Wolof, although French is never a working language in such groups. Thus the Niassène *daaira* in Fatick, for example, elects members to fill some twenty official positions. The *Président* is aided by a *premier vice-président* and a *second vice-président*, a *Secrétaire Administratif* is in turn assisted by *premier, second,* and *troisième vice présidents*, the *Trésorier Général* has his various assistants, and so on down the line. In some cases a separate women's section is created; the main Mouride daaira in Fatick has an elected *Présidente des femmes*, and some of the Tijans similarly choose a *Responsable cellule feminine*. As in various state-sponsored organizations, the proliferation of official positions increases group cohesiveness by tying members in directly. Although it is difficult to generalize given the degree of variation, the "typical" *daaira* includes somewhere in the order of thirty to fifty genuinely active members among its one to two hundred (and in some cases more) official members. A multiplicity of offices, therefore, gives a significant percentage of interested members a direct stake in the organization.

Further paralleling state structures, "federations" have been formed to group together *daairas* to the same marabout within a given administrative area, usually at the level of the *département* or of the region. These

Table 5.1. *Active* daairas *in Fatick, 1989*

Order or marabout	Number	Status
Qadir	one	Functioning, but with some divisions. Head of federation of Qadir *daairas* for the region lives in Fatick, but alienated from *daaira*.
Tijan – Niassène	one	Active, unified, and well organized.
Mouride	two	Both to *xalifa*. Split due to personal differences within one original *daaira*, now reflecting some generational differences. Original *daaira* far more active.

Tijan – Sy family:
  Current *xalifa*
  Ababacar Sy
	three
	three
		There are three functioning *daairas* to each of the rival branches of the Sy family, organized by neighborhood, but in each case one main *daaira* (under the direction of a local marabout) dominates.

Dahiratoul Moustarchidina wal Moustarchidaty[a]	four	Originally five "sections" (i.e. *daairas*) of this movement were formed in Fatick. One was defunct in 1989, and the others varied in their degree of activity, with only one being particularly active.
Ma Ansou Niang	two	Followers of this marabout are divided into two *daairas* on the basis of age, but both work closely together and maintain close ties.
M. Ngom (Rufisque)	one	Single unified *daaira*, active.

Note:
[a] A special case, to be discussed below.

groupings have met with mixed success, primarily because they do not clearly contribute to the purpose of maintaining the affective ties between marabouts and followers, and thus there is no clear incentive for either group to encourage such organization. Federations seem to exist mainly due to the interest of important *taalibes* of a given national marabout – those most likely to serve as *daaira* presidents – in enhancing their standing in the order through participation in such structures.[13] Although Mouride federations exist, the two Mouride *daairas* in Fatick do not maintain contacts with any of them. And the federation of Tijan *daairas* to the Sy family for the region of Fatick, based in the town of Diofior where the president of the federation lives, in fact includes only *daairas* to the Ababacar Sy side of that family.[14] A Qadir federation is based in Fatick, but the president of that organization has been alienated from the only Qadir *daaira* in town, and thus even the relationship between the local *daaira* and the federation is rather tenuous. Federations, therefore, are most interesting as an effort to organize religious structures in direct reaction to state structures, but in terms of their impact on the structuring of religious activity and affiliation in Senegal they are largely negligible.

A special case of *daaira* organization has been the effort launched by the young Tijan marabout Moustapha Sy, son of Cheikh Tidiane Sy (and thus grandson of Ababacar and great-grandson of the founder), to create a comprehensive national organization of Tijan disciples, intended to appeal in particular to the youth of the order. The inspiration for the "Dahiratoul (*daaira*) Moustarchidina wal Moustarchidaty," (DMWM) which he has founded must be traced at least in part to reformist Muslim groups, a point that will be discussed further in the following chapter. In terms of the elaboration of new religious structures, however, it presents the most obvious case of borrowing from the French-based political model. This fact is explicitly acknowledged: "when the *tubaabs* (whites, i.e. colonialists) were here," says one of the leaders of this organization in Fatick, "they created regions, sectors, and such. So that's why the Dahira is organized that way."[15] The result is a highly centralized and hierarchical structure in which the levels of organization and the numerous offices are all described in French bureaucratic terminology. Having reserved the term *daaira* (dahira) for the organization as a whole, the local cells which would normally be known by that name (and are referred to that way ordinarily) have been labeled "sections." Table 5.2 illustrates the structure of the organization.

Although it is important both as a political actor in its own right (as we shall discuss in the next chapter) and as an indication of the extent to which religious structures in Senegal can be shaped by the state context, the DMWM is in many respects exceptional. Its strictly defined hierarchy, high degree of centralization, and often explicitly political activity distinguish it qualitatively from the more traditional *daaira* structures of the country. Most significantly, the creation of the DMWM was a "top-down" process, in sharp contrast to the "bottom-up" procedure that gives rise to most *daairas*. Those features which result from the movement's creation "from above" have placed particular constraints on its ability to attract new followers, a fact which is at least partially responsible for the swings in the movement's political orientations. With the very survival of Moustapha Sy's movement at stake, the earlier quest for state patronage which might have given it a certain lasting power beyond its ability to recruit autonomously has more recently been replaced by an appeal to Senegal's disenfranchised youth via an explicitly anti-government stance. These shifts have

Table 5.2. *Organizational structure of the Dahiratoul Moustarchidina wal Moustarchidaty*

Bureau National
Located in Dakar, headed by Moustapha Sy as "responsable morale"

Bureau de Coordination
One in each regional capital except Fatick and Ziguinchor, plus several in Dakar area

Bureau de Secteur
Several in each *Coordination*. There is a Fatick *Secteur* under the Kaolack *Coordination*.
Each highly organized to include the following positions:
    Chef de Secteur
    Vice Chef de Secteur
    Secrétaire Général
    Moniteur (in charge of Arabic and religious instruction)
    Trésorier Général
    Responsable Cellule Féminine
    Responsable Action Sociale
    Secrétaire à l'Organisation
    Responsable Commission Coorpo. [?]
    Chargée des relations avec les cadets
    Représentant CPAJ (Comité du programme Année de la Jeunesse)[special one year
      position]
    "Père du Secteur"
    "Mère du Secteur"
    Responsables cellules de recherche et de contact

Zone
Subdivision of *Secteurs*. Four *Zones* in Fatick's *Secteur*, two in the town of Fatick
Also includes various official positions:
    Responsable de Zone
    Secrétaire
    Responsable Action Sociale
    Responsable Cellule Féminine
    Moniteur de Zone

Section
Subdivision of *Zones*, local "daairas" *per se*. Tend to be restricted and neighborhood
    based, maintaining close ties with other sections in the *Secteur*

---

been intermingled with various efforts to reinforce the movement by appeals to the more traditional bases of maraboutic legitimacy. In this respect the DMWM might be usefully contrasted with the two *daairas* in Fatick dedicated to the Serer marabout Ma Ansou Niang. In this latter case, the organization of the marabout's disciples was a purely local initiative and took place without any participation by the marabout – in fact, despite the marabout's express ambivalence about such structures.[16] Such origins from below, at the level of local disciples, is the more standard pattern of *daaira* formation, and is reflected quite clearly in their functioning and appeal.

The appeal of the daaira

Asked about the functions of *daairas* and the reasons for their existence, marabouts point to a series of factors which demonstrate their clear understanding of the important role these institutions play in the Senegalese social structure.[17] *Daairas* serve first to build a sense of community among a group of followers. This is particularly useful as a basis for the mutual aid that such groups can provide for dealing with the expense and the preparation of life-cycle celebrations. In addition, *daairas* regularly help to facilitate the participation of disciples at the major celebrations of the order, usually held at important religious sites. They also frequently organize local-level celebrations and religious events. Finally, *daairas* facilitate the collection and delivery of funds to be contributed to the marabout. Their role in filling all of these functions is fundamental to the virtually universal acceptance of the institution of the *daaira* in Senegal.

Although its particular formulation is unique to Senegal, *daairas* in fact closely approximate a type of institution which has flourished throughout Africa in the wake of the social transformations brought on by colonial rule. Aili Mari Tripp, for example, has documented the proliferation of similar institutions in Tanzania.[18] Such "voluntary associations," explored by Immanuel Wallerstein shortly after independence and frequently discussed since then as one of the bases of African social structures, are not usually religious groupings. Nevertheless *daairas* share the essential features of such groups: "they were formed within the colonial social structure for a limited objective by groups of individuals who were almost never recruited exclusively on a traditional base. The individual had to join these associations through a process of formal entry; he chose his leaders. Each organization had some form of responsible, autocephalous government." Most significantly, they arose predominantly in response to the new challenges posed by urbanization and the accompanying weakening of the capacity of the older rural forms of organization to meet the social needs of individuals.[19]

The psycho-social benefits of group membership must be considered an important part of the appeal of *daairas*, as for all voluntary associations. These, of course, are inherently difficult to specify, apart from the obvious universal human need for community. More concrete is the aid which *daairas* offer members at the occasion of major life-cycle events, notably birth and death. Helping members meet the immediate need of payment for funeral expenses is a virtually universal function of voluntary associations,[20] and one which *daairas* regularly fill. This takes on particular importance for the Mourides, for whom burial in the cemetery at Touba carries special spiritual benefits, including expedited entry into paradise. The Mouride community in Fatick keeps a casket to be used for transportation purposes, and when a death occurs among the members or their relatives, the *daaira* helps to guarantee the necessary funds to rent a vehicle to transport the body to Touba. Likewise other unexpected expenses resulting from difficulty or tragedy may be met by fellow *daaira* members. *Daairas* also periodically raise funds among their members for such quasi-obligatory social celebrations as a *ngente*, the naming ceremony held for an infant a week after birth. Given the expense of such events, and the lack of resources available to most individuals, mutual aid often represents the only feasible means of meeting them.

Daairas can also at times usurp the functions normally filled by more formal organizations. In research on labor unions within the urban Dakar context, Geoffrey Bergen found that workers who belonged to *daairas* not only frequently considered them complementary to unions, but even at times see them as alternative – and more effective – means of organizing for protecting collective interests. Indeed, while workers in urban factories willingly pay *daaira* dues of some 500 FCFA per month, they systematically refuse to raise union dues from their very modest 150 FCFA per month level. And in at least one defunct plastic shoe factory, workers identified the absence of *daairas* in the workplace as a factor in their failure to defend their interests successfully.[21] In such contexts, then, the appeal of the *daaira* may spring from the very real material benefits which this means of organization can provide its members.

In addition to these internal functions, *daairas* provide individuals with a place in wider social networks based on the affective ties that unite marabouts to disciples within the Sufi orders. At the local level the role of *daairas* in organizing periodic religious ceremonies gives members an opportunity to both work with local marabouts and to demonstrate their allegiance and devotion to the more important marabouts of the order, who are usually invited to serve as "honorary presidents" of such events. More importantly, the *daairas* organize attendance at the principal celebrations of the orders which, as we shall see, play an important role in maintaining their cohesion and their political leverage. At both of these types of events, the *daairas* also serve as vehicles for the collection and delivery of the *addiya*, the financial contributions made by an individual to his or her marabout. One of the crucial functions of *daairas* is that of serving as the institutional channel for this method of establishing an individual's claim to an affective tie to a marabout, a tie that can be called on should circumstances require it. This important issue will be explored further below.

In accordance with its innovative character, the Dahiratoul Moustarchidina wal Moustarchidaty has officially sponsored various other activities not normally performed by *daairas*, ranging from the overtly political to the social. In Fatick, for example, *daaira* members have marched in the 4th of April Senegalese Independence day parade, all dressed in their signature white. They have also collected goods which were prepared into gift packages and distributed at the local hospital on the feast of *Tabaski*. Similarly, the group has taken up collections for the cause of a leper colony in the region.[22] Enthusiasm appears to have waned for these officially sponsored activities, however, which in any case can have only a symbolic significance in the context of the poverty of Fatick. The DMWM sections have in various cases thus undertaken activities more in keeping with the established pattern. In one case of mutual aid, for example, a DMWM section in Fatick organized a collection to the benefit of the family of a man who had been injured and lost all of his belongings before being repatriated to Fatick from Mauritania following the May 1989 violence against Senegalese in that country. The successful sections of the DMWM, in fact, may be those that manage to move closer to functioning in the normal *daaira* pattern.

This pattern includes most significantly a system of organization which is controlled at the local level and responsive to local concerns – that is, a system which is designed to meet the perceived needs of disciples. *Daairas* meet on a regular basis, occasionally monthly but most frequently weekly, usually on Thursday evenings (referred to in Wolof as *guddi ajumaa*, meaning roughly "Friday eve"). Meetings are devoted to discussion of upcoming events and plans, socializing, frequently a moralistic sermon or presentation by a leader of the group, and devotional exercises such as the *sikar* or, in the case of Tijans, singing the devotional poem known as the *Teysir*.[23] Meetings may be held at the compound of the *daaira's* president or, perhaps more frequently, on a rotating basis at the homes of different members. At times the host of the evening may provide tea or biscuits as refreshments, although the cost of this is such that at least one *daaira* in Fatick explicitly agreed to limit the burden of hosting to the provision of iced water.[24] The more active of the two Mouride *daairas* in Fatick keeps a twice-weekly meeting schedule; Saturday meetings are held at the president's house and devoted largely to organization and planning, while Thursday evenings rotate among the members and are more purely devotional and social. In reality one or the other (sometimes both) are frequently cancelled for various reasons. Occasionally other meetings are held; *daairas* may, for example, meet for the purposes of a *sarax*, a gathering held on the third, eighth, or fortieth day following a death.

Daaira members pay regular dues, invariably referred to by the French term *cotisation*, the amount of which is set by the members themselves. These thus vary locally, so that dues in a town like Fatick tend to be significantly lower than those in the more prosperous cities of Kaolack or Dakar. While even within towns there is no fixed standard, the Mouride *daaira's* rate of 100 CFA francs per month for women and 200 FCFA for men might be taken as average for Fatick.[25] To facilitate payment, members can also contribute at a weekly rate of 25 or 50 FCFA. The irregularity of most people's income in Fatick, and the severe budgetary constraints under which most people lead their daily lives, means that despite their relative modesty, dues payment is usually quite flexible. The rates set might thus be better understood as officially suggested contributions for those who can meet them.[26] In addition to regular dues, special collections are occasionally taken up, either for the benefit of a particular member, to make a contribution to the group's marabout, or for purposes of funding a larger-scale local celebration. For their annual night of religious chanting and celebration, for example, the Mouride *daaira* decided on a *cotisation* of 1500 FCFA per member. Again, however, actual contributions varied widely; some gave nothing at all, while at least one member contributed the extravagant sum of 5000 FCFA.

Leadership of *daairas* is decided upon by the members themselves. The various officers are usually chosen via discussion and consensus, although certain individuals, either because of their social status or their particular interest in the organization, tend to exert particular influence in such decisions. The association with a local marabout affiliated with the order may also mean that leadership of the *daaira* in effect devolves on him. Interestingly enough, in this respect the Mouride *daaira* in Fatick enjoyed particular autonomy; the local Mouride marabout plays little direct role in the activities of the *daaira*, and never attends meetings, though he is regularly consulted on important issues.

There is no compulsion, however, to accept leadership with which one is dissatisfied. The second Mouride *daaira* in Fatick was formed precisely because of a disagreement about organization on the part of some, mostly younger, members. In an even more telling case, the Qadir *daaira* in the town, dissatisfied with the man who by virtue of wealth and social standing served as president, abandoned him *en masse* to establish a *daaira* without him. This was made possible when a political figure, a *député* from the town of Diakhao, donated a set of the distinctive Moorish drums used in Qadir ceremonies, thus enabling the group to strike out on its own. The original president remains as president of the regional federation of Qadir *daairas*, but enjoys only politely cordial relations with other Qadirs in the town.[27]

While, as noted above, men tend to control the important posts in a *daaira*, a structure for formal representation is usually established for female members. Women, in addition, generally have a fair amount of say in the *daaira's* operations. When an especially risky decision (concerning whether or not to schedule a major event in July, during the rainy season) had to be made at a meeting of the Mouride *daaira*, for example, the "women's president" was repeatedly called on to state an opinion. The decision had to be consensual, the officers of the *daaira* insisted, so that later neither the women nor anyone else could criticize the decision should it prove faulty.[28] Although they of course function within the stratified social structure and the resulting hierarchical cultural norms of Senegal, in terms of gender as in other respects *daairas* are clearly voluntary associations organized to serve the interests of their members.

This fact is further underscored by a unique case in Fatick of an all-women's *daaira* which claims no affiliation with any one order.[29] Organized predominantly on a neighborhood basis, the *daaira* includes women affiliated with *all* of the different orders represented in Senegal. They meet regularly, as all *daairas* do, and collect dues from the members. Once a year a large celebration is organized, and a religious singer from Kaolack named El Hajj Tidiane Mbodj is contracted for the event. He is chosen especially for his ability to conduct the singing and the devotional recitations free of any single maraboutic affiliation, while at the same time making occasional mention of *each* of the important marabouts in Senegal, regardless of order. Monies are also kept for the purpose of allowing each of the members of the *daaira*, when the time comes, to attend the major annual celebrations of her order at Touba, Tivaouane, Ndiassane, or elsewhere. In 1988 at least two of the members, one a Tijan and the other a Mouride, had together under-taken the pilgrimages to *both* Touba and Tivaouane at the respective events in those sacred towns.

This unique case, therefore, demonstrates the possibility for *daairas* to exist while answering to no authority in the hierarchy of an order and underscores the extent to which the *daaira* is capable of functioning as a strictly local organization serving to meet the needs of its members. And although this "ecumenical" *daaira* does not serve the purposes of any one particular marabout, it clearly facilitates the functioning of the maraboutic *system* as a whole. It thus also underlines the points made in the preceding chapter: while there is a general consensus in favor of the maraboutic system, and widespread agreement that it is good to follow a marabout, there is no established socio-political cleavage along religious lines. The choice of *which* marabout to follow remains at least partly a question of individual preference.

The rituals: *gàmmus*, *màggals*, and other ceremonies

In addition to the regular periodic chanting ceremonies held in members' homes, the more dynamic *daairas* will, usually on an annual basis, sponsor a public and much larger religious ceremony to which all important local officials are formally invited. These events are small-scale versions of the principal ritual ceremonies organized annually by the major maraboutic families of the country, and the local ceremonies are explicitly patterned on the model provided by the larger ones. The *daaira* as an institution plays a central role in the successful orchestration of these ritual events, and together they comprise the crucial components of a socio-religious system that both reinforces and reflects the relationship between marabouts and their mass followings. Indicative of the linkage between the institution and the ritual, as well as of the importance of the rituals themselves, is the fact that both marabouts and *daaira* members are virtually unanimous in citing the role of facilitating attendance at these events as one of the crucial functions of *daairas*. The all-women's *daaira* discussed above exists largely for the purpose of helping each of its members attend the ceremonies of her order. And the son-in-law and primary spokesman for the Serer marabout Ma Ansou Niang says quite explicitly that facilitating attendance at the *zawiya's* ceremonies is the single most important, and virtually only justifiable, reason for the followers of the marabout to form *daairas* at all.[30]

While the functions they fill are parallel, there are also some differences in these major ceremonies across orders. Mouride events are usually referred to by the term *màggal*, from a Wolof verb meaning "to celebrate" or "to exalt." By far the most important of the *màggals* is the annual celebration in the order's "holy city" of Touba, known appropriately as the "*grand màggal*." First held in 1928, the year following Amadou Bamba's death, at the instigation of his son and first *xalifa* Mamadou Moustapha Mbacké, the *grand màggal* was originally intended to commemorate the anniversary of that death. After the accession of the second *xalifa* to leadership of the order in 1945 the date and motive for the *màggal* were changed to commemorate the anniversary of Amadou Bamba's return from exile in Gabon.[31] Indicative of the relative lack of importance of the "official" reason for the event, however, is that many – perhaps most – Mouride *taalibes* today are unclear as to the actual event commemorated, and when asked disciples variously refer to the founder's death, his departure, and his return from exile as reasons for the *màggal*.

In addition to the *grand màggal*, numerous other *màggals* are held by Mouride marabouts throughout the country, or under the auspices of Mouride *daairas* in urban areas. The actual events commemorated by these may vary, but they are always linked to the history of the order itself and to its major figures.[32] Although their fortunes have fluctuated over the years, most of the important secondary *màggals* were launched in the early years of the order. Occasionally, however, new ones are organized under the auspices of successful marabouts. In the 1970s, for example, a new *màggal* was organized in St. Louis at the site where Amadou Bamba was called for interrogation by the French, and said to commemorate his defiant performance of two prayer prostrations (*ràkka*) there. This *màggal*, the only one held on the Western (rather than Muslim lunar) calendar, has since become one of the more significant secondary celebrations of the order.

For Tijan ceremonies, as indeed for those of most other non-Mouride religious groups in the country, the Wolof term *gàmmu* is used, borrowed from the name for an older (non-Islamic) celebration which at one time was held shortly before the start of the rainy season. The most significant of the *gàmmus* in Senegal is the one held annually at Tivaouane under the auspices of the Sy family marabouts on the occasion of the Muslim feast of *Mawlud*, or celebration of the prophet's birthday.[33] All significant Tijan marabouts, as indeed the Qadirs and many others (including some Mourides), hold *gàmmu* celebrations on this date. But *gàmmus* are also held at many other times of the year. Unlike those of the Mourides, however, these do not normally commemorate (even nominally) specific events in the order's history; at most they are simply said to be dedicated to "the honor of the founders of the *zawiyas*, their [dead] *xalifas*, and the glory of the Prophet." *Sëriñ* "Baldé," the local marabout in Fatick most closely tied to the Sy family, actually claims that all *gàmmus* commemorate the Prophet's birthdate; it is insignificant that they are held on many different dates throughout the year, since "one can celebrate the Prophet's birthdate at any time."[34] The ambiguity, once again, clearly points to the relative unimportance of the "official" or formal reason for these events.

Variations on these ritual forms are occasionally referred to by other terms. Most notably, the word *siyaare* (from the Arabic verb *ziaara*, "a visit") has been appropriated as a noun to refer to a communal visit by disciples to a marabout, and in various cases these visits have been institutionalized as ritual events comparable to *màggals* or *gàmmus*. Thus Ma Ansou Niang, the Serer marabout whom I have referred to several times above, sponsors two large ceremonies annually: the first known as his *siyaare*, and the second a *gàmmu* on the feast of *Mawlud*. Moustapha Sy, in addition, has adopted the term to refer to the annual ritual (discussed below) which he has instituted on the feast of *Tamxarit*, the Muslim new year, as the major ceremony of the Dahiratoul Moustarchidina wal Moustarchidaty.

As for *màggals* and *gàmmus*, the significance of these *siyaares* lies much deeper than the purely nominal justifications for their existence. Although there is some diversity – and a great deal of ambiguity – in the stated reasons for these various ceremonies, they serve clearly parallel purposes – and are indeed treated as functional equivalents by most *taalibe*. I now turn, therefore, to an examination of the similarities and differences in the patterns of these large and intentionally orchestrated rituals which bring disciples and marabouts together, and then offer an interpretation of these events as they affect the structure and organization of Senegal's religiously based civil society.

Patterns and variations

Although the important rituals of all of the orders blend some degree of entertainment, commerce, and devotion, there are nevertheless some potentially significant variations in their actual practice. Rather than attempting to describe these in the abstract, however, and in the interest of presenting the reader as complete a description of these celebrations as possible, I offer below accounts of three specific events of national importance, followed by brief descriptions of how the themes and patterns of these events are reflected in several local ceremonies.

The grand màggal *of Touba.*[35] No other event in Senegal, religious or secular, attracts as much attention as the *grand màggal* at Touba. The state elite is of course always careful to display a comparable degree of public solicitude (by such things as presidential patronage and banner headlines in the official newspaper *Le Soleil*) towards the Tijan *gàmmu* and other religious ceremonies – including even the celebrations of the small Catholic minority.[36] But the *màggal* outstrips all others in the degree to which it annually dominates several days in the life of the country.

On the eve of the day set for the *màggal* every available taxi and *car rapide*, transport trucks and trailers of all sorts, and even the buses of the state-owned public transport company, SOTRAC, join a stream of private vehicles in heading out of the Cap Vert peninsula towards the Mouride heartland in Baol. All are filled to overflowing and beyond, and crowds of people line the main road hoping to find space in one of the passing vehicles. The more daring young men simply climb aboard a moving truck, usually already overflowing with people. The volume of traffic on the road stretches the normal two to three hours of the drive to many more, until at the final approach to Touba the pace becomes a slow crawl. Throughout the night vehicles negotiate the last few miles at snail's pace, and as they get nearer to the city some strike out from the road to head across the fields, guided by the light of the Great Mosque's minaret which is visible for several miles.

Similar exoduses flow from all major cities and towns in the country into the Mouride capital, while carts and wagons pulled by horses and donkeys bring the faithful from the villages of Touba's hinterland. Until the flow is reversed two days later the normal bustle of traffic in Dakar gives way to an almost surreal calm, government offices deprived of the majority of their Mouride staff function even more slowly than usual, if at all, and the sprawling Sandaga marketplace where Mouride merchants have their stalls is virtually abandoned.

In Touba itself the normally dusty and quiet town is transformed into a continuous open-air festival celebrating the dynamism of the order. At any hour of the day or night crowds fill the public areas. In the courtyard of each residential compound scores – indeed usually hundreds – of people who have come as guests sit in groups and talk or find a place to stretch out on a mat to sleep for a few hours. Those without a connection to one of these households sleep wherever they can find a spot; the crowd simply flows around them as it makes its way from one attraction to the next. Food is cooked and sold in hundreds of make-shift "restaurants" around the town, and meat roasters in particular do brisk business as people splurge on this treat. Herders guard their small flocks of goats or sheep which they have brought to market and which provide a supply of fresh meat to the restaurants and to households obliged to feed innumerable guests and visitors. In the evening, particularly in the vicinity of the Great Mosque, *daairas* or other groups of disciples gather to engage in devotional chanting. The larger and more prosperous of these have erected awnings with electric lights and an amplifying system. Some in the crowd that swirls around them may stop to listen to the chanting, while others continue their rounds in search of spiritual as well as material benefits. For two nights and the day in between the city of Touba becomes the devotional, commercial, and entertainment capital of Senegal.

The whole event goes on in this fashion, and to the outside observer it is not immediately evident that there is any distinct ritual purpose being fulfilled. In an indication of the high degree of institutionalization which the Mouride order has achieved in independent Senegal, no single orchestrated public ceremony occurs at the *màggal*. During the colonial period and on into the early years of Senegalese independence, when President Senghor skillfully used this forum for political purposes, a closing ceremony publicly seated the leaders of the order, notably the *xalifa général* and his entourage, with the political elite. Private meetings are now held instead, frequently on the day following the *màggal*, with the ministerial delegation which represents the government, the heads of major political parties, numerous foreign ambassadors to Senegal, and other important dignitaries who make the trek to Touba for the event. Each of these delegations is received by the *xalifa*, and the meetings are later given prominent coverage in the national media. But for the vast majority of disciples at the *màggal* these formal meetings are largely insignificant; to the extent that they are discussed it is only as proof of the power and importance of the marabouts.

The occasion is instead an opportunity for Mouride faithful throughout the country to undertake a pilgrimage which allows them to visit and therefore reinforce, maintain, or develop ties with their marabouts, as well as benefit from the *baraka* to be derived from the various holy sites. It presents at the same time an occasion for fun and a chance to enjoy the spectacle, as well as an opportunity for many to engage in profitable commercial transactions. And engaging in all of these activities serves directly to renew the experience of the strength of the order and reinforce the sense of the benefits of allegiance and participation in its activities. For the disciple the *màggal* is the celebration *par excellence* of the joys of Mouridism.

Of the numerous holy sites to be visited during the course of the *màggal*, the most important are the mausoleums of Amadou Bamba himself and that of his son and first *xalifa* Moustapha Mbacké, which lies nearby. The two tombs are located inside the walls of the Great Mosque of Touba, the disproportionately massive edifice which dominates the town. Day and night during the *màggal* disciples wait in line to enter the mosque. They can expect to wait for many hours before having their turn, and to avoid any breaking in line they try to maintain physical contact with the person immediately in front. Access is controlled by a group of young Baye Fall, members of the colorful Mouride sub-sect distinguished by their clothing, dreadlocks, and large wooden clubs. Working side by side with some Senegalese *gendarmes*, the Baye Fall swing their clubs violently to keep the crowd from rushing the mosque. Inside the mosque other Baye Fall periodically move people along, discouraging excessive dawdling so that a new group can be admitted. Having gained admission pilgrims circle the mausoleums, praying with their hands outstretched and touching the walls and doors to receive the saint's blessing. Many will also drop coins inside the fenced off area around the actual tomb, and these are collected periodically to be used for the upkeep and expansion of the mosque.

In addition to the tombs inside the mosque several other sites have emerged as important places to visit during the course of the *màggal*. The sprawling and chaotic cemetery at Touba (where all Mouride faithful whose families can afford it are buried) draws crowds, many visiting the tombs of the numerous less important marabouts who are buried there. The "library"[37] is also a pilgrimage site. In 1988 the Mouride Students' Association of the University of Dakar had prepared a large exhibition entitled *"L'Hagiographie du Mouridisme"* which presented just that in numerous large displays and various languages. To protect it from the crowds, however, it was arranged behind the locked gates to the building and thus only visible through a fence to all but special guests. In 1989 the courtyard to the library became a new pilgrimage site because of the burial there of the *xalifa* Abdou Lahatte following his death in June. In that year a simple tin shed was erected over the tomb, pending construction of a mausoleum. Amadou Bamba's "house," a new and lavishly decorated structure standing on the original site of the founder's compound, is also visited by disciples who wander through the arcade that surrounds it and peer through its many windows at the well-furnished reception hall inside. Nearby a smaller structure houses various of the founder's personal effects: trunks which he allegedly carried into exile with him and his earthenware water cistern. Here also, in the presence of these artifacts, the faithful pray and leave offerings of coins.

In addition to the pilgrimage sites commemorating the history of the order, an integral part of the *màggal* are visits to one or more of the numerous living marabouts of the order, and in particular the one which the disciple might identify as his or her own. Numerous disciples spend the entire *màggal* in each of the houses of Bamba's many descendants. Others visit all day long, so that the compound is constantly filled with huge crowds. The marabout spends hours giving blessings and receiving disciples, some *daairas* coming collectively to bring offerings of cash or kind. Although the disciples show extreme deference in the presence of the marabouts, the latter are also careful to be solicitous of their followers and to display both piety and generosity. In the compound of one grandson of Amadou Bamba's I watched as the relatively young marabout lay on an imposing purple cushion of artificial fur and received one by one a line of disciples who crawled forward to receive his blessing and speak with him briefly. Yet despite this almost ostentatious display of submission, when the son of a relatively wealthy Mouride businessmen with ties to the marabout had his turn, the brief conversation concerned principally the marabout's concern about whether the young man's father had received the *laissez passer* which he had sent over to allow him to drive within the city limits during the *màggal*. In more public ways also the marabout must demonstrate generosity and wealth. Numerous animals are slaughtered in each of the most important households and countless disciples fed. Lines of Baye Fall or of women, each carrying a huge bowl of food on the head, occasionally pass through the streets as meals for large numbers of disciples and dependants are sent to or from the compounds of important marabouts. As we shall discuss below, at least part of the funds provided to marabouts circulate rather freely, thus building in an important degree of reciprocity in exchanges with their disciples.

Although physical conditions are rather harsh, and those amenities which exist are quickly overwhelmed by the huge crowds, the entertainment aspect of the *màggal* also plays an important part in its appeal. People tend to describe the event as "fun,"[38] and many spend the majority of their time there in eating and socializing. The large amounts of meat and other relatively expensive items consumed add to the air of feasting which characterizes the event. Around the town there are numerous diversions which attract crowds of spectators, perhaps the most popular being the *sikar* chanting sessions performed by groups of Baye Fall who eventually work themselves into a trance and take turns engaging in wild self-flagellation with their large and heavy clubs, to the delight of many spectators. And for those interested in even more entertainment, diversion of a different sort is available just seven kilometers away in the village of Mbacké where the nights are spent in smoking, drinking, and other licentious activities prohibited in Touba.

As I have indicated above, the commercial side of the *màggal* also cannot be ignored in an explanation of its appeal. Touba's status as a virtual free-trade zone (or, rather more accurately, as a center of the parallel economy) means that goods otherwise unavailable in Senegal can be found there and more standard goods sell at lower prices, leading people to make the *màggal* an opportunity to buy. In addition, merchants of all sorts of other items – medicines and potions, *gris-gris* amulets and magical items, clothing and perfumes, toys and dolls, and especially portraits of marabouts and other religious paraphernalia – flock to Touba from other towns for the *màggal*. The large amounts of money brought into the city encourage both legitimate and illegitimate efforts to accumulate some of it. Many thieves work the crowd, risking a serious public beating – or worse – by Baye Fall "police" or the crowd itself if they are caught. The worldly and the metaphysical are closely intertwined in the celebration of the *màggal*.

There are occasional small hints that some degree of tension is felt in the disjuncture between Mouride tradition, particularly as reflected in the *màggal*, and the more "mainstream" Islam of the Arab world. This was, for example, evident in some of the cautious and circuitous wording of the hagiographic exhibit prepared by the Mouride university students. For the overwhelming majority of disciples who attend, however, these issues do not present themselves. The *màggal* exemplifies the highly self-contained nature of the order and serves to reinforce its internal cohesion; it carves out for disciples a place in the world of Islam while clearly directing their attention inward. The explicit drawing of parallels between aspects of Mouride tradition and the broader Islamic one thus has the effect not only of legitimating the practices of the order, but also of reducing or eliminating any need to go outside the order itself. Among the various banners which hung in the central areas of the town during the *màggal* of 1988 were several quoting Amadou Bamba's request to God that He make the *màggal* a substitute for all those unable to make the *hajj* to Mecca. One need go no further than Touba in search of salvation. While the ritual logic of the *màggal* is perhaps not readily apparent in its colorful chaos, it fulfills largely the same purposes in the marabout-disciple relationship as the far more carefully orchestrated events I will discuss below.

A major gàmmu *at Tivaouane.*[39] The "Gamou Dahiratoul Abrar," as the announcement for the 1989 event in the national newspaper noted, is "commonly called the Gamou Serigne Abdoul Aziz Sy, Junior."[40] The appellation is significant in that it identifies the event as the work of one side of the family, indeed of one marabout. While the official reasons for such celebrations evoke the broader themes of Islam or of the order as a whole, it is quite clear that each *gàmmu* "belongs" to one particular marabout; the event represents *his* efforts to demonstrate maraboutic legitimacy at once to his disciples and to government officials.

With the exception of the main *gàmmu* held at the feast of *Mawlud*, Sy Junior's *gàmmu* is probably the most important of those held at Tivaouane every year. Like the others, it is carefully prepared in advance by the marabout with assistance from family members, numerous disciples, local marabouts, and *daaira* presidents who meet in Tivaouane several weeks before the scheduled date for the event. By now a well-rehearsed pattern exists for these ceremonies, and Sy Junior's 1989 *gàmmu* followed this model in all significant respects.

As at most of the numerous ceremonies in Senegal, the public and most ritualized part of the event takes place overnight, lasting until dawn. Throughout the day preceding the 1989 ceremony, therefore, people made their way to Tivaouane from all over the country. During the day and well into the evening the focus of attention is the marabout's house in the center of town, near the main mosque, where disciples might hope to see Sy Junior before the evening's events. At the house itself several of the marabout's sons and numerous other assistants were posted as guards, struggling to maintain order and control access to the inner rooms where the marabout himself spent the day. Groups of people, often identified as a *daaira* from a particular town or neighborhood, were periodically ushered into a reception room. When the marabout finally appeared he would spend some time with the group, speak to them and thank them for coming and for their work on his behalf, hear praise and well-wishing, and bless the group before departing. Once the group was ushered out, others would crowd into the room to wait their turn. All the while the sons and assistants carried in and arranged boxes of gifts – milk, sugar, rice, fruit, and such – sent to the marabout or brought by disciples.

In accordance with Senegalese custom the marabout also received people, in particular the more important guests, in his private bedroom, and over the course of the evening a group of dignitaries and others close to the marabout gradually assembled there. Sy Junior made periodic appearances, sitting for a while to chat with those present, between time spent with the successive groups of disciples who crowded into the reception area. As the evening wore on the marabout spent more time in the bedroom, still occasionally receiving delegations of disciples there. These were most frequently *daairas* that had travelled together to attend the *gàmmu*. The head of the delegation usually spoke for the group, and then presented the marabout with an envelope containing a cash offering collected by the *daaira*.[41] After receiving thanks and a blessing the group would exit, returning outside to await the *gàmmu* ceremony.

The group that gathered in the marabout's room for the evening represented a cross-section of the people with whom an important marabout like Sy Junior would regularly interact. Various political figures were there: the *préfet* and *sous-préfet* for Tivaouane, a magistrate of some importance, and a former very high official in the Ministry of Finance who greeted Sy Junior with a friendly "*Marabout! Ça va?*" Also in the room were other people close to the marabout, relatives and local representatives of the family in different towns. The gathering clearly provided an opportunity for an "inner circle" to meet and discuss issues important to the maraboutic cause. This particular *gàmmu* happened to coincide with an "International Colloquium on Muslim Youth" which the Dahiratoul Moustarchidina wal Moustarchidaty, under the direction of Sy Junior's nephew Moustapha Sy, had organized in Dakar with government assistance. The issue of the colloquium provoked a spirited debate in the room. In particular the close collaboration of the DMWM with the government – which made it a point to stress the theme of *laïcité* (the secular state) and which was evidently responsible for the presence at the conference and prominent coverage in the press of the Catholic archbishop of Dakar – was the subject of sharp criticism by several of the people there. The event had potentially significant consequences for the family, as we shall see below, and the reunion that was occasioned by the *gàmmu* provided those most affected with an opportunity to debate these important issues.

It must be stressed here that this debate should in no way be taken to indicate any necessary hostility to the secular state or to the Catholic minority arising from any "fundamentalist" orientation on the part of the family, nor can one read into it a dichotomous antagonism between the religious and the political in Senegal. Rather it reflects an astute political understanding on the part of those closely tied to the maraboutic system about the basis of the relations between the political and the religious elite. It is noteworthy that this debate was carried out in both French and Wolof and that the most vocal in the debate were clearly more comfortable in French; the entire discussion, in fact, had a distinct French intellectual air to it and reflected the highly Westernized side of the Sy marabouts which distinguishes them most clearly from the Mourides. The family is quite comfortable in interactions with officials of the secular state and with leaders of other religious groups, and this also is something in which various family members take pride and, as we shall see below, which they use in their efforts to appeal to disciples.

Somewhat after one o'clock in the morning, after a large and lavish meal had been served to the numerous guests, the marabout's entourage moved outside to the area where many thousands of disciples had gathered. Elaborate preparations had been going on all day; an expansive open tent had been put up, a platform or dais with several armchairs erected at one end of it, and an amplification system installed and tested. Microphones were placed on the dais and in front of it where the marabout would speak, as well as at a series of tables where the singers took their place in chairs facing the dais. The entire area was brightly lit with electric lights installed for the occasion, and colored paper streamers and other decorations provided a festive atmosphere. In a roped-off area in front of the dais the most important guests, including those who had spent the evening in the marabout's room, were seated. Guards kept order as others jostled for good positions within view of where the marabouts were to sit.

The first important marabout to arrive was Sy Junior's older brother, Mansour Sy. Accompanied by various assistants and richly dressed in a canary yellow *boubou* (robe) and a red Fez hat, he took his place in one of the armchairs placed directly in front the dais. He was followed by his uncle Abdoul Aziz Sy, the *xalifa* of the order, an old and quite frail man who was helped to another of the chairs. Mansour spoke first to introduce the event, followed by his uncle who gave a general blessing and a short speech. Sy Junior then made his appearance, and also spoke briefly from the ground in front of the dais, referring in particular to the unity of the family around the figure of El Hajj Malik, the founder. Only after the *xalifa* had left, escorted by his numerous guards, did the two brothers mount the dais to begin the ceremony.

The *gàmmu* ceremony itself was distinguished by no one single climax or central point. Rather the entire night was spent in a series of speeches, moralistic stories, and sermons delivered principally by Sy Junior, but with his brother's assistance. The initial talk was slow and rambling, consisting primarily of an exhaustive listing of all of the many people who had facilitated the preparations for the event – including president Abdou Diouf himself and his then Minister of State Jean Collin – and all of the most important people in attendance. Other speeches alternated between serious or moralistic and witty entertaining anecdotes. Much attention was paid to the family and its history, with special and repeated mention of the father of the two men, the previous *xalifa* Ababacar Sy. The show-like quality of some of the monologues included numerous jokes told by the marabouts at which the audience laughed gladly; for many in the crowd the event was clearly a lot of fun. Occasionally someone in the audience would stand up to speak in praise of the marabouts, addressing them directly and at times passing up money to be handed to them. Speeches were punctuated by sessions of religious chanting performed by the men who sat at the tables facing the marabouts. Money which had been given was then frequently and publicly passed back to the singers by the marabouts in a display of unconcern for worldly goods. The entire night was spent in this manner, and the event finally ended with a general blessing at dawn. Before leaving many in the audience entered the nearby mosque to pray at the mausoleum of Ababacar Sy, an act which it was said would guarantee anything one requested at that special event.

The lack of any single central message transmitted directly in the numerous speeches may again obscure the purpose of this elaborate and expensive event. Yet at the same time this points, I believe, to the fact that the crucial ritual functions served by the *gàmmu* must be sought outside the explicit reasons given for the event. As will be seen even more clearly in the case described below, and as the subsequent discussion will emphasize, the ritual primarily serves the broader purpose of maintaining and reinforcing the ties between marabouts and their followers, in this case at least partly in opposition to other marabouts within the same family. In addition, and very importantly, it presents the state elite with a clear indication of the potential political clout of the marabout. It thus has implications for both the internal and the external relations of the maraboutic movement.

The siyaare tamxarit *of the Dahiratoul Moustarchidina wal Moustarchidaty.*[42] *Tamxarit* is the Wolof term for the Muslim new year, traditionally celebrated in Senegal as a children's holiday when treats are given out. It is the innovation of Moustapha Sy to make it the occasion of the major ritual celebration of the Dahiratoul Moustarchidina wal Moustarchidaty. In contrast to most other ceremonies, the *siyaare* is held during the daytime, on the day following the evening celebration of *Tamxarit*. In 1989 this should have been a Saturday, but for unspecified reasons which must be linked to the Mourides' late announcement that, not having seen the moon, they would celebrate the feast a day later than expected and also to the fact that a Sunday would ensure a larger turnout, the celebration was postponed by one day with only a little over a day's notice. It was, nevertheless, a clear success.

As I have noted above, the DMWM is an innovative organization which has adapted and modified various aspects of the Senegalese maraboutic model. The movement had at least implicitly demonstrated its intent to "rationalize" and modify the predominant model of Islamic organization in Senegal, in part by the establishment of an elaborate institutional structure. The originality of the DMWM – and the ambiguity of its future – lies in its high degree of organization and in the efforts of Moustapha Sy to make explicit political use of his position at the head of the organization. The search for a political posture appealing to his targeted young clientele and also likely to provide him with real political leverage has led to various, seemingly erratic, shifts in the organization's public image. While he earlier pursued a policy of close collaboration with the government of Abdou Diouf, as in the 1989 colloquium which had provoked the debate in his uncle's bedroom, within just a few years Sy had moved to a radically opposed position. His attack on the president at a public meeting of the DMWM in Thiès during the 1993 electoral campaign must be understood as an effort to appeal to the large numbers of highly dissatisfied urban youth, and a gamble that the opposition might win the election.[43] In fact, it seems clear that the extent to which it will be able to sustain and develop its following in the long run must be linked most closely to the possibility for Moustapha Sy to draw on the traditional sources of maraboutic legitimacy; Sy's position as the founder and head of the DMWM is currently based primarily on his claim to the inherited charisma of the family. His 1989 *siyaare*, which drew a large number of Tijan disciples, represented an effort to establish his maraboutic legitimacy on firmer ground, and thus reflected very clearly the functions which these rituals fulfill. This apparent effort to align himself more closely with the family must certainly be linked to the (private) criticism to which he had been earlier subjected.

Attendance at the *siyaare* was almost totally organized along the lines of the institutional structures of the DMWM. A large van rented from a local Lebanese businessman brought members from the various Fatick *sections*, each of whom paid 1500 FCFA for round-trip transportation. An additional, voluntary, collection (*une participation*) was taken up for the marabout during the trip. The arrival of groups of *taalibes* in Tivaouane was carefully orchestrated to enhance the sense of an important and popular event. Delegations from the many *sections* of each *coordination* were timed to arrive together. Each such group was preceded by a police car with sirens blaring, followed by one or two vehicles displaying flags, signs identifying the *coordination*, and huge portraits of the marabouts, most conspicuously Ababacar Sy. These were in turn followed by vehicle after vehicle carrying disciples from the *coordination*. From the cities of Dakar and Thiès lines of SOTRAC buses brought the urban *taalibes*. The impression was of an unending stream of disciples pouring into Tivaouane.

A crowd started to form many hours before the ceremony began, sitting patiently and listening to the continuous and loudly amplified religious singing of a group of chanters seated near the dais. The songs were almost all in Wolof and concentrated heavily on singing the praises of the marabouts of the family, both living and dead. The single most mentioned marabout was Ababacar Sy, but (his father) El Hajj Malik and (his son) Cheikh Tidiane Sy as well as the founder of the Tijaniyya itself, *Shaykh* Ahmed at-Tijani, all received a fair amount of attention. Other family members and the Prophet Muhammad likewise were invoked in the course of the singing. The tempo of the chanting picked up gradually over the course of the several hours, and at various times the crowd would be moved to applaud or to break into a rhythmic swaying back and forth while snapping their fingers with the arms held high. By the time of the actual ceremony the crowd was in a receptive mood.

In addition to the carefully orchestrated arrivals a high degree of organization, noteworthy for its reliance on modern equipment, was evident throughout the event. Police guards, in addition to controlling traffic, guarded the dais on which the marabouts were to sit and controlled access to the central area under the tent reserved for the more important people. Numerous members of the marabout's entourage circulated, ordered chairs arranged and rearranged, communicated via walkie-talkies with others stationed elsewhere, and adjusted and tested amplification and recording equipment and photography, video, and television cameras which had been set up near the dais.

In the early afternoon, after the crowd of thousands had assembled, the wail of police escort sirens announced the arrival of the marabout Moustapha Sy and his entourage in a flurry of activity. The crowd buzzed with excitement, and as he left his car and moved toward the dais there was a surge forward which obliged the police and family guards present to struggle to clear a path for him to pass. The dais was arranged so that one large armchair faced the crowd with microphones arranged in front of it. Two other chairs flanked this main seat, and a series of others were arranged behind this front row. Eventually all of the seats were to be filled by family members and various political figures, including the *préfet* of Tivaouane. Moustapha Sy made his way to the dais and then mounted it to greet the various people already present there. In a gesture that highlighted the Franco-Arabic acculturation that later in the ceremony was to be admiringly invoked, he greeted most of those present with three kisses – a decidedly non-Wolof touch. Turning to the crowd he waved in recognition of their attention, touched his right hand to his heart, and clasped both hands together in a pious greeting to various unidentifiable members of the audience.

Having made his appearance, the marabout then left the central area again to undertake the symbolic visit to the tomb of his grandfather, Ababacar, which apparently is the basis for calling the ritual a *siyaare*. A small delegation from each *coordination* waited outside to accompany him, and the color of the flag each should follow was announced over the microphones. During his absence the lead singer, a *taalibe* named Mbaye Donde who works closely with the family at various ceremonies, mounted the dais and announced that it was time for the *siyaare* ritual to begin. He then led the crowd in a simple and repetitive litany in Arabic (which few in the audience would understand), spoken one or two words at a time and lasting a half-hour or so. The prayer was addressed principally to *Sërñ* Ababacar, but both Cheikh Ahmed at-Tijani and the Prophet were periodically invoked, thus linking Ababacar directly to both the broader world of Islam and to the founder of the Tijaniyya order. At the conclusion of this litany Mbaye Donde led the gathering in another long prayer, specifically for *Tamxarit*.

As these prayers drew to a close, Moustapha Sy returned to the central arena, making an entrance as before, and this time accompanied by his uncle Abdoul Aziz Sy Junior. After greeting the important officials who had arrived in the meantime, Moustapha Sy positioned himself on the ground in front of the dais, where a microphone had been set up, while the main seat on the dais was taken by his uncle. Before the beginning of the long monologues by each of the two marabouts which were to take up the remainder of the afternoon, a younger family member spoke, thanking an exhaustive list of important people who had helped to make the event possible and contributed to its success. This public exercise, a litany of a different genre, provided an impression of close and cordial relations between the maraboutic family and the other powerful men of Senegal.[44] The importance of the family and the involvement of so many people in the day's events thus invoked, Moustapha Sy got up to speak.

Like his uncles and his father, the young marabout is an effective speaker; like them he has a good sense of working a crowd, building up to a point, getting a laugh, then turning it serious, all the while mixing in parables and moralistic stories to drive home his points. Among those points on this particular occasion were the crucial issues that appear regularly in such contexts: the relationship between disciples and marabouts, and that of the state to the marabouts. Thus on the first of these he developed the theme of the importance of having a (maraboutic) guide for living a good life, and on the second alluded to the importance of the marabouts in Senegalese political life. Turning to the *préfet*, he discussed the current economic crisis of the country. Addressing him directly as the representative of the state, he directed him to tell President Diouf that, if the state was serious about improving the situation, they need only "come to Ababacar." The suggestion implicitly, but clearly, referred to more than the spiritual guidance the dead marabout could provide the politicians; Ababacar's heirs also insist on their centrality in the temporal domain.

Given the specific circumstances of Moustapha Sy's movement, the theme of the family and its internal relations was intermingled throughout the entire hour-long talk with these more common themes of maraboutic discourse. He referred to his "special relationship" within the family with his uncle, Abdoul Aziz Sy Junior. He spoke defensively about his father, Cheikh Tidiane Sy, who has maintained a relatively low profile since the 1988 elections during which he campaigned actively for Abdou Diouf, and who had spent most of the previous year in Paris. Most importantly, he attempted to position himself unambiguously in the hereditary line of *baraka* by constant references to family members, notably his grandfather Ababacar. The heavy focus on Ababacar throughout the event was directed towards reinforcing the late *xalifa's* position as a source of original charisma in his own right, rather than as the simple heir to that of El Hajj Malik. This insistence must be understood as an effort by the marabouts directing the event to strengthen their own positions both by their greater proximity, in genealogical terms, to this charismatic figure and by limiting the number of potential claimants to important hereditary status. Most significantly, and somewhat surprisingly, Moustapha Sy addressed the rift that was evident in the family quite directly. He may have had little choice since this fact was by then public knowledge, and avoiding it would thus have been to risk an even greater harm. In any case, the issue having been raised, his uncle was clearly prepared to deal with it when his turn came to speak.

Abdoul Aziz Sy Junior's talk, which also exceeded an hour in length, was meant to be conciliatory and resolve the tensions which Moustapha's had raised. He also touched on the important common themes of such events, but most importantly he adopted the tone of the wiser uncle, smiling benevolently at some of the excessive enthusiasm of a favorite nephew, while gently correcting him and also explaining him to the rest of the family – and the thousands of assembled disciples. Recalling his own youthful excesses, he recounted a conversation he had had with then president Senghor concerning the Union Culturelle Musulmane (UCM), the important Islamic organization of which he was president in the 1960s. Senghor, he said, had listened patiently to Sy Junior's fiery enthusiasm for an initiative he had undertaken, then counselled him by saying, "You're right – but remember, if one tries to hurry an ass along too quickly, it is likely to fall." Now, he noted, he found himself in the reverse role, with Moustapha following in the footsteps of the young Sy Junior. And despite his youthful shortcomings, the marabout emphasized the traits in his nephew that the family has generally billed as some of their great strengths. His cosmopolitanism, his adeptness and ease in three cultures and three languages – Arabic, French, and Wolof – all made him, the senior marabout pointed out, an invaluable "intermediary" for Senegal on the international scene.

Abdoul Aziz Sy Junior's talk had the desired effect. The crowd was obviously pleased as a final blessing brought the ceremony to a close. In the car on the return to Fatick the *daaira* members discussed the day's events. The ceremony had been a success on all counts. They conceded that there had been a disagreement in the family, but *it was all resolved now*, they unanimously emphasized. The event was unusual in that it publicly recognized criticism of a marabout. But it clearly served its purposes first by deflecting the criticisms both from the maraboutic system as a whole and from the Sy family in particular, and also by restoring Moustapha Sy to the family fold, the maraboutic and charismatic mainstream. It also thus revealed with little ambiguity the importance of such ritual encounters in shaping and maintaining the ties between marabouts and followers.

Local adoptions of the ritual models.[45] In addition to these large-scale national ceremonies, innumerable smaller ceremonies all over the country pursue the same themes and serve parallel functions. These may be organized by a local marabout and aimed at his own local clientele, by a *daaira* intent on demonstrating and celebrating local loyalty to a national marabout, or in the case of local marabouts who serve as representatives of more important ones these events may be hybrids which serve the causes of both the local and national marabouts simultaneously. And although there are again variations in terminology and format the essential elements of the model are always found in these rituals.

In Fatick the two Tijan marabouts who serve as representatives of the two branches of the Sy family each organize an annual *gàmmu* under the auspices of the respective *daairas* which they head. Both of these events follow the model provided by the Sy family's ceremonies in all essential respects, and the one presided over by *Sëriñ* Baldé in May 1989 attempted to replicate almost identically the format of the national ceremonies organized by that family and discussed above. Beginning late, under a tent set up and decorated especially for the occasion, the small crowd gathered there was entertained by a group of religious chanters while awaiting the arrival of the locally important people. In a small coup, Mbaye Donde, the lead singer at the *siyaare tamxarit*, was brought from Tivaouane to help preside over the night's ceremony. The arrival of *Sëriñ* Baldé, and a little later of the state delegation headed by the governor of the region himself, was dramatically signaled by a few whistles of the siren of the police car that escorted them. As at Tivaouane, speeches were made thanking those who had contributed to the event and addressing the political delegation. The governor was invited to speak (in a Wolof that he himself described as "not very nice"[46]) and he took the occasion to praise the marabouts of the order for their collaboration with the state elite. Also in accordance with the model, the rest of the night was spent in a mixture of funny and moralistic monologues interspersed with frequent references to Ababacar Sy and his descendants, as well as to the Tijaniyya itself.

The *màggal* organized by the main Mouride *daaira* in Fatick, postponed till December in 1989 due to the death of the *xalifa* earlier that year, adapted the essential elements of the *grand màggal* into a somewhat more structured format. Narrowly escaping a disappointing cancelation when an electric failure was finally resolved around midnight, members of the *daaira* gathered under the tent set up for the event after an evening of feasting made possible by the gift of a cow from the local elected deputy to the Senegalese parliament. Less focused than the Tijan events, the night was spent principally in devotional songs dedicated to Amadou Bamba under the direction of a well-known lead singer hired especially for the event. And as in the *grand màggal*, the atmosphere of fun and the spectacle provided by the dancing and self-flagellation of the various Baye Fall in attendance attracted a large crowd. In addition to Mourides from outside Fatick who had been invited, many non-Mouride Fatick residents gathered at the site to enjoy the spectacle. As at Touba, the evening provided a public sign and a celebration of the dynamism of the order, at the same time that it reinforced the benefits of adherence for the members of the *daaira*.

An example of the use of these rituals by local marabouts faced with the need to cultivate a personal following while also maintaining a position in the order is provided by the case of a *màggal* sponsored by a Mouride Baye Fall marabout in the town of Gaindiaye, some twenty kilometers from Fatick. The marabout, *Sëriñ* Maas Sèye, is the second *xalifa* of his late uncle, *Sëriñ* Baye Seck, the original marabout there.[47] During the course of the day set for the celebration, in October 1989, young Baye Fall from the area and other *taalibe* of the marabout trickled into Gaindiaye. In preparation for the night-time event, arriving guests feasted on meat from a cow slaughtered for the occasion and were entertained by occasional *sikar* cycles complete with self-clubbing performed by the *taalibes* of the household. In the evening the local state official, the *sous-préfet* of Gaindiaye, made an appearance to sit publicly with the marabout for several hours as more and more people arrived in the marabout's compound. With the arrival of a large delegation made up of a *daaira* from nearby Kaolack the ceremony began in earnest. In a large open area near the marabout's compound, facing a tent where some chairs had been prepared for the marabout and other important people, the crowd assembled to watch or participate. The passage of the marabout from his compound to the site of the celebration was accompanied by a show of chanting, vigorous drumming, dancing, self-flagellation, and even fire-eating by one especially enthusiastic Baye Fall. The spectacle went on in this fashion through the night.

Significantly, the large number of disciples assembled in Gaindiaye represented the membership of three different *daairas*. A *daaira* from Kaolack was composed of disciples of an important Baye Fall marabout from Diourbel, *Sëriñ* Modou Abdoulaye Fall, a grandson of the sect's founder, Cheikh Ibra Fall. A second *daaira* from Gaindiaye itself was dedicated directly to the late marabout Baye Seck, while only the third "belongs" to the current marabout, Maas Sèye. While this third *daaira* was responsible for organizing the celebration every year, the two other *daairas* regularly participate in the annual *màggal* at Gaindiaye, greatly enhancing its success by their dynamic and numerous presence. The event, therefore, celebrates charisma and maraboutic affiliation simultaneously at several levels; in one iteration it serves to reinforce the ties of disciples both to the main marabouts of the order and to local marabouts.

These multiple levels are, as we shall see, crucial to understanding the functions not only of the *màggal* at Gaindiaye, but indeed of all such ceremonies. Throughout the discussion of these specific events of both national and local significance I have alluded to their importance both in reinforcing the internal relations of the maraboutic following and in demonstrating its cohesion to those external to the movement. Their centrality to both of these purposes, I argue, serves to explain the frequency and the dynamism of religious rituals in Senegal, and I now turn to a more complete analysis of the rituals in terms of these two dimensions.

Reflections and reinforcers of allegiance

In a fascinating study of Muslim saint cults in Tanta, Egypt, Edward Reeves offers an explanation of "how the cult of saints has been involved in the governance of Egyptian society."[48] The "hidden government" which he analyzes is, he argues, an integral part of a cultural model which legitimates the patron-client system that characterizes Egyptian society and politics. Central to the articulation of that cultural model are the numerous "commemorative festivals" which are at the heart of the cult of saints. The most significant of these in Tanta is the big *mulid* of the great thirteenth century saint Sayyid Ahmad al-Badawi, an event which in his description bears a striking external similarity to the *grand màggal* at Touba.[49] These festivals, Reeves notes, are important primarily for the ritual functions they fulfill, most significantly their role in legitimating a pattern of social

organization. "Legitimacy," he argues, "is won through ritual perfor-
mances" which are themselves "the arena in which persons and groups
struggle to have legitimacy defined."[50]

Most significantly in the context of the role of the ritual ceremonies I have
discussed in Senegal, Reeves points to the fact that rituals actually address
two different types of audiences, one internal and the other external:

> Rituals intensify common feelings and beliefs within a group and assert its
> legitimacy vis à vis another group. Thus a ritual has two audiences, inside members
> of the group and outsiders or members of competing groups. The intent of the ritual
> performance is to dramatize the differences between these two social categories so
> that greater legitimacy is accorded the insiders.[51]

Similarly, Marc Swartz has argued that "[r]ituals foster unity between
participants, but they also assert differences and establish the *exclusiveness*
of the group which celebrates."[52] Adhering to this pattern, *màggals*,
gàmmus, and other ritual expressions of marabout-disciple ties in Senegal
serve both to demarcate the distinctiveness of a marabout's following as a
group and to reinforce the internal cohesion of that group.

The external audience for the message of group allegiance transmitted by
the rituals includes, of course, other maraboutic groups. As we have seen in
the previous chapter, there is always an element of rivalry in the need for
marabouts to distinguish themselves from others, an imperative which is
further complicated in the case of local marabouts tied to national *zawiyas*.
More important, however, is the audience of state officials whose drive for
incorporation and transformation of populations brings them into competition with the religious elite. The role played by rituals in this domain can
be stated quite simply: maraboutic leverage in the sense of influence over
the actions of political elites is a direct function of the size, and in a less
quantifiable sense the fervency, of the followings they command. And the
ritual celebrations of religious allegiance are the occasions when the size
and devotion of followings is demonstrated most clearly and publicly. For
the state official sitting on the dais beside the marabout while crowds of
thousands chant the glories and powers of the saintly family the message is
abundantly clear: the marabout as a force cannot be ignored. For the
marabout, therefore, wide attendance at his public ceremonies is a *sine qua
non* of elite status.[53] Mass attendance, in addition, serves the interests of the
citizen-disciple. In the uneven power relationship which marks the interactions of normal individuals with the representatives of the state, the
capacity to invoke, directly or implicitly, a connection to a marabout whose
importance and power have been publicly demonstrated can introduce a
measure of reciprocity – however limited – into an otherwise highly
unbalanced interaction.

In a discussion with significant relevance to the understanding of Senegal's Sufi orders, William Miles has analyzed the functions of political campaign rallies in northern Nigeria during the ill-fated national elections of 1983.[54] His discussion of the "rally as ritual" considers the importance of rhetoric, style, and format in the political effect of the events; the importance of form leads him to describe the rallies as instances of "dramaturgical politics." Miles describes the arrival of busloads of chanting and singing supporters at the site of the event, the meetings between the religious and the political elite, and a "warm-up" speaker whose task involved leading the audience in a sort of secular litany analogous to the maraboutic version. This speaker "would mount the podium and lead the crowd in a politico-liturgical dialogue, or *responsa*. He would cry out the name or slogan of the party, and have the crowd shout back the appropriate response."[55] In addition these rallies are seen as occasions for fun and socialization, an aspect that is important for attracting people and which the party leaders thus intentionally cultivate. These similarities between ostensibly distinct types of events – the Nigerian being explicitly political while the Senegalese is formally religious – are not simply superficial coincidences of style. Rather they point to the fact that the sponsors of the two activities are engaged in parallel efforts: to attract a following and build binding ties while simultaneously demonstrating their capacity to do so to an outside audience. In a very real and concrete sense, the numerous religiously sponsored events in Senegal can be understood as continuous and ongoing maraboutic "electoral" campaigns, rituals as rallies.

In terms of building group ties – that is of addressing, in Reeves' terms, the *internal* audience of the ritual – Miles' analysis is particularly suggestive concerning the ambiguity which must accompany any effort to define a sub-community or a sub-system of allegiance without calling into question the primary community or the system of primary allegiances. Ritual expressions of group identity are faced with the need to incorporate a reaffirmation of the "first-order" importance of the broader system into the evocation of the "second order" issues of the particular allegiance being cultivated. In the case of Miles' study this first-order allegiance concerns the broader ethno-religious community of the Muslim Hausa. The rallies, he notes, were always structured to communicate at these two levels:

Despite second-order differences between and among communities that the existence of competing parties reflected, all rallies, regardless of ideological persuasion, reaffirmed the first order unity of *addini* and *jamaʿa*, Islam and community. Having established their social legitimacy by placing themselves squarely under the "Islamic umbrella," ... each party would then go on to present its particular platform as being the best. Fundamental unity within Islam having been professed, the populace was relieved of any ulterior religious anxiety fostered by the political process.[56]

When the particular allegiance or sub-group solidarity being encouraged depends on the continued functioning of an existing socio-political system of organization, it becomes particularly important to reaffirm the first-order legitimacy of the system itself. Thus in successful and stable democratic systems, for example, competing elites regularly demonstrate a primary commitment to the system of democracy; through both explicit statements and symbolic public activity rival elites must signal the primordialness of common allegiance to the democratic system before making an appeal to individual allegiances.

For the Senegalese marabout concerned with building and maintaining ties to his followers, the first-order need involves the legitimation and reaffirmation of the Sufi maraboutic model itself. Not surprisingly, the ceremonies which celebrate the ties of disciples to marabouts include a variety of elements serving to reaffirm that legitimacy. In addition to the advantages of the specific maraboutic affiliation in question, speeches at public rituals frequently make reference to the generic benefits of having a marabout. A particularly clear example of this was included in Abdoul Aziz Sy Junior's speech at the *siyaare tamxarit*. Insisting on the need for *everyone* to have a marabout, he cited a proverb to the effect that even "a good person, if he has no leader (*kilifa*), will no longer remain a good person."[57] Then, to underscore this point, he described at great length his patronage of a young Mouride whom he personally funded every year so as to enable him to attend the *grand màggal* at Touba. He had no interest, he protested, in trying to persuade this young man to change his affiliation. The important thing, he insisted, is that he recognize the importance of maintaining his ties to his marabout and that he have available the means of doing so.

The insistence on the commonality of purpose of all marabouts, and consequent public demonstrations of mutual respect, are central to the strengthening of the first-order issues. In local ceremonies in particular this is demonstrated and emphasized by the common practice of inviting marabouts of competing orders to the events. At the two ceremonies in Fatick discussed above, for example, other local marabouts made an appearance at the event and were publicly thanked for their support. At *Sëriñ* Baldé's *gàmmu* all of the significant religious figures of the town were thanked, and the local marabout *Sëriñ* Diakhaté, whose own connections are to the Niassène Tijans, came early in the evening with a group of his disciples to entertain the gathering crowd with religious chanting in a sort of "warm-up" act. Similarly, at the Mouride *màggal* sponsored by the Fatick *daaira*, other marabouts including the Tijan *Sëriñ* Alpha as well as the imam of the mosque, himself a *taalibe* of the Niasse family Tijans, arrived early and spent several hours sitting in a place of honor before leaving. The pattern of these two examples is, in fact, the normal one; religious figures of competing orders will usually make an appearance and then leave the celebration as the more important activities are about to begin. The primordial, first-order, importance of the maraboutic system thus signaled, the organizers can then proceed to the second-order affirmation of the desirability of the specific relationship in question. Clearly secularization, or to a lesser extent Muslim anti-maraboutic movements, present a greater threat than the risk of reinforcing the position of rivals.

The descriptions above provide, I believe, an indication of the manner in which Senegalese Sufi rituals also reinforce the "second-order" issues of developing the internal ties within the maraboutic movement. Credible threats to the Sufi system, while perhaps increasing, are still rather rare in Senegal, and thus the second-order issues remain the prime motivation for the rituals. The overwhelming concentration of attention on the marabout or maraboutic family sponsoring the ceremony, despite its broader "official" justification, clearly indicates the importance of this function. Certainly the most direct manifestation of this is the repetitive and insistent chanting of prayers and praises replete with references to the marabout-sponsor. In addition the images of the marabouts are omnipresent at ritual events; large posters and banners displaying iconographic representations of the marabouts are prominently displayed,[58] and photos or artistic renderings for sale to the public are always readily available, and in high demand. To attend a ritual ceremony is to infuse yourself for its duration in a world dominated completely by the maraboutic aura.

The numerous ways in which the ritual events reinforce the unity of the community of disciples should also be evident from the descriptions above. Attendance at a *màggal* or a *gàmmu* provides the disciple with a sense of belonging to a much larger, and more important, social order than the purely local world in which he or she normally dwells. Amar Samb's observation about the *màggal* in the 1950s is equally relevant to all such rituals: "The pilgrimage to Touba permits the Mouride sect to take the temperature of its strength and its cohesion."[59] Direct personal ties with other co-disciples around the country further add to the sense of community. In the roped-off area nearest the dais where chairs are reserved for people of some importance at the Tivaouane events, heads of delegations or *daairas*, older male *taalibes* of some social stature, town or neighborhood representatives of the family, and other people of some distinction gather over the course of several hours. As they arrive, people greet each other effusively as they catch sight of old friends. The reunion of *taalibes* whose common interests include primarily a shared religious affiliation at marabout-sponsored events thus serves to solidify at one and the same time both the horizontal ties among disciples and the vertical ties of disciples to marabouts.

Finally, in this discussion of the ways in which ritual ceremonies serve to address both internal and external audiences and of the need to reaffirm first-order issues concerning the larger system while also insisting on the specific allegiance in question, special mention should be made of the ambiguities of this dual purpose for marabouts at the local level. The issue is particularly difficult for local marabouts who claim more than an intermediary role; these religious leaders are, in effect, obliged to take *three* orders of issues into account. In addition to support for the maraboutic system as a whole, they must display a concern for the Sufi order or the specific *zawiya* with which they are affiliated, while at the same time insisting on their own *individual* claims to religious leadership. They are obliged, in effect, to simultaneously attempt to claim "reflected" charismatic authority without relinquishing a claim to some degree of "original" charisma.

One way in which this difficulty has been moderated in the organization of the ritual celebrations of allegiance has been for the local marabout to sponsor *two* annual events, one at the same time as the major event of the order, and the other at a separate occasion. Maas Sèye, the Baye Fall marabout in Gaindiaye, thus holds two *màggals* every year. The first is held at the time of the *grand màggal* at Touba, and the ceremony thus serves as a local substitute for the celebration of the Mouride order for those unable to make the trip to Touba. But since he is unlikely to be able to compete in attracting many local disciples at that occasion, notably from *daaira* members in Kaolack, a separate ceremony – the one discussed above – is held annually to reaffirm his own position. *Sëriñ* Diakhaté, in Fatick, has developed a particularly innovative justification for a similar practice. At *Mawlud*, the feast of the prophet's birthday, when all major Tijan *zawiyas* sponsor their most important *gàmmu*, he himself holds a *gàmmu* in Fatick. Then, on the eighth day following *Mawlud* he sponsors a second event, which he refers to as a *"ngente" gàmmu*, using the term for the eighth day ceremony at which an infant is traditionally given a name. The first event thus provides an occasion for emphasizing "reflected" charisma, and thus claiming the allegiance of local Tijans who cannot make the trip to one of the major *zawiyas*, while the second event presents an opportunity for local disciples to affirm their loyalty to Diakhaté without needing to choose this local tie over the national one.

There are a great number of religious ceremonies in Senegal. As the above descriptions and their analysis indicates, these are important components of the maraboutic system which forms the predominant basis of social organization in Senegal. This system, which arises from the conjuncture of the needs of marabouts to recruit disciples to maintain their positions on the one hand, and the centrality of marabouts to the lives of individuals on the other, is built largely on the institution of the *daaira* which facilitates the organization and guarantees attendance at the ritual events. And while these rituals vary in the degree and manner of their orchestration, there is also an important underlying similarity in the functions they serve within the maraboutic system. *Màggals, gàmmus, siyaares,* and other such celebrations are both instruments for building religiously based social networks and the means of communicating the strength and vitality of these networks to the state. In their manifestation of the clear distinction between the realm of the state and that of Senegalese society the ceremonies thus constitute an essential component of Senegalese civil society, of "society in its relations with the state" with some degree of consciousness of its "externality and opposition to the state." The proliferation of these rituals in the country, therefore, is more significant than a simple indication of a new or revived religious devotion.

The balance of exchanges in the relationship

Throughout the discussion of relations between marabouts and disciples so far I have alluded regularly to the economic aspect of this relationship, frequently in terms of the offerings of goods or cash which marabouts receive from disciples. The issue is clearly a centrally important one, yet it is also one that by its very nature presents virtually insurmountable obstacles to any efforts to study it quantitatively.[60] Given the relative affluence of many marabouts and the seeming illogic of very poor people donating even a small portion of their meager incomes to these men, there is a seductive temptation to interpret the phenomenon in terms of Marx's characterization of religion as the "opiate of the people"; the rhetoric of devotion appears quite clearly to mask a very real material exploitation of the faithful. This in fact is the approach taken by Jean Copans in a study of the Mourides in which he concludes that the order is "an infernal machine," dedicated to the confiscation of the fruits of peasant labor.[61] The interpretation of religion as an instrument of economic exploitation has appeared regularly in the literature on Senegal. Robert Fatton, for example, writes that "the *taalibe's* religious convictions and submission are . . . transformed into the material gains of the *marabouts* . . . It is because they perceive him as an intermediary with God that they consent to such sacrifices."[62]

There is no denying that the nationally important marabouts in Senegal enjoy, thanks to their position, a higher standard of living than most of the population – although, as Cruise O'Brien notes, not necessarily higher than that of even middle-level functionaries in Dakar.[63] But in light of the characterization described above, it is important here to insist on two general points clearly supported by my research. First, the costs to disciples in terms of the actual "sacrifices" made for the marabout are rarely, if ever, onerous. And secondly, there is an important degree of reciprocity in exchanges with a marabout – at least in the sense of the insurance against catastrophe which a relationship with a marabout affords a disciple.

This more moderate view of marabout-disciple economic interactions is in fact essentially equivalent to that proposed by both Coulon and Cruise O'Brien in their respective landmark works on the orders in Senegal. Coulon, for example, describes the relationship as follows:

> The submission of the *taalibe* is not as blind as it might appear to be at first glance. The marabout also has obligations *vis-à-vis* his disciple; and without actually reposing on a true reciprocity in terms of gift and return-gift [une véritable réciprocité du type don contre-don], it nevertheless presents certain typical traits of a patron-client relationship . . . In general, in fact, the marabout is expected to help his disciples in all circumstances. He should be ready even to feed them in case of scarcity, to help them to find work, or even to find them a wife. Each time that the *taalibe* is in need, or that he has problems of whatever kind, he will confide in his marabout and will expect advice from him, but also a more tangible aid.[64]

And in his consideration of the economic sociology of the Mouride order, Cruise O'Brien concludes that the costs and benefits to disciples are generally on par. "Economic tribute," he argues, "is in fact roughly proportional to the real material services provided by the saints [i.e., marabouts]."[65] For the other orders, where the ideological emphasis on submission is less developed than among Mourides, this evaluation is certainly at least equally valid.

It is nevertheless true that some marabouts do control large amounts of money and other resources such as land. Their control, however, is carefully circumscribed by a cultural system which requires them to serve as conduits for redistribution if they are to maintain their following, and their position. The most important marabouts in Senegal are thus located at the center of great networks of economic exchanges, a position which obviously provides them with the means of maintaining an elevated standard of living, but which also requires that they facilitate and contribute to the circulation of those resources.

Historically land has been the major resource controlled by marabouts, especially among the Mourides. The revenues provided by fields cultivated with volunteer labor have been an important component of rural maraboutic income.[66] More recently certain marabouts, most notably perhaps those of the Sy family, have invested in business ventures which provide them with an additional source of revenue.[67] From the point of view of the analysis of the marabout-disciple relationship, however, and particularly outside the rural peanut basin, the most important source of maraboutic revenue to consider is the direct contributions of disciples. A voluntary gift to a marabout is usually referred to as *addiya*. Given the continued urbanization of Senegal and the decline of export agriculture that has characterized the country, *addiya* contributions have almost certainly surpassed agriculture as a proportion of maraboutic income in many – perhaps most – cases.

While the more wealthy *taalibe* may occasionally make individual contributions directly to their marabout, for most disciples the collective offerings of the *daairas'* "envelopes" are the means of giving the *addiya*. The donations made by *daairas* to a marabout are raised in various ways. Money collected via dues or by the contributions of small coins which *daaira* members or others make at the weekly chanting sessions are kept in the *daaira's* treasury and may be added to the *addiya* when other expenses have been met. In addition, the annual public ceremonies organized by *daairas* are the occasion of significant fundraising in the form of donations both from those present at these events and from bureaucrats or other more well-off locals. Typically the members of a *daaira* will reproduce "invitations" requesting the "support" (*soutien*) of influential individuals and these will be distributed in envelopes to those people, who are then expected to return the envelope with a cash contribution. The ceremonies are themselves very expensive, and thus consume a significant percentage of the revenues raised, but they nevertheless normally generate monies which the *daaira* may also direct to the *addiya*.[68] Finally, the most direct collection of the *addiya* takes place before the major ritual ceremonies at which most *daairas* present their "envelopes." At that time the members of the *daaira* will agree on a sum for each to contribute, frequently referring to it with the French term *participation*, implying a share in a group effort.

The amounts collected for the *addiya* of course vary widely depending on the membership and situation of the *daaira*. As a general rule, however, while these sums are significant for the marabouts due to the large numbers of disciples, from the perspective of any one individual the requirements are relatively modest. On one occasion, for example, the main Mouride *daaira* in Fatick sent a gift of some 15,720 CFA francs to the *xalifa* in Touba as its contribution to the continued expansion of the great mosque. In that instance each member had been requested to contribute only 150 FCFA, although those who were able to gave more.[69] A "typical" sum (to be treated with great caution, given the great variations) for the group *addiya* delivered at the time of the *gàmmu* or *grand màggal* might be in the range of 30,000–40,000 FCFA for the "average" *daaira*, although one occasionally hears stories (which may be exaggerated) of large urban *daairas* making contributions in the 100,000–200,000 FCFA range.

Given the poverty of most Senegalese *any* sum contributed as *addiya* must be treated as significant in that it means the disciple must forego some other good. Nevertheless it is also clear that the individual donations that are required for a *daaira* to present an *addiya* of this magnitude are never so high as to involve a substantial "sacrifice." The fact that the actual sums set for each individual's share, like *daaira* dues, are met only to the extent that a disciple is able to do so makes them even less onerous. Participation in a *daaira* thus regularly involves a disciple in the *addiya* even at times when economic hardship makes an individually significant contribution difficult or impossible. Standing in the *daaira*, and consequently the benefits to be derived from membership, are of course linked in part to the extent of a disciple's "participation" – a fact that mitigates the "free-rider" problem which might otherwise appear. But for the vast majority of disciples whose poverty precludes the possibility of individually establishing a significant position in a major marabout's social network, the relatively modest demands of a *daaira* allow him or her to share in a larger effort which is sure to command maraboutic attention, and may thus serve as a basis for requesting maraboutic patronage should the occasion arise.

Although few people receive tangible material returns from their marabout with any regularity, at times the benefits to disciples can be quite significant. The case already referred to concerning the preferential access to lots of land for a number of Mouride disciples in Fatick at the time of the *lotissement* is a prime example of the benefits to be had from participation in the maraboutic system. The most likely means by which this was achieved is as follows: the Mouride *daaira* would organize and draw up a list of members whose applications for lots was pending; this would be presented to the local Mouride marabout, *Sëriñ* Cissé, who would refer the list to the *xalifa* or another important marabout in Touba to request their help; the marabouts in Touba would then approach the higher levels of the relevant bureaucracies in Dakar, who would in turn instruct the local office concerning the handling of the relevant applications. For those involved, then, even years of participation in the *daaira* without any single tangible benefit may thus pay off on one issue. It should also be noted that for a small handful of individuals at the national level there are large payoffs to association with a marabout. Although these rare and exceptional cases cannot be explored here, it is nevertheless significant for what it reveals about the role of marabouts that the wealthiest men in Senegal are actually often businessmen with a close *taalibe* relationship with a major marabout.[70] The multifaceted commercial empire of the late Ndiouga Kébé, an extraordinarily rich Mouride businessman, might be pointed to as an example of this phenomenon.

For most people at most times, however, the economic (as distinct from the spiritual, psychological, or social) benefits that are derived from maintaining a *taalibe* relationship are in the form of the insurance which involvement in the network of economic ties provides.[71] In the precarious economic situation in which most Senegalese lead their lives, ties to a network of individuals to whom one can appeal in case of exceptional difficulties is a benefit of very real and concrete proportions. Marabouts, as a result, tend to portray their economic function precisely in terms of facilitating or providing help for those experiencing particular difficulties. A good example of this in Fatick concerns *Sëriñ* Baldé's portrayal of an agricultural project, sponsored by Cheikh Tidiane Sy and Abdoul Aziz Sy Junior, in which he regularly participates.[72]

At the village of Medina Boulel, some 17 kilometers from the town of Kaffrine in Saloum, the two brothers have some "very large" peanut fields. These fields are worked annually by disciples of the family, and at the time of the harvest in the fall disciples come from all over Senegal to participate. Working through the night the volunteers are able to harvest somewhere between one and two thousand tons of peanuts in just a couple of days. These are then sold, and the resulting money is divided up into "envelopes" of "ten, fifteen, twenty, or even fifty or one hundred thousand FCFA" to be distributed to those in need. All of the proceeds, *Sëriñ* Baldé insisted, are given away; the marabouts themselves do not profit from these fields. Moreover, necessity is the only criteria used in deciding on the beneficiaries. On the question of how the needy are identified, however, he noted that the marabouts most often rely on local intermediaries like himself to indicate those individuals undergoing particular difficulties. These, of course, are most likely to be disciples who are well-known to the intermediary, namely those who participate most regularly in the local structures of allegiance. Given the possible pay-off in case of need, such participation thus represents again a form of "insurance premium" against the constant threat of economic crisis.

The marabouts, then, are located at the centers of networks of economic exchanges from which the benefits are such that it makes clear rational sense for the disciple to participate. This system is reflected in and reinforced by a cultural code which rewards the elite both for having money and for giving it away. As I have discussed in chapter 2, this cultural characteristic is found throughout the Sahelian region and applies not only to the religious elite but to any individual claiming a position of power and influence in the social hierarchy. In the context of northern Nigerian political parties, Miles notes, extravagantly generous gestures are expected of political leaders, so that "the more a patron gives away, the greater his virtue and reputation."[73] Thus at *gàmmus*, for example, the public circulation of money given to the marabouts, while involving only a small portion of what is contributed, is important as a symbolic demonstration of the marabout's generosity. This cultural model explains such otherwise puzzling features of Senegalese attitudes towards marabouts as the "goodness" of both wealth *and* of a lack of concern for money. One Mouride disciple, for example, expounded to me with great pride about the huge quantities of money which are brought to the marabouts in Touba at big occasions and described in highly complimentary terms the great wealth of the late Mouride marabout-businessman Djilly Mbaye at Louga, and then proceeded to discuss in equally favorable terms Amadou Bamba's reputed total lack of concern for the money he was brought and which he promptly gave away.[74]

This duality is even more clearly manifest in an anecdote concerning Abdoul Aziz Sy Junior's finances which a Tijan *taalibe* admiringly recounted.[75] Speaking to the group of people who had gathered at Tivaouane to prepare the big *gàmmu* at *Mawlud*, Sy Junior described the constant struggles to meet the many expenses of running his household – including the feeding of countless *taalibes* who came to him daily for assistance. One day, he recounted, he woke up to find that five million francs were required, and that he had nothing at all to his name. He informed his household that they would have to see what they could do to feed themselves for the day, and that he would figure out a way to get enough money to put gas in his car and go to Dakar. Arriving at the house he keeps in the capital, he discovered that he had a message waiting from a *tubaab* (white, European) who had just arrived in Senegal. He met the *tubaab* at his hotel, and it turned out that he had some business deals to propose the marabout. The two got down to work, and within a few hours Sy Junior had made a profit of five million francs. The marabout went home and paid up his expenses.

The story is particularly noteworthy in that the status of the marabout as an intermediary responsible for procuring funds which are then redistributed extends in this case beyond the domestic network of *taalibes* into the international domain. From the perspective of the *taalibe* who recounted the incident, the identity of the anonymous *tubaab* and the nature of his business proposition were irrelevant. Rather, for him, the story illustrated the merits of a marabout whose interest in money was motivated by the need to meet his obligations toward his many dependants, and whose qualifications included the ability to engage in inscrutable negotiations with foreigners at great, indeed almost miraculous, profit. This image of an intermediary with little or no accumulated capital but with many obligations which he must constantly scramble to meet is carefully cultivated by the marabout.

It is important to note that only a very few of the many marabouts in Senegal are located at centers of exchange where they can exert control over such large sums. The economic clout of other marabouts varies widely depending on their location in the networks of the orders. In Fatick local marabouts control very few economic resources and must, in fact, engage in a variety of activities to meet their expenses. I have noted how in almost every case local disciples have volunteered labor for the construction and upkeep of these marabout's houses. *Sëriñ* Diakhaté provides Qur'anic instruction to children, whom he additionally sends out to beg to help meet their boarding expenses. And *Sëriñ* Alpha depends almost exclusively on teaching in his schools to meet his financial obligations. In all cases these may be supplemented with other occasional income from the making of amulets or the performance of some religious rite.

Although it cannot be accurately quantified, the most significant source of income for local marabouts, particularly those who serve most directly as representatives of national ones, seems to derive from fulfilling the functions required by this intermediary position. Thus *Sëriñs* Baldé and Cissé both receive some assistance from the marabouts they represent, and they can certainly count on these marabouts to provide emergency help should the need arise. In addition, a local *taalibe* may occasionally make a gift in cash or kind to one of these men, or the *daaira* may decide to meet some of their expenses from the organization's treasury. The income of local marabouts is therefore quite irregular, and while by strictly local standards these men all make a reasonable living for themselves, none could be considered in any sense rich. Indeed all of them display some frustration with the limitations imposed on their activities by the relatively limited resources at their disposal. Their stable but modest economic position thus mirrors the value of their work to local disciples, whose insertion into the broader maraboutic networks may be facilitated by, but does not depend on, local marabouts.

It is not my intent here to argue that the economic exchanges that take place within the orders are some sort of ideal system of social insurance. It is undeniable that the system incorporates many unjust inequalities. Not only do the mostly hereditary holders of important maraboutic positions enjoy a standard of living that is well above the masses of their disciples, but many of the funds provided by disciples are not in fact redirected downwards. Prestige expenses such as the construction of ever larger and more elaborate mosques take up a large share of the revenues that pass through a marabout's hands. And, although most of their wealth is likely to result from preferential access to state-controlled goods, at least some of the capital which is accumulated by the few well-placed *taalibes* must come, directly or indirectly, from the quasi-taxation represented by the *addiya*. Rather my point here has been to argue that despite these inequalities there is a logic to the disciple's participation in this system that goes beyond mere submission to a hegemonic ideology in the Gramscian sense. This argument is further reinforced by a consideration of the fact that, while loyalty tends to prevail in the allegiance of disciples, it does encounter limits, which may be manifested by exit or camouflaged by voice.

The limits of allegiance

The argument throughout this chapter and the preceding one should, I trust, give an indication of the high degree of stability that characterizes the maraboutic system in Senegal. I have tried to indicate how this stability is rooted not only in ideological formulations of Sufi theology but also in the logic of rational calculations by both marabouts and disciples within the framework of local knowledge. Disciples, we have seen, have an interest in emphasizing loyal allegiance given the fact that an alternative relationship requires time to establish and that the very act of declaring loyalty improves their position with the marabout and/or the intermediary organizations of allegiance. Marabouts, in addition, have an interest in perpetuating the myth of total control over disciples as a means of increasing the leverage they enjoy *vis-à-vis* the state. And because in this respect the more powerful one's marabout the better one's position, disciples in turn have clear incentives to claim the total allegiance which can reinforce the marabout's position.

But as I have also argued, and as indicated by the unending series of religious rituals which indicate the need to constantly reinforce these ties, the stability of the marabout-disciple relationship can neither be taken for granted nor does it imply the omnipotence of marabouts; there are limits to allegiance. Disciples who find themselves dissatisfied with the demands made on them may opt for two types of responses. There exists, first of all, the possibility of simply switching marabouts. Secondly, disciples can reduce their affiliation with a marabout or an order to a purely nominal level, thus resulting in a loss of real maraboutic influence over the actions of a disciple. A brief discussion of these two types of response to maraboutic limitations can thus serve to conclude our analysis of the internal structures and organization which make the orders crucial institutions of Senegalese civil society.

The potential for realignment

Despite its relative rarity, the potential for switching to a marabout one somehow finds more appealing is widely recognized as a viable option for disciples. This is, perhaps, more likely to take place within the order, or even within the maraboutic family itself. The great number of options presented to disciples by the proliferation of direct descendants of each of the founding fathers will undoubtedly make this type of realignment even more frequent in the future, but the potential has been present from early on in the evolution of the system. Cruise O'Brien, in his monograph on the Mourides, discussed "the possibility that a follower will disavow his allegiance" to a marabout. "When very dissatisfied with his *shaikh*, the *talibé* can leave and do the *njebbel* with another," he observed, noting further that this "undoubtedly does act as a restraint on the power of his *shaikh*."[76] This possibility for realignment also extends across orders and maraboutic families. It is, in addition, not restricted to cases of explicit dissatisfaction with one's marabout, but can be simply the result of the perennial interest of most people in ever more powerful marabouts.

There is a broad agreement among Senegalese of all affiliations that there is currently a greater likelihood of someone's switching *to* rather than *from* the Mourides. In response to direct questioning people consistently claimed that this was especially true for youth; it was quite unlikely, they insisted, that the children of Mouride parents would become Tijan, while it was far more likely that the children of Tijans might become Mourides. This is in keeping with accounts of the Mouride appeal to youth in urban areas, most notably in Dakar, which is linked to the greater economic opportunities offered by Mouride commercial solidarity in crucial import markets.[77] But, despite one case with which I am familiar in Fatick in which a son of a Tijan Serer family decided to become a Baye Fall (despite the family's initial efforts to discourage him), there are no indications that this occurs with any degree of frequency in the town. The demographic data from the 1988 census likewise bears this out. As Table 5.3 indicates, while there are some modest variations in religious affiliation across age groups, no clear trend towards the Mourides (or any other order) can be seen. The possibility for realignment, that is, exists in any direction.

In addition, it is not universally agreed that it is "easier" to quit the Tijans than others. In an extended comparison of the various orders, one woman who had herself switched affiliation from Qadir to Tijan at marriage insisted that, had her husband been Qadir and she Tijan, she would have requested – and he would have granted – permission to keep her original affiliation.[78] This, she explained, was because the Tijan order was "heavier," by which she meant harder to follow, more demanding, and therefore not readily abandoned. As evidence she pointed to the strict requirements of the Tijaniyya concerning ablutions and to the greater complexity of the Tijan *wird*, both of which clearly distinguished it from the more "popular" and accessible, but less rigorous practices of both Qadirs and Mourides. Independently of the extent to which the specifics of her evaluation are representative of popular sentiment in Fatick, the discussion is significant

Table 5.3. *Religion by age cohorts in Fatick*[79]

(in percentages)

Age in years	Qadir	Mouride	Tijan	Other Muslim	Christian
0–10	8.0	27.5	54.0	3.9	6.5
11–20	7.4	23.8	58.7	3.3	6.7
21–30	7.6	22.2	59.4	3.9	6.7
31–40	8.1	25.1	55.5	4.8	6.4
41–50	9.7	22.6	60.0	2.2	5.5
51–60	10.9	19.9	64.4	1.8	2.9
61–70	9.7	17.3	67.7	1.9	3.4
70+	9.7	20.2	64.8	1.8	3.1
Average	8.1	24.4	57.7	3.5	6.2

in that it points to the fact that these issues are at times explicitly addressed; a change in maraboutic or *tarixa* affiliation is an option, even if not frequently exercised.

The option, however, does not exist only in theory; although rare, it is in fact occasionally exercised. In Fatick I was able to confirm several important cases of changes in maraboutic affiliation. The most significant of these was the wide-scale and ethnically linked abandonment by many Serer of their previous ties to the Tijan marabouts at Tivaouane to declare themselves disciples of the "new" marabout Ma Ansou Niang. This case is discussed at some length in the final chapter of this book and consequently will not be pursued further here.

A very different type of switch, one involving an individual with a high level of religious knowledge and based on a careful consideration of the competing maraboutic messages, was that of the Tukulor merchant "Thierno Tall," who also serves as one of the adjunct imams of the main mosque in Fatick.[80] His father had been a *taalibe* and a *muqàddam* of El Hajj Malik Sy, having accepted him as his marabout after being instructed in a vision to walk from the Futa Toro to Dakar to declare his allegiance. He was eventually sent to represent El Hajj Malik in Sine, in a village some ten kilometers from Fatick, where Tall was born. Although he had adopted his father's affiliation, in 1972 Tall broke with the Sy family to declare himself a *taalibe* of Ibrahima "Baye" Niasse. He maintained the affiliation with the family even after Baye Niasse's death in 1975. Tall, who spent many years in religious studies in the Futa Toro as well as in Dakar before establishing himself in commerce to support the family after his father's death, explains this switch in religious terms. In his view, the history of religion – from the time of Adam himself – has been one of divine revelations of the "true path" and subsequent human distortions of that message. In Tall's view, Islam in Senegal, and by implication the Sy family with it, has deviated significantly from the correct path; only Baye Niasse had the vision to restore it to its proper track. Significantly, Tall's conversion was followed by that of the majority of his extended family, so that today the Niasse family counts many *taalibes* among an important segment of the Tukulor community in Fatick.[81]

As these cases show, the possibility for realignment is generally recognized and occasionally exercised. And although it is rare, the fact that it can easily come to involve other members of an individual's social network, whether family or ethnic kin, means that it is a possibility that any marabout would do well to take seriously.

Words louder than actions

It is perhaps not apparent from the discussion thus far that, while *claiming* a maraboutic affiliation is virtually universal in Senegal, a significant minority of the population neither actively participates in any of the ritual practices of allegiance nor seeks maraboutic guidance in taking action; a purely nominal affiliation is quite conceivable. In such cases, of course, the marabout carries little or no weight with his putative disciples. Even when the affiliation cannot be said to be purely nominal, however, there are clear limits to the demands which marabouts can place on their disciples. If the benefits are unclear and the potential sanctions limited, disciples may, quite simply, ignore the marabout's advice while continuing to protest their allegiance.

An important part of maraboutic "sanctions" in eliciting the compliance of disciples is, of course, moral. The acceptance by disciples of the Sufi notion of the appropriateness of seeking guidance from *shaykhs* is crucial to the influence of marabouts. This foundation, however, is limited and not totally reliable – hence the constant need felt by marabouts to emphasize the importance of following a religious guide. An additional sanction for defection from the relationship involves the loss of the benefits which are derived from a place in a network of relations. This, we have seen, is significant and is at least partially responsible for the stability of marabout-disciple ties. At times, however, it is possible for disciples to quite simply ignore their marabout's advice, while maintaining their allegiance, without suffering a loss of their position. This is most likely to be the case in situations involving a large number of a marabout's disciples or in those where the action is beyond the immediate surveillance of the marabout or a representative. This factor, as a result, imposes a real limitation on the power of the marabouts to elicit broad compliance from disciples as a group, particularly on non-religious issues.

A clear and particularly important recent example of the limited power of marabouts to control the actions of their disciples is presented by the case of Mouride involvement in the 1988 elections. Before the election, the *xalifa* of the order issued a *ndigal*, a command, directing all Mourides to vote for the ruling party and the re-election of President Abdou Diouf. "Any Mouride who did not vote for Abdou Diouf," he told the faithful, "would betray Serigne Touba Mbacké [i.e. Amadou Bamba]," adding that "voting for Abdou goes along with prayer" [va dans le sens de la prière].[82]

Although there are no exact data on voting by religious group, and any efforts at estimating it by region would be questionable given the widespread fraud which accompanied the election, it is nevertheless very clear that the command was widely ignored among Mourides.[83] Many people, it seems, opted for abstention from voting rather than going against the *ndigal* or making the (to them) distasteful choice of casting a vote for the beleaguered president.[84] Many others, however, simply disobeyed the marabout's command and voted as they saw fit. This was apparently most prevalent among younger urban Mourides, who joined their cohorts in strongly supporting opposition candidate Abdoulaye Wade's Parti Democratique Sénégalais (PDS) and his promise of "*soppi!*" (change). Even among otherwise quite fervent Mourides this response was widespread. Typical in his reaction was a young disciple from a strongly Mouride family who – in Touba at the occasion of the *màggal* – shrugged off my question about the *ndigal* with the suggestion that such matters were not within the competence of the marabouts.[85] This rejection, however, in no way called into question his affiliation with the Mouride order or the marabouts themselves, a devotion he also eagerly stressed.

This case of ignoring maraboutic advice is particularly significant because elections in Senegal have typically been identified as the place where the "blind obedience" of disciples plays the most direct political role. It suggests that the political stability of Senegal which has allowed for regular elections cannot be attributed simply to the ability of the marabouts to "deliver the vote" independently of the calculations of citizen-disciples. This is not to say, of course, that a maraboutic endorsement cannot be quite influential in the outcome of an election. But such an influence must result from a marabout's ability to persuade disciples via moral sanctions – an undertaking which the 1988 elections showed to be quite tricky. There was a widespread belief in Senegal following the elections that the Mouride *xalifa* had made a strategic miscalculation, and that he would have been unlikely to repeat the *ndigal* again. Although this cannot be answered definitively –

he died the following year – the error was clearly costly to the marabout in two domains. First of all it did damage to his own position and that of the order in terms of his credibility with disciples. It demonstrated, in addition, the limits of his influence, thus costing him in leverage with the state officials, whose patronage of the marabouts has always been understood to be based precisely on the power of marabouts to influence the actions of their disciples. Strong evidence that marabouts in the country understood the impact of the 1988 experience precisely in such terms is provided by the stance taken by the most important marabouts during the February 1993 elections. "At Touba as at Tivaouane the famous *ndigal* did not fall," noted the Islamic weekly *Wal Fadjri* ("And the Dawn") in late 1992. "At the occasion of the *màggal* as at the *gàmmu* the *xalifas-général* of the Tijans and of the Mourides placed themselves above the political *mêlée*. 1993 will therefore not be like 1988 with the categorical injunction of the late Abdou Lahad to support Abdou Diouf."[86] Indeed, aside from Moustapha Sy's attempt to position himself as spokesman for dissatisfied and angry urban youth via his scathing attack on the incumbent president, only a very few relatively minor marabouts made any partisan political pronouncements during the campaign.

The double danger of hurting relations both with disciples and with the state prescribes caution on the part of marabouts. To demand the unpopular, which they have in addition no means to enforce, is to invite the erosion of maraboutic prestige, and hence their authority. Marabouts, therefore, must be responsive to popular sentiment. This understanding, reinforced by the experience of the 1988 *ndigal*, was certainly central to the immediate maraboutic reaction to the violent events of April 1989. During the course of the ethnic violence against Moors that exploded in Senegal at that time, the major marabouts of the country were conspicuous by their almost complete silence – this despite the fact that the attacks and killings took place during the holy month of Ramadan and against a Muslim population.[87] This surprising (indeed almost scandalous) silence, I believe, can only be explained by the marabouts' understanding of their own inability to control the actions of disciples in the situation, along with the calculation that, in the climate of ethnic animosity which pervaded all levels of society, making unpopular pronouncements could only result in further erosion of their reputational prestige.

These two cases are of course exceptional; in most situations a widespread defiance of maraboutic authority such as that displayed by Mourides during the 1988 election is highly unlikely. But similarly, as in the case of the 1989 ethnic violence, marabouts are also unlikely to make demands which test too strongly the limits of their own authority. This again adds to the stability and the cohesiveness of the orders which these two chapters have examined. As well organized institutions with an extraordinarily high degree of popular legitimacy, based both on an ideological religious foundation and on their responsiveness to popular concerns, the orders have been able to provide Senegalese society with a degree of "strength" in interactions with the state which is virtually unparalleled elsewhere in Africa.

6 · The state–marabout relationship: collaboration, conflict, and alternatives

The ambiguity towards Islam which marks the attitudes of the contemporary political elite in Senegal is a product of the same dilemma as that which characterized the relations between political and religious authorities in pre-colonial Senegambia. In Sine the *buur*, like other monarchs in the region, maintained good diplomatic ties with various important religious leaders, but he also recognized that they offered an alternative system of allegiances to that which maintained his position. Coumba Ndoffène Diouf *fa ndepp*, the second-to-last *Buur-Siin* who reigned from 1898 to 1924, kept particularly good ties with a Moorish maraboutic family from the town of Boutilimit in today's Mauritania. Cheikhouna ould Dada, a marabout from that family who was later to die in Fatick and be buried in the family cemetery of the *buur's* descendants, served as the *buur's* emissary to Amadou Bamba, founder of the Mouride order. Good relations with Bamba were cemented when the *Buur-Siin* intervened with the French to defend Bamba against the incriminating allegations made by a disgruntled son of Lat Dior Diop, the *Damel* of Cayor.

Cordial relations have been maintained among the descendants of all of these men. El Hajj Farba Diouf, the now quite old son of Coumba Ndoffène Diouf, regularly receives Moorish marabouts of ould Dada's family as guests. One of his sons, grandson to the *buur*, was given to the Moorish family to educate and subsequently spent seven years in Boutilimit, where he acquired a sound Arabic education. Farba Diouf also maintains close personal ties with Amadou Bamba's descendants, particularly since his own conversion over the course of the 1950s. In 1983 Abdou Lahatte Mbacké, Bamba's son and successor as head of the Mouride order, came to Fatick personally to pay a visit to Farba Diouf in recognition of the service which the latter's father had performed for that of the former. The visit rekindled close ties, and since that date Farba Diouf has regularly attended the *grand màggal* at Touba as a guest of the Mbacké family. Yet despite these ties, when asked whether the *Buur-Siin* had himself ever converted, his son quickly answered "Never!", indicating how unthinkable such a move would have been. Had he done so, he explained, all of Sine would have followed, and the result would have been that the *Siin-Siin* would have become followers of Amadou Bamba rather than of the *buur*, and he would have consequently lost his power and authority.[1] While for many reasons, both personal and political, princes and politicians may cultivate good relations with marabouts, the two are also clear rivals for authority.

The authority which both seek, of course, is over the masses of the Senegalese population; to maintain their positions of power governments need obedient citizens just as marabouts need faithful disciples. We have seen in chapter 3 how the dynamics of the post-colonial situation leave the state with only limited direct authority over much of the population, in Fatick as elsewhere in Senegal. Marabouts, for their part, enjoy a considerable degree of authority within the limits of their capacity to diffuse a broad popular appeal. The highly organized and ritualized interactions of leaders and followers within the orders, as I have portrayed them in the two previous chapters, serve to reinforce – but also to delimit – the authority of marabouts over their followers. Considering these two sets of relations, then, I now turn to the examination of the patterns of interaction that have characterized relations between the religious and the political elite in Senegal.

In contrast to the picture of strict collaboration – based on a putative common interest in maintaining the status quo – which observers of Senegal have frequently painted in discussing this relationship, I will argue that while the incentives for collaboration are significant, the relationship is ultimately more tenuous and contingent. This is the result of divergent long-term interests. While the political elite finds itself regularly in the position of working through the marabouts, their ultimate goal is to be able to function without them. Marabouts, for their part, seek to maintain and ensure the state's dependence on them. They thus alternately have incentives to cooperate or defect depending on the situation. This chapter explores the strategies which each pursues in this regard, and concludes with an examination of how the existence of Muslim alternatives to the Sufi orders has affected these relations.

The development and evolution of the relationship

The Sufi orders in their contemporary, and distinctively Senegalese, manifestation are only about as old as the Senegalese colonial state itself. The orders are based, of course, on a broader Sufi tradition, and more particularly on the characteristic pattern of the Maghrebian interpretation of that tradition. But, as we have seen in the preceding chapters, they also incorporate many uniquely Senegalese elements. Because they originated and evolved in the context of the colonial conquest of Senegal, the distinctive forms of religious organization in Senegal can only be fully understood in light of political considerations. This has had a particularly important impact in terms of the relations between religious structures and the state in the country today. The history of French relations with the Muslim elite in West Africa effectively established parameters for Muslim political activity which are still broadly relevant. In the post-colonial period, however, these have also been modified by various factors. A discussion of the current dynamics of state-marabout relations, therefore, must begin with an understanding of their origins and evolution.

Colonial sources: the bases of a relationship

It is remarkable, and certainly not simply coincidental, that the founders of the three most significant maraboutic dynasties of contemporary Senegal were almost exact contemporaries, and that the period in which their religious movements knew their greatest expansion coincided largely with the establishment of colonial control. Amadou Bamba, El Hajj Malik Sy, and Abdoulaye Niasse were all born within a few years of each other in the middle of the nineteenth century and died within a five year period from 1922 to 1927.[2] They were thus all small children as the French began expanding into the interior of Senegal from their coastal enclaves after the naming of Louis Faidherbe as Governor of "French Senegal" in 1854. And by 1886, when the Wolof armies that had continued to resist the French in the central zone of the country were finally defeated, each was established in a maraboutic career. In 1895, the same year that the Federation of French West Africa was formally created, the French deported to Gabon the enigmatic Amadou Bamba, whose rapidly growing following had begun to be seen by colonial authorities as a threat to their rule. Despite the initial seven year exile – which was followed by another period (1903–1907) in Mauritania after a brief return to Senegal – Bamba's following continued to grow. El Hajj Malik Sy likewise attracted thousands of new followers during this period, first in Cayor, in the village where he had established a school after his return from the pilgrimage in 1889, and then later in Tivaouane after his definitive move there in 1902. And in Kaolack, the rival Tijan *zawiya* led by Abdoulaye Niasse also developed a broad popular following in the years around the turn of the century. By the time of the death of each of these men in the 1920s, the social movements that had formed around them had been sufficiently consolidated and routinized to survive the transition to a second generation of maraboutic leadership. The movements were thus born and built simultaneously with the colonial state.

A crucial factor in the rise of the Sufi orders in their Senegalese form was the urgent need to reconstruct a social order in the wake of the disruption occasioned by the colonial conquest. And as they developed into the cohesive and routinized organizations which they represent today the orders evolved in opposition to, but were also adapted and shaped by, the newly emerging institutions of the colonial state. In this respect the Mouride order, in contrast to the Tijaniyya or the Qadiriyya with their Arab origins and longer history in the region, was of particular importance. F. Quesnot, who undertook a study of Senegalese Islam as an attaché to the colonial administration in its final years, argued that the Mouride model became the paradigm of religious organization for all other maraboutic movements in Senegal, and especially the Tijaniyya, in the years following the deaths of the founding fathers. "The dogma of 'sanctification' through labor no longer remained the exclusive domain of the Mouride sect but became more and more a general rule of Senegalese Islam which each marabout strives to put into practice." Most importantly, he noted, the colonial administration's emphasis, after 1943, on intensifying peanut production, "endorsed this tendency, and thus contributed involuntarily" to the emergence of a new model of marabout-agriculturalist. Thus, Quesnot argued, "'Maraboutism' in accordance with the *Mouride* conception has become the rule in Senegalese Islam."[3]

While Quesnot is certainly correct in arguing that the Mouride example was of particular importance in the development of Senegalese Sufism in the colonial period, most notably in terms of rural agricultural organization, it would be incorrect to see all of the other orders in Senegal simply as imitators of the Mouride model. Rather, throughout the colonial period, the model was modified and developed in accordance with influences from each of the major religious movements of the epoch. Most significantly, as we have seen, the institution of the *daaira*, which is almost certainly of Tijan origin, emerged as a central component of Senegalese religious organization. And what is most important to note here is that the adaptation of religion took place in accordance with the imperative of interacting and responding to the evolving state structures which the French were erecting during this period. Indeed, at various times the French played a direct and active role in determining outcomes which were subsequently to establish lasting precedents, the system of succession to major marabouts being a particularly important example. Religious and political structures in colonial Senegal arose simultaneously and were formed and developed alternately in collaboration with and in opposition to each other – a history which, as we shall see, continues to inform their interaction within the independent state.

There was a real ambivalence in French attitudes toward Islam at the time of the conquest and early in the colonial period. A British colonial study of French West Africa bluntly stated the sources of this ambivalence: "Nor can it be denied that the Mohammedans are as a whole superior in moral outlook to the heathen negro; so that adoption of Mohammedanism is a real advance in the scale of civilization, though probably a bar to further development."[4] The contradictions in policy which resulted from this ambivalence have led to a debate among later historiographers concerning the extent to which a consistent French "Islamic policy" can be discerned in this period. Cruise O'Brien has argued that the "considerable impulsion to the spread of Islam" which the French provoked in setting up an administrative system "was not conscious policy, but the result of a series of administrative initiatives, and some common value judgements as to the relative worth of Islamic and non-Islamic culture. In particular, the early administrators took a number of measures, the results of which they did not perhaps foresee, which gave a crucial position to Muslim intermediaries."[5]

In a rebuttal to this argument, David Robinson argues that there existed a well-defined French position on Islam throughout the nineteenth century, and that it consisted first in systematically distinguishing between Muslim leaders hostile to France and those more amenable to cooperation with colonial authorities, and then encouraging the latter while suppressing the former. This, he argues, was the reason for "the recurrent patterns of reaction, rhetoric and quarantine, the consistent fear of the Islamic state, and the equally consistent encouragement of francophile marabouts."[6] Whether such a policy existed in some clearly defined form or not, however, students of the period agree that by more or less the time of the First World War, the French had successfully defined the acceptable political parameters of Islamic social movements. Most significantly, in Robinson's phrase, they had "succeeded in producing a Muslim society ready to accept French domination."[7]

Having successfully contained the threat of "militant Islam," the French turned to the task of elaborating a colonial system and shaping it to meet metropolitan needs. In the period leading up to and during the First World War colonial policies were guided largely by the need for military recruitment and the desire to expand agricultural, and especially peanut, production in the newly conquered territories. Their reliance on Muslim intermediaries in both of these tasks gradually forced the French to move by the late 1920s from their earlier "complacency" to "an active realization that they had acquired a considerable stake in Islam in AOF, a stake which was both economic and political and which was so important that it had to be carefully protected."[8] This stake was concentrated in the major marabouts of the Sufi orders, so that the "realization of the existence of this community of interests between the French and the Sufi brotherhoods . . . became most obvious at the deaths of such people as el-Hajj Malik Sy, Sheikh Sidia and Ahmadu Bamba."[9]

The earlier distrust of Amadou Bamba had given way by the time of his death to a very close reliance of the colonial authorities on his new Mouride order. And despite the greater ambivalence in French attitudes towards Tijan marabouts in general – in part the legacy of the opposition of El Hajj Umar Tall to the colonial conquest – similarly close relationships had been established with such important Tijan figures as El Hajj Malik Sy and his son-in-law (and grandson of El Hajj Umar Tall) Seydou Nourou Tall. The deaths of several important maraboutic allies in the 1920s forced the French to make decisions concerning future policies towards the orders, and it was in this period that the patterns of interaction were established. Harrison identifies three central aspects of French relations with the Muslim elite in the inter-war period. First, colonial officials demonstrated their willingness and capability for intervening directly in the affairs of the orders, particularly in determining the outcome of succession struggles. Secondly, the French embarked on a policy of reinforcing the cohesion of the orders, in contrast to the earlier tendency to attempt to divide and rule Muslim societies. Finally, French relations with the orders were "fossilized" in that the earlier ambivalence was replaced with a firm belief in the compatibility of the interests of the colonial state and the marabouts.[10]

The courting of the marabouts as allies reached its peak after 1936, when J. M. de Coppet was named Governor-General of French West Africa. De Coppet actively pursued the policy of encouraging maraboutic causes by such things as providing state help in the construction of mosques – the concessionary transportation terms which he gave Ibrahima Niasse to facilitate the construction of the mosque at Kaolack is a prime example. He also inaugurated a series of symbolic gestures, such as the gifts and visits to marabouts on important Muslim feastdays, which remain part of the symbolic repertoire in relations between the Senegalese political and religious elites, as we shall see below.

The traumatic experience of the Second World War and the political chaos of the French Fourth Republic shattered the cohesion of French policy as the colonial empire began to crumble. Thus, willy-nilly, the component units of the Federation of French West Africa moved to independence. The politics of the immediate post-war period were characterized by the multiplication of indigenous political demands and an increased rivalry among the Westernized African elite as "it became increasingly obvious that the prize for the winners was likely to be control over an independent state."[11] In an effort to maintain control of the process the French attempted, down to the last-ditch effort to preserve some semblance of the empire by means of de Gaulle's 1958 referendum on the "French Community," to counter the influence of the new political forces by re-emphasizing their ties (via gifts and concessions) to the more conservative "traditional" authorities. In Senegal the most important of these were the marabouts of the major *zawiyas*. As independence approached, therefore, the religious and the indigenous political elite of Senegal found themselves struggling – at times in collaboration, at others in conflict – with each attempting to maintain its pre-eminence in the newly emerging order. The period was fraught with dangers for both sides as their relative power to influence events was tested, and the outcomes were thus partially responsible for later relations.

The 1958 referendum asked the African colonies to choose either continued ties with France within a federal arrangement or immediate independence. Throughout French West Africa the political elite was divided on the issue. Political parties found themselves in the difficult situation of having to choose between compromising their nationalist credentials in campaigning for a "yes" vote (in favor of the French Community, and hence against independence) or of campaigning for a "no" vote and risk certain political marginalization if the vote went against them.[12] The debate about the appropriate response raged as de Gaulle made a tour through Africa in August of 1958 to encourage support for the Community. In Senegal, before any of the leading political parties had had time to announce its stance, the major marabouts of the country – including Ibrahima Niasse, Falilou Mbacké, and the young Cheikh Tidiane Sy – joined together to announce their loyalty to de Gaulle and their support for the French Community. The marabouts' action in effect forced the hand of the leaders of the political parties, shifting the balance of power within the parties in favor of those opposed to independence. Within Senghor's Union Progressiste Sénégalaise (UPS), which had participated at the meeting of the mass territorial party, the Parti du Regroupement Africain (PRA), in Cotonou in July, those who had emerged as spokesmen for independence found themselves marginalized and the more "moderate" element gained the upper hand following the marabouts' pronouncement. When the vote was held in September it went overwhelmingly in favor of the Community, an outcome which a French journalist labeled "*le oui des marabouts.*"[13]

The ill-planned Community was short-lived, however, and almost immediately African leaders throughout the former French empire found themselves negotiating the processes of acceding to formal independence. Capitalizing on the momentum gained from their influence in the referendum, and fearful of the challenge to their positions which they had reason to believe independence would bring, the most important marabouts in Senegal joined together before the end of 1958 to form the Conseil Supérieur des Chefs Religieux du Sénégal in defense of their interests. But the group was unable to maintain its cohesion as the various members maneuvered to protect their personal positions in the rapidly changing political situation. When the Tijan marabout Ibrahima Niasse sent a

.telegram to de Gaulle protesting the new constitution which the Senegalese government was proposing for the Mali Federation (intended to unite Senegal with the French Soudan) most of the other important marabouts quickly distanced themselves from his move.

Others, however, continued to challenge the political elite, most significantly through the creation of a political party under the leadership of Cheikh Tidiane Sy and Ibrahima Niasse, along with various other secular leaders who had reason to oppose Léopold Senghor's UPS. The Parti de la Solidarité Sénégalaise (PSS) which the dissident marabouts founded espoused a "progressive politics based on a symbiosis of the values of Islam and those of the universal and fertile French culture," a platform that led one observer to call it "a Muslim Gaullist movement."[14] Largely due to the opposition of other important marabouts, notably the *xalifas* at Tivaouane and at Touba, the PSS failed to win any significant support in the legislative elections of March 1959. Cheikh Tidiane Sy's continued activism led to his eventual arrest and imprisonment for six months, until Ibrahima Niasse interceded to gain his release. By the summer of 1960, when Senegal achieved full independence after the failure of the Mali Federation, the unity of the maraboutic opposition had been shattered, but the marabouts had nevertheless displayed their capacity for significantly influencing political outcomes. As Coulon puts it, "The Muslim religious leaders had, for the first time, taken a political initiative instead of being satisfied with following in the steps of the parties."[15] As we shall see, this demonstration of their strengths – and its limits – began to set the parameters of the relationship within which marabouts and the state have interacted throughout the post-colonial period.

Continuities and changes in the post-independence relationship

The Conseil Supérieur des Chefs Religieux had been formed in opposition to the nascent independent state and for the express purpose of dealing with it. The statutes of the organization listed five goals that defined its "mission":[16]

1 To protect, watch over, and maintain the dogmas of Islam in their true sense.
2 To supervise and verify that the constitution to be submitted for popular approval grant absolute liberty to Islam in the new Senegalese state.
3 To secure acceptance for any constitution which conforms to the interests of Islam and practicing Muslims, and to secure rejection of any constitution whose terms could injure, no matter how slightly, Islam, the practice of Islam, and the expansion of Islam.
4 To serve as mediator in all existing disagreements or those which might

exist among Muslims or religious leaders, or between them and the administration, with the goal of a perfect reconciliation and a cordial understanding for the common peace.

5 To defend both the general and specific interests of the members of Islam [sic, *des membres de l'Islam*] in all domains – economic, political, social, cultural, and judicial – through advice and by presenting claims to the public and judicial authorities.

The marabouts who had organized themselves in the Conseil clearly meant to establish their right, and willingness, to define limits beyond which the Senegalese state could not go. Although, as I have noted, the group effectively ceased to function after the accession to full independence, it was to re-emerge a decade later in the one major confrontation in which the state appeared to be exceeding the limits: the passage of the *Code de la Famille*, which I will discuss below.[17] The potential for confrontation between the religious and the political elite of the country, although sparsely used, was nevertheless evident from the birth of the new Senegalese state.

The relative lack of direct confrontation in the relationship and the predominance of the collaborative mode of interaction must be understood in light of the fact that the "moderate" political faction which won control of the state at independence had clearly displayed its willingness to consider the interests of the marabouts. Indeed, the marabouts had played a large role in that outcome. Léopold Senghor had been the most prominent of those who found themselves marginalized at the 1958 PRA Congress in Cotonou. Consistent with his longtime support for a variety of federal arrangements with France, Senghor had initially downplayed the demand for independence. However he quickly found himself repudiated by the rest of the delegates as demands for "immediate and unconditional" independence came to dominate the meeting.[18] Although Senghor ultimately endorsed the idea of independence, his ambivalence had clearly compromised him. Indeed, in the highly charged and volatile atmosphere of those months, *any* public position on the referendum presented enormous political risks, and politicians proceeded with great caution. (Senghor, along with his long-time collaborator Mamadou Dia, actually managed to arrange to be in Europe, and thus out of the fray, at the time of de Gaulle's visit to Africa at the end of August.) It was only after the marabouts had pronounced themselves in favor of a "yes" vote that Senghor and Dia undertook and were able, in two "tumultuous meetings," to secure the support of the majority of the executive committee of the UPS in favor of the French Community.[19] The act provoked a split in the party, but with the eventual victory of the "yes" vote, due largely to the support of the marabouts, Senghor and the UPS reemerged as the most powerful political forces in Senegal. In a very real sense it was the marabouts' stance which allowed Senghor to reclaim the upper hand within the UPS.

The negotiations concerning independence within the framework of the Mali Federation, as we have seen, were even more complicated and eventually resulted in divisions within the maraboutic front. But again with the support of important marabouts Senghor was able first to win support for the Federation and then get approval for aborting the effort when it became clear that the Soudanese were to dominate the organization. Finally, in 1962, Senghor was able to garner the backing of the most important marabouts in the crisis that pitted him against his erstwhile (and, unlike him, Muslim) comrade, Mamadou Dia.[20] The collaborative relationship between Senghor and the religious elite – which had begun early in his political career when with their support he first defeated the venerable Lamine Guèye – was definitively consolidated.

The marabouts thus appeared to have saved Senghor, just as Senghor's victory in 1958 had apparently saved the marabouts. While one can hypothesize about alternative outcomes that might have pitted these two against each other, at the moment of independence both the newly dominant political elite and the religious leaders of Senegal certainly had reason to believe in the complementarity of their interests. Each, however, also had reason to be wary, because neither could be assured of surviving a challenge to its position by the other; there was a rough parity in the balance of power between the new state and the representatives of the most significant societal groups in the country.

This parity, which in any case left the two elite groups few alternatives but to reach a *modus vivendi*, also provided an additional incentive to focus on their complementary interests. The collaborative aspect of the relationship between marabouts and the state has been, quite justly, the pre-eminent one explored by scholars of Senegalese politics. Most notable in this regard is Coulon's superb exposition of the dynamics of the relationship which remains highly relevant today.[21] Coulon approaches the issue by describing the exchange of services between the state and the marabouts. The marabouts, he notes, provide two types of important services to political authorities. First, in a continuation of the role they had played during the colonial period, maraboutic support serves as a source of legitimation for a regime which has few direct ties to its society. Secondly, the state frequently finds itself in the position of having to rely on maraboutic authority in pursuit of policy goals. This function of "auxiliary to the administration" has been particularly pronounced in the implementation of rural agricultural development programs.[22]

These services are reciprocated with parallel support provided by the state to the marabouts. First, by showing respect for maraboutic authority, agents of the state increase their apparent importance in the eyes of their disciples and thus serve to reinforce the position of marabouts. This is the reason for the constant courtesy visits by state officials to marabouts, particularly at the time of religious feastdays or major ritual celebrations. Secondly, the state serves to protect and advance the material interests of marabouts, at times in terms of their direct personal resources, but also in terms of facilitating or sponsoring projects important to the maraboutic cause, such as the construction of mosques or the organization of ritual celebrations. As Coulon discusses, the system of maraboutic collaboration with the colonial state was in many ways continued in the mutually beneficial exchange of services after 1960.

But these continuities should not hide the existence of real political differences too. The transition from a colonial regime to an independent state entailed a concomitant change in the goals pursued by the political authorities, thus inserting a new dimension into the relationship. Despite their many real affective and intellectual ties with France, the new political elite in independent Senegal were not simply black colonialists. However much they may have identified with the metropole in an earlier period, their goals and their orientations were transformed with their change of status, a transformation that has been solidified by the process of Africanization of the regime. This change resulted in the seemingly paradoxical, but actually quite explainable, simultaneous emergence of two different aspects of the relationship: on the one hand there was an intensification of contacts with a broader diversity of marabouts, especially at the local level, and at the same time there emerged new sources of tension in the recognition of a divergence in the long-term interests of the state and the marabouts. While the French colonial attitude towards relations with the marabouts had been conditioned by more immediate and pragmatic short-term goals which were well served by the reliance on religious authorities as intermediaries, the political elite of independent Senegal answered to a different set of motivations.[23]

As we have seen in chapter 3, one aspect of functionaries' approach towards the population at the local level, in Fatick as elsewhere in Senegal, is motivated by the hegemonic drive to transform the juridical reality of the African state into an empirical dominance over that population. This is the search for a more direct control over the citizenry, driven by the twin ideological goals of incorporation and transformation. Because the independent state seeks goals more ambitious than the colonial ones of stability and agricultural exploitation, it is driven to pursue a more intensive intervention at the grass roots level. This search for rapid modernization and transformation by a relatively weak or "soft" state, however, requires help and intermediaries. Given their ready availability, the result in many cases has been a greater reliance on marabouts as intermediaries, particularly at the local level.

While in the short run, then, the local level agents of the independent state may be motivated to increase contacts and collaboration with marabouts, and hence reinforce the power and authority of the religious elite, the same goals of the state also produce an opposing attitude towards maraboutic authority. The goal of *direct* incorporation of the population into the state and their transformation into the citizenry of a modern republic necessitates, in the long run, the marginalization of maraboutic authority, or at least its limitation to the metaphysical domain. Collaboration with marabouts is thus ultimately seen by state officials as a sub-optimal strategy, and one that conflicts with the longer term goals of the state.

The ambivalence in state actions and attitudes resulting from these two contradictory motivations provokes marabouts to respond in various ways. Marabouts need to maneuver to limit the expansion of state power over the population so as to maintain state dependence on them. But they must simultaneously demonstrate their utility to the state as intermediaries with social groups. They must also always seek to increase their appeal to disciples in order to demonstrate to the state their capacity for exerting influence over the population. This becomes all the more important insofar as it is their collaboration with the state which allows them to secure the benefits which constitute part of their appeal to *taalibes*. Specific local circumstances and diverse judgments as to the most effective way to juggle these forces leads to a diversity of attitudes towards the state as marabouts alternately attempt to limit, counter, or share in the state's power over their common clientele.

Although his work stresses the continuities, comments in two interviews cited by Coulon in his discussion of the "exchange of services" actually hint quite clearly at the transformed sensitivity of marabouts towards the state in light of the ambiguities in the post-colonial relationship. In one, a local Tijan marabout from the village of M'Pal remarked: "At the time of the French, administrators rarely came by to visit me. For them I was certainly nothing more than the lieutenant of the *xalifa* in Tivaouane. Since independence it is not the same. The prefect and even the governor come by to see me frequently. They treat me like an important person." In another, a local functionary discussing the respect for maraboutic authority which was part of the state's side of the exchange noted that, "relations with marabouts are delicate. The marabouts must not see us very often with their peasants, because they would see in that a threat to their power."[24] From the maraboutic perspective, the independent state is thus recognized as being both responsible for the increased importance of marabouts' positions *and* a threat to the long-term maintenance of their authority. Throughout the remainder of this chapter we will see how this marks the relations between the state and marabouts, seen primarily from the local level.

The ambivalence of the state: working and dealing with marabouts

Turning once again to a discussion of aspects of the state in its local manifestation we encounter familiar difficulties in drawing the lines which demarcate it from other societal actors. In a parallel to the way in which the "economy of affection" blurs the lines between state and local society, what we might call the "spiritual economy" bridges and unites state and maraboutic organizations at various times and in various ways. The close alliances and ties between state officials and religious figures, established for the purposes of maintaining their personal – rather than organizational – positions, are widespread in West Africa and signify another departure from the colonial model of these relations. Stories of political leaders consulting with marabouts for personal advancement within the state are frequent and common in Senegal, as elsewhere in the region.[25]

Relations of this sort are based on an understanding of the utility of a marabout to a political figure in the metaphysical domain. This is, of course, an aspect of their potential influence of which most marabouts are well aware. And again, there is a parallel to relations with traditional authorities. The father of *Sëriñ* Diakhaté, one of the local Tijan marabouts in Fatick, received a gift of a parcel of land on which to build a house and mosque from Farba Diouf, the *Buur-Siin's* son, when he settled in the town in the early 1950s. The gift was granted when Ibrahima Niasse, with whom the elder Diakhaté had good ties, came to visit Diakhaté in Fatick and approached Diouf to request his help. Diouf offered to donate or contribute (*sarax*) the land to the marabout, and showed him several sites before the marabout found one acceptable. About the nature of these relations that would prompt such generosity, *Sëriñ* Diakhaté insists that Diouf was not a *taalibe* of Niasse at all, but rather that it was motivated by personal considerations of what the marabout's spiritual renown might do for the *buur's* descendant. "Governments (*ngur yi*)," *Sëriñ* Diakhaté says, "are like that; they always want marabouts to come and pray for them so that they'll last a long time."[26]

It is quite possible, of course, that considerations of a more temporal nature also played a role in this particular case, as they no doubt frequently do. But it is nevertheless beyond doubt that the personal beliefs of state officials and bureaucrats at times affect their relations with marabouts. Most functionaries, like other Senegalese, accept the general premises concerning the centrality of marabouts to their personal lives. These connections, however, are mitigated today by other aspects of the world-view of officials. Both their positions in the state and their Westernized (frequently foreign) education and training lead most state officials to accept the notion of secularism, of separating the domains of the spiritual from that of the worldly. There is no perceived contradiction between believing that personal ties with a marabout are important in terms of the spiritual, and acting to delimit the socio-political influence of marabouts.

In Fatick this orientation is embodied in three of the local officials with a clearly demonstrated interest in the spiritual domain. The prefect of the region at the time of fieldwork was a *taalibe* of a Moorish Qadir marabout, and he played an important personal role in such things as the organization of the marabout's annual visits to Fatick. The municipal administrator was a devout Mouride, who regularly attended the *màggal* in Touba and paid visits to his marabout, and the chief regional medical officer was a committed Tijan who took his faith very seriously. Yet all three of these men at various times explicitly bemoaned the excessive influence of marabouts in administrative questions and argued that marabouts should not be involved in non-spiritual issues. While these personal ties thus do complicate and influence the relations between the state and the religious elite, this issue should not be overstated. The notion of secularism is widely accepted in Senegal, almost universally among state officials. Personal ties cannot be ignored when considering the relations of the state to the marabouts, but while they may occasionally blur they do not eradicate the lines that separate these two groups.

Cohabitation without affection

The intensification of efforts by the post-colonial state to penetrate society and reach down to the local level prompted an increased degree of contact with a diversity of local elites, most significantly marabouts. As a result, the patterns of interaction with the important religious elite of the country which had been developed under colonial rule were expanded and adapted to serve as a model for interactions between any state official and a religious figure, even down to the level of marabouts with very restricted audiences. At the same time, these relations have provoked a significant degree of frustration among local officials, who find that the need to pass through intermediaries restricts their capacity for decisive action in the pursuit of policy goals. State officials, therefore, consider their form of "indirect rule" a distinctly sub-optimal situation, and maintain the long-term goal of relegating maraboutic authority exclusively to the personal and spiritual domain.

As I have noted above, the attitudes of state officials themselves (and consequently the analysis of the relations) are complicated by the personal ties of officials to marabouts. In addition, there are also at times significant incentives for personal collaboration between these two groups in undertakings that might lead to their mutual material benefit. To these temptations, of course, individuals will respond in different ways. As a result, no single pattern characterizes the nature of relationships between functionaries and different marabouts. What is important, however, is that both sides are obliged at all times to negotiate and balance the tension and ambiguity which marks the relationship. Although there exists a potential for distancing one from the other, neither can opt to ignore the other completely if it hopes to preserve and expand the basis of its status.

Given the ambiguity and the variations, it may be useful to organize the discussion of these issues in this section by focusing primarily on one marabout's itinerary and evolving relationship with the state over the course of two decades in Fatick. This case can then serve as a point of comparison by which to consider the generalizable aspects of the pattern of relations.

In the brief biographical sketches of local marabouts in chapter 4, I noted that the Tijan marabout *Sërin* Alpha had come to settle in Fatick at the invitation of local officials. The origins and extent of the aid he received, in fact, indicate that his establishment in the town must be understood as an example of the independent state's efforts to encourage local authorities who could serve as intermediaries for the state.[27] Alpha's initial decision to move to Fatick in the late 1960s was undertaken at the initiative of a town official, the *Secrétaire Municipale à la Mairie*, who first sponsored him after his arrival. Within a couple of years, the prefect (then the highest state official in Fatick itself), whose name was Idi Karas Bocoum, suggested that Alpha should set up his own household, and arranged for him to be granted a lot in the next *lotissement*. Bocoum's successor continued the sponsorship, and Alpha eventually received a large lot on the edge of town, where he would have room to expand his activities. The next step of constructing a permanent dwelling was made possible when Alpha was given a gift of two tons of cement by the Senegalese Minister of Culture of the time, a native of Fatick named Alioune Sène.[28] Sène also funded a trip to Mecca for the *hajj*, which of course added to *Sërin* Alpha's status. Thanks to this support, therefore, within a few years of his arrival as a relatively young man *Sërin* Alpha was well established as a religious figure of some stature in the town.

The personal convictions of officials certainly played a role in Alpha's establishment; the *secrétaire municipale* who made the initial contact, for example, was apparently committed to bringing someone capable of providing solid religious instruction to Fatick. But the efforts of state officials to help him get established were also part of a pattern of setting up religious intermediaries. In Fatick there were several parallel concessions, involving important government officials, made to strengthen the local position of the Mouride order in the same period. During his brief tenure as governor of the old region of Sine-Saloum, before his appointment to the president's staff in 1963, Abdou Diouf paid a visit to *Sëriñ* Cissé, the Mouride marabout who still heads that community in Fatick. At about this time *Sëriñ* Cissé wrote a letter to the town's mayor requesting the concession of a lot of land for the Mouride community to use as a meeting and prayer place. The mayor in turn approached then Prime Minister Mamadou Dia with the request, and the Mourides were allotted a large lot of land near the center of town.[29] Then a few years later, Idi Karas Bocoum, the prefect who had been instrumental in *Sëriñ* Alpha's establishment on his own lot, granted the Mourides another large lot on which to build a school and a Mouride center. Named *Kër Sëriñ Touba* (the house of the marabout from Touba, i.e., Amadou Bamba), the lot was closed in by a cement wall and a large gate, and over the years various buildings have gradually been constructed. By the mid-1980s, however, the economic downturn had halted further progress and the rooms stand empty and unused. Although they have fallen short of their ambitious plans, the Mourides benefited from the state's interest in aiding the spread of what seemed to be the most useful of maraboutic communities. We see in Fatick, then, that the effort to revive and integrate a town that had become a relatively insignificant commercial backwater into the new post-independence Senegal involved at times the participation of high-level state officials in the establishment and expansion of maraboutic communities. While in the case of *Sëriñ* Alpha the aid was mostly personalized, and in the case of the Mourides it was directed more generally at the local members of the order, this should not be misleading. In both cases the effort was to establish and reinforce the material bases of maraboutic authority. In dealing with the more centralized and cohesive Mourides, this could be done most effectively by means that encouraged the order's local expansion, and hence strengthened the potential extent of the *xalifa-général's* authority.

Although they may have received state aid in their establishment, however, this in no way guaranteed the subservience of marabouts to state interests. On the contrary, the demonstrated willingness (indeed eagerness) of the state to cater to maraboutic interests might easily serve to reinforce maraboutic cognizance of their utility to the state, and hence a sense of their capability for exerting significant leverage in the relationship. Such questions of perception and evaluation, of course, are inherently difficult to measure and define. What is certain, however, is that even when the state has been instrumental in advancing their careers, marabouts have not been automatically willing to relinquish their autonomy. In this respect *Sëriñ* Alpha is again illustrative. Over the course of the years Alpha has developed highly tenuous and occasionally even conflictive relations with subsequent state officials in Fatick.

Alpha's posture is built both on his understanding of the proper relationship between the realms of politics and religion (they should respect each other but remain distinct), and on his evaluation of the comportment of the specific political regime in question (the politicians of the new generation have enriched themselves, and locked away in their air-conditioned rooms in Dakar they have forgotten the Senegalese masses). Although hardly a political activist, Alpha is nevertheless willing to express his opinions publicly. As a result, he has been tagged by state officials as one of the local marabouts likely to question and perhaps even resist state policy decisions – and one they would today happily do without. One state official labelled Alpha *the* marabout in Fatick most likely to cause difficulties for the state. Interestingly, the comment was made in response to my anonymous reporting of a statement by a different marabout, on which I asked the official to comment. The somewhat critical tone of the statement led him to guess that Alpha was the source. Another official, who had invited Alpha to speak on the question of water and purification in Islam in conjunction with a public health program, generalized his dissatisfaction with the outcome of that experience to regret more broadly the need to work through marabouts at all, whom, he said, "no one elected anyway."[30]

In the specific case of *Sëriñ* Alpha, part of the tension with state officials must be attributed to the marabout's stated refusal to collaborate in questionable activities in the pursuit of mutual gain. He is in fact highly critical of what he describes as state efforts to corrupt marabouts by gifts that are only meant to recruit the marabout and his *taalibes* for political purposes, as well as of marabouts who compromise themselves in this manner. An incident which Alpha readily recounts is highly telling of how this occasionally occurs.[31] Alpha once received a letter from an acquaintance in a ministry in Dakar, informing him that as a marabout with a large number of dependants (*njaboot*) to support, Alpha would be granted some rice that was available as free aid. When he arrived in the town of Kahone to see about receiving it, the official in charge proposed that Alpha take an extra large share – as much as three tons – sell it, and share the profits with the official. Alpha refused to take part in this scheme, and was eventually sent away with only a fifty-kilo sack, a quantity he justified accepting since it would be used exclusively to feed those for whom he was responsible. Alpha's principled stance may be exceptional, but it does point to the fact that the state cannot always count on maraboutic cooperation even in such endeavors.

A more generalizable manifestation of the ambivalence in the state's relationship with Alpha, and a central source of his dissatisfaction with the state, concerns the question of the official status of the Arabic-language school which is Alpha's primary concern. The school was founded in 1971, shortly after Alpha's arrival in Fatick, and has been functioning with some ups and downs since then. The student fees of 1000 FCFA per month are paid directly to the teachers, whom Alpha must subsidize for food and housing if they are to survive.[32] The school offers students the opportunity to study through the *brevet*, the state certificate necessary for admission to a *lycée*, though few have gone that far. Despite its modesty, the school is relatively successful by local standards. Indeed, at the Ndiaye-Ndiaye mosque across town, the imam's daughter has started a small school with Alpha's help which is officially organized (in terms of the necessary permits) as a branch of his school.

Relations with state officials, however, are marked by a constant struggle which appears to be aimed at maintaining limits on Alpha's influence. This must be understood in the light of the long history of discussions and negotiations in Senegal concerning the place of "Arabo-Islamic" schools in the country's educational system. While such schools can be recognized legally, they must meet numerous conditions imposed by the state and conform to a state-dictated curriculum.[33] The reluctance to relinquish control over a domain as important as education, however, has led to regular, if subtle, obstruction of Arabic language education by the state. In Alpha's case, the major source of frustration has been his inability to secure the particular status which would allow state officials to collect the educational subsidy of 2000 FCFA per month for sending their children to his school. Although all of his papers are in order with the Regional Inspector of the Ministry of Education, the police, and the Governor's office, bureaucratic hurdles of various sorts have regularly prevented him from getting this status, something which he believes would add significantly to the appeal of his school.

Even the arrangements concerning the physical organization of the school reflect the currently uneasy coexistence of the state and the marabout. The classrooms for the school are located in a privately owned old colonial building near the defunct port, and there are also several classes belonging to one of the nearby state schools housed in the same building. At one time the building was lent by its owner to the state, which then in turn conceded several rooms to Alpha. Concerned that the state might at some point displace him, however, Alpha approached the owner of the building and was able to secure the reverse situation: the building is now officially lent to Alpha, and it is he who in turn grants the state use of part of the building.

This cohabitation, uneasy though it may be at times, points to the fundamental understanding concerning their interdependence which both parties share. While Alpha could perhaps not be categorized as "typical" of marabouts in Fatick in his specific attitude towards the state, he is certainly not exceptional in the acceptance of the established formal patterns of interaction with the state. (In any case, as we shall see, there is little uniformity in these attitudes.) In particular, despite his ambivalence Alpha shares the general maraboutic recognition of the need to reach a *modus vivendi* with the state, based on the fact that both sides depend on each other. The widespread recognition of this mutual need in spite of underlying tensions is the basis for the pattern of formalized relations and interactions, symbolically legitimating each other's authority, which are almost universally followed in interactions between state and marabouts.

I have already noted that state officials are always prominently represented at the many religious ceremonies and rituals. In addition, on important religious feastdays, especially on *Korite* (*Id al-fitr*, the end of the Ramadan fast), *Tabaski* (*Id al-adha*, the feast of Abraham's sacrifice), and *Mawlud* (the Prophet's birthday), state officials are obliged to make the rounds to visit marabouts within their jurisdiction. What is particularly significant is that these practices, which began with Governor de Coppet's policy of making such visits to the most important marabouts of the country during the colonial period, have been extended today to include marabouts at even the most localized level. These visits, in addition, must usually include a large and important delegation of officials. In the typical pattern, the marabout will arrange chairs and a reception area and will be accompanied by local *taalibes*, perhaps engaged in religious chanting, while awaiting the arrival of the delegation.

The visits, of course, indicate the government's recognition of the marabout's importance, and as such are a source of prestige for a marabout. They must, therefore, be large and public; "At least ten cars were parked at my door!" bragged one local marabout recounting the importance of the delegation that had visited him on the *Korite* feastday.[34] Despite the fact that it has become increasingly onerous, time-consuming and expensive, this practice has become an absolute obligation for local officials, which they dare not ignore. As one rather critical official explained it, "if we do not visit the marabouts, they will write to the big marabouts at Touba, Tivaouane, or elsewhere, and complain that the governor and his staff do not pay sufficient attention to them. If the big marabouts then complain to the government in Dakar, we risk considerable political problems."[35]

A more materially significant practice that has also emerged as an expected pattern in state dealings with marabouts – and an especially interesting one in light of my argument in the previous chapter – is the state's role in facilitating the organization and execution of ritual ceremonies. I have noted the sometimes massive collaboration of the state in major national ceremonies through contributions in such areas as transport and security. And again, this practice has extended to include official participation in the numerous such ceremonies at the local level. *Sëriñ* Alpha, despite his ambivalent attitudes towards the state, noted quite matter-of-factly that *of course* religious leaders were obliged to deal with the state, since it is the state which provides them with the materials necessary for their activities. For a *gàmmu*, he noted, you need electricity, wiring and an amplification system, perhaps a tent or chairs, maybe even the services of the police – all of which must be secured from the state. State officials, in turn, are very careful to meet these expectations. The secretary to the prefect commented to me that it was fortunate that no state-sponsored wrestling matches were planned for the night during the season when *Sëriñ* Diakhaté had scheduled his second *gàmmu*, and thus no conflict existed over who should have use of the amplification system. In any case, he noted, there would have been little choice; state patronage of popular sport activities is important, but the marabout would of course get priority because "c'est la politique d'abord," politics comes first.[36]

Sources of dissatisfaction

Political considerations have maintained these patterns, and to date there has never been a coordinated assault on maraboutic power by the state in Senegal. But although many officials are more or less resigned to the need to deal with marabouts on a regular basis, there is no enthusiasm for the system. At no point in interviews with state officials did any of them even imply that the advantages for the administration outweighed the disadvantages of working through marabouts. On the contrary, although the public rhetoric at ceremonies tends to extol the help of marabouts in the "development of the country," in private discourse there are regular complaints and critiques of the need to deal with marabouts in administrative work. This dissatisfaction, which feeds the long-term goal of bypassing the marabouts to interact directly with the population, has various sources. Personal, ideological, and political reasons are all noted by officials critical of the system.

While seemingly somewhat idiosyncratic, the complaints of officials about the personal inconveniences of having to deal with marabouts should not be discounted, if only because they predispose officials to accept other arguments for their objections. Many officials expressed their dislike of having to spend significant portions of their time on symbolic visits to and ritual interactions with marabouts. On the major feastdays a large number of local officials, from the governor down, are all obliged to make the rounds from one marabout to the other. Since the regional or departmental delegation may well have to visit marabouts in various towns, virtually the entire day can be spent in these activities. In addition, given the large number of ceremonies organized by marabouts, functionaries are also regularly obliged to attend many such events throughout the year, usually well after midnight when the crowd has gathered, or at the very least to contribute in some way to such ceremonies. One mid-level official who declined to attend *Sëriñ* Alpha's annual *gàmmu*, for example, nevertheless sent ten kilos of sugar in response to the *"carte d'honneur"* he had received inviting him.[37] These constant demands on their time and resources are frequently resented by state officials, who blame the inconveniences on the excessive power of marabouts in domains which properly belong to the state.

The perceived need to pursue a policy of secularization, that is, to establish and maintain the separation of the temporal and the spiritual domains, forms the major ideological argument espoused by state officials in their critique of the current system. The notion of the secular state has been one of the pillars of Senegalese independence, and it is one that is virtually unquestioned within the administration. This sentiment is at times reinforced by a French-style anticlericalism which is rarely articulated publicly today, but is nevertheless very much alive among Senegal's small Westernized segment of the population – from which the state's staff is recruited. Writing before Abdou Diouf's accession to the presidency, Coulon cited the thesis on Islam in Wolof society which Diouf had written as a student at the Ecole Nationale de la France d'Outre-mer shortly before independence. "The majority of marabouts," the future president wrote, "are ignorant of the notion of the public good; they are nothing but feudal lords [*des féodaux*] who represent absolutely nothing and who live only in the pursuit of their own interests."[38] Discussing the ideology of the political party which brought Senegal to independence (the precursor to today's Parti Socialiste) Behrman echoed this rhetoric: "The philosophy of the UPS leaders leaves no room for privileged feudal lords like the marabouts."[39] Such stinging remarks were quickly muted as the realities of politics obliged more diplomatic language, but the ideological foundations of these critiques are still widely shared.

Finally, officials frequently point to political and administrative reasons for disliking the system of working through marabouts. There is particular frustration with the fact that the need to take marabouts into account in formulating technical developmental decisions interferes with the implementation of policy goals. An example given by the prefect is typical of the sort of maraboutic leverage in policy domains which officials regularly regret. The question of insuring that peasants save an appropriate stock of seed for the following year, he said, is a technical agricultural issue which should have *nothing* to do with religion. Yet state development agents frequently find themselves obliged to go through religious figures for these purposes. And the result is that in addition to interfering with the efficient exercise of administrative tasks, "religious chiefs come to think they are essential, and then they become demanding," he complained.[40] Tellingly, as an illustration of what religious leaders might demand in return for their collaboration, the prefect pointed to the necessary support, materials and infrastructure for *gàmmus*, *màggals*, and *jàngs*.

The combination of personal, ideological and administrative complaints about maraboutic power are at the base of the long term goal of secularization, which I have already indicated. From the point of view of state officials, secularization is an essential component of development, although whether it is considered a necessary precondition or a side-effect is not always clear. In any case, the belief in the interlinked nature of these processes and the desire to pursue both can be traced back to the expansion of state goals at independence to include direct incorporation and transformation in addition to the colonial goal of domination. In discussing the ideology of the political elite in the first few years of independence, Behrman pointed to the manner in which the goal of development led to a secular ideology committed to the marginalization of maraboutic power:

> The politicians are ... working toward the modern development of Senegal, a goal that may well destroy a large part of the Muslim leaders' power. Furthermore, UPS [party] leaders are continually trying to win the support of the people in Senegal apart from their leaders ... In the long run they would like to be able to offset the traditional leaders with a block of popular votes not dependent on the marabus.[41]

Of course, the more immediate need to deal with marabouts results in a high degree of ambivalence in the expression of such sentiments by state officials. But these goals have nevertheless remained central to the exercise of state power in Senegal.

The autobiographical memoirs of a former Senegalese prefect provide an insightful example of the way this interpretation informed state attitudes towards a particularly important maraboutic movement in the upper Casamance region.[42] During the three years in the early 1980s when he was posted as prefect in the department of Velingara, Abdourahmane Konaté found the "essential task of development" complicated by conflicts which stemmed from what Konaté referred to as the "religious totalitarianism" of a local marabout. The marabouts in charge of the highly isolated religious community of Médina Gounass have always maintained a cautious distance from the state. "A simple contract seemed to regulate relations between the religious community and the holders of temporal power: 'We will turn over the taxes,' this community said to the administration, 'but leave us alone.'"[43] Not content with such an arrangement, which effectively isolated the town's population from state control, Konaté saw it as his task upon arriving as prefect to "establish [faire prévaloir] the primacy of the state." In his description, this goal is both aided by and essential to the process of modernization. He attributes conflict within the community to the decision by certain younger members to "adapt themselves to the practices of modern life." And "modern" politics leads naturally to secularization in his view: "The reform and the democratic opening favored by the multiparty political system provided ... the opportunity for finalizing the divorce with the spiritual guide."[44]

Konaté is diplomatic and cautious in his wording – the community after all is not only still very powerful but also pays its taxes. He somewhat ambiguously claims to have found a compromise allowing for good relations with the new marabout (who succeeded upon his father's death in 1980) by holding to "a simple principle: establishing the respect due to religions and to their chiefs and the respect of individual human rights, both recognized in the Constitution of the State."[45] But it is clear that although recognizing the need to continue to work with the maraboutic authorities for the time being, the prefect's long-term vision – and goal – is the preeminent one for the state: a secularized society in which the administration will be able to reach local populations directly, without the need for maraboutic intermediaries.

Engagement, isolation, contestation: Sufi style

Caught between the state's ambivalence – resulting from the immediate incentives to collaborate and the long-term desire to marginalize – and their own need to maintain the allegiance of disciples, marabouts react in various ways. I have argued in the preceding chapters that marabouts must always keep an eye on popular opinion if they are to preserve the followings which translate into leverage with the state. Likewise, religious elites must constantly define and redefine their relationship with the state if they are to preserve the position as privileged intermediaries which constitutes part of their attraction to disciples. As a result, and as I have already indicated in various cases, no single pattern defines maraboutic attitudes towards the state in Senegal. The ambivalence of positions on all sides means that each must react to the other as conditions change.

Marabouts, for their part, must demonstrate flexibility in their responses to state actions. Coulon has described how this has been practiced:

The whole political art of the marabouts consists in playing on the ambiguity of their positions in political society: on the one hand by using the resources they procure from the state, and on the other by keeping their distance from the same state. The balance will lean more towards one side or the other depending on the political situation. During normal times, or in the case of a limited crisis, the marabouts will function mainly in collaboration with the state. But if the crisis is more profound, if popular dissatisfaction develops, especially in rural areas, the marabouts will be much more reticent towards the state, although without always going as far as condemning it.[46]

While under normal circumstances the patterns of collaboration prevail, the possibility exists for other modes of interaction.

In the terminology proposed in the theoretical discussion of state-society relations in the first chapter of this book, the predominant pattern in maraboutic interactions with the state has been that of "engagement." Both sides have adhered to patterns of interaction based on established "rules of the game" that both sides accept – albeit at times reluctantly. But, again as I have argued, maintaining this pattern in the face of the state's hegemonic impulses requires an effective capacity to pursue – or at least credibly threaten – alternative responses. Without such alternatives, there exists a real potential for the state to succeed in its goal of marginalizing maraboutic power. As a result, marabouts have regularly attempted to demonstrate their capacity and willingness to limit state power in various ways. The option of "contestation," directly challenging the state's right to define the rules of the game, has been occasionally exercised, and although serious confrontations have been rare, frequent subtle challenges to state authority comprise an implicit constant threat of a more direct challenge. Perhaps more importantly the potential for "isolation," refusing to acknowledge the validity of state-imposed rules, has provided a persistent theme in maraboutic dealings with the state. The variable recourse to these options has been central to negotiating the balance between state and society in Senegal.

Patterns of engagement

While engagement has tended to dominate as the primary pattern of interaction in the marabout-state relationship, the specific forms of such interactions vary in accordance with numerous factors. Most important is the calculation of how disciples will respond. As Coulon concludes in the passage cited above: "If some marabouts continue to support the government in such a context [of popular dissatisfaction], they risk their authority,

because in all of Senegalese political culture ... the marabouts are associated with a protective role against oppressive powers."[47] Being thus
obliged to strike certain postures in accord with popular sentiment to
maintain their followings, marabouts in effect serve as the representatives
of broad societal sentiment *vis-à-vis* state actions. And concern for disciples
will not only inform a marabout's relations with the state as a whole, but it
may in addition lead religious leaders to distinguish between elements of the
state in defining the nature of their ties.

A telling illustration of this in Fatick is provided by the contrast drawn by
the state regional medical officer between the governor's position and his
own in terms of relations with marabouts in the town. The governor, he
noted, is obliged to be much more solicitous of the marabouts and cater to
them by such means as regular attendance at ceremonies. He, on the
contrary, could afford to maintain a greater distance and allow the
marabouts to take the initiative in cultivating ties with him instead. This, he
pointed out, was due to his greater utility to marabouts in their relations
with disciples. If he were to have a sick *taalibe*, who did not have the
resources or connections necessary to get access to the medical officer on his
own, a marabout who maintains good ties can serve as an intermediary to
arrange such access. Thus, in addition to helping the sick individual, the
marabout is able to reinforce the loyalty of the disciple to his benefit.[48]
While a relationship of engagement with the governor proceeds directly
from a marabout's importance in terms of his influence over disciples,
satisfactory engagement with the medical officer – who controls more
important resources from the limited perspective of local marabouts – may
require the active solicitude of the marabout.

These factors mean that within the broad range of specific actions
encompassed by the engagement mode there is a high degree of variation.
Marabouts play on the ambiguities of the relationship to attempt to
preserve the involvement and dependence of the state, while limiting the
expansion of state power in ways that would result in the erosion of
maraboutic authority. Even in the restricted context of Fatick we thus see
significant variations in local maraboutic attitudes towards the state, some
of which have been touched on already. I have discussed above *Sëriñ*
Alpha's ambivalent position; while seeing no alternative to engagement
with the state, Alpha is distrustful of the state's interpretation of this
relationship. In his view, engagement should include a clear definition of
separate domains of authority for each. He is thus willing to cooperate and
to grant certain realms to the state, but he demands in return that other
realms be exempted from state authority. His distrust and dissatisfaction
stems from the recognition that his demands clash with the state's interest in
extending its direct influence over society. *Sëriñ* Cissé and his Mouride

disciples, by contrast, tend to concern themselves much less with defining the borders between state power and that of the marabouts. The high degree of cohesion of the order and its well tested strengths translate into a confident sense that the state is highly unlikely to be able to dislocate maraboutic positions for the foreseeable future, and consequently a simple disregard for much state initiative. Engagement on the Mouride model, instead, tends to center on direct exchanges based on explicit demands for material goods and benefits.[49]

A still different attitude towards the state is struck by *Sëriñ* Baldé, who follows in this respect his Sy family patrons, the sons of the late *xalifa* Ababacar. As we have already seen in the biographical sketches of local marabouts, Baldé has by far the closest relationship with the state of all marabouts in Fatick. He alone expresses unambivalent praise for the installation of the new region in Fatick, and he readily extols the work of state officials in the causes of peace and development. At the time of the 1988 elections Baldé headed the local committee of the national organization founded by Cheikh Tidiane Sy in support of the reelection of President Abdou Diouf. He received in this capacity a large amount of fabric printed with the movement's logo from SOTIBA, the major Senegalese textile enterprise, which he distributed as part of the campaign.[50] As a result, Baldé has emerged as the preferred marabout among local state officials, who do not hesitate to praise him as an "intellectual and modern marabout," in contrast to some others "who think having prayer beads and a turban is enough for them to call themselves real marabouts."[51] Engagement with the state for *Sëriñ* Baldé signifies a direct and collaborative participation in state-initiated activities.

Despite these seemingly very different attitudes, however, all marabouts share a primary concern for maintaining an intermediary position that will ensure them a place between the state and the population it attempts to incorporate. Variations in maraboutic orientations are based on varying evaluations of the best means of ensuring such a position. At times religious leaders may espouse pragmatic reasons for the centrality of the marabouts' intermediary role. In this vein a Niassène Tijan marabout and a group of important *taalibe* in Kaolack made a strong argument that not only the Senegalese government, but even foreign aid agencies, could only be successful in promoting development if they worked through marabouts, "the true representatives of the people."[52] The commonalities underlying the variations in maraboutic evaluations of their positions is illustrated by the contrasting answers offered by two local marabouts to the direct question of what the political role of marabouts should be. The job of marabouts, according to *Sëriñ* Baldé, is to *help the state in its dealings with people* (adding that of course the state should also help marabouts), while

Sërñ Diakhaté answers instead that marabouts' role is to *help people deal with the state*.[53] Each finds himself more closely allied with one or the other, but both agree that they should be positioned between the two to provide a linkage, a basis of engagement, between state and population.

Contestations: active and passive

As I have argued and as Coulon indicates in the passage cited above, however, maintaining an intermediary position requires not only a formula for effective engagement with the state, but also a basis for a continued appeal to disciples. And at times such a basis may require that marabouts break the pattern of engagement to either challenge the state directly or to move to shield local populations from state actions. These alternatives, of course, have been only rarely exercised in their most radical form. Within the ambiguities I have discussed, the pattern of engagement and interaction between political and religious authorities has been remarkably stable in Senegal. One can point to various reasons for this stability. In part, no doubt, the relative rarity of direct Muslim challenges to the state in Senegal is due to the highly "conformist" nature of the version of Sufi Islam which was carefully cultivated by colonial officials, and further encouraged by the independent state.[54] Marabouts, however, have not been simple lackeys of the state, as should be apparent in the discussion by now. The stability of the relationship must also be attributed in large part to the fact that the mutual recognition of each side's strength has led each to respect the well-established system of interaction. This system allows for the reconciliation of differences within the established parameters of engagement, and it is precisely the constant redefinitions of the nature and limits of the relationship which produce the ambiguities noted above.

Importantly, the parameters of the relationship have been defined on the one hand by demonstrations of maraboutic potential to threaten the system itself, and on the other by the demonstrated limits of maraboutic power. Several important "test cases" have been central to the definition of these parameters within the context of independent Senegal, and although more recent years have seen few direct confrontations, more subtle reminders of the potential regularly mark maraboutic interactions with the state. The first tests of relative maraboutic strength *vis-à-vis* the Senegalese state arose, quite naturally, at the transition to independence. I have discussed above the marabouts' success at the time of the 1958 referendum in forcing the political elite to adopt a posture defined in accordance with perceived maraboutic interests. In the following period leading up to full independence, the political activity of the marabouts on such issues as the shape of the constitution further demonstrated the need for the political elite to cautiously weigh maraboutic concerns. But their failure to maintain a united front in challenging the political elite also showed the limits of maraboutic strength. The basis for a new version of the system of shared authority was thus set.

A more important case of maraboutic contestation that is still debated in Senegal and which was central to the further demarcation of the relative strength of each side was the struggle surrounding the adoption of the new legal code on family issues, the *Code de la Famille*, which was championed by Senghor. The laws regulating such domains as marriage, polygamy, divorce, inheritance, and women's status, have frequently been among the most readily politicized issues in Muslim societies, due to their centrality in the corpus of Muslim law, the *shari'a*. In Indonesia, for example, Piscatori notes that the "usually compliant" *ulama* "reacted very strongly against the government's attempt to implement a new marriage law that would have departed significantly from Islamic family law."[55] And in "socialist" Algeria the process that finally resulted in the passing of a relatively conservative family code in 1986 after years of debate also demonstrated the importance of this issue to Muslim leaders.[56] Similarly in Senegal the French-inspired code proposed by the state elicited the immediate and vocal opposition of the country's religious elite.[57]

The Conseil Supérieur des Chefs Religieux which had been created to contest various elements of the proposed constitution in 1958 virtually ceased to exist almost immediately following independence, due largely to the rivalries among the orders and maraboutic families that comprised its membership. Ten years later, however, in 1970, when the government first announced the proposed *Code de la Famille*, the united maraboutic front quickly resurfaced under the name Conseil Supérieur Islamique du Sénégal to express its opposition. The extent of maraboutic activity and organization in contesting the law was unprecedented, and the group launched direct challenges to the law both before and after its eventual adoption. Tellingly, the marabouts pointed out that this action, which they considered an attack by the state on their domain, was a departure from the colonial system which by comparison had demonstrated a higher degree of respect for their authority.[58] In this they were certainly correct; the code was constructed as a central component of the state's goal of transforming Senegal in accordance with a vision of a "modern" country and, as such, signaled again a departure from the bases of colonial practice.

The Conseil set up three commissions to study the proposed laws and make recommendations concerning it. Three separate documents were drawn up as a result: one categorically rejecting the proposition in its entirety; a second which pointed out each of the articles deemed to be in contradiction with the *shari'a*, and noting in each case the position of

Muslim law on that point; and the third critiquing the document and suggesting the addition of a special advisory chamber on religious matters to the National Assembly, as well as listing without comment over eighty articles in the proposed code which contradicted Muslim law. This third document was presented by the Conseil to the government in January of 1971, and the marabouts made clear their expectations that their voice be heard before any further action was taken.[59]

When it appeared that despite their opposition the government was to go ahead with its plans to adopt a version of the code, the Conseil followed with another letter regretting that, although they had "the right to expect it," the revised project to be soon considered by the National Assembly had not been submitted to their inspection, and emphasizing once again their position. This letter merits citing for the cautiously polite but nevertheless unwavering, and indeed subtly threatening, tone which it adopts:

We insist on specifying that it is absolutely not and will not be our intention to insinuate ourselves [nous inféoder] into the management of the nation's affairs, which falls on you by the sovereign will of the people.

But by virtue of the obligations that result from the roles assigned to us by our religious positions, we must necessarily remove any ambiguity about our position by solemnly reaffirming our unshakeable conviction *to categorically reject any measure, even an official one, which does not respect the sacred principles of our religion.*

It is true that Islam includes recommendations that can be accommodated to local circumstances, but it also incorporates *obligatory and immutable prescriptions that nothing can change for whatever reason.*

Under the circumstances it seemed to us appropriate to be clear on this matter so that your decision might be made in full knowledge of the facts.[60]

Despite this final warning, however, the code was indeed adopted in 1972 without maraboutic input. This outcome must be understood in light of the extreme importance attached to the family code measure by the state, and particularly by Senghor himself. At various times Senghor stated categorically that the code could not be amended under any circumstances, claiming that it was the result of ten years of work.[61] The conflict over the *Code de la Famille* thus seemed to define the upper limits of the power of marabouts to contest state actions.

The victory of the state, however, was more apparent than real. Marabouts were still left with the alternative I have called "isolation," a means of limiting state power which, by its very nature, is more difficult for the state to resist and counteract. Indeed, in the case of the family code, the potential for falling back on isolation must be understood as central to the lack of any further significant maraboutic reaction to this apparent setback. Following its passage by the National Assembly, several marabouts publicly proclaimed that they would in effect simply isolate their disciples from its impact. In matters of marriage, divorce, or inheritance, disciples were directed to turn to the marabouts rather than the state judicial system. And the *xalifa* of the Mourides announced that the code would not reach the town of Touba.[62] The years since then have demonstrated the effectiveness of the tactic. Coulon notes the official finding by the president of the Supreme Court some five years after its adoption that "the family code is not rigidly applied in our countryside," a dramatic understatement.[63]

Recent research by Amsatou Sow Sidibé not only confirms the continuity of this pattern, but indicates how the state has been obliged to make *de facto* concessions. One example from her study of the application of the code is based on inheritance cases in a Dakar legal jurisdiction, one where Westernization is likely to be significantly higher than elsewhere in the country. Of 4,607 cases considered, not even ten percent were decided in accordance with "modern" law. By contrast, in 4,150 (some ninety percent) of the cases, the "exceptional" system of Muslim law was applied. Sow Sidibé is led to conclude: "The goal sought by the Senegalese state, in this case the search for the economic and social development of the country, is commendable. Nevertheless, the method utilized, that of Westernizing the law, does not appear to be appropriate ... The wary reaction of the population is made evident by the statistics. Modern law has not entered common practice."[64] Still committed to the original goals, however, the state is obliged to campaign actively to attempt to secure anything more than nominal compliance with the code. Such efforts as the visits by the group of young lawyers to Fatick discussed in chapter 3 attests to the continued quest by the state to give some empirical reality to its juridical decision.

The isolationist potential has remained absolutely central as a limiting device on state power in Senegal. The highly restricted resources of the state effectively undercut the potential for any forced compliance with state initiatives in most domains, a move that in any case would almost certainly be met with active resistance and contestation. In the context of Senegalese poverty, the simple refusal to acknowledge state-imposed rules grants a high degree of societal autonomy. This tactic is all the more powerful because of the possibility of defining an ideological basis for it in Islamic thought, in the concept of *hijra*. In its literal sense the concept has been used in the Senegambia, as throughout the Muslim world. In the mid-nineteenth century El Hajj Umar called on the inhabitants of areas that had been occupied by the French to flee to Muslim areas, and he thereby "crystallized the imperative of *hijra* (emigration) for Senegalese Muslims, an imperative which was obeyed throughout the late nineteenth century."[65] And in its more figurative sense implying a distancing from illegitimate authority the concept has also supplied a justification for the postures of maraboutic movements in Senegal. In discussing the range of responses based on "Islamic doctrine" and taken by Muslim leaders to colonial rule, Harrison notes that of "the alternative strategies open to all Muslims the possibility of withdrawing from political life altogether and attempting to restrict contact with the colonizing power to a minimum was more common than outright hostility."[66] This trend continues today. In the case of Médina Gounass discussed above, the community has explicitly appealed to disciples on the basis of practicing *hijra* from the Senegalese state. Likewise in the maraboutic movement which will be discussed in the final chapter the concept lends ideological legitimacy.

Certainly the most significant use of the isolationist potential is that of the Mouride marabouts in their fief at Touba. The town provides the very paradigm of a maraboutic state-within-a-state, and by extension Mouride activities even outside the physical boundaries of the city are often effectively off-limits to state control. As a result the town has long served as a center of parallel market activities in Senegal. The well-known isolation goes so far, for example, that in a technical discussion of the peanut trade in Senegal, a state official commenting on the ban on peanut processing by private enterprises could remark quite casually that, of course, this did not apply to Touba.[67] The resulting sense of the order's autonomy is at times virtually flaunted by its leaders. At the occasion of the *grand màggal* in 1988 and 1989, large banners draped throughout the city of Touba proclaimed in Arabic, French, Wolof, and English: "The day of the *màggal* is the celebration of our independence." Despite the ambiguity of the possessive, the banners could only refer to *Mouride* independence – presumably from any other authority, including the state.

Within the well-established parameters which have emerged, more indirect techniques of contestation and isolation maintain maraboutic power *vis-à-vis* the state. Coulon speaks of "silent maraboutic contestations," including the potential for marabouts in the peanut zone to advise their disciples to concentrate on consumption crops, namely millet, in response to state decisions on marketing or pricing.[68] And much less materially significant but politically important symbolic acts of defiance also serve to mark the inherent potential for confrontation. Antecedents to the use of such "popular modes of political action" can again be found in the French colonial experience in West Africa.

Harrison documents the fascinating case of the controversial *Shaykh* Hamallah's relations with colonial officials in the inter-war period. Fearful of Hamallah's supposed contestatory potential, the marabout's ritual practice of repeating a specific Tijan prayer eleven rather than the usual twelve times became a virtual obsession of French officials, who came to refer to the movement as the *Tidjaniya onze grains* for its adherents' shortened prayer beads. In 1936, upon his return from ten years of French-imposed exile, Hamallah adopted another controversial ritual practice, that of abridging his prayers, a practice said to be allowed to Muslims only when travelling, threatened, or at war. Again the French saw a threat to their rule in the symbolic practice. Harrison cites a colonial report: "Even if he does not himself go so far as to indulge in specifically criminal activity that would justify a sanction, he makes use of indirect means, which superficially bear the marks of detachment and disdain but which are carefully thought out and adapted to achieve the required aim."[69] These French fears clearly indicate the political significance and power of symbolic gestures organized by leaders of social forces which escape state domination.

Although less directly threatening in intent or perception, one might point as a contemporary parallel to such symbolically powerful activity to the constant controversy concerning the announcement of the dates of feastdays. The frequent discrepancy between initial official announcements and the actual date of celebrations is widely interpreted as a maraboutic statement about the state's inability to control or dictate in certain matters. The issue, in fact, seems at times to be manipulated intentionally to embarrass the state. In 1988, for example, the official government daily, *Le Soleil*, announced in banner headlines the date for the *grand màggal* several days in advance, and then had to rectify when the marabouts of the order announced it instead for one day later. Likewise the following year, the paper also carried headlines announcing that all of the orders would celebrate *Tamxarit*, the new year, on the same day, only to have the Mourides postpone their celebration by one day. Since this feast falls on the tenth day of the lunar month and the government announcement had only come two days in advance, the discrepancy cannot be attributed to different sightings of the moon. Such incidents are in fact very common, and must be understood as intentional defiances of the state by the marabouts, most frequently in these cases the Mourides.[70] The political elite in Senegal are thus constantly reminded of their limited control over maraboutic power.

The ambiguity of relations between state and marabouts is thus heightened, and as we have seen this distrust extends down to the local level. Because of the network of connections which unites component parts of the system, the important battles that have been fought at the top have served to define the major parameters of the patterns of interaction at all levels of state-society relations. These patterns, we have seen, are at times ambiguous and are constantly subject to negotiation and manipulation, but they have also been remarkably stable. While in certain important domains the state has demonstrated its capacity to stand up to maraboutic opposition and impose its decisions, the marabouts have also demonstrated their capacity for effectively limiting the state's hegemonic power over society. While stable, therefore, the arrangement is one with which the state remains uneasy and dissatisfied. And this dissatisfaction is complicated by another source of challenges to the system, which the state must also factor into its calculations.

Playing with fire: flirting with the alternatives

In Senegal, as in various neighboring Muslim countries, a segment of the population has come to espouse a variety of Islamic ideologies loosely labeled "reformist" and notable primarily for being critical of the established system. The origins of reformist movements are religious, arising from a perception that there exist "major threats to Islam in the prevailing participation in religious brotherhoods and in various maraboutic practices."[71] But such an ideology quickly comes to include a political component, particularly in the context of the close relations between the two realms in Senegal. The existence of reformist critics has dogged Senegalese politics from the colonial period. And for various reasons – not all internal to Senegal – by the early 1980s there was a widespread belief that the apparent "resurgence" or "renewal" of Islam and the seeming proliferation of groups espousing this ideology posed a threat (if a somewhat amorphously defined one) to both Senegalese politics and Sufism. By the end of the decade, however, the threat appeared to have receded – or perhaps simply to have been initially rather overstated. Momar Coumba Diop and Mamadou Diouf have linked the increased interest in Islam in Senegal following the Iranian Revolution of 1979 to the "crisis of the regime" which provoked the transition from presidents Senghor to Diouf. They argue, however, that it was the Sufi orders who benefited the most from these events, and that the initial advantage enjoyed by the Mourides in exploiting the situation was countered by the Tijans with help from the state itself.[72]

There is no doubt that the reformist tendency has influenced the shape of both religion and politics in the country. But although the evidence is somewhat sketchy, there also appears to be no basis for the conclusion that it has provoked major changes in the system. From the perspective of Fatick quite the opposite seems to be the case; the maraboutic system remains wholly unchallenged by any organized reformist opposition in the town. The situation, however, is clearly somewhat different elsewhere in the country, notably in major urban areas. Even there, however, the impact of reformism appears to have been quite limited. There is, in fact, reason to believe that the long-term effects may be of strengthening the existing patterns of religion and politics in Senegal.

The impact of the "arabisants"

The origins of reformist groups in Senegal can be traced to the gradual concentration in urban areas of returned students who had been sent abroad to study in the Arab world, frequently at religious centers in Morocco, Algeria, or the ancient university of Al Azhar in Egypt. Because of their Arabic training and acculturation, such people have come to be know as *arabisants* ("arabizers") in the French language literature on Senegal. The integration of these people into an administrative and educational system built on a French model and operating in the French language posed real difficulties, first for the colonial state and then its independent successor. To defend their interests as their number grew in the colony, various associations of *arabisants* were formed, some as early as the 1930s. Their most significant flowering was to come in the 1950s, however, with the founding of the historically most important reformist organization, the Union Culturelle Musulmane, or UCM, which in the years immediately preceding independence was to be the most vocal Muslim critic of both colonialism and the maraboutic system.

Since independence there has been a dual aspect to state relations with the various reformist groups, not unlike state-marabout relations, and with similar origins: these groups are both potentially useful and threatening to the state. Two general reasons can be identified for why the state found it useful to court reformist groups. First, the critique of the maraboutic system espoused by reformists has served the state well as a means of offsetting the power of marabouts. To the extent that the reformist argument concerning the "un-Islamic" nature of ties with a spiritual intermediary like a marabout are accepted, the state can hope to reduce these allegiances and claim some of the hegemonic space denied it by maraboutic power. There is, of course, a risk in encouraging such ideas: the reformist ideology frequently also includes elements of a political critique of such central tenets of Senegalese politics as the secular state. Secondly, *arabisants* have been useful for the state as effective intermediaries at the international level in the quest for aid and influence in international fora based on common Islamic ties.[73] This has been especially significant in Senegal because both Senghor and current president Abdou Diouf have sought (rather successfully) to establish themselves as influential international statesmen in African and Third World, and indeed even broader, circles. Again, however, this strategy carries risks; the cultivation of close ties with Arab and other Muslim countries by the intermediary means of societal groups in Senegal facilitates the possibility of channeling outside aid directly to "radical" religious groups capable of challenging the state.

In attempting to balance these two aspects of dealing with reformist groups – the fear of their possible contestatory nature and the sense of their utility – the state since independence has largely pursued a policy of attempting to coopt *arabisants* in various ways. At the same time, in the search to establish international ties, to manage and supervise the spread of Arabic education, and in dealing with marabouts, the state effectively provoked a significant increase in the number of young *arabisants*. Following independence a greater number of students was sent to pursue formal education in North Africa, many from maraboutic families and provided with state-sponsored scholarships. Given their origins, most pursued studies in religious domains. There was thus a need to find ways to meet the demands of this group upon their return, and the state provided the only recourse for most of them. As Mamadou Ndiaye has described the process: "Upon their return to Senegal, they did not head for the mosques to lead prayers as one might have expected, rather they came to knock on the door of the public services to demand a salaried employment. This placed the Senegalese state in the obligation of finding an adequate solution allowing for their insertion into the economic circuits of the country by granting them employment." And "despite the diversity of their diplomas and specializations," Ndiaye notes, most were eventually employed in education, as teachers of Arabic in the country's secondary schools.[74]

Less numerous but perhaps in some ways more important have been those *arabisants* coopted by receiving a position in a state-sponsored organization either within Senegal or at an international agency or association. This has in effect been practiced primarily in cases of individuals who have been successful in organizing movements or building organizations with the potential to significantly challenge the state, and it has frequently taken the form of state patronage for that movement. As a result, there has been an incentive to undertake such activities in the pursuit of advancement. The reality of these incentives is indicated in the frequently heard mutual recriminations about others "playing the Muslim game" as a means of exploiting state ambivalence and fears and thus securing jobs or other benefits.[75]

Various *arabisant* groups or individuals have at times attempted to develop ties and secure aid from outside Senegal, in particular from sources in the Arab Gulf states or Iran willing to fund Islamic alternatives. The exact extent of such aid remains rather nebulous, but most indications point to a gradual drying up of such funds over the course of the 1980s, if indeed they ever existed in any significant quantities.[76] The fate of the most widely distributed publication of the Islamic press in Senegal, the weekly *Wal Fadjri*, illustrates this trend. The publication is edited by Sidy Lamine Niasse, an *arabisant* from a branch of the maraboutic Tijan family in Kaolack who studied for some time at Al Azhar, where he served as president of the Association of Senegalese Students in Cairo. Like his controversial elder brother Ahmed Khalifa Niasse (known mainly for his failed effort to found an Islamic party in Senegal) Sidy Lamine was involved in numerous political activities in the 1970s and early 1980s. While in Paris in this period he had contact with many Iranians, some of whom allegedly funded him to return to Senegal to found *Wal Fadjri*. The magazine's goal, Sidy Lamine says, is to further the idea that "what is necessary is not to modernize Islam, but rather to Islamize modernity."[77] In its early years the publication had a strongly reformist tone with a distinctly pro-Iranian orientation.[78] Over the course of the decade, however, the journal moved squarely into the mainstream of the Senegalese independent press (indeed, it was among the best of that press), shedding almost completely its reformist tone. It had, in addition, evident fiscal problems, and by the end of the decade Sidy Lamine was attempting to sell an advertising supplement to the American Embassy in Dakar.[79]

The search for outside funding is complicated by the lack of popular appeal of the message propagated by many reformists. The uneasy coexistence of the Sufi majority with reformist groups at the popular level has led to political imbroglios and a relative lack of success of these groups which can only discourage further "investments" by outsiders. In one telling case, a mosque constructed with financial assistance from a prince of one of the Gulf states was eventually closed by political authorities after a dispute disintegrated into violence between Tijan members of the mosque and the adherents of a reformist group with Wahhabist overtones known as the "Mouvement Al-Fallah pour la Culture Islamique Salafiyya."[80] The original impetus for its construction had come from a group of Tijan residents of the Parcelles Assainies neighborhood of Dakar. The group approached the Arab prince, a classmate of the project's organizer who had studied abroad, to request a gift for construction. The money was made available but, wary of the potential for misappropriation, the prince insisted that it be channeled officially through an established organization. The group's leader then approached the Al-Fallah to request that they serve that purpose, and they agreed. The mosque was built and for some time served as a neighborhood mosque for Muslims of all affiliations. Conflict arose, however, when the Tijans, who comprised the majority, began to use the mosque for a uniquely Tijan prayer ritual known as the *wazifa*.[81] The Al-Fallah group, with their "purist" interpretation of Islam, objected to this practice and, claiming control due to their role in the mosque's construction, they attempted to put an end to it. The resulting violence led to the intervention of political authorities, and by order of the prefect the mosque was closed indefinitely.

The conflict with popular religious sentiments which this story illustrates has ultimately been highly influential in the evolution of most such Islamic organizations in Senegal. Those that have adhered to a strictly reformist line have tended to remain limited to a small group of urban Muslims with virtually no resonance among the majority of Senegalese. In addition to the Al-Fallah, another group known as the Jamaatou Ibadou Arrahmane, a UCM offshoot, is the most significant of these. A fascinating seven-page open letter from the head of this organization, Alioune Habiboul Lâh Diouf, who takes the title of "Amir of the Jamaa," provides clear indication of the difficulties faced by these organizations.[82] The document is a spirited defense of the organization, and the opening lines make clear that it has been the subject of serious criticism by other Muslim groups:

> We had never thought for a single instant that our following the path of the Daʿwa ["the call," i.e., the teaching of Islam] would be free of obstacles. But that these obstacles should come more from our brothers in the Daʿwa than from the traditional enemies of Islam is, however, a fact that is both strange and surprising.
>
> We are not led to write these lines because of the false news spread in their press by the Freemasons, Communists, or the Secular Fifth Column with the goal of damaging the good reputation of Islam; rather we are led to this by the persistent rumors circulating in the milieu of the Daʿwa which claim that the Jamaatou Ibadour Rahmane is either of oriental or occidental persuasion, depending on who the spreader of rumors is addressing!!!

The letter continues with a detailed defense of the organization against three specific charges: (1) that it is hostile to the Sufi orders; (2) that it is devoted largely to political activities (and thus presumably not concerned primarily with religion); and (3) that the organization has adopted the Shiʿa legal school. The thrust of the response is that the group is concerned primarily with the defense of Islam against its (secular) enemies, and that it consequently refuses to make distinctions among Muslims because these can only lead to a weakening of the Muslim world. The highly defensive nature of the document demonstrates the vulnerability of reformist organizations to political battles both within Senegal and in the Muslim world at large. It also demonstrates the ultimate need for groups that wish to exert a popular appeal to bring themselves into the mainstream of Senegalese Islamic belief.

The moderating search for a popular appeal

These limitations have meant that only those organizations that have allied themselves more closely with popular sentiment have managed to survive as significant groups. This has come at the expense of getting intertwined with maraboutic organizations, and consequently with the state, and indeed it is these ties which have allowed such groups to survive. The itinerary of the UCM is very telling in this regard. The organization was founded in 1953 by Cheikh Touré, an *arabisant* who was to become known in Senegal for the publication of a reformist tract in the form of a brochure entitled *Afin que tu deviennes croyant* ("That you may become a believer"). The UCM did not immediately declare its opposition to the entire maraboutic system, at least in part for pragmatic considerations, but rather it only argued against certain practices associated with it.[83] Certain marabouts, in fact, affiliated themselves with it from the beginning, many for equally pragmatic reasons.[84] Nevertheless, the UCM eventually emerged under Touré's leadership as a highly vocal critic of the marabouts and in particular of the attitude towards France which provoked maraboutic endorsement of continued ties rather than independence.

Immediately after independence, however, the UCM went into eclipse as Touré was brought into the government in various capacities and as difficulties arose in reconciling the diverse ideological strains which had combined in the organization. Touré was to re-emerge some years later as a sharp critic of Westernization and corruption, using the discourse of reformers elsewhere in the Muslim world. Having vowed never to collaborate with the government again, he heads today a new association called "L'Organisation pour l'Action Islamique," which cautiously appears to advocate the establishment of an Islamic republic in Senegal. Despite his fame, however, he has virtually no popular following. As for the UCM, it has only barely managed to survive over the years by accepting state patronage, and hence control. It is currently led by El Hadj Ahmed Iyane Thiam, an enthusiastic member of the Parti Socialiste who serves as titular president of the organization although he has spent years posted to Morocco as a Senegalese diplomat. Its main activity in recent years has been to organize "cultural weeks" devoted to the hagiography of major maraboutic figures of Senegalese Islam. In Fatick *Sëriñ* Diakhaté was visited by representatives of the UCM to try to recruit him as a member and to discuss his cooperation in the next such conference, which may be devoted to Baye Niasse.[85] It has thus unabashedly moved to a position of accepting the Senegalese Sufi system in its entirety; "Islam is a house in which the rooms are the Sufi orders," its official publication, *Le Reveil Islamique*, has noted.[86]

The largest official organization of Islamic groups in Senegal also demonstrates the close entangling with both the orders and the state. The predecessor to what was to become the Fédération des Associations Islamiques du Sénégal (FAIS) was founded at the eve of independence as an umbrella organization uniting fourteen different Islamic associations in "the defense of the interests of Islam."[87] While it has regularly exhorted a greater adherence to Islamic moral values and practices, the organization has maintained itself squarely at the center of Senegalese religion and politics. Its leadership reflects this orientation; the president of the association since its founding has been Abdoul Aziz Sy Junior and its Secretary General, Moustapha Cissé, is a special counselor to Abdou Diouf who additionally serves as Senegal's ambassador to several Arab states including, since 1989, to the Palestinian state.[88] The association now includes thirty-six different member groups. As one critic has noted, however, these include some "which are nothing more than *daairas* faithfully attached to their religious leader, or [others which are] the results of personal efforts that only unite a few individuals incapable of anything important."[89] Its relative inactivity and extreme closeness to the state has provoked the more recent creation of a rival organization, the Coordination des Associations Islamiques du Sénégal (CAIS). There is little reason, however, to suspect that this group will exert either an increased popular appeal or a greater challenge to the established order.

By the late 1980s, therefore, there were no clearly distinguishable boundaries between maraboutic and reformist Islamic organizations in Senegal. Rather there existed a proliferation of groups with varying degrees of ties to the state on the one hand and to the Sufi orders on the other. (One might even speculate, though the issue would require closer consideration, that these organizations serve as institutional channels for the negotiation of state-marabout relations.) While in some senses the marabouts have "captured" non-Sufi Islamic organizations (as Abdoul Aziz Sy Junior's position shows), in another sense reformist groups seem to have "penetrated" maraboutic structures. One important example in this respect is the Cercle d'Etudes et de Recherches Islam et Développement (CERID) which includes a number of Dakar intellectuals and professionals with ties to virtually all significant maraboutic families in Senegal. The group's members espouse, among other things, the renunciation of the secular state in Senegal, but they are ambiguous about whether an Islamic republic should replace it.

Although it includes Mourides and others among its membership, the group seems to carry special influence in Tivaouane, due in particular to the relationship between one of its members, a cardiologist named Daouda Diouf, and the *xalifa* Abdoul Aziz Sy. Diouf has emerged as a spokesman for the aged *xalifa*, and currently appears to have significant influence over him. In 1989, when the affair concerning the Ayatollah Khomeini's death sentence on the novelist Salman Rushdie shook the Muslim world, the *xalifa* gave a sermon on the controversy at Friday prayers in Tivaouane. Virtually identical French versions of the speech (which would of course have been delivered primarily in Wolof) were published in the government daily *Le Soleil* and in *Wal Fadjri*. Only at one crucial point, however, did the wording of the two versions differ; while the text in *Le Soleil* reported the *xalifa's* pronouncement that Rushdie "should be condemned," *Wal Fadjri's* version added "to death." The texts had been made available to the two publications by Daouda Diouf, who claimed (though he was not pleased to be asked) that the government newspaper had changed the text. *Wal Fadjri* editor Sidy Lamine Niasse, however, also noted the possibility that Diouf had provided two different versions in order to ensure publication.[90] Regardless of which of these versions is true, the incident is an indication of Diouf's influence in a domain as important as the public posture adopted by one of the two most important marabouts in Senegal. It thus also indicates that there does exist a potential for reformist influence on maraboutic positions.

To date, the blending of reformism and Sufism is most notable among the Tijans, in particular the Sy family. And the family seems well disposed – and well prepared – to take over some of the functions which the state had previously assigned to reformist *arabisants*. One might note, for example, their insistence that they have a role to play as intermediaries between Senegal and the international Muslim world. The family's maraboutic stature, in fact, provides them with a great advantage in appropriating elements of the *arabisants'* role: none of the non-Sufi Islamic organizations in Senegal to date have emerged as anything resembling a mass organization, while the Tijans can claim disciples in the millions.

The blending is seen most clearly in – and must be understood as being at the source of – the creation of Moustapha Sy's Dahiratoul Moustarchidina wal Moustarchidaty. The DMWM has borrowed from reformist groups in terms both of its themes and its rhetoric, and it has played on state concerns about controlling such groups. But it has emerged as a mass movement only by building on its base as a maraboutic and a Tijan movement. It is thus ultimately better understood as a maraboutic movement influenced by modern reformist Islam than as a reformist movement that happens to be led by a marabout. In many respects the stated ideology of the movement resembles the modern form of *da'wa* organizations found throughout the Muslim world. Although the original meaning of the term implied missionary activity among non-Muslims, Piscatori documents its transformation into the ideological basis for organizations devoted to educational and political activity among Muslims, with the theme of making Islam relevant to life in the modern world.[91] The DMWM reflects this orientation by, for example, occasionally organizing educational conferences and seminars on such issues as the relationship of Islam to modern entertainment, sex and birth control, and social problems.[92] These issues, of course, are inherently political and the existence of such organizations concerns the state directly. In Senegal the state's initial response to the DMWM was primarily aimed at attempting to capture the movement and use it to its own purposes via official sponsorship and aid.

The DMWM emerged as a mass movement to fill a political space opened up by the increased activism of urban youth, and this origin has determined its relations with the state. Over the course of the 1980s, and especially following the rioting and social unrest of the 1988 elections, Senegalese youth (and in particular urban groups) developed into a potent and potentially destabilizing political force. An organization which could effectively unite large numbers of young people and exert influence over them thus had the potential for translating such clout into great leverage on the state, and it is this role which Moustapha Sy's movement assumed. As with other maraboutic organizations, state officials quickly saw the advantage of a "bridge" to a social group that had otherwise escaped their influence, and they moved very promptly to offer some patronage to the organization. Moustapha Sy thus enjoyed the enthusiastic solicitude of state officials in his endeavors. During a visit to Fatick in 1986, for example, he was received with great fanfare by political officials, including the local deputy to the National Assembly and the governor himself, in whose residence he spent the night.[93]

For his part Moustapha Sy demonstrated a willingness – some might say eagerness – to deal with the state. The most explicit and public indication of the collaboration between the state and the marabout was the highly touted "International Conference on Muslim Youth" held in Dakar in February of 1989. The week-long conference gathered some 2000 delegates, reportedly representing some twenty countries, forty-three youth movements, and twenty-seven international organizations. The conference was planned to debate issues of concern to young people throughout the Muslim world, although its centrality to Senegalese politics was immediately evident. "It is very appropriate that the head of state, president Abdou Diouf, has chosen this forum of youth who have come from the four corners of the globe to pursue a direct dialogue with his own youth," noted an editorial in *Le Soleil* on the first day of the conference.[94] The president spoke at the opening ceremony, addressing Sy directly as "My dear Moustapha, my dear son." His message about the importance of youth in the search for solutions to the world's problems and his promise of commitment to them was, interestingly enough, interspersed with strong statements about the secular nature of the Senegalese state, described as "one of the great virtues of our country." Accounts in the official press also gave great attention to the invited presence of the Catholic archbishop of Dakar, Cardinal Thiandoum, who was photographed sitting among the important delegates

throughout the proceedings of the conference. While the political imperative of establishing ties to the nation's youth led to close state participation
in the conference, such close collaboration clearly posed a dilemma for the
state, and the anomalous focus on secularism and important Catholic
figures must be understood as an effort to mitigate the potential negative
effects of collaboration.

The marabout, however, was also careful to do his part. Speaking in
Wolof (and thus to the Senegalese and not the international participants),
he addressed Abdou Diouf: "You have before you all of the youth of
Senegal, without regard to religion or Sufi order. All of our youth is
gathered around you and this opportunity to build a new Senegal should be
seized; and let no one come between you and the youth. Give us the order
and we shall carry it out!"[95]

With such explicit displays of collaboration it is no surprise that the
DMWM quickly became highly controversial, both among secularist
Senegalese and within maraboutic circles, and by the end of the 1980s its
long-term prognosis was rather unclear. For many youths the initial
promise of the organization appears to have faded quickly. In Fatick, as we
have seen, an active core remained but several sections had an only nominal
existence. At various times young people who had been active in the
organization in the town indicated their disillusionment with it. One young
man decried Moustapha Sy's excessive political ambitions and the overem-
phasis on what he called the "folkloric" and "touristic" aspects of the
organization at the expense of the "mystic, which should be the only
important one."[96] And in a thesis presented at the University of Dakar,
Demba Koné notes the case of a young university graduate who had been a
member of the DMWM but had quit because, "far from providing him with
a truly religious culture," it only served instead to "keep him under
domination."[97]

The attitudes displayed in these anecdotes point to the salience of the
movement's relationship with the maraboutic mainstream. The reformist
promise of teaching "true Islam" which the DMWM had seemed to offer
the interested university student proved disappointing by its excessive
conformity to the "domination" of standard marabout-disciple relations,
yet this latter pattern was more likely to win the group a mass following. By
such means as the DMWM's 1989 *Tamxarit* celebration which we saw in
the previous chapter, therefore, Moustapha Sy worked to realign his
movement with family tradition. And while this readjustment cost him
some disciples who had been attracted by the reformist alternative, the shift
also allowed the movement to maintain significant vigor to draw crowds to
Tivaouane for its major celebrations. Building on these more standard
sources of maraboutic legitimacy not only facilitated the survival of the

movement, but it clearly contributed to a lessened dependence by Mousta-pha Sy on state patronage, with subsequent consequences for those relations. Coulon has argued that, "Paradoxically, the reformists are less agitating and more controllable than certain marabouts whose base and legitimacy are more independent."[98] He is no doubt correct, but perhaps this is not so paradoxical; reformists ultimately depend on the state since they enjoy little or no popular support, a constraint which does not limit marabouts in any comparable fashion. To the extent that Moustapha Sy developed his maraboutic legitimacy, he in fact enhanced his capacity to be rather more "agitating."

The young marabout quickly proved his willingness to strike a confron-tational political stance when the opportunity arose in early 1993 by the convergence of several factors: a period of escalating tensions between Sy and the government of Abdou Diouf; a continued erosion of Diouf's popularity among Sy's principal clientele, urban youth; and a variety of changes in the Senegalese electoral code that seemed to promise the real potential for an opposition victory in the February elections.[99] The conflict culminated in a long and scathing personal attack on Diouf – complete with sex scandals and more – delivered by Sy at a meeting of the DMWM in Thiès only a few days prior to the election. Cassette copies made of the hours-long speech were quickly circulated and available for sale in Dakar's Sandaga market area. The attack struck a chord with highly disillusioned urban youth who willingly believed even Sy's wildest allegations. Senior marabouts of the Sy family distanced themselves from Moustapha Sy's attack, most directly in a sermon delivered by Abdoul Aziz Sy Junior the following Friday, and the incident led to Sy's implication in a series of political imbroglios throughout the rest of the year. But there is no doubt that it also re-established him as the spokesman for an important segment of urban youth. Several months after the election both DMWM members and critics in Fatick noted that the organization was doing rather well, in large part because it had tapped into the widespread disillusionment provoked by the elections' failure to yield change. As one official in a local "section" explained in offering a justification for the movement's political about-face: "Marabouts should love the president, but they should love the population even more."[100] And doing so, he clearly implied, might entail moving from collaboration to contestation when "the population" found itself at odds with the president.

In an annex to the thesis noted above, Demba Koné reflects critically on Coulon and Magassouba's portrayal of the alleged new "dynamism" of Islam in Senegal, which he understands to mean "a process tending to appropriate certain mechanisms so as to react against domination," that is, a contestatory movement against the existing order. Considering the impact of the Muslim reformist tendency in Senegal in the 1980s he concludes that "what we have seen here was nothing more than a religious fervor, which was displayed in a renewed zeal, evidence of a strong spiritual aspiration. This aspiration was unable to produce a 'dynamism,' precisely because it was channeled and diverted by the marabouts to the benefit of the dominant order to which they belong."[101] On the basis of both the evidence from Fatick and a consideration of the historical evolution of non-maraboutic Muslim alternatives, I am led to concur with his assessment. The relations of the state to religion in Senegal remain as strongly as ever a process of collaboration and conflict with marabouts at all levels over the relative control of each over their common clientele.

7   Bureaucrats, marabouts, and citizen-disciples: how precarious a balance?

The relations between any two of the three sets of actors we have considered in this work – the state, the marabouts, and the citizen-disciples of Senegal – can only be understood in the context of relations with the third. Moustapha Sy's DMWM illustrates this well: the state has been obliged to deal with the marabout given his clientele; the marabout has sought to define a relationship with the state adapted to the ties he has attempted to build with his followers; and citizen-disciples have moderated their response in accordance with their view of the relationship between the marabout and the state. In addition, the movement's evolution demonstrates the extent to which such a three-sided pattern of socio-political interactions remains absolutely central to Senegalese social life. The maraboutic model has provided the "normal," default manner of organizing Senegalese society outside of the state. Because the state must then deal with society organized in this manner, the maraboutic system is the essential institutional structure defining the processes of state-society relations.

The extent to which the system has been routinized is clearly indicated by a maraboutic movement of some importance in Fatick, that led by the Serer marabout Ma Ansou Niang from a village near the Gambian border. I have referred to this movement at various times in the preceding chapters, but have reserved a fuller exploration of it until now because it provides a useful means of tying together many of the themes of this work. In particular, the history of the movement to date provides a clear indication of how the maraboutic model has been central to the negotiation of relations between state and society in Senegal. While the movement has flourished over the past decade or so, its ultimate success in the sense of institutionalization as one of the significant centers of Senegalese Sufism is not necessarily assured. Precisely because the relations are still being negotiated, however, it presents a unique opportunity to consider how each of the sides of the triangular set of relations is dependent on the other. In this final chapter, then, I will consider this case, and use it as a point of departure for drawing some conclusions about the role of the Sufi system in Senegal's distinct pattern of state-society relations.

244

A consideration of the case highlights the question of why a maraboutic movement emerges around a given religious figure, and what connection this has with the relations of both the followers and the marabout to the state. To address this issue, it may be useful to reconsider briefly the notion of charisma in Max Weber's classic formulation. So far I have used the term "charisma" only in the broad sense of a personal ability to attract popular attention, in the case of marabouts referring to the source of the appeal that draws disciples. This type of attraction, however, cannot be understood only by a consideration of the qualities of the individual leader himself. From the fact that marabouts always need to seek to exert a popular appeal it follows that the interests and concerns of the disciples must also be taken into account to explain the establishment of marabout-*taalibe* ties. We thus need to consider what Cruise O'Brien has labeled "the contributions of the charismatic clientele, the populist underpinnings of extraordinary power."[1] Such an approach involves a closer adherence to the Weberian sense of the term.

In its Weberian prototype or ideal form a charismatic movement entails a break with an established system in a context of social crisis to follow a leader who personally embodies qualities that offer alternative sources of allegiance and guidance.[2] Charisma, therefore, is not simply a quality of an individual, but an aspect of a type of relationship between leaders and followers. Two elements are generally recognized as central to the emergence of charismatic movements: (1) the quality of the message which is offered as an alternative to the old order, particularly in terms of its "newness" or originality, and (2) the social context of the movement in terms of the "ripeness" of the historical moment, most frequently understood as a perceived popular need for change. It is this latter element which represents the "populist underpinnings" of charisma. Some combination of these two elements appears to be a necessary condition for the emergence of a charismatic movement.

Charisma on this model provides important explanatory insights into the careers of the great popularizers of Islam in Senegal, in particular, of course, the three men who indelibly marked the history of Islamic organization in the country: Amadou Bamba, El Hajj Malik Sy, and Abdoulaye Niasse. Each of these men was obviously gifted with some extraordinary qualities, but what seems most significant in the formulation of the movements around these personages was their ability to answer to the historical exigencies of the moment. As charismatic movements they were able to address popularly perceived needs in such a way as to earn them each a mass clientele. Studies of Amadou Bamba's life, which has been more closely examined than that of his contemporaries, point to the importance of the social context. The masses of disciples whom he attracted in his lifetime seem neither to have been especially desired by Bamba himself, nor explainable solely in terms of his personal qualities. This phenomenon is so noteworthy that one scholar has been led to conclude of Bamba's movement: "He was, indeed a factor *despite* himself."[3] As charismatic movements on the Weberian model, the followings developed around the turn of the century by these Sufi leaders are thus distinguished primarily by the relative importance of the social context in determining their success. As in Weber's ideal type, the wide acceptance of the marabouts' charisma appears to have been most fundamentally "an attribute of the belief of the followers and not of the quality of the leader."[4]

The direct descendants of these founders, as we have seen, continue to benefit from the success of the original movements. While "pure charisma" is radical and involves a break with the established order, the association of the charismatic figure with an existing institution or the formation of a new organization around his or her person may result in the "routinization" of charisma. As a source of legitimacy such charisma is thus depersonalized, and can evolve into a form of "charisma of office," "lineage charisma," or "hereditary charisma."[5] This step is the ultimate test of the "success" of a charismatic movement, and the broad popular acceptance of the legitimacy of inherited charisma indicates that it was achieved by the great Senegalese maraboutic movements of the turn of the century. These movements were thus able to manage successfully the transition to a routinized charisma.

But what of more recent *new* maraboutic movements? Are they instances of the same phenomenon as that which resulted in the establishment of the main *zawiyas* of Senegalese Sufism, or is there a qualitative difference in their sources? I have noted in chapter 4 that new sources of maraboutic charisma have occasionally managed to recruit popular followings and produce distinct movements. None to date have had the phenomenal success of the earlier generation of religious leaders, but various movements have nevertheless made their mark, at least in local terms. In this regard I pointed as an example to the once quite significant, but currently bankrupt, movement led by *Shaykh* Ousmane Sountou Badji in the lower Casamance, near the town of Bignona. To what extent can more recent cases such as his be explained in terms of "charisma" on a par with those of the earlier epoch? That is, what element of "newness" is present in the maraboutic message, and what social crisis serves as the source of the "populist underpinnings" of the movement?

Clearly some elements of each of these criteria can be discerned in most cases. In Badji's movement, for example, his own idiosyncratic interpretations of the Sufi tradition gave his mission an innovative aspect that may have been part of his appeal (and probably ultimately of his decline). And the pressure felt by Diola society threatened by northern (especially Wolof) domination seems to have fed a sense of crisis which created the demand for a local Diola marabout. In Badji's movement like most other new ones, however, the similarties to the existing model are far more striking than any innovative characteristics. Even those who claim to reject the Sufi model actually fit the pattern quite closely in most significant respects; their "newness" is at times reduced to simple questions of terminology and style.

In new movements the more properly charismatic elements in terms of the intersection of innovative leadership and a situation of social crisis, which leads to a new form of organization and new sources of legitimacy, are only present in very muted form, if at all. In the context of contemporary Senegal these movements must be understood instead as the result of the fact that the entire maraboutic *system* has been, in a sense, "routinized." The rise and institutionalization of the great charismatic movements of the turn of the century resulted in the establishment of the Sufi model as the acceptable mode of socio-political organization in interactions with the colonial state, and later its independent successor. The symbiotic relationship which developed between the religious elite of the Sufi orders and the political elite of the country, as explored in the previous chapter, served to cement that pattern. The result is that today a social group under pressure (including at times, as we shall see, an ethnic group) finds that the most readily available model for organizing a claim to the attention of the state is the maraboutic one. Because relations between Senegalese society and the state are mediated predominantly via the religious structures of that society, such structures appear as the most legitimate and effective organizational model available to social groups.

In this context then the legitimacy of the very notion of maraboutic charisma has been routinized. The potential bases for the appeal of a marabout are present even in the absence of a personal radical and new charisma. It may be only the "pseudocharisma" of the politician, rather than the pure charisma of the prophet that is required to attract a following.[6] Resorting to this diluted version of Weber's concept may help to account for some of the ambiguities and difficulties noted by Cruise O'Brien of applying the Weberian ideal type to African Sufism.[7] As the discussion of Ma Ansou Niang will illustrate, the concept of a routinized charisma which legitimates the entire maraboutic *system* provides both a plausible means of explaining the rise of new movements in the world of contemporary Senegalese Sufism and an indication of the centrality of the maraboutic system to Senegalese state-society relations. A consideration of the sources of such new movements highlights the extent to which recourse to the maraboutic system has shaped patterns of societal reactions to the state, and state dealings with society.

Disciples, bureaucrats, and a marabout: a case study

We have seen that, in Fatick, the relations between the Serer population of Ndiaye-Ndiaye and the Senegalese state have been particularly ambiguous. The fact that the Serer represent the most numerous ethnic group in the town has not translated into any particular importance in either economic or political terms. And the reinforcement of the state's presence, with the elevation of Fatick to regional capital, did nothing to alleviate, and in fact seems to have exacerbated, the tension between this group and the state. Lacking the economic or political organization that would allow for engagement with the state on more equal terms, the Serer have been unable to command state attention and have been relatively marginalized in the governance of Fatick. It is in this context that, over the course of the late 1980s, most of the Serer of Ndiaye-Ndiaye affiliated themselves with the maraboutic movement led by Ma Ansou Niang. Faced with the growing size and dynamism of this movement, state officials in Fatick have had no alternative but to respond.

The ultimate fate of this movement is still unsettled, but its evolution clearly has important implications for an understanding of state-society relations – both locally in Fatick and more broadly in contemporary Senegal. To explore these implications, then, I will consider the movement first in terms of why people have chosen this particular maraboutic affiliation (that is, in terms of the nature of maraboutic charisma in this case), and then consider how the state has been obliged to respond and the aspects of the maraboutic movement that appear central to the determination of its (still evolving) relations with the state.

The marabout and his community[8]

Cheikh al Islam El Hadj Ousmane Mama Ansou Niang, as his letterhead identifies him in both French and Arabic, was born in 1925 in the Serer coastal village of Niodior. He belongs, therefore, to the branch of the Serer known as the Serer-Niominka, or *séeréer-u-ndox* ("water Serer") in Wolof. Ma Ansou's studies were undertaken under a relatively unknown Gambian marabout named Ibrahima Kante, in whose household he remained until the decision to strike out on his own. His *taalibes* tend to describe his life in parallels to that of the Prophet. This move, consequently, is said to have occurred when the marabout was forty – the age at which Muhammad was first called to his prophetic mission – and is explicitly compared to the Prophet's *hijra*, his flight from Mecca to establish his fledgling community in Medina. Like the Prophet, Ma Ansou found it difficult to teach in his own community, and thus in 1968/69 he moved to the small village of

Sirmang, just a few miles from the Gambian border, with two wives, some children, and a handful of followers.

His first undertaking was the construction of a mosque, which was achieved within the first three years and which remains the focal point of the village – a structure far more imposing than the mosques found in many significantly larger towns. As the community grew over the years further construction was carried out, so that today it comprises a physical complex of impressive proportions in the context of rural Senegal. The marabout's personal compound includes a large waiting room for visitors, along with a small library, his private quarters where he receives many guests, a separate area for women and children, and further housing for other married family members. Nearby, a large one-room building serves as the main school, awaiting the completion of a much larger structure. Surrounding an expansive open quadrangle some ten concrete houses have been built, each divided into eight to ten rooms. Many of these are occupied by disciples who live in the community and by the numerous students whom they care for. Others are reserved for guests and frequent visitors to the community. In another sign of relative prosperity, a large tin and cement shed houses a gasoline-powered electric generator which is run for several hours in the evenings to permit night-time study.

This prosperity is built almost entirely on agriculture. The soils in the area of Sirmang are quite rich by Senegalese standards, so that garden vegetables, as well as millet and peanuts, are produced by the community. In addition, the marabout owns numerous head of cattle and other livestock. The labor for this production is provided by local disciples, who voluntarily work the marabout's fields on Thursdays, as well as by the young students who have been entrusted by their parents to the marabout. Between two and three hundred boys were in residence in the community in 1989, engaged predominantly in study but also, during the summer rainy season, in doing agricultural work.

Education in Arabic and the religious sciences is, in fact, the primary occupation of the community, and its organization turns around this activity. Other than in periods when their help is required in the fields, the students adhere to a rigorous schedule of studies: they are awakened at four in the morning and study until the call to dawn prayers. After breakfast they return to their classes until a lunch break at noon, then again study from three to five, and in the evenings from eight to nine-thirty. Adhering to the Muslim work-week, no classes are held on Thursdays or Fridays. The tasks of caring for the children is done by adult disciples who live in the community. Upon arrival each child is assigned a surrogate "father" and "mother" who take responsibility for him, including in particular the responsibility for feeding and housing him. Clothing, however, must be provided by the child's real parents, and the tattered rags that many wear indicate that a significant percentage in fact receive nothing from outside the community.

The vast majority, but not all, of the students at the community are Serer. Among Ma Ansou's disciples are also numerous Manding (Socé) from the surrounding region, including many from Gambia, along with a handful of Peul. Serer influences, however, are clearly dominant in the community, and Serer is the primary language used; non-Serer children who do not speak the language on arrival are quickly obliged to learn at least enough to function in day-to-day activities. Social movements in Senegal, of course, are only rarely (if ever) rigidly exclusionary on an ethnic basis, and Ma Ansou Niang's is no exception. There is no doubt, however, that the identity of the community is intricately linked to Serer ethnicity.

This of course is not an explicit aspect of the ideological or intellectual foundations of the Sirmang community as formulated by Ma Ansou Niang himself. In terms of guiding principles that structure its functioning, two other elements are particularly noteworthy for an explanation of the community's appeal. First, in religious terms, although the marabout insists that the community practices what he terms "orthodox" Islam – by which he clearly means to distance himself from some of the critiques leveled against Sufism by reformists and align himself more closely with the Arab world – there is abundant evidence that the movement actually falls squarely and unambiguously into the established pattern of Senegalese Sufism as it has been described throughout this book. Secondly, within the range of possible types of relations which marabouts have maintained with the state, Ma Ansou has to date emphasized the "isolationist" potential in his movement, choosing to maintain the maximum distance possible from the state.

Ma Ansou acknowledges no affiliation with a Sufi order, although various of his disciples note that he first studied and received the Tijan *wird*. Questioned about the orders he shrugs them off as rather insignificant, but he also refuses to condemn them. The *tarixas*, he explains, are simply paths which all lead to the same final destination. The difficulty, however, is that these paths are at times rather circuitous. Rather than take any of these, then, the marabout has preferred simply to go directly to the final destination. For those who wish, however, such paths are acceptable, and it is even said that he will personally teach whatever *wird* a disciple might desire – Tijan, Qadir, or other, he has mastered them all – if someone comes to ask. Taking this position, of course, grants Ma Ansou an independence from the orders, and avoids placing him in a position of spiritual dependence *vis-à-vis* any of the established maraboutic lineages in Senegal. Building on his "original" charisma, Ma Ansou has chosen to make no claims to "reflected" charisma. The possibility thus remains open that Ma Ansou may himself, at some later point, propose to teach a more direct "path" of his own.

The logic of the marabout's rejection of the orders is an indication of his adherence to mystical beliefs of the very type which are generally said to characterize the Sufi tendency. No sociological categories, explains Ma Ansou, have any significance for human life; governments, ethnicity, or even the *tarixas* are only constructs which, if given any importance, can become barriers to the direct experience of God by men. Moreover, he stresses, the ultimate experience of this relationship is peace, a cause not often well served by any of these human structures. Study, meditation, and prayer in the search for a personal understanding of the good and the true are the essential elements of Ma Ansou's mystical message – a formula directly in the Sufi tradition.

And in its vocabulary, structures, and ritual practices the movement led by Ma Ansou Niang replicates exactly much of what I have described as the uniquely Senegalese version of that tradition. Borrowing from the Mourides, the Wolof word *njébbal* is used among disciples to describe the act of declaring allegiance to the marabout. Most notably, the disciples have adopted the established organizational patterns, organizing themselves into *daairas*, which function in the same manner as all *daairas*, including coordinating attendance at the ceremonies organized at Sirmang. The services which Ma Ansou performs for his disciples are also directly in the tradition of Senegalese marabouts. *Gris-gris* amulets are written for those that desire them, and a constant line of disciples arrives daily at Sirmang to consult the marabout and request guidance and advice. On one weekday morning, for example, a group of jean-clad young men, a quiet young woman alone, a soldier in military uniform, a local villager, a mother with a child, and a well-dressed and obviously rather prosperous middle-aged couple from Dakar, all sat patiently in the marabout's waiting room as he received such visitors one after the other. The interactions of the disciples with the marabout are marked by a deferential submission, and although he does not seem to cultivate it directly, a personality cult surrounds Ma Ansou as it does all other Senegalese marabouts of significance; his photograph is sold at ceremonies held in Sirmang, and songs in his praise are composed and sung by groups of disciples.[9] In all significant respects, the "orthodoxy" of Ma Ansou's movement is directly in the tradition of *Senegalese* Islam, though this fact seems to be something that he has not intended, nor with which he is particularly satisfied.

More directly in accord with the marabout's explicit formulations is the other defining characteristic of his movement, the relations between the community at Sirmang and the Senegalese state. When interaction is required formal relations with government officials are polite, but ties with the Senegalese state are neither sought nor encouraged. Rather, the marabout and his assistants insist, the community is marked by the distance and detachment it maintains from the state and its non-involvement in Senegalese politics. At times the state has been *allowed* to undertake projects that affect the community – most notably the construction of an (unpaved) road from the main Gambia road to Sirmang, and the drilling (with Belgian financing) of a deep well that provides water to various villages in the area, including Sirmang – but these projects did not target the community directly. Nothing is asked of the government, and nothing is accepted which would give the state any degree of leverage over the school or the community. Ma Ansou's disciples are proud of this fact, and point to his success without state help as indicative of his personal attributes. Officials in Fatick also acknowledge the veracity of this claim: the marabout makes no requests of the state.

Illustrative in this regard of how Ma Ansou has signaled his (polite) distance from the state was his reception of the governmental delegation that made the two-hour trip from Fatick to Sirmang at the time of the 1989 *gàmmu*. In contrast to what we have seen is the practice among most other marabouts, when the important delegation composed of the governor of the region, the prefects of Fatick and Foundiougne, the regional police commissioner, the secretary general of the Fatick chamber of commerce, and various other officials arrived at Sirmang at the time of the *gàmmu* a place was prepared to receive them in the courtyard of the marabout's compound, rather than under the large tent that had been set up for the ceremony. The audience for the reception was thus effectively restricted. Most significantly, although the various officials were seated in chairs provided for the occasion, the marabout himself did not leave his room to greet them publicly.

The delegation was received instead by the marabout's personal secretary and son-in-law, who began his speech for the occasion by explaining that the governor came as the representative of President Abdou Diouf to the marabout, and that the marabout had accordingly chosen to delegate the secretary as *his* representative. In a cryptic and unexplained comment he also noted that the marabout could equally have chosen *also* to name the governor himself as a representative, since the governor already knew both what Abdou Diouf had to say and what the marabout would answer. By implication, of course, the marabout thus placed himself at the level of the president. Only after the speeches were done were the officials briefly escorted into the marabout's rooms to receive a private blessing, then accompanied to their vehicles without any fanfare by the secretary. Any public interaction between the marabout and the state officials was thus avoided. Somewhat flustered members of the delegation later explained the marabout's non-appearance as due to the fact that he was not feeling well. No such excuses were made at Sirmang, nor was any concern expressed for the marabout's health.

The choice of whether to maintain or soften the isolationist mode of interaction with the state will certainly be crucial in shaping the future development of the community. The new influx of disciples that the community has experienced in recent years has fed an interest in expansion, largely under the managerial guidance of the marabout's son-in-law and secretary, a young *arabisant* who joined the community in 1983 upon his return from years of study in Cairo. Under his direction an ambitious new project was launched to build what he labels an *Institut Islamique* – a school focused largely on Arabic and religious studies – capable of housing up to two thousand students in residence. By late 1989 the buildings for the school were about half-finished, and some 10 million francs CFA[10] had already been invested, without any outside help. The economic downturn, however, had significantly slowed construction. A more serious problem concerned how that number of students would be supported without charging fees, an option that was absolutely ruled out, when construction was finally completed.

The plan which the marabout and his secretary have devised centers around the development of an irrigated garden project to produce market vegetables for sale outside the community. The gardens would be worked part-time by the students, who would thus earn their keep. The need to secure significant initial financing to launch the project, however, poses the most serious bottleneck to the future growth of the community along these lines. The secretary had contacted various non-governmental organizations (NGO's) to request help, and actually entered into negotiations with one that expressed an interest in a project involving *private* ownership of garden plots in Sirmang and several neighboring villages. The secretary was unwilling, however, to enter into such an agreement, insisting that the project must be communal, and controlled by the marabout. Clearly this presents a major stumbling block; it is highly unlikely that an NGO would seriously consider such an investment. Without outside help in overcoming this constraint, however, the expansion and institutionalization of the marabout's position as a major center of Senegalese Islam may prove impossible. That status has been achieved by other marabouts at Touba or at Tivaouane only via some degree of engagement with the state. But given the importance of his isolationist posture in attracting disciples, accepting state help (which the leaders of the community insist they would not do) could well hurt the marabout in his efforts to attract new disciples or students for the school. The community, therefore, is now faced with a dilemma of major proportions, and how this bottleneck is resolved (or not resolved) will be a major factor in determining the future of Ma Ansou's movement.

Actions and reactions in Fatick: disciples and bureaucrats

Sometime around 1984 – the same year Fatick was named a regional capital – Ma Ansou Niang paid a visit to the town in the course of a tour of the region. During his stay, in the compound of a long-time disciple in Ndiaye-Ndiaye, he gave a series of talks on religious themes, both in Fatick and in nearby villages, which won him the allegiance of many local Serer. The visit, in fact, was even said to have inspired the "real" or "sincere" conversion of some villagers (in contrast to an earlier, nominal, conversion), who had their heads shaved publicly to mark the event. In Fatick, disciples speak of this visit as the time when Ma Ansou chose to "make himself visible," using the Wolof term *feeñu* with its implications of a mystical experience or apparition. In Ndiaye-Ndiaye many people became his disciples, a number that quickly grew to include by 1988 virtually all of the neighborhood's Serer population which defined itself as Tijan.

This realignment took place directly at the expense of the Sy family marabouts who had managed at least nominally to claim a wide clientele among the Serer of Ndiaye-Ndiaye. As I have already noted, a Tijan *daaira* had been established in Ndiaye-Ndiaye to the family of El Hajj Malik Sy in 1965, and when this group first organized a *gàmmu* in May 1966, Cheikh Tidiane Sy was invited to preside. In 1970 construction was begun on a Friday mosque for the neighborhood, purportedly at least in part because the central mosque in Fatick was a long walk, but quite clearly a decision with important *ethnic* resonance – particularly since the central mosque tends to be also Tijan dominated. When the Friday mosque for Ndiaye-Ndiaye was finally ready to be inaugurated in 1980 after ten years of work, Abdoul Aziz Sy Junior presided over the ceremony marking the first prayers. While there is no indication that these ties ever developed into any particularly close relationship with the majority of Ndiaye-Ndiaye's Muslims, certain religious leaders in Ndiaye-Ndiaye did court close ties with the Sy family, and a *daaira* to the Sy family marabouts drew disciples in the neighborhood. The most visible and significant organizational impact of the realignment was the collapse of that *daaira* and the emergence of two new *daairas* dedicated to Ma Ansou Niang – one composed primarily of younger disciples and the other for older people. In its day the Sy family *daaira* had maintained an active membership, but "people are fickle," says the old imam of a small mosque in Ndiaye-Ndiaye who still remains its titular president, "always looking for something new," and this membership had simply evaporated in short order.[11]

The fact that the switch in religious affiliation was initiated and driven at the popular level, that is, among ordinary disciples rather than by local elites or "opinion leaders," is indicative of the importance of the "populist underpinnings" of Ma Ansou's movement. The imam who had headed the Sy family *daaira* found himself virtually alone in the organization, a leader with no followers. Similarly, the imam of the new Friday mosque in the neighborhood, who had been instrumental in its construction and in inviting Abdoul Aziz Sy Junior to preside over its opening, has maintained his allegiance to the family at Tivaouane, but retains no followers. He cautiously, in fact, admits to having heard good things about Ma Ansou, and suggests that he might someday consider visiting Sirmang himself.

Yet if the religious realignment in Fatick was clearly a *popular* movement, what popularly perceived interests were the motivating forces behind it? Asked directly about the switch, disciples answer with a combination of two reasons: the appeals of an ethnic allegiance, and the virtues of the marabout himself. The ethnic attraction is unambiguous, and readily recognized both by disciples and outside observers, notably state officials knowledgeable about the movement. About the marabout's personal qualities, however, disciples are less clear; few can specify attributes more specific than those generally said of marabouts as a class, that is that they are the possessors of great knowledge and powers (*ay boroom xam-xam*). At no point in numerous discussions of Ma Ansou did disciples specify attributes that clearly distinguished him from other marabouts in Senegal with broad followings.

But if there is no doubt about the fact that the attraction of Ma Ansou Niang to Fatick's Serer population is largely ethnic, it is less clear why ethnicity should in this case prove to be the basis for social organization. As we have seen throughout this work, ethnic affiliation has never been a significant cleavage on which to organize politically in Senegal and religious movements, while at times dominated by one group, are never rigidly exclusionary on ethnic grounds; as I have already noted, Ma Ansou himself claims Manding and Peul disciples in Sirmang. The answer, I believe, must be sought in the conjuncture of the new state presence and the specific local implications of ethnicity along with the relative appeals of the predominant patterns of interaction with the state which the Sy family and Ma Ansou have respectively adopted: close and collaborative engagement versus cautious isolation. As we have seen in various discussions of Fatick, the Serer of Ndiaye-Ndiaye have come to be identified and to identify themselves as a group apart in the town's ethno-religious mosaic. In the context of Fatick society, the Serer have clearly come to perceive both a disproportionate intrusion by the state into their domain and an inequality in their degree of access to the few goods available.

An anecdotal illustration of Serer expression of dissatisfaction with the representatives of the new state presence in Fatick is provided by an event that echoes both the marabout's reception of the governmental delegation to the *gàmmu* and the Serer *saltigis'* reaction to the state at the inauguration of the traditional medicine center at Fatick. At the occasion in 1988 of a traditional Serer celebration held annually in Fatick, the governor was late for an expected appearance at the arena where the celebration culminated.[12] The increasingly annoyed crowd waited patiently, but then at the moment when he finally appeared, quietly dispersed and went home, leaving the governor and his delegation at the near-empty arena. There was no direct confrontation, but the message was unambiguous.

The same message was delivered via the very broad support in Ndiaye-Ndiaye for the opposition Parti Démocratique Sénégalais (PDS) at the time of both the 1988 and the 1993 elections. But as the results of those elections demonstrated, such overt political action is only of very limited utility. And the already limited range of effective possibilities for formal political expression of opposition is further reduced by the ability of local officials of the state to manipulate the sources of citizens' ambivalence through the selective and conditional distribution of benefits. Yet the Serer have not been totally powerless. As Jean-François Bayart has said of African societies more generally, "there is a long list of popular practices that limit and relativize the state's domain, thus also assuring society a degree of revenge over it."[13] Forms of socio-religious organization have been among the most politically significant "popular practices" throughout Africa, and we have seen that the choice of maraboutic affiliation is an act with clear political resonance in Senegal, due in particular to the varying postures which religious leaders have struck *vis-à-vis* the state.

No specific grievance to explain the dissatisfaction with the Sy marabouts is publicly articulated among Fatick's Serer, but there is a widespread distrust of the closely collaborative position with the state and the ruling party which, as we have seen in various places, the marabouts of that family have adopted in recent years. Particularly notable among these are, of course, such overtly political acts as Cheikh Tidiane Sy's active campaigning for Abdou Diouf's re-election in 1988. And in Fatick itself *Sëriñ* Baldé's enthusiasm for the new region and his close ties with state officials emphasize that the collaboration between Dakar and Tivaouane has local implications. In contrast to this position, descriptions by disciples frequently remark as a point of pride and an indicator of great powers that Ma Ansou's entire community has been developed by the marabout *without* any help or involvement by the state. In the Fatick context of the late 1980s, where a close relationship with the political elite held few attractions for the Serer population, a marabout who could demonstrate his capacity for success in *isolation* from the state was attractive indeed.

The new religious affiliation, therefore, reflects local Serer attitudes about the state in Fatick, but the organization of that affiliation follows the existing patterns of Sufi organization in Senegal. Because Ma Ansou has made no explicit statement of his wishes for the organization of his followers or about the practices that characterize his "path," the established organizational model has been adopted. If asked, most of Ma Ansou's disciples continue to refer to themselves as Tijan, for lack of any other label to apply. And the adoption of the *daaira* structure by the followers has already been noted. This adoption is particularly noteworthy given that Ma Ansou expresses clear reservations about whether these organizations are appropriate in Islam. In the weekly meetings which Ma Ansou's *daairas*, like most *daairas*, holds on Thursday evenings, religious chanting is based on El Hajj Malik Sy's *Teysir*, a devotional poem recited by disciples of that family in their gatherings. The Serer community in Fatick has readily adopted the existing pattern to organize their affiliation with a maraboutic movement that has a greater appeal in the *secular* domain. The movement thus reflects, as René Otayek has noted in the case of another religious movement in Burkina Faso, a desire for a "spiritual, if not temporal, independence," a will which becomes, as Cruise O'Brien rephrases it "surrogate to the political, a sacred proto-nationalism."[14]

Clearly, attempting to decipher the charismatic element in Ma Ansou Niang's movement is an ambiguous task. While there is no denying that he is an erudite and in many ways exceptional individual, his current success in attracting followers appears to be more closely linked to his appearance "in the right place at the right time" than to his personal qualities or any readily identifiable characteristics of his religious message. In the setting of Fatick, at least, the "right place" is most significantly an ethnically linked locus; ethnicity, more than original charisma, has proven to be at the source of the allure of the maraboutic image. And most significantly for the argument of this work, it is noteworthy that it has been the Sufi model which has emerged as the legitimate alternative for organizing the socio-political concerns of an ethnically defined group. Ma Ansou's movement, therefore, owes its rapid expansion largely to the existence of this model and its widespread acceptance. Legitimacy of this sort, in Weber's formulation, is the product of the routinization of charisma in the institutional structures that arise from the original charismatic movement, and thus passes to those who can successfully lay claim to being the founder's heirs. While at Touba, Tivaouane, or Kaolack, the heirs of Amadou Bamba, El Hajj Malik, and

Abdoulaye Niasse all owe their positions to a large extent to such routinization, in Ma Ansou's case legitimacy is derived indirectly from the routinization of an entire *system* of organization. Ma Ansou is heir to the legacy of *all* – and none in particular – of the great proselytizers of Islam in Senegal.

Ma Ansou Niang's movement demonstrates how this system has been central to state-society relations. Borrowing Cruise O'Brien's formulation in his discussion of the importance of "populist underpinnings," it can be said that Ma Ansou has been "in an unusual sense popularly elected."[15] Presented with this *fait accompli*, state officials discover a need to court the marabout's cooperation. "It is of no use," one bureaucrat in Fatick acknowledged, "to deny sociological reality" – however much one might have wished it to be otherwise. The leverage which this provides the marabout, and by extension his elector-clientele, is by no means purely local. President Abdou Diouf is said to have personally ordered the governor's solicitude toward the community, and has at least twice paid visits to the marabout at Sirmang himself, once at the time of the inauguration of the government-built and Belgian-financed well (a visit intended no doubt to underline the presidential patronage of this project of great value to the maraboutic cause), and again during the course of the 1988 electoral campaign. And as the difficulties of financing the community's expansion indicate, the marabout may yet have occasion to consider the benefits of greater engagement with the state. Should it be possible to arrange this to their mutual satisfaction, without provoking the defection of the elector-clients whose acquiescence is indispensable, all may yet stand to gain. By establishing the parameters of the relationship via a clear demonstration of the marabout's capacity to sustain an isolationist posture, it may be possible to move towards a greater engagement between marabout and state, an engagement by which the marabout's *taalibes* – and Serer society more broadly – would find themselves better represented than has been the case to date.

Conclusion: religion as civil society

The ready adoption of the religious model to address ethnic concerns in the case of Ma Ansou Niang's movement points to the flexibility of the maraboutic system. The Sufi pattern has become the basis for the establishment of a religiously based "civil society," that is, of a mode of social organization *vis-à-vis* the state, which has bestowed a considerable degree of power in the societal side of the state-society equation. The maraboutic system is thus central to Senegal's relative success in maintaining the "precarious balance" between state and society, and to the consequent avoidance of the unchecked authoritarian excesses that result from a disruption of this balance. Throughout this work I have been concerned with the ways in which the shape of Senegalese society and the exercise of state power have interacted and influenced each other. The centrality of religious organization in particular has been my focus, particularly the question of how this method of organizing civil society has determined the politics of relations with the state. It may be appropriate at this point, then, to summarize and comment on various aspects of the picture I have presented as a means of conclusion.

The argument has been widely accepted among scholars of Africa, and of comparative political systems more broadly, that variations in the exercise of state political power must take into account the structure or "shape" of the societies over which states rule. Many analysts have argued in particular that a well-developed civil society is necessary to the establishment of a stable or democratic order. Most frequently, however, it is assumed that the emergence of such a civil society must come from the expansion of "modern" institutions – unions, trade groupings, interest groups, and the like. The Senegalese case suggests that this need not be the case, and a central argument of this work has been that religious institutions in Senegal have been able to fill the role prescribed for civil societies in current theories about African politics. In making that argument, I have attempted to detail how a religiously based civil society has moderated relations between state and society in practice. The characteristics of the Sufi orders which I explore – their capability to aggregate interests; sufficient strength and autonomy to require state efforts to engage them in the effort to govern society; and the potential for flexibility in the range of responses to state actions – would appear to be general characteristics which are required of any civil society capable of balancing state power.

In the consideration of the importance of civil society in the determinants of politics in Africa which I cited in laying the theoretical groundwork for this work, Patrick Chabal argued that:

under the conditions of Africa's independences, the reality and consequences of political representation (that is, working political accountability) depend almost entirely on the ability of civil society to curb the hegemony of the state. An effective government can be bad. Government can only be good (that is, of benefit to its citizens) where civil society matters. Absolute hegemony corrupts governments absolutely.[16]

Following his formulation, it is clear that the relative "goodness" of government in Senegal must be attributed largely to the fact that the hegemony of the Senegalese state has been curbed quite effectively because a unique form of civil society has indeed mattered. In the institution of the

Sufi orders Senegalese society has been organized in such a way that the exercise of state power must be tailored to societal structures. As "bevies of institutions for protecting collective interests,"[17] these structures have the capacity for alternately challenging the state or limiting its influence by isolating social groups from state initiatives. There thus exists a sound basis, and important incentives, for state and society to engage on a relatively even footing.

We have seen in examining the internal dynamics of the orders that marabouts need to keep an eye out for popular support. In the case of new movements like that of Ma Ansou Niang, in fact, it is not unreasonable to describe them as *popular* movements based on the maraboutic model. Given the large number of local religious leaders, the organization of a movement around one particular figure must be understood largely as a function of popular perceptions and answering to popular needs. Even without going as far as Cruise O'Brien's assessment that the Mouride order, "with its qualified but effective defence of peasant interests against governmental economic hegemony, may be asserting a claim to recognition as Africa's first autonomous peasant trade union," it is clear that maraboutic organizations *do* represent societal concerns in the face of state actions.[18]

In addition, certain structural aspects of the organization of maraboutic movements make them particularly effective in interactions with the state, and hence as vehicles for transmitting the popular concerns they embody. They are, first of all, relatively cohesive organizations. The system of *daairas* and the regular attendance at broader celebrations which they facilitate makes true mass organizations of the orders, and thus renders them social forces which the state can ignore only at peril to its authority. The gathering of thousands of disciples under the patronage of important marabouts poses a significant contestatory potential to the state. The cohesiveness of the orders also facilitates the isolation of societal activities from state control and this potential is further enhanced by the organization of economic exchanges within the orders. The resources from internal taxation and fundraising activities such as the collections taken up by *daairas* and the requests for contributions at the time of ceremonies, although at times relatively modest, nevertheless provide an important element of independence to local groups of *taalibes*.

More significantly, all of the more successful maraboutic organizations are built on an additional economic resource base independent of the state. In most cases, and perhaps most notably with the Mourides, agriculture originally provided that base. Increasingly other activities, whether smuggling or international trade by Mourides or investments in industrial ventures by the Sy marabouts, have served to strengthen and diversify it. In the case of Ma Ansou Niang it is quite clear that the agricultural resources which he controls have made possible his isolationist attitude toward the state, as well as the establishment of his large community and the recruitment of a mass clientele. Indicating the importance of the economic factor in this aspect of state-society relations is an important lesson of the Senegalese case. In his review essay on African associational life Bratton concludes that it "may well be correct that effective organization within civil society requires an independent economic resource base."[19] The effectiveness of Senegalese maraboutic organizations provides important evidence in support of this assessment.

In addition, the Senegalese case suggests that a stable – even perhaps a (quasi) democratic – relationship between state and society does not necessarily require a high degree of economic development. Despite Senegal's poverty, the diffusion of control over economic resources to include groups outside of the state has created diverse centers of power, thus effectively limiting any hegemonic monopoly of political control. This interpretation suggests consequences that differ somewhat from those following from a view of the orders as simple patronage networks for the distribution of resources. Cruise O'Brien was certainly quite correct when he pointed out that the "prognosis for a spoils system cannot be good when the means of corruption become exhausted."[20] But the fact that despite twenty years of dwindling means in Senegal the system to which he refers – that involving state officials, Mouride marabouts, and peasant cultivators in the Wolof regions – is still largely in place indicates that it has been maintained by something other than the simple distribution of spoils.

While an independent resource base allows for a degree of societal independence, the current situation of Ma Ansou's community also appears to indicate the economic limits of a radical isolationism. All of the more important maraboutic movements in Senegal have developed and consolidated their position at the cost of some degree of engagement with the state. As I indicated above, Ma Ansou's movement is at an important juncture and its future may hinge on his willingness to seek an accommodation with the state. From the state perspective, of course, there are many reasons to cultivate this possibility. Thus there exist significant incentives on both sides to interact and establish a pattern of relations marked principally by engagement. And as we have seen throughout, this situation has direct political effects. Behrman, among others, has noted that from the immediate post-colonial period political parties in Senegal have tailored their platforms and positions in accordance with the need to seek maraboutic support.[21] Islamic societal organizations have consequently played an agenda-setting function in the country, helping to bridge the gap between the juridical reality of the imported state system and the empirical one of Senegalese society.

We have also seen, however, that the pattern of engagement has included an important element of contestation and rivalry between the state and the marabouts. The long-term survival of the system might thus appear to be called into question if the contestation is understood as a struggle for control of the state between two elite groups, the "traditional" religious elite and the "modern" secular one. Nothing I have explored in this work, however, would support such a depiction of the relationship. There is, in any case, abundant evidence that the position of each is sufficiently consolidated so as to make an assault on the position of the other unlikely to succeed. But the non-centrality of Islam to the severe political battles which Senegal has experienced in recent years also indicates that the political importance of Islam in Senegal has been concentrated in the domain of state-society relations and not in the struggle for control of the state.

For a period of over two years following the February 1988 elections Senegal was embroiled in what was arguably the most severe political crisis since independence, and one which seemed quite capable of destroying the Senegalese political system. The conflict hinged on the claims by opposition groups that the electoral results had been manipulated to give the ruling party the victory and the demand that power be relinquished by the party and by President Abdou Diouf. Various incidents of this period have been referred to in this work: the demonstrations and rioting which accompanied the announcement of electoral results and the public appearances of opposition leader Abdoulaye Wade; the crisis in the school system which cost students a year of study and threatened to entail much more; and the ethnic violence which targeted the Moorish population of Senegal and which again required calling the army into the streets for the government to reassert its authority to maintain order. Although the reconciliation of the political elite which brought Wade and his Parti Démocratique Sénégalais (PDS) into the government in 1991 temporarily defused the crisis, throughout this period the continued hold of the existing political elite over the state was at least open to question. In somewhat more muted form, the same political battles were to resurface during the 1993 campaign and especially in the intense controversies which followed the announcement of Diouf's re-election and the assassination of Babacar Sèye, the widely respected vice president of the Constitutional Council.[22]

Yet nowhere in this struggle for control of the state was the rhetoric of religion central, and the marabouts at no point involved themselves directly in the struggle. At various times important religious leaders, most notably perhaps the *xalifa* Abdoul Aziz Sy, made broad calls for "national reconciliation" or for peace, but all important marabouts maintained themselves carefully above the fray, or at least out of it. Even the death of the Mouride *xalifa* Abdou Lahatte, who had issued a *ndigal* ordering a vote for Abdou Diouf in 1988, and his replacement by his brother Abdoul Qadir, widely said to be Abdoulaye Wade's personal marabout, in no way changed the balance of power between the rivals for control of the state. Rather it became clear that even if the crisis were to lead to a change in the political elite, the new administrators of the Senegalese state would find themselves obliged to deal with maraboutic organizations in their search to govern society. And there is every reason to believe that there would be a high degree of continuity with the existing system.

The most important official of the PDS in Fatick takes a virtually identical tack to that of the state officials when discussing the question of maraboutic power. "We are Muslims," he said, "and consequently we must consult marabouts [on est obligé de fréquenter les marabouts], but we have no obligation to allow them to lead us by the nose in non-religious affairs."[23] In addition, he noted, the PDS maintains good ties with marabouts; at major *màggals*, *gàmmus* and other such events a delegation is frequently sent and, if appropriate, "something was given to the marabout." The official noted that certain marabouts have called for a vote for Abdou Diouf, but that many people ignore such "inappropriate" maraboutic pronouncements. And it is clear that the relations with marabouts are not seen as central to the PDS in its efforts to win state power. Rather those relations are simply something with which the party will need to contend when and if it takes control of the state.

As the campaign for the February 1993 elections began to heat up in the last months of 1992, marabouts around the country and at different levels all maneuvered to adopt the most advantageous position possible in terms both of their relations with the state and with their disciples. Under a banner headline which proclaimed "Elections of 1993: The 'little *ndigals*' in position," the Islamic weekly *Wal Fadjri* noted the actions of both religious and political leaders:[24]

The *xalifas-général* of the Mourides and of the Tijans have abstained from giving voting advice for the upcoming electoral consultation and have opted for a strict neutrality which places them above the *mêlée*. These positions were confirmed by the absence of a *ndigal* during the *màggal* at Touba as well as at the *gàmmu* at Tivaouane.

But this reserve in no way marginalizes the religious vote ... The occasion is in fact too good for the 'little' marabouts who have decided to cash in their support for politicians. Some of them have already positioned themselves, others are still waiting in hope. And the opposition parties, which have understood all of the benefits which the PS has always received from the *ndigals* of religious dignitaries, have no intention of being left behind. They do not all admit it, but the roads to Tivaouane, Touba, Kaolack, etc. are well in the sights of political leaders who only yesterday were unyielding [réfractaires] to the religious milieu.

These actions indicate the relativity of the position of marabouts who need to always move carefully between the state and the Senegalese population to maintain their intermediary position. The reluctance of the major marabouts to make explicit political pronouncements must be understood in light of their concern not to alienate disciples in what was to be a highly contested election. I argued above that there was good reason to believe that the Mouride *xalifa* in particular had been hurt by his explicit *ndigal* in 1988, an interpretation which is reinforced by his successor's failure to follow his example five years later.

At the same time, the willingness of "little" marabouts to engage in some religious entrepreneurship is clearly the result of the opportunities which the elections presented. If the gamble of making an explicit political endorsement were to pay off by the victory of the endorsee, the capability for securing access to state-controlled goods and services may in turn be translatable into larger followings via an increased attraction to disciples. The diversity of political positions within any given maraboutic family – perhaps most notably among the Mourides where, one marabout noted, "each member has struck out on his own" – provides disciples with a wide choice of whom to follow in accordance with strictly political consider-ations. Under these conditions marabouts in more delicate positions must be cautious. Moustapha Sy, like some Mouride marabouts, refrained from making an explicit political endorsement early in the pre-election period, but he pointedly directed his followers within the DMWM to register themselves on the electoral lists *en masse*. Likewise in this context political leaders found it expedient to proceed cautiously. Abdoulaye Bathily, the candidate of the officially Marxist LD/MPT party thus declared it "comple-tely normal for political organizations to approach the religious leaders because they are the responsible representative of currents of opinion which one cannot ignore when one wishes to preside over the destiny of this country." Considering the possibility that they might indeed win an election, the leaders of opposition parties are confronted with the same need as the ruling PS to find a basis for engagement with marabouts. Stated more generally, the patterns of interaction which have marked the relation-ship between marabouts and the state is in no way a function of the Parti Socialiste's control of that state. These arise, instead, due to broader structural factors concerning the nature of state power and the "shape" of Senegalese society.

State power and maraboutic power in Senegal coexist and interact. The two rival each other in many domains, and there is an important degree of uncertainty and ambiguity in terms of the negotiation of where the power of one begins and that of the other ends. The dimensions of this space are uncertain, and they are thus subject to constant negotiation. But while the ambiguity may never be resolved, the system allows for a means of addressing it. It may be an overstatement to say that the structures of Sufi organizations in Senegal are the basis of a democratic relationship between state and society, but to the extent that we accept Adam Przeworski's definition of democracy as "institutionalized uncertainty," there is clearly an important democratic element in the system.[25]

The coexistence of two rival elite groups that vie for influence over society is the basis of this institutionalized uncertainty. Having begun this work with an anecdotal illustration of the extent to which Senegalese Islam has been "conformist" in terms of its acceptance of the institutions of the nation-state, it may be appropriate to conclude with another highlighting popular satisfaction with the consequent sharing of authority.

In February of 1989 Abdou Diouf made his first trip out of Dakar after the turmoil and social unrest that had accompanied the previous year's contested elections. He was awarded a carefully orchestrated reception in the town of Foundiougne, where he had come to inaugurate the twenty-two kilometer road and the small ferry which now link the formerly quite inaccessible town to Fatick. In the style of such events, the hours-long ceremony involved drumming, singing, and dancing by women's groups, school classes, and party sections from various towns in the region, as well as speeches by all of the local officials, the Algerian ambassador (whose country had helped pay for the road), and the president himself. When the event finally ended and the crowd moved towards the field where the many vehicles had been parked, an old man, clearly a local figure, distributed various versions of a badly photocopied poem on small slips of paper to all who passed. In a mixture of French and Wolof, the verse, referred to by its author as "The Three Abdous," read:[26]

LI LA YALLA DEF	[This is what God has done
Abdou Lakhat à Touba	Abdou Lahatte in Touba
Abdoul Aziz Sy à Tivaouane	Abdoul Aziz Sy in Tivaouane
Abdou Diouf à Dakar	Abdou Diouf in Dakar
Le Sénégal est complet	Senegal is complete
C'EST FAIT PAR DIEU	It was done by God]

The poem, no doubt, was motivated in part by the element of personal flattery of the president which had marked the entire ceremony, and which not all citizens of Senegal would be willing to endorse. Indeed, a few copies of a tract by one of the small opposition parties (criticizing Diouf's government for its handling of that year's locust infestation) were also circulated outside the event. But in terms of its depiction of the complementarity of divided authority between marabouts and the state, the unabashed verse pithily captured the consensus of opinion among the masses of Senegal's citizen-disciples.

Notes

INTRODUCTION: GOOD AFRICANS, GOOD CITIZENS, GOOD MUSLIMS

1 The speech, entitled "L'Islam et la Négritude," was delivered by Cheikh Tidiane Sy some years earlier at an occasion I was unable to determine. It was delivered in eloquent French, with occasional passages in Arabic. The cited passage in the original went as follows: "Les musulmans sénégalais ne sont pas seulement des musulmans. Ils sont aussi les citoyens d'une république, les militants d'un parti. Ils sont aussi des nègres. Et ce que l'Islam exige d'eux, c'est d'être à la fois de très bons nègres, de très bons citoyens, et d'excellents militants."

2 James P. Piscatori, *Islam in a World of Nation-States* (Cambridge: Cambridge University Press, 1986). Piscatori's work examines the relationship between Islam and the modern international system based on the nation-state. His argument is that Islam has been far more capable of adaptation ("conformism") than most scholars of Islam have believed.

3 It may merit emphasizing here that race *per se* is not particularly central to political or religious discourse in contemporary Senegal. As noted, its inclusion in the marabout's comments is significant primarily as an indication of how far some Senegalese religious leaders have been willing to bend.

4 A claim scholars have also supported; note, for example, the title of Robert Fatton Jr.'s work: *The Making of a Liberal Democracy: Senegal's Passive Revolution, 1975–1985* (Boulder: Lynne Rienner, 1987).

5 On the 1988 elections, see Crawford Young and Babacar Kanté, "Governance, Democracy, and the 1988 Senegalese Elections," in *Governance and Politics in Africa*, ed. Goran Hyden and Michael Bratton (Boulder: Lynne Rienner, 1992), 57–74, and on the more recent ones see Leonardo A. Villalón, "Democratizing a (Quasi)Democracy: the Senegalese Elections of 1993," in *African Affairs* 93:371 (April 1994).

6 Goran Hyden, "Governance and the Study of Politics," in *Governance and Politics in Africa*, 7. The concept of "governance" has been recently proposed by several Africanist political scientists as a more useful dimension than that of "democracy" for comparing African regimes. The Hyden and Bratton volume represents the first major effort to apply the concept to a diversity of cases.

7 Donal B. Cruise O'Brien, in *Political Domination in Africa: Reflections on the Limits of Power*, ed. Patrick Chabal (Cambridge: Cambridge University Press, 1986). In a much quoted analysis of the specific case of the Mouride order, on which most of his work has been concentrated, Cruise O'Brien goes so far as to remark that with its "qualified but effective defence of peasant interests against

governmental economic hegemony," the order "may be asserting a claim to recognition as Africa's first autonomous peasant trade union." "Ruling Class and Peasantry in Senegal, 1960–1976: The Politics of a Monocrop Economy," in *The Political Economy of Underdevelopment: Dependence in Senegal*, ed. Rita Cruise O'Brien (Beverly Hills: Sage, 1979), 226.

8 Crawford Young, "The African Colonial State and its Political Legacy," in *The Precarious Balance: State and Society in Africa*, ed. Donald Rothchild and Naomi Chazan (Boulder: Westview, 1988), 60. This volume includes the contributions of many scholars working in this domain.

9 "Civil Society in Africa," in *Political Domination*, ed. Chabal, 114.

10 "Beyond the State: Civil Society and Associational Life in Africa," *World Politics* 41:3 (April 1989), 411.

11 The most significant of his writings are gathered into a two volume set: Paul Marty, *Etudes sur l'Islam au Sénégal* (Paris: Leroux, 1917).

12 The main works by these scholars are as follows: Lucy Behrman, *Muslim Brotherhoods and Politics in Senegal* (Cambridge: Harvard University Press, 1970); Christian Coulon, *Le Marabout et le prince: Islam et pouvoir au Sénégal* (Paris: A. Pedone, 1981); and Donal B. Cruise O'Brien, *The Mourides of Senegal: The Political and Economic Organization of an Islamic Brotherhood* (Oxford: Clarendon Press, 1971), and *Saints and Politicians: Essays in the Organization of a Senegalese Peasant Society* (Cambridge: Cambridge University Press, 1975). In addition each has published numerous articles on these topics.

13 Ravane Mbaye, "L'Islam au Sénégal," unpublished *thèse de doctorat de troisième cycle*, Faculté des Lettres et Sciences Humaines, Département d'Arabe (Université de Dakar, 1976), and Cheikh Tidiane Sy, *La Confrérie sénégalaise des mourides: Un essai sur l'Islam au Sénégal* (Paris: Présence Africaine, 1969).

14 Jean Copans, *Les Marabouts de l'arachide: La confrérie mouride et les paysans du Sénégal* (Paris: Le Sycomore, 1980)

15 The one important work which has been published on the Tijaniyya is: Jamil M. Abun-Nasr, *The Tijaniyya: A Sufi Order in the Modern World* (London: Oxford University Press, 1965). This now somewhat dated but nevertheless seminal work does include an historical account of the order in West Africa in the nineteenth century and under colonial rule, but it is primarily concerned with the birth and evolution of the order in Algeria and Morocco.

16 An example which illustrates the utility of a comparative local perspective is provided by the fact that even as astute an observer as Cruise O'Brien has been led to assume an inherently greater rivalry at the local level among disciples than among marabouts, thus implying established socio-political cleavages by order – an assumption my research has called into question. See his article "Sufi Politics in Senegal," in *Islam in the Political Process*, ed. James P. Piscatori (Cambridge: Cambridge University Press, 1983).

17 Perhaps the most famous of the attempts to specify a cultural explanation for a political outcome, Gabriel A. Almond and Sidney Verba's *The Civic Culture: Political Attitudes and Democracy in Five Nations* (Princeton: Princeton University Press, 1963) has been plagued by this issue; the direction of causality in the civic culture-democracy correlation which they demonstrate cannot ultimately be established.

18 Piscatori, *Islam in a World of Nation-States*, 74.
19 John Lukacs, *Confessions of an Original Sinner* (New York: Ticknor and Fields, 1990).
20 John Lonsdale, "States and Social Processes in Africa: A Historiographical Survey," *African Studies Review* 24: 2/3 (June/September 1981), 140.
21 Forrest D. Colburn, "Statism, Rationality, and State Centrism," *Comparative Politics* 20:4 (July 1988). The phrases cited are from pages 488–490.
22 The expression comes from the name of a research group, the "Groupe d'Analyse des Modes Populaires d'Action Politique" organized at the Centre d'Etudes et de Recherches Internationales of the Fondation Nationale des Sciences Politiques, Paris. Much of my discussion of state and society in Africa is influenced by various publications by members of this group, most notably Jean-François Bayart. See his most recent work, *L'Etat en Afrique: La politique du ventre* (Paris: Fayard, 1989), translated as *The State in Africa: the Politics of the Belly* (London: Longman, 1993)
23 Michael G. Schatzberg, *The Dialectics of Oppression in Zaire* (Bloomington: Indiana University Press, 1988), 144.
24 David D. Laitin, *Hegemony and Culture: Politics and Religious Change among the Yoruba* (Chicago: Chicago University Press, 1986), 204, 240. Laitin's superb methodological appendix to this work guided much of my thinking about these issues as I prepared to carry out fieldwork for this study.
25 Unless otherwise indicated, all interviews cited were carried out in Fatick.
26 Schatzberg, *The Dialectics of Oppression in Zaire*.
27 Donald Rothchild and Naomi Chazan, eds., *The Precarious Balance: State and Society in Africa* (Boulder: Westview, 1988).

1   ISLAM IN THE POLITICS OF STATE–SOCIETY RELATIONS

1 The expression is from Thomas M. Callaghy, *The State-Society Struggle: Zaire in Comparative Perspective* (New York: Columbia University Press, 1984).
2 See, for example, the otherwise excellent work by Manfred Halpern, *The Politics of Social Change in the Middle East and North Africa* (Princeton: Princeton University Press, 1963). Writing of the struggle to secularize politics in the Middle East, Halpern states: "There will still be battles, but this particular war is over in the great majority of Middle Eastern states," 130.
3 James P. Piscatori, *Islam in a World of Nation-States* (Cambridge: Cambridge University Press, 1986), 25.
4 William R. Roff, "Islamic Movements: One or Many?" In William R. Roff, ed. *Islam and the Political Economy of Meaning: Comparative Studies of Muslim Discourse* (London: Croom Helm, 1987), 47.
5 See, for example, the debate about the post-colonial state discussed in Colin Leys, "The 'Overdeveloped' Post Colonial State: A Re-evaluation," *Review of African Political Economy* 5 (January-April 1976). The term "conceptual variable" is J. P. Nettl's, an early advocate of state-centered theorizing. See his "The State as a Conceptual Variable," *World Politics* 20:4 (July 1968).
6 The most influential of recent works focused on the state has been Peter B. Evans, Dietrich Rueschemeyer, and Theda Skocpol, *Bringing the State Back In* (Cambridge: Cambridge University Press, 1985), but see also: Bertrand Badie

and Pierre Birnbaum, *Sociologie de l'état* (Paris: Bernard Grasset, 1979); and James A. Caporaso, *The Elusive State: International and Comparative Perspectives* (Newbury Park, California: Sage, 1989). On the African state, see Zaki Ergas, ed., *The African State in Transition* (New York: St. Martin's Press, 1987); Donald Rothchild and Naomi Chazan, eds., *The Precarious Balance: State and Society in Africa* (Boulder: Westview, 1988); and Jean-François Bayart, *L'Etat en Afrique* (Paris: Fayard, 1989).

7 See Theda Skocpol. "Bringing the State Back In: Strategies of Analysis in Current Research," in *Bringing the State Back In*, ed. Evans et al., for an elaboration of the state-centric model and its differences with society-centered ones.

8 Ibid., 9.

9 Forrest D. Colburn, "Statism, Rationality, and State Centrism," *Comparative Politics* 20:4 (July 1988), 488.

10 Naomi Chazan has thus argued that the nature of state-society relations is properly seen as a dependent variable in need of explanation. See her "Patterns of State-Society Incorporation and Disengagement in Africa," in *The Precarious Balance*, ed. Rothchild and Chazan, 123.

11 Max Weber, *The Theory of Social and Economic Organization* (New York: Free Press, 1947), 154, italics in original. The definition is restated and expanded on p. 156.

12 Lisa Anderson, "The State in the Middle East and North Africa," *Comparative Politics* 20:1 (October 1987), 2–3.

13 Michael G. Schatzberg, *The Dialectics of Oppression in Zaire* (Bloomington: Indiana University Press, 1988), 5–6.

14 For one of the more insightful of these, see the essay by Crawford Young, "The African Colonial State and Its Political Legacy," in *The Precarious Balance*, ed. Rothchild and Chazan, in which Young discusses seven "defining characteristics" of states.

15 Colburn, "Statism, Rationality, and State Centrism," 485.

16 Michael Bratton, "Beyond the State: Civil Society and Associational Life in Africa," *World Politics* 41:3 (1989), cites the definition in Victor Azarya, "Reordering State-Society Relations: Incorporation and Disengagement," in *The Precarious Balance*, ed. Rothchild and Chazan, 10. In a footnote Bratton modifies Azarya's "organization" to "a *set* of organizations – legal, coercive, administrative – whose functionaries do not always act cohesively," 409, italics in original. My restatement modifies the wording slightly to integrate the revision.

17 John Lonsdale, "States and Social Processes in Africa: A Historiographical Survey," *African Studies Review* 24:2/3 (June-September 1981), 141.

18 Gunnar Myrdal, *Asian Drama: An Inquiry into the Poverty of Nations* (New York: Twentieth Century Fund, 1968) first used the term "soft state" to refer to the countries of South Asia.

19 Joshua B. Forrest, "The Quest for State 'Hardness' in Africa," *Comparative Politics* 20:4 (July 1988).

20 For a concise discussion of the Gramscian notion of "hegemony," see Martin Carnoy, *The State and Political Theory* (Princeton: Princeton University Press, 1984), esp. chapter 3, "Gramsci and the State," 65–88.

21 Jean-François Bayart, "Civil Society in Africa," in *Political Domination in Africa: Reflections on the Limits of Power*, ed. Patrick Chabal (Cambridge: Cambridge University Press, 1986), 112. Italics in original.

22 Goran Hyden, *No Shortcuts to Progress: African Development Management in Perspective*, (Berkeley: University of California Press, 1983), 7. See also Badie and Birnbaum, *Sociologie de l'Etat*, who write: "L'état reste en Afrique comme en Asie un pur produit d'importation, une pâle copie des systèmes politiques et sociaux européens les plus opposés, un corps étranger de surcroit lourd, inefficace et source de violence," 181. Quoted in Bayart, *L'Etat en Afrique*, 27.

23 For a richly textured examination of the historical development of the colonial state, and its implications for the contemporary crisis of the African state, see Young, "The African Colonial State." On the evolution of the Senegalese state in response to indigenous political forces in the post-independence period, see Catherine Boone, "State Power and Economic Crisis in Senegal," *Comparative Politics* 22:3 (April 1990), 341–357 and *Merchant Capital and the Roots of State Power in Senegal, 1930–1985* (Cambridge: Cambridge University Press, 1992). In fairness to Hyden, it should be noted that he also notes that "the post-colonial state, in spite of a superficial structural resemblance with its colonial predecessor, is very different," 19. Hyden sees this change, however, as the result of the rupture brought about by independence rather than the product of evolutionary changes resulting from interactions with society.

24 Bayart, *L'Etat en Afrique*.

25 Robert Fatton, Jr., "The State of African Studies and Studies of the African State: The Theoretical Softness of the 'Soft State,'" *Journal of Asian and African Studies* 24:3/4 (1989), 172.

26 Bratton, "Beyond the State," 409.

27 Schatzberg, *The Dialectics of Oppression*.

28 Anderson, "The State in the Middle East," 2.

29 Bratton, "Beyond the State," 410, 411.

30 Robert H. Jackson and Carl G. Rosberg, "Why Africa's Weak States Persist: The Empirical and the Juridical in Statehood," *World Politics* 35:1 (October 1982).

31 Ibid., 16.

32 Ibid., 23.

33 For a discussion and critique of the concept of "nation-building" see Sheldon Gellar, "State-building and Nation-building in West Africa," in *Building States and Nations*, vol. 2, ed. S. N. Eisenstadt and S. Rokkan (Beverly Hills: Sage, 1973). On the European state, see Gianfranco Poggi, *The Development of the Modern State: A Sociological Introduction* (Stanford: Stanford University Press, 1978).

34 Robert H. Jackson, *Quasi-States: Sovereignty, International Relations, and the Third World* (Cambridge: Cambridge University Press, 1990). This book is a further development of Jackson's work with Carl Rosberg cited above.

35 Young, "The African Colonial State," 56.

36 Callaghy, *The State-Society Struggle*.

37 See Timothy Mitchell, "The Limits of the State: Beyond Statist Approaches and Their Critics," *American Political Science Review* 85:1 (March 1991), 77–96, for an interesting argument about the *political* production of the state-society distinction.

38 See Callaghy, *The State-Society Struggle*, 89–93 and *passim*.
39 Bratton, "Beyond the State," 427.
40 Ibid, 411. Bratton later cites Alfred Stepan, *Rethinking Military Politics: Brazil and the Southern Cone* (Princeton: Princeton University Press, 1988), 3–4, in defining civil society as an "arena where manifold social movements . . . and civic organizations from all classes . . . attempt to constitute themselves in an ensemble of arrangements so that they can express themselves and advance their interests," 417. The term "civil society" can be confusing because of the multiple uses to which it has historically been put. Used by both Hegel and Marx with different – and not always consistent – meanings, the term was later adopted by Gramsci in his formulation of a theory of the state. For Gramsci "civil society" comprises part of the ideological superstructure through which the state establishes its "hegemony." For a thorough discussion of these issues, see Carnoy, *The State and Political Theory*, especially chapter 3, "Gramsci and the State," 65–88.
41 Bayart, "Civil Society in Africa," 111, citing R. Fossaert, *La Société. Les Etats*, vol. 5 (Paris: Seuil, 1981), 146–7.
42 Patrick Chabal, "Introduction: Thinking about Politics in Africa," in *Political Domination in Africa*, ed. Chabal, 15. The sense of "externality and opposition" to the state, I believe, is crucial to distinguishing the term from society more broadly, and is thus emphasized here. Not all usages have done so, however; Martin Doornbos cites from the same passage in Chabal, but truncates the definition before the final clause cited here. See his "The African State in Academic Debate: Retrospect and Prospect," *The Journal of Modern African Studies* 28:2 (1990), 191.
43 Goran Hyden, *Beyond Ujamaa in Tanzania: Underdevelopment and an Uncaptured Peasantry* (London: Heinemann, 1980).
44 For a fascinating account of such activity in Zaire, see Janet MacGaffey, *Entrepreneurs and Parasites: The Struggle for Indigenous Capitalism in Zaire* (Cambridge: Cambridge University Press, 1987.) More broadly, Robert Bates has described the various ways in which individual peasant producers have been able to use the market *against* the state in Africa. See his *Markets and States in Tropical Africa: The Political Basis of Agricultural Policies* (Berkeley: University of California Press, 1981), especially pp. 82–87.
45 Julius E. Nyang'oro, "The State of Politics in Africa: The Corporatist Factor," *Studies in Comparative International Development* 24:1 (Spring 1989), 5–19.
46 James C. Scott, *Weapons of the Weak: Everyday Forms of Peasant Resistance* (New Haven: Yale University Press, 1985).
47 Nathan J. Brown, *Peasant Politics in Modern Egypt: The Struggle Against the State* (New Haven: Yale University Press, 1990).
48 "La liste est longue des pratiques populaires qui limitent et relativisent le champ étatique, assurant ici aussi une certaine revanche de la société sur celui-ci et contribuant à sa faillite économique." Jean-François Bayart, "La Revanche des sociétés africaines," *Politique Africaine* 11 (September 1983), 102. See also by the same author, "Les Sociétés africaines face à l'état," *Pouvoirs* 25 (1983); and "Le Politique par le bas en Afrique Noire: Question de méthode," *Politique Africaine* 1 (January 1981). Bayart has more recently expanded on this theme in *L'Etat en Afrique*.
49 Bratton, "Beyond the State," 415.

50 These reactions are frequently described in the terminology of Hirschman's analysis of possible responses to organizational decline – one can "exit" the firm, or one can "voice" a complaint. Albert O. Hirschman, *Exit, Voice, and Loyalty: Responses to Decline in Firms, Organizations and States* (Cambridge: Harvard University Press, 1970). For an effort by Hirschman to apply these concepts directly to relations with the state, see his "Exit, Voice, and the State," *World Politics* 31:1 (October 1978).

51 Victor Azarya, "Reordering State-Society Relations: Incorporation and Disengagement," in *The Precarious Balance*, ed. Rothchild and Chazan, 6. See also Naomi Chazan's article in the same volume, as well as their co-authored "Disengagement from the State in Africa: Reflections on the Experience of Ghana and Guinea," *Comparative Studies in Society and History* 29:1 (January 1987).

52 Bratton, "Beyond the State," 424–425. In light of this modification Bratton also suggests a four-fold framework for classifying state-society relations by considering the type of relation ("engagement" or "disengagement") and the source (state-sponsored or society-sponsored).

53 Edward Mortimer, *Faith and Power: The Politics of Islam* (New York: Random House, 1982), 396.

54 Dale F. Eickelman, "Changing Interpretations of Islamic Movements," in *Islam and the Political Economy of Meaning*, ed. Roff, 19–20 discusses the use of the term. See also Abdul Hamid M. El-Zein, "Beyond Ideology and Theology: The Search for the Anthropology of Islam," *Annual Review of Anthropology* 6 (1977), 227–254. El-Zein concludes that "neither Islam nor the notion of religion exists as a fixed and autonomous form referring to positive content which can be reduced to universal and unchanging characteristics. Religion becomes an arbitrary category which as a unified and bounded form has no necessary existence. 'Islam' as an analytical category dissolves as well." (p. 252). For a critique of this approach see Bruce B. Lawrence, "Muslim Fundamentalist Movements: Reflections toward a New Approach," in *The Islamic Impulse*, ed. Barbara Freyer Stowasser (London: Croom Helm), 134 and fn. 29.

55 An excellent collection of essays focused on the question of the shared discursive elements in Muslim societies is Roff, ed., *Islam and the Political Economy of Meaning*. Roff, who is himself quite critical of the "essentialism" of much writing on Islam, concludes his contribution to the book with the observation that: "If there is not an 'Islamic World,' perhaps at times not even a 'Muslim World,' there is an evident World of Muslims, to whom Muslim discourse speaks," 48.

56 Thus Charles Stewart suggests that the term "popular Islam" which – like that of "islams" – implies "denial or fragmentation within the Great Tradition or 'orthodoxy' in Islam" also reflects "a degree of hostility on the part of those Islamicists and Muslims whose understanding of the oneness of God extends to the indivisibility of His Community." "Introduction: Popular Islam in Twentieth Century Africa," in *'Popular Islam' South of the Sahara*, ed. C. C. Stewart and J. D. Y. Peel (Manchester: Manchester University Press, 1985), 363. (Originally published as *Africa: The Journal of the International Africa Institute*, 55:4).

57 Daniel Pipes, *In the Path of God: Islam and Political Power* (New York: Basic

Books, 1983), 11 and 7. Given the frequent tendency of politicized Islamic movements to refuse to acknowledge the validity of others' Islam, Pipes' definition of "mainstream Muslims" is highly problematic. Still, Pipes clearly means "the vast majority of Muslims," including here both Sunnis and Shiʿa since, he states, "Shiʿa laws differ most dramatically from those of the Sunnis in that they permit temporary marriage," 11.

58 For examples of works structured in this way see: Tareq Y. Ismael and Jacqueline S. Ismael, *Government and Politics in Islam* (London: Frances Pinter, 1985) and Don Peretz, Richard U. Moench, and Safia K. Mohsen, *Islam: Legacy of the Past: Challenge of the Future* (np: North River Press, 1984) Although more nuanced, the argument in John L. Esposito, *Islam and Politics* (Syracuse: Syracuse University Press, 2nd edn. 1987) also proceeds in a similar fashion.

59 Esposito, *Islam and Politics*, 17–18.

60 For a thoughtful contemporary example of the continuing relevance of Islamic theology for Muslim intellectuals grappling with the issue of defining an appropriate political system, see Abdulrahman Abdulkadir Kurdi, *The Islamic State: A Study Based on the Islamic Holy Constitution* (London: Mansell Publishing Ltd., 1984). For a more boldly titled example, by a writer who has had a profound impact on the subcontinent, particularly in Pakistan, see Syed Abul Aʿla Maududi, *System of Government Under the Holy Prophet (Peace Be Upon Him) with Discussion on the Method for Implementing it in Pakistan Today* (Lahore, Pakistan: Islamic Publications Ltd., 1978).

61 It bears noting here that there is also a certain ambivalence in the feelings of Senegalese Muslims about Arabs, and by extension Persians and other non-Black Muslims. Tensions produced by suspicions of racism coexist with admiration and fraternal feelings as fellow Muslims. Feelings of distrust of "Arabs" were heightened by the tension between Senegal and Mauritania which followed the violent clashes between Black Senegalese and Moors in April of 1989.

62 Esposito, *Islam and Politics*, xvi.

63 Emmanuel Sivan, *Radical Islam: Medieval Theology and Modern Politics* (New Haven: Yale University Press, 1985), 181.

64 Ali Merad, "The Ideologisation of Islam in the Contemporary Muslim World," in *Islam and Power*, ed. Alexander S. Cudsi and Ale E. Hillal Dessouki (London: Croom Helm, 1981), 38.

65 Lawrence, "Muslim Fundamentalist Movements," 31. For a somewhat different, and highly insightful, approach which proposes a typology of varieties of Muslim "ideological orientations," see William E. Shepherd, "Islam and Ideology: Towards a Typology," *International Journal of Middle East Studies* 19 (1987), 307–336. Shepherd attempts to place Muslim ideological positions on a two-dimensional scale on which the axes are "modernity" and "Islamism." By the latter he means the degree to which the notion of Islam as a "blueprint" for all of social life is accepted. In this sense, this dimension might be defined by its other pole: secularism. The argument I make here is most relevant for movements that Shepherd would place high on the "Islamism" scale – which is in fact where ideologies which labelled themselves "Islamic" would be found.

66 Esposito, *Islam and Politics*, xvi.

67 Jean-Claude Vatin, "Popular Puritanism versus State Reformism: Islam in Algeria," in *Islam in the Political Process*, ed. Piscatori, 98. Roff makes a similar point in discussing "the importance of the state as a primary determinant of Islamic discourses." He notes the ways in which the state establishes the "dominant terms of discourse" and the opposing use of "'Islamist' discourse ... [by] social groups which are in certain ways at odds with state power." "Editor's Introduction," in *Islam and the Political Economy of Meaning*, 5–6.

68 Ismael and Ismael, *Government and Politics in Islam*, 127.

69 The Muslim calendar enshrines the importance of Mohammed's *hijra* by counting the years from that event. The AH of Muslim dates (as distinct from AD) thus refers to *Anno Hejirae* ("In the year of the *hijra*").

70 Esposito, *Islam and Politics*, 41.

71 David Robinson, *The Holy War of Umar Tal: The Western Sudan in the mid-Nineteenth century*. (Oxford: Clarendon Press, 1985), 217. For a discussion of the debate on the relative merits of *jihad* and *hijra*, see also John Hanson, "*Jihad* and the *Talibé* Colonization of Karta: the Genesis of a Dissident Tradition in the Umarian Movement." (Paper presented at the 36th annual meeting of the African Studies Association. Boston, MA, 4–7 December 1993.) An anthology of English translations of original historical sources on the debates of this period is available in John Hanson and David Robinson, *After the Jihad: The Reign of Ahmad al-Kabir in the Western Sudan*. (East Lansing: Michigan State University Press, 1991.)

72 Ismael and Ismael, *Government and Politics in Islam*, 127.

73 Cudsi and Dessouki, "Introduction," in *Islam and Power*, 5.

74 Sami Zubaida, *Islam, the People and the State: Essays on Political Ideas and Movements in the Middle East* (London: Routledge, 1989), ix.

75 Mortimer, *Faith and Power*, 406.

76 Although of course not all. James P. Piscatori, most notably, has argued strongly for the pre-eminence of politics. As he puts it: "It is the opposite ranking, religion first and politics second, or a different assumption, religion determining politics, which we have seen in the literature, that troubles me ... [P]olitics has a life of its own and influences the evolution of values more often than this literature would have us believe; politics is more often independent of than dependent on religion." *Islam in a World of Nation-States*, 13.

77 The impact of state structures on religion is reflected in such studies of "national islams" as Dale Eickelman's excellent work, *Moroccan Islam: Tradition and Society in a Pilgrimage Center* (Austin: The University of Texas Press, 1976).

2   THE STRUCTURE OF SOCIETY: FATICK IN THE SENEGALESE CONTEXT

1 Martin A. Klein, *Islam and Imperialism in Senegal: Sine-Saloum, 1847–1914* (Stanford: Stanford University Press, 1968), 43, 56ff, 115, 120ff, and 203.

2 See the exhaustive description of Senegal's economy by Régine Nguyen-Van-Chi-Bonardel, *Vie de Relations au Sénégal: La circulation des biens* (Dakar: Mémoires de l'Institut Fondamental d'Afrique Noire No. 90, 1978), especially chapter 1, "Le poids de l'arachide," 55–178, for a discussion of the role of peanuts in Senegal's economy. The adherence of Fatick to this classic colonial

pattern was emphasized to me by the Secretary General of the (now rather inactive) Fatick Chamber of Commerce, Interview, 31 August 1989. This was also confirmed at various times by the few individuals who remained as remnants of the Lebanese families that once played an important part in this system.

3 The figures are from J. Fouquet, *La traite des arachides dans le pays de Kaolack et ses conséquences économiques, sociales et juridiques* (St. Louis du Sénégal: Institut Français d'Afrique Noire, 1958), cited in Martin A. Klein, "Colonial Rule and Structural Change: The Case of Sine-Saloum," in *The Political Economy of Underdevelopment: Dependence in Senegal*, ed. Rita Cruise O'Brien (Beverly Hills: Sage, 1979), 79.

4 For a discussion of the role of the peanut trade in the transformations of the region of Sine-Saloum and the growth of Kaolack, see Mohamed Mbodj, "Un Exemple d'économie coloniale, le Sine-Saloum (Sénégal) de 1887 à 1940: Cultures arachidières et mutations sociales." Unpublished *Thèse de 3eme Cycle*. Université de Paris VII, 1977–78 (Three volumes).

5 See Edward J. Schumacher, *Politics, Bureaucracy and Rural Development in Senegal* (Berkeley: University of California Press, 1975) for a discussion of the transition from the colonial to the post-independence organization of the peanut economy.

6 The *lycée*, opened in the early 1980s shortly before Fatick was named a regional capital, now counts some 1200 students of which over half are drawn from outside the town.

7 HLM is the acronym for "Habitations à loyer modéré," housing projects built with government participation and which, despite their name, are highly desirable and beyond the reach of the vast majority of people in a place like Fatick.

8 Interviews, 3 November 1989, 17 November 1989, 26 June 1989.

9 Aside from Klein's history of Sine-Saloum, little has been published on the Serer *per se*, and virtually nothing on Islam in the Serer regions. The three-volume study in progress by the French priest and scholar Henry Gravrand will do much to fill this need. To date the first two volumes have been published: *La Civilisation Sereer: Cosaan: Les origines* (Dakar: Les Nouvelles Editions Africaines, 1983), and *La Civilisation Sereer: Pangool: Le génie religieux Sereer* (Dakar: Les Nouvelles Editions Africaines, 1990). To this should be added several monographs produced by French research organizations. Note in particular Jean-Marc Gastellu, *L'égalitarisme économique des Serer du Sénégal*, Travaux et Documents de L'ORSTOM, 128 (Paris: ORSTOM,1981); and Jean-Claude Reverdy, "Une Société rurale au Sénégal: Les structures foncières, familiales, et villageoises des Serer" (Aix-en-Provence: Centre Africain des Sciences Humaines Appliquées, collection des Travaux du CASHA, n.d.)

10 For a series of interviews on ethnic relations in Senegal, see *Two Studies on Ethnic Group Relations in Africa: Senegal; The United Republic of Tanzania* (Paris: UNESCO, 1974).

11 See Clifford Geertz, "The Integrative Revolution: Primordial Sentiments and Civil Politics in the New States," in *Old Societies and New States: The Quest for Modernity in Asia and Africa*, ed. Geertz (London: The Free Press of Glencoe, 1963) for an early and comprehensive statement of this perspective.

12 The contextual and fluid nature of cultural identity has been widely documented in African studies, and is perhaps most thoroughly analyzed in Crawford Young, *The Politics of Cultural Pluralism* (Madison, Wisconsin: The University of Wisconsin Press, 1976). See especially chapter 4, "Patterns of Identity Change and Cultural Mobilization," 98–139.

13 This position has been convincingly argued by Robert A. Bates. See his "Ethnicity in Contemporary Africa," (Eastern African Studies XIV, Program of Eastern African Studies, Maxwell School of Citizenship and Public Affairs, Syracuse University, 1973), and "Modernization, Ethnic Competition, and the Rationality of Politics in Contemporary Africa," in *Governing in Black Africa*, ed. M. E. Doro and N. M. Schultz (New York: Africana, 1986).

14 David D. Laitin, "Hegemony and Religious Conflict: British Imperial Control and Political Cleavages in Yorubaland," in *Bringing the State Back In*, ed. Peter B. Evans, Dietrich Rueschmayer, and Theda Skocpol (Cambridge: Cambridge University Press, 1985), 286–287. See also Laitin's book-length exposition of this argument, *Hegemony and Culture: Politics and Religious Change among the Yoruba* (Chicago: Chicago University Press, 1986). The issue of "motivation" in Laitin's definition is clearly applicable in the case of African states but, as the discussion in chapter 2 indicated, African states are (despite variations that are of interest for comparative purposes) generally characterized by the *weakness* of their power to shape social structures. There is, therefore, reason to doubt the extent to which state hegemony can be usefully said to remain as the primary determinant of politicized social cleavages in Africa.

15 This is the position of Guy Nicolas, who argues that in the predominantly Muslim states of Black Africa, "the common adherence to the Muslim religion can reinforce national cohesion." See his "Islam et 'constructions nationales' au sud du Sahara," *Revue Française d'Etudes Politiques Africaines* 165/166 (September/October 1979), 93.

16 This census was carried out in May 1988, and national results are now available in République du Sénégal, Ministère de l'Economie, des Finances et du Plan, Direction de la Prévision de la Statistique. "Recensement général de la population et de l'habitat, mai–juin 1988: Résultats définitifs." (1990) With the help of an official at the Direction de la Prévision et de la Statistique, I was able to get most of the census results for the town of Fatick, including information not otherwise released (namely religion) as well as cross-tabulation of certain variables. Unless otherwise attributed, all demographic figures and tables for Fatick or Senegal given in this work were compiled by the author from this data set. Small variations in figures from one table to another are almost always the result of the fact that two slightly different data bases were used; one for legal population ("population de droit") which counted residents present at time of census plus regular residents absent at that time, and another for actual population ("population de fait"), which counted all of those actually present at time of census, including those normally resident elsewhere.

17 The most thorough ethnographic study of the Wolof available is Abdoulaye-Bara Diop, *La Société Wolof: Tradition et Changement: Les Systèmes d'inégalité et de domination* (Paris: Karthala, 1981). See also David P. Gamble, *The Wolof of Senegambia, Together with Notes on the Lebu and the Serer* (London: International African Institute, Oxford University Press, 1957).

18 See Donal B. Cruise O'Brien, "Langue et nationalité au Sénégal: l'enjeu politique de la Wolofisation," in *Année africaine 1979* (Paris: A. Pedone), and Leigh Swigart, "Cultural Creolization and Language Use in Postcolonial Africa: The Case of Senegal," in *Africa* 64:2 (1994) for a discussion of this evolution in ethnic identity.

19 An insightful consideration of the meaning of "being Wolof" in an urban setting is provided in Leigh Swigart, "Wolof, Language or Ethnic Group? The Development of a National Identity," paper delivered at the annual meeting of the African Studies Association, Baltimore, Maryland, November 1990.

20 Speakers of various dialects of this language are found throughout West Africa, and it is variously referred to by the terms Fula, Ful, Peul, Fulfulde, and Fulani.

21 These are probably the descendents of people who have inhabited this area since Paleolithic times, and consequently antedate the "true" Serer. These groups speak languages of the Cangin group, only distantly related (if at all) to the West Atlantic language family subgroup which includes Wolof, Serer, and Pulaar. See J. David Sapir, "West Atlantic: An Inventory of the Languages, Their Noun Class Systems and Consonant Alternation," in *Current Trends in Linguistics* 7, ed. Thomas Sebeok, 58. In this work the term Serer used alone will always refer to the majority Serer, exclusive of these smaller groups.

22 Gravrand, *La Civilisation Sereer: Cosaan*, 55, lists these kingdoms and their periods of origin. One of the two other kingdoms, Djonik, disappeared early, while the third, Saloum, lasted along with Sine into the colonial period. The French combined the two into the administrative unit of Sine-Saloum, which became one of the regions of Senegal at independence. The 1984 administrative reforms that established ten regions in Senegal, each bearing the name of its capital city, divided Sine-Saloum into two. The new region of Kaolack corresponds roughly to the traditional area of Saloum, while the region of Fatick includes most of Sine. It bears noting that this reform seems to have been targeted primarily at the Casamance, which was divided into the two regions of Kolda and Ziguinchor, thus eliminating the last regions of the country to bear names with pre-colonial or ethnic connotations.

23 This lack of connections between the heirs to Sine's political structure and those of its cultural traditions represents one of the most paradoxical aspects of the political sociology of Fatick. While both E. H. Farba Diouf and the descendents of the last *Buur-Siin*, Mahecor Diouf, maintain large households in Fatick (neither of them in Ndiaye-Ndiaye), I frequently found in interviews with many Serer that I needed to explain who they were when referring to these descendents of the royal families.

24 Gravrand, *La Civilisation Sereer: Cosaan*, especially chapters 4, "La Vallée du Sénégal, 'sanctuaire national'," and 5, "L'Exode Serer," 79–127. Linguistic research corroborates this history. See Fiona McLaughlin, *Noun Classification in Seereer-Siin*, Ph.D. dissertation, The University of Texas at Austin, 1992.

25 This is reported in an interview about the use of the *kaal* with the historian and 1993 presidential candidate Iba der Thiam, *Wal Fadjri* 175 (25 August 1989). A related article in the same source recalls that former president Senghor (himself a Serer) made extensive political use of the *kaal* in dealing with the Tukulor population. Paul Pélissier notes that the *kaal* ties have meant that Tukulor have traditionally been well received when settling among the Serer, *Les paysans du*

Sénégal: Les civilisations agraires du Cayor à la Casamance (Saint-Yrieix, Haute-Vienne: Fabrègue, 1966), 194.

26 Interview with the imam of the Ndiaye-Ndiaye mosque, 17 March 1989.

27 Interview with the prefect, 17 January 1989. Others at times expressed similar sentiments.

28 In research on urban language use in Dakar, Leigh Swigart found that when asked what language they associated with Islam, the majority of her informants answered Wolof, rather than Arabic, regardless of their own ethnicity. Personal communication. See also, Leigh Swigart, "Practice and Perception: Language Use and Attitudes in Dakar," Ph.D. dissertation, University of Washington, 1992.

29 While the generalizations to be made below are valid for the three main groups discussed here, it should be noted that the Diola people of the lower Casamance area represent a noteworthy exception to these shared Sahelian cultural traits – a fact that is certainly of relevance if we consider that the Diola have been the source of Senegal's most significant ethnic political movements, and its only separatist one. On Diola society see: Louis-Vincent Thomas, *Les Diola: Essai d'analyse fonctionnelle sur une population de Basse-Casamance*, volumes 1 and 2 (Dakar: Institut Français d'Afrique Noire, 1959).

30 Diop, *La Société Wolof*. Although I remain unconvinced of the validity of her contention that hierarchy should not be considered a defining characteristic of the caste system, a nevertheless excellent discussion of the significance of the caste system in Senegambian societies is provided by Bonnie Wright, "The Power of Articulation," in *Creativity of Power: Cosmology and Action in African Societies*, ed. W. Arens and Ivan Karp, (Washington: Smithsonian Institution Press, 1989), 39–57.

31 Also variously described as oral historians, genealogists, musicians or entertainers, the position of griots is a particularly enigmatic one. While on the one hand they are frequently looked down upon by others as the very lowest caste – a position justified and reinforced by various myths of their origins – the fact that they fulfill certain indispensable social functions also endows them with significant power. Both Diop, *La Société Wolof* and Wright, "The Power of Articulation," contain good discussions of this caste.

32 Wright, Ibid., makes this point and I borrow from her insights here. *Xeet* also refers to a matrilineage, and it is probable that this is in fact the original sense of the word.

33 Interview, imam of Ndiaye-Ndiaye mosque, 13 September 1989. For further discussion of the survival of the caste system see Ousmane Silla, "La Persistance des castes dans la société wolof contemporaine," *Bulletin de l'IFAN (L'Institut Fondamentale d'Afrique Noire)*, 28, B: 3–4 (1966), 731–770.

34 Quoted in Gerti Hesseling, *Histoire politique du Sénégal: Institutions, droit et société* (Paris: Karthala, 1985), 82.

35 A rare example of political action along caste lines was reported in the Islamic weekly, *Wal Fadjri*, No. 334, 9–15 October 1992. As the campaign for the February 1993 presidential campaign got underway a Laobé association, described in the article as "an ethnic group which also has elements (*des allures*) of caste," made a public promise to support President Abdou Diouf in his re-election efforts. The article also reports a "bewildering" (*effarant*) episode in

Kaolack in which a group of *ñeeño* held a meeting to announce the support of casted people for the president.

36 Thomas A. Hale and Paul Stoller, "Oral Art, Society, and Survival in the Sahel," in *African Literature Studies: The Present State/L'Etat Présent*, ed. Stephen Arnold (Washington: Three Continents Press, 1985), 164.

37 See Lucie G. Colvir., "The *Shaykh's* Men: Religion and Power in Senegambian Islam," in *Rural and Urban Islam in West Africa*, ed. Nehemia Levtzion and Humphrey J. Fisher (Boulder: Lynne Rienner, 1987), for a discussion of the historical centrality of the notion of personal dependence to the political-economic culture of the Senegambia region.

38 Diop, *La Société Wolof*, 84 and note.

39 Hale and Stoller, "Oral Art."

40 Tellingly, the only information on religion provided by the government is the proportion of Muslims to Christians, a cleavage with little political significance. The data on religious affiliation in Fatick presented in this work was provided to me by the official at the Direction de la Prévision et de la Statistique mentioned above, who prefers to remain anonymous.

41 The Roman Catholic priest who serves as pastor of the Church in Fatick described quite candidly the ways in which the Senegalese Catholic Church has been influenced by the predominant Sufi Muslim forms of organization. Most interestingly, he described various advantages and disadvantages of this status in relations with the state. Christians, he said, were at a disadvantage at times in that priests were reluctant to follow the marabouts' example in automatically defending disciples regardless of the circumstances. At the same time, given the state's extreme care to avoid the appearance of favoritism, they benefited from such innovations as state patronage and financial assistance in the organization of an "annual pilgrimage to the holy places of Christianity," a purely Senegalese innovation clearly patterned on the *hajj*. Interview, 8 November 1989.

42 For surveys of that history, see: Mervyn Hiskett, *The Development of Islam in West Africa* (London: Longman, 1984), and Peter B. Clarke, *West Africa and Islam: A Study of Religious Development from the 8th to the 20th Century* (London: Edward Arnold, 1982). An older work is J. Spencer Trimingham, *Islam in West Africa* (Oxford: Oxford University Press, 1959). A review of this history focused primarily on Senegal is available in El Hadji Ravane Mbaye, "L'Islam au Sénégal," Thèse de doctorat de troisième cycle, Department of Arabic, The University of Dakar, 1976. For discussions of a number of the central figures in this history, see John Ralph Willis, ed., *Studies in West African Islamic History. Volume 1: The Cultivators of Islam* (London: Frank Cass, 1979).

43 This hypothesized correlation of the two processes has been suggested by various scholars, and is perhaps most fully developed in Christian Coulon, *Le Marabout et le prince: Islam et pouvoir au Sénégal* (Paris: A. Pedone, 1981). See in particular part I of that work, entitled "Le Phénomène maraboutique comme reconstruction sociale et politique."

44 Mbaye, "L'Islam au Sénégal," 106. Mbaye argues that only the Wolof were eventually able to convert the Serer. He does not mention the Mouride order, though it seems clear that to the extent that he is right such conversion would have been limited to the rural areas of the expanding peanut frontier. In Fatick

this pattern certainly does not hold. To the extent that an ethnic tie can be attached to the conversion of Fatick's Serer, it is the Tukulor who must take the credit.

45 On Ma Ba's *jihad* see, in addition to chapter 4 of Klein, *Islam and Imperialism*, the following: Kélétigui S. Keita, "Maba Diakhou Ba dans le Rip et le Saloum (1861–1867)," Mémoire de Maîtrise, Université de Dakar, 1970; and Charlotte Alison Quinn, "Maba Diakhou and the Gambian Jihad, 1850–1890," in *Studies in West African Islamic History. Volume 1: The Cultivators of Islam*, ed. John Ralph Willis (London: Frank Cass, 1979). A hagiographic work, presenting Ma Ba as a Senegalese national hero is Iba Der Thiam, *Maba Diakhou Ba, almamy du Rip (Sénégal)* (Paris: ABC, "Grandes Figures Africaines" series, 1977).

46 Keita, "Maba Diakhou Ba."

47 Interviews, griot, 27 February 1989, and with the marabout, 9 March 1989.

48 Klein, *Islam and Imperialism*, 219. The correlation between socio-economic and political change and Islamization in explaining the differences between Sine and Saloum is one of Klein's main points in chapter XI, "The Triumph of Islam."

49 Paul Marty, *Etudes sur l'Islam au Sénégal*, 2 volumes (Paris: Leroux, 1917); figure cited in Klein, *Islam and Imperialism*, 220.

50 Ibid., 219.

51 Donal B. Cruise O'Brien, "Islam and Power in Black Africa," in *Islam and Power*, ed. Alexander S. Cudsi and Ali E. Hillal Dessouki (London: Croom Helm, 1981), 159.

52 "Marabout" and its Wolof equivalent, *sëriñ* are actually much broader terms, referring simply to any religious notable of any stature. *Shaykh* is a more precise term, used in Senegal by the Mouride and the Qadir orders to refer to a notable of the appropriate stature in an order to be capable of transmitting the *wird*. The equivalent term used by the Tijan order is *muqàddam*. In keeping with conventional usage in Senegal, I will prefer the term "marabout" unless the discussion requires the more precise term.

53 There is significant variation in Senegal on this issue. Many followers of the Tijaniyya order, particularly among the Tukulor ethnic group, adhere more closely to the "classic" Sufi pattern. In the Mouride order, on the contrary, the act of declaring submission is absolutely central. For a more extensive discussion of Sufism see, Julian Baldick, *Mystical Islam: an Introduction to Sufism* (London: J. B. Tauris and Co., 1989).

54 In Cruise O'Brien's terms, the orders "may properly be understood as a vehicle for the mass inculcation of a form of Sunni orthodoxy by a literate and learned few." In "Islam and Power," 158.

55 Interview, 28 March 1989.

56 Assane Sylla and El-Hadji Mamadou Sakhir Gaye, *Le Mahdi: Mouhamadou Seydina Limamou Laye du Sénégal* (Imprimerie Nationale Rufisque, 2nd edn, May 1985). This local publication easily available in Dakar makes the argument for accepting Laye as the long-awaited *mahdi*.

57 It may be useful at this point to clarify names. The terms "Tijaniyya" and "Qadiriyya" are based on the Arabic forms of the nouns that identify these orders. The parallel term for the third order would therefore be "Muridiyya." Although it is occasionally used by some Arabist scholars this term is unknown in Senegal, where the order is always referred to by its Franco-Wolof name of

Mouride (Murid). I thus prefer this non-parallel but more locally accurate use of terms in this work.

58 For a history of the Boutilimit founder and his times, see Charles C. Stewart, *Islam and Social Order in Mauritania: A Case Study from the Nineteenth Century* (Oxford: Clarendon Press, 1973). A brief sketch of the Qadiriyya and of the relations of these three families is available in René Luc Moreau, *Africains Musulmans: des communautés en mouvement* (Paris: Présence Africaine, 1982), 152–165. For an account of the bewilderingly complex Kunta genealogy, see A. A. Batran, "The Kunta, Sidi al-Mukhtar al-Kunti, and the Office of *Shaykh al-Tariqa'l-Qadiriyya*," in *Studies in West African Islamic History*, ed. Willis, 113–146. A rather arcane study by a Senegalese scholar devoted to the Sufi vision of the Qadiriyya's founder is Ibrahima Boye, *Sayyidi Abdal Qadr Djilani: Imam Suprême de la 'Walaya'* (Paris: Publisud, 1990).

59 Until his death in 1988, the *xalifa* at Nimzatt was *Shaykh* Sidaty Aïdara, a grandson of the founder, Saad Bou. He was succeeded by his brother, *Shaykh* Mohamed Ma'al Ainine, who presided over the family until his death in Dakar on 7 October 1991. The current *xalifa*, another brother, is named Saad Bou after his grandfather, but also known as "Cheikhna Atnafayil." Their brother Abdoul Aziz Aïdara is the marabout in Thiès, and the brother with the more important ties in Fatick is named Bou Nana Aïdara. There are some claims that this youngest brother "should" have been the *xalifa* from their father's death, having been so designated by the elder marabout. He however, refuses to press the issue. The family has clearly not fully resolved succession issues; in 1989 tension erupted into open conflict among the brothers, and the unity of the lineage occasionally appears to be threatened. Interviews with a stepson of Bou Nana and with Qadir *taalibes*, 5 and 9 December 1989.

60 Donal B. Cruise O'Brien, "Sufi Politics in Senegal," in *Islam in the Political Process*, ed. James P. Piscatori (Cambridge: Cambridge University Press, 1983), 132.

61 Interviews, 5 and 6 December 1989.

62 The most complete account of the order's founding and subsequent development is that of Jamil M. Abun-Nasr, *The Tijaniyya: A Sufi Order in the Modern World* (London: Oxford University Press, 1965). There are relatively few works devoted specifically to the order in Senegal, but see Ibrahima Marone, "Le Tidjanisme au Sénégal," *Bulletin de l'Institut Fondamentale d'Afrique Noire*, Série B: Sciences Humaines 32:1 (January 1970), 136–215; and Demba Koné, "Tidjanisme et pouvoir politique au Sénégal (1950–1987)," Mémoire de Maîtrise, Université Cheikh Anta Diop de Dakar, 1988.

63 Whether Bello in fact was converted or not is a matter of contention, but it nevertheless seems clear that El Hajj Umar was largely responsible for establishing the Tijaniyya in Sokoto. For a review of the historiographical debate about the reported initiation see: John N. Paden, *Religion and Political Culture in Kano* (Berkeley: University of California Press, 1973), 76ff.

64 For more on El Hajj Umar's life, see: Cheikh Moussa Kamara, "La Vie d'El Hadji Omar," translated and annotated by Amar Samb, *Bulletin de l'Institut Fondamentale d'Afrique Noire*, Série B: Sciences Humaines 32:1 (January 1970), 44–135; David Robinson, *The Holy War of Umar Tal: The Western Sudan in the Mid-Nineteenth Century* (Oxford: Clarendon Press, 1985); and John Ralph

Willis, *In the Path of Allah. The Passion of Al-Hajj Umar: An Essay into the Nature of Charisma in Islam* (London: Frank Cass, 1990).

65 Among the more important of these are the Dème family of Sokone, the Bâ family of Médina Gounasse, and the Cissé family in Pire. The exact chain of transmission of the *wird* (i.e., the *silsila*, or spiritual genealogy) of these various families is highly complicated and a frequent source of contention. The central importance of El Hajj Umar for all of them and the significance of variations in the chain was made clear to me in an interview with an Arabic teacher active in mosque affairs in Fatick (whose position is nevertheless ambiguous due to uncertain caste status). This man, who might accurately be described as a Tukulor nationalist and a Tijan supremacist, gave me his own complicated version of over a dozen such spiritual genealogies. Interview, 21 November 1989.

66 The Arabic term *zawiya*, which refers to a Sufi center usually organized around the tomb of a saintly figure, is not in common usage in Senegal. No adequate substitute exists, however, and I will therefore follow the literature in adopting this term to refer to the centers of the major maraboutic lineages.

67 For a discussion of the Niasse family ties with Nigeria, see Ousmane Kane, "La Confrérie 'Tijaniyya Ibrahimiyya' de Kano et ses liens avec la zawiya mère de Kaolack," *Islam et Sociétés au sud du Sahara* 3 (May 1989), 27–40. Indicative of the continuing relevance of the ties is that throughout the Hausa areas of northern Nigeria and Niger, photos, badges and other religious memorabilia of Baye Niasse are displayed and readily available for sale.

68 The most noteworthy of this work is the *oeuvre* of Donal Cruise O'Brien, whose name in scholarly circles is virtually synonymous with Mouride studies. Note in particular his two book-length works: *The Mourides of Senegal: The Political and Economic Organization of an Islamic Brotherhood* (Oxford: Clarendon Press, 1971) and *Saints and Politicians: Essays in the Organization of a Senegalese Peasant Society* (Cambridge: Cambridge University Press, 1975). Other works on the order include: Jean Copans, *Les Marabouts de l'arachide: La confrérie mouride et les paysans du Sénégal* (Paris: Le Sycomore, 1980); and Cheikh Tidiane Sy, *La Confrérie Sénégalaise des Mourides: Un essai sur l'Islam au Sénégal* (Paris: Présence Africaine, 1969).

69 Jean-Louis Triaud, "Le Thème confrérique en Afrique de l'Ouest," in *Les Ordres mystiques dans l'Islam: Cheminements et situation actuelle*, ed. A. Popovic and G. Veinstein (Paris: EHESS, 1986). Donal B. Cruise O'Brien notes this critique in his "Introduction," in *Charisma and Brotherhood in African Islam*, ed. Cruise O'Brien and Christian Coulon (Oxford: Clarendon Press, 1988), 26(n).

70 From 1895 to 1902 Amadou Bamba was exiled to Gabon by the French who feared the large crowds of converts he was attracting following the collapse of Baol. His return sparked even more conversions, and within a year the colonial authorities exiled him once more, this time north to Mauritania. Although always wary of his influence, a more cooperative relationship with the French was eventually established over the twenty-year period from his return to Senegal in 1907 until his death. For more on Amadou Bamba's life, see Donal B. Cruise O'Brien, "The Saint and the Squire: Personalities and Social Forces in the Development of a Religious Brotherhood," in *African Perspectives: Papers*

in the History, Politics and Economics of Africa Presented to Thomas Hodgkin,
ed. Christopher Allen and R. W. Johnson (Cambridge: Cambridge University
Press, 1970); and Lucy E. Creevey, "Ahmed Bamba 1850–1927," in *Studies in
West African Islamic History,* ed. Willis.

71 "The peanut marabouts," this from the title of Copans' work, *Les Marabouts de
l'arachide.*

72 See Donal B. Cruise O'Brien, "Charisma Comes to Town: Mouride Urbanization 1945–1986" in *Charisma and Brotherhood,* ed. Cruise O'Brien and Coulon,
for a discussion of this process, and Victoria Ebin, "A la recherche de nouveaux
'poissons': Stratégies commerciales mourides par temps de crise," in *Politique
Africaine* 45 (March 1992) for a case study of the development of international
trade networks by a Mouride family.

73 Unconvinced that many would soon return to Senegal, Embassy officials
granted few visas. My thanks to Capie Polk for having provided me with a copy
of this invitation. Concerning the communities in Europe, I personally met one
group of traders in Granada, Spain in the summer of 1988 and have been
informed of other well established communities in Italy. France, of course, has
long had a large Senegalese community.

74 These estimates, for which no precise dates are given, are based on a survey done
by the Centre de Hautes Etudes Administratives sur l'Afrique et l'Asie
Modernes (CHEAM), and reported in that organization's publication, *Notes et
études sur l'Islam en Afrique Noire* (Paris: Peyronnet, 1962), 193–194. All
estimates cited here are from this source.

75 République du Sénégal, Ministère des Travaux Publics, de l'Urbanisme et des
Transports, Direction de l'Urbanisme et de l'Habitat, *Ville de Fatick: Monographie* (Paris: BCEOM, 1974), 24.

76 Interview with the current imam of the Ndiaye-Ndiaye mosque (now a *jumaa,* or
"Friday mosque"), 17 March 1989.

77 This marabout's elder brother, Cheikh Tidiane Sy, had been invited to preside
over the first religious singing ceremony (*gàmmu*) organized by Serer Tijans in
Fatick in May 1966. Interview with the current imam, 17 March 1989. Both of
these events were also recorded into a log book maintained by the old griot
referred to above, and pointed out to me in an interview, 27 February, 1989.

3 THE STATE–CITIZEN RELATIONSHIP: STRUGGLE OVER BRIDGES

1 The examples given are intended to be only illustrative of the nature of requests,
not exact records of each.

2 Timothy Mitchell, "The Limits of the State: Beyond Statist Approaches and
Their Critics," *American Political Science Review* 85:1 (March 1991), 78.
Various critiques of this article and Mitchell's response to them were subse-
quently published as John Bendix, Bertell Ollman, Bartholomew H. Sparrow,
and Timothy P. Mitchell, "Controversy: Going Beyond the State?" in *American
Political Science Review* 86:4 (December 1992), 1007–1021.

3 Ibid., 81. Emphasis in original.

4 Michael Crowder, *Senegal: A Study in French Assimilation Policy* (London:
Oxford University Press, 1962), 1–2. This brief overview to French colonial
policy and its effects in Senegal remains an excellent introduction to the topic.

5 For a superb history of this period see G. Wesley Johnson, Jr., *The Emergence of Black Politics in Senegal: The Struggle for Power in the Four Communes, 1900–1920* (Stanford: Stanford University Press, 1971). On the debate about military service see also Crowder, *Senegal*, 19–20.

6 See Robert H. Jackson and Carl G. Rosberg, *Personal Rule in Black Africa: Prince, Autocrat, Prophet, Tyrant* (Berkeley: University of California Press, 1982).

7 One of the most visible African statesmen on the international scene, Senghor has been the subject of numerous writings. Although many of these are laudatory, uncritical works, several excellent studies have also been published (interestingly enough, in English). See Jacques Louis Hymans, *Léopold Sédar Senghor: An Intellectual Biography* (Edinburgh: Edinburgh University Press, 1971); Irving Leonard Markovitz, *Léopold Sédar Senghor and the Politics of Négritude* (New York: Atheneum, 1969); and Janet G. Vaillant, *Black, French, and African: A Life of Léopold Sédar Senghor* (Cambridge: Harvard University Press, 1990).

8 For an artful exposition of the complex politics of this period, see William J. Foltz, *From French West Africa to the Mali Federation* (New Haven: Yale University Press, 1965). For a more wide-ranging work, see also Ruth Schachter Morgenthau, *Political Parties in French-Speaking West Africa* (Oxford: Clarendon Press, 1964).

9 For a now somewhat dated sympathetic history of that party (under a later name) written by a French official who has held various important administrative posts in independent Senegal, see François Zuccarelli, *Un Parti politique africain: L'Union Progressiste Sénégalaise* (Paris: R. Pichon et R. Durand-Auzias, 1970). Many of the subsequent changes in the party are discussed in Zuccarelli's more recent, *La Vie politique sénégalaise (1940–1988)* (Paris: CHEAM, 1988).

10 Gerti Hesseling, *Histoire politique du Sénégal: Institutions, droit et société* (Paris: Karthala, 1985), 364. This thorough study of Senegalese constitutional history is devoted to an exploration of the continuities and modifications of the French statist model in Senegal.

11 An English version of Senghor's own statement of this ideology is available in Léopold Sédar Senghor, *On African Socialism* (New York: Praeger, 1964). Senghor's published writings are voluminous. In addition to his poetry, the following are useful for an understanding of Senghor's political thought: *Ce que je crois: Négritude, francité, et civilisation de l'universel* (Paris: Bernard Grasset, 1988); *La Poésie de l'action: Conversations avec Mohamed Aziza* (Paris: Stock, 1980); and *Pierre Teilhard de Chardin et la politique africaine* (Paris: Editions du Seuil, 1962). In addition, a series of five volumes of Senghor's collected essays and speeches have been published by Editions du Seuil: *Liberté I: Négritude et humanisme* (1964); *Liberté II: Nation et voie africaine du socialisme* (1971); *Liberté III: Négritude et civilisation de l'universel* (1977); *Liberté IV: Socialisme et planification* (1983); and *Liberté V: Le Dialogue des cultures* (1993).

12 The government's own figures, from the 1988 census, indicate that some 78 percent of the population is illiterate in French. This figure, which in any case may be an underestimate, also conceals the fact that outside the regions of

Dakar and Ziguinchor (the latter being an area where missionary education was relatively concentrated) the rate of illiteracy is significantly higher. There are important generational and gender-based aspects to this phenomenon: younger people and males are far more likely to be literate than older people or women. For a discussion of the role of French and indigenous languages in Senegal (in a book dedicated to Senghor himself, and with a preface by the president), see Pierre Dumont, *Le Français et les langues africaines au Sénégal* (Paris: Karthala, 1983), especially part two: "Langues en contact: Problèmes politiques et pédagogiques." Hesseling, *Histoire politique*, also discusses the political debate on language policy in Senegal, 348–358.

13 Carol Myers-Scotton, "Elite Closure as Boundary Maintenance: The Case of Africa," in *Language Policy and Political Development*, ed. Brian Weinstein (Norwood, New Jersey: Ablex, 1990), 25, 27.

14 Fatou Sow, *Les Fonctionnaires de l'administration centrale sénégalaise* (Dakar: IFAN, 1972), 117. This monograph, although now quite dated, presents the results of a lengthy survey of 234 bureaucrats carried out in Dakar, and is still valuable for the insights it offers into the staffing of the Senegalese state.

15 Pathé F. Diagne, *Sénégal: Crise économique et sociale et devenir de la démocratie* (Dakar: Sankore, 1984), 90. Cited in Robert Fatton, Jr., *The Making of a Liberal Democracy: Senegal's Passive Revolution, 1975–1985* (Boulder: Lynne Reinner, 1987), 80.

16 Edward J. Schumacher, *Politics, Bureaucracy, and Rural Development in Senegal* (Berkeley, University of California Press, 1975), 127–128, discusses these programs, particularly in relation to technical training of development specialists. Among the most important of these training centers are the Polytechnical Institute, (*Institut Polytechnique*) which trains engineers, and the National School of Applied Economics (ENEA, Ecole Nationale d'Economie Appliquée), which produces the personnel for many development related programs.

17 See Harold D. Nelson, et. al, *Area Handbook for Senegal*, (Washington DC: Foreign Area Studies Division of American University, 2nd edn 1974), 188. Senghor's expression, of course, refers to the tendency of officials to "wash their hands" of responsibility for taking important or difficult decisions.

18 Republic of Senegal, *Projet de loi portant révision de la constitution: Exposé des motifs*. Cited in Hesseling, *Histoire politique*, 263. The discussion following this citation examines the demands for deconcentration and their effect on the 1970 constitution, see 263–272.

19 Hesseling, *Histoire Politique*, 297–300. Citation from 298.

20 *Jeune Afrique* 1575 (13–19 March 1991), 10–11, and 1581 (17–23 April 1991), 20–24. For an interview with Habib Thiam on the issue of the new government and his role within it, see *Jeune Afrique* 1582 (24–30 April 1991), 20–23.

21 Sow, *Les Fonctionnaires*, 55.

22 For a description of Senegalese "overcentralization" and a review of the politics of decentralization, see Sheldon Gellar, "State Tutelage vs. Self-Governance: The Rhetoric and Reality of Decentralization in Senegal," in *The Failure of the Centralized State: Institutions and Self-Governance in Africa*, ed. James S. Wunsch and Dele Olowu (Boulder: Westview, 1990).

23 Sheldon Gellar, *Senegal: An African Nation Between Islam and the West* (Boulder: Westview, 1982), 39–42. Citation from 41.

24 Richard Vengroff, "The Transition to Democracy in Senegal: The Role of Decentralization," in *In Depth* 3:1 (Winter 1993), 40. This article surveys the history of decentralization in Senegal, and analyzes the post-1988 reforms in terms of their contribution to Senegalese democratization.

25 *Area Handbook for Senegal*, 186–187.

26 Amadou Latyr Ndiaye, speech given at the celebration of the 70th anniversary of the Commune of Fatick, January 1, 1988. The photocopied written text of this speech contains a brief history of the status of Fatick.

27 Interview, Administrateur Municipal, 18 November 1989. It bears noting that this official nevertheless thought that the system was unlikely to be changed soon because it was the brainchild of the powerful French-born Senegalese politician Jean Collin, at the time of the interview Ministre d'Etat and Secrétaire Général à la Présidence de la République. Jean Collin's fall from power in late 1990, therefore, may indeed bave been a factor facilitating the eventual abolition of the system.

28 Amadou Latyr Ndiaye, speech given at the celebration of the 70th anniversary of the commune of Fatick, photocopied text.

29 The tension arising from the competing incentives and pressures for both decentralization and deconcentration are not unique to Senegal. Goran Hyden, in fact, notes the relevance of this problem throughout Africa, and the widespread "preference for deconcentration" on the continent. See his *No Shortcuts to Progress: African Development Management in Perspective* (Berkeley: University of California Press, 1983), especially 84–91.

30 "L'Etat, c'est l'expression de la Nation, c'est surtout le moyen de réaliser la Nation." Léopold Sédar Senghor, *Congrès Constitutif du P. F. A. (Dakar, 1er-3 Juillet 1959): Rapport sur la doctrine et le programme du parti* (Paris: Présence Africaine, 1959), 35. The P. F. A. (Parti de la Fédération Africaine) was founded in 1959 after the breakup of the larger interterritorial parties, and disappeared with the breakup of the Mali Federation in August 1960.

31 *Le Soleil*, 22 September 1988, 2.

32 Michael G. Schatzberg, *The Dialectics of Oppression in Zaire* (Bloomington: Indiana University Press, 1988).

33 Hyden, *No Shortcuts*, 8. Hyden is primarily concerned with the effects of the economy of affection on the behavior of peasants, but notes that the concept "also throws important light on such issues as governance, policy-making and management in these societies," 8. For a richly textured review of the concept of the "economy of affection," see René Lemarchand, "African Peasantries, Reciprocity, and the Market: The Economy of Affection Reconsidered," *Cahiers d'Etudes Africaines* 113, 29:1 (1989), 33–67.

34 Ibid., 10.

35 Sow, *Les Fonctionnaires*, 174–176. The figures given here are drawn from the tables on those pages. Sow concludes, 175, that "aid to family, which is frequently denounced as parasitic, constitutes a very tight link between the elite fraction and the social milieu."

36 Interview with Secretary General of Fatick Chamber of Commerce, who complained of being inundated with requests from all sides, 31 August 1989. The system was never implemented, at least in part because a greater number of

private shops sprang up than had been expected. In Fatick, several such shops were opened with the help of state officials who provided dependents with the capital or the guarantees necessary to secure credit from wholesalers.

37 For the most eloquent examination of the phenomenon, see Donal B. Cruise O'Brien, *Saints and Politicians: Essays in the Organization of a Senegalese Peasant Society* (Cambridge: Cambridge University Press, 1975), chapter 5: "Clans, Clienteles and Communities: A Structure of Political Loyalties," 147– 185. Concerning the legitimation within the values of the economy of affection of certain actions which might appear quite illegitimate to the outsider, Hyden's general observation that, "It is not at all uncommon in Africa that a person who can demonstrate generosity at public expense is not only forgiven by his people but also seen as having acted correctly" is equally valid for Senegal. *No Shortcuts*, 38.

38 Crawford Young and Thomas Turner, *The Rise and Decline of the Zairian State* (Madison: University of Wisconsin Press, 1985), 183, 244. Cited in Schatzberg, *The Dialectics of Oppression*, 143.

39 This description is drawn from interviews with that official, the second in command at the *Service Régional de l'Urbanisme et de l'Habitat*, 13 and 14 September 1989.

40 The *Loi sur le Domaine Nationale* (Law on the National Domain) of June 1964 was intended to supersede traditional land-tenure and distribution systems, mostly centered on the positions of *lamanes*, traditional chiefs who controlled land. The law established the state as the proprietor of all undeeded land, giving *de facto* owners a fixed time period in which to establish deeds if they could demonstrate that they personally occupied or had developed the land via cultivation or construction. Various modifications have subsequently been made in the law, but in many areas traditional land-holding patterns persist.

41 Interview, 13 September 1989.

42 Interview, 19 January 1989. I also accompanied the two officials to the site on that date.

43 Interview, 18 March 1989.

44 This is a main point of Schatzberg's analysis in *The Dialectics of Oppression*.

45 Sow, *Les Fonctionnaires*, 205. The second study is Pierre Fougeyrollas, *Modernisation des hommes: L'exemple du Sénégal* (Paris: Flammarion, 1967).

46 Interview, president of local youth organization, 18 February 1989.

47 Interview, Secretary General of the Fatick Chamber of Commerce, 16 March 1989.

48 The difficult issue of polygamy, for example, resulted in a compromise by which individuals must choose to adhere to either a monogamous or a polygamous regime at the time of first marriage, and this choice is then binding for life. In reality this has had little effect; most marriages outside of major urban areas are still arranged under customary law, and in the urban areas the standard default option for men consists in keeping their options open, regardless of their plans, by opting for the polygamous regime. The Maliki legal school, followed by virtually all Senegalese religious scholars, is one of four legal schools accepted within Sunni Islam. The crucial political battle surrounding the adoption of this code will be discussed in more depth in chapter 6.

49 The issue is particularly complex because of the coexistence of three contrasting systems: traditional Serer inheritance is matrilineal, passing from maternal

uncle to nephew; Muslim law prescribes inheritance by legitimate children, with unequal distribution among sons and daughters; the French-based family code calls for equal inheritance of all children.

50 Sow, *Les Fonctionnaires*, 123.

51 République du Sénégal, Ministère du Plan et de la Coopération, "Plan régional de développement intégré de la région de Fatick: Synthèse du bilan-diagnostic et enjeux majeurs," (photocopied text, 1987).

52 SOTIBA is one of the most important Senegalese industrial enterprises. Textile manufacturing has historically been a sector of some importance in the Senegalese economy, but one that has been in steady decline since the 1970s. For an outstanding study of this evolution, see Catherine Boone, *Merchant Capital and the Roots of State Power in Senegal, 1930–1985* (Cambridge: Cambridge University Press, 1992).

53 Interview, 9 December 1989. I heard the same sentiment expressed innumerable other times by different officials.

54 Michael Bratton, "Beyond the State: Civil Society and Associational Life in Africa," *World Politics* 41:3 (April 1989), 414–15.

55 These examples are not chosen for any intrinsic importance or because of their frequency, but rather are simply intended to be indicative of the range of such needs. All are based on at least one real case in Fatick with which I am personally familiar.

56 A mysterious prohibition. Various people explained it to me locally as necessary because drumming might prevent good rains, though the practice probably derives from the colonial period when celebrations were banned during this season from a paternalistic concern that peasants might irresponsibly stay away from their fields during crucial periods.

57 A government document dating from 1978, thus before the influx of state officials that came with the new region in 1984, estimated that only ten percent of the "economically active" population was salaried. Most of those, it can be assumed, were teachers or others on the state payroll. République du Sénégal, Ministère de l'Urbanisme, de l'Habitat et de l'Environnement, Direction de l'Urbanisme et de l'Architecture, "Région du Sine-Saloum, ville de Fatick: Lotissement d'extension, rapport justificatif," (photocopied document, dated September 1978), 5.

58 An example: one of his long-time apprentices requested and received the money necessary to cover the funeral expenses for his father, who had died unexpectedly.

59 Interview, Secretary General of the Fatick Chamber of Commerce, 31 August 1989.

60 The allusion is to Bratton's characterization of the African state, cited in chapter 1.

61 International smuggling may be the most important exception to this rule in the Senegalese case. For an excellent discussion of this process in Zaire, see Janet MacGaffey, *Entrepreneurs and Parasites: The Struggle for Indigenous Capitalism in Zaire* (Cambridge: Cambridge University Press, 1987) as well as her "Economic Disengagement and Class Formation in Zaire," in *The Precarious Balance: State and Society in Africa*, ed. Donald Rothchild and Naomi Chazan (Boulder: Westview, 1988), 171–188.

62 Interview, 9 December 1989.

63 République de Sénégal, Ministère des Travaux Publiques, de l'Urbanisme, et des Transports, Direction de l'Urbanisme et de l'Habitat, *Ville de Fatick: Monographie*. (Paris: BCEOM, typed document with maps, 1974), 44–47. The government official responsible for maintaining the civil registry confirmed the persistence of this pattern, indeed pointed to even greater non-compliance than suggested by the report – this despite efforts to persuade more people to comply via educational meetings held in the neighborhoods. Only those with sufficient ties to the state and the modern sector to require a death certificate for purposes of inheritance or pensions declare deaths, he noted. Interview, 15 November 1989.

64 $.033 at the then current rate of about 300 CFA francs/$1.

65 Interview, 15 November 1989. The account of the distribution of the kiosks was first recounted to me by this same official, whose position was at a state office involved with granting the required permits. Although the specifics could obviously not be verified with those involved, the essential facts were corroborated later by others in the town.

66 Interview, 10 April 1989. The goals of the organization were printed in the brochure prepared for the inauguration of the center on January 30, 1989. The brochure also contains an organizational chart explaining the structure of "The Association of Healers of Sine," which follows the administrative divisions of the state itself, and which lists, in the practice of proliferating titles described above, *eleven* officers of the central bureau of the association, including *four* vice-presidents.

67 Maghan Keita, "The Integration of Traditional and Modern Health Care Revisited," paper delivered at the annual meeting of the African Studies Association, 5 November 1989, 10–11. This research is the basis for a dissertation, "The Political Economy of Health Care in Senegal" (Ph.D. dissertation, The African Studies and Research Program, Howard University, 1988). The brochure of the Center cited above itself places the percentage of the population who consults healers at 85 percent.

68 Keita, "The Integration," 12.

69 Interview with a Western doctor associated with the project in Dakar, 30 January 1989. Much of my knowledge of this aspect of the center derives from this and subsequent discussion with this doctor. I am also indebted to Catherine Bicknell for information on the evolution of the center after the completion of fieldwork for this study.

70 Interview, president of the Fatick Departmental Federation of the PDS, 6 November, 1989.

71 The phrase is Bratton's, "Beyond the State," 415.

72 Interview, 31 October 1989.

73 Interview, 15 November 1989.

4   THE MARABOUT–DISCIPLE RELATIONSHIP I:
    FOUNDATIONS OF RECRUITING AND FOLLOWING

1 Clifford Geertz, "The Integrative Revolution: Primordial Sentiments and Civil Politics in the New States," in *Old Societies and New States: The Quest for Modernity in Asia and Africa*, ed. Clifford Geertz (New York: The Free Press of Glencoe, 1963).

2 Gerti Hesseling, *Histoire politique du Sénégal: Institutions, droit et société* (Paris: Karthala, 1985), 90.

3 Lucy Behrman, *Muslim Brotherhoods and Politics in Senegal* (Cambridge: Harvard University Press, 1970). The research for this study was carried out in 1965–66, but much of the analysis is still quite relevant today.

4 Ibid., 13–18, citation from 16. Emphasis added.

5 Ibid., 68.

6 Ibid., 17.

7 Christian Coulon, *Le Marabout et le prince: Islam et pouvoir au Sénégal* (Paris: A. Pedone, 1981).

8 Ibid., 102.

9 Ibid., 103–115.

10 Ibid., 108.

11 Ibid., 111.

12 Ibid., 106 and 112–113.

13 Ibid., 102. Coulon notes here that the centrality of "charisma" may be attributed to the fact that *tarixas* in Senegal have not evolved to the "routinized" stage described by J. Spencer Trimingham in his study of Sufi orders.

14 While Mourides account for no more than 30 percent of Senegal's population, somewhere between one-half to two-thirds of peanut producers are Mourides. See Donal Cruise O'Brien, "Ruling Class and Peasantry in Senegal, 1960–1976: The Politics of a Monocrop Economy," in *The Political Economy of Underdevelopment: Dependence in Senegal*, ed. Rita Cruise O'Brien (Beverly Hills: Sage, 1979), 221.

15 See Donal Cruise O'Brien, *The Mourides of Senegal: The Political and Economic Organization of an Islamic Brotherhood* (Oxford: Clarendon Press, 1971), especially part one, "Origins and Growth," for more information on this process.

16 Not to be confused with "*daaira*," the predominantly urban "cells" of an order to be discussed in the following chapter. The Wolof word *daara* (from the Arabic *daar*, or house) means primarily a place of religious instruction, particularly in the expression "*daara alxoran*," Qur'anic school. The word is also used today to mean simply "school." The Mouride sense of the term reflects the pedagogic origins of this agricultural institution. For the fullest discussion of the *daara* institution, see Cruise O'Brien, *The Mourides*, chapter 8, "The Dara."

17 Ibid., 186–187.

18 The verb form of this Wolof term is *jébbalu* meaning to place oneself in someone's hands. The non-reflexive form, *jébbal*, is also used in the context of marriage, when a wife is delivered into her husband's hands.

19 Donal Cruise O'Brien, *The Mourides*. See especially chapter 4, "The Followers," for a discussion of this ideology and the ritual of the *njébbal*.

20 Donal Cruise O'Brien discusses this phenomenon in chapter 11 of *The Mourides*, "The Urban Brothers." See also his recent "Charisma comes to town: The Urbanization of the Mouride Brotherhood," in *Charisma and Brotherhood in African Islam*, ed. Donal Cruise O'Brien and Christian Coulon (Oxford: Clarendon Press, 1988).

21 See chapter 2, "Land, Cash, and Charisma: An Economic Sociology of the Mouride Brotherhood," in *Saints and Politicians: Essays in the Organization of a*

Senegalese Peasant Society, (Cambridge: Cambridge University Press, 1975). Cruise O'Brien notes there that "Mouride ideology, however logically coherent on its own terms, in fact serves to conceal or disguise important aspects of the real relation between the saint [marabout] and his disciple," 62–63.

22 Irving Leonard Markowitz, *Léopold Sédar Senghor and the Politics of Négritude*, Atheneum, 1969. It bears noting here that even in the absence of specific material benefits it is misleading to see the choice of submission as necessarily "irrational." An eternity of heavenly bliss in exchange for a mere several years, or even a lifetime, of submission and sacrifice – to the extent one believes that is the choice – can be a very "rational" choice indeed.

23 Gerti Hesseling, *Histoire politique du Sénégal: Institutions, droit et société* (Paris: Karthala, 1985), 376, emphasis added.

24 François Zuccarelli. *La Vie politique sénégalaise (1940–1988)* (Paris: CHEAM, 1988), 107.

25 Robert Fatton, *The Making of a Liberal Democracy: Senegal's Passive Revolution, 1975–1985* (Boulder: Lynne Rienner, 1987), 97–98.

26 Ibid., 104–105.

27 Aminata Sow Fall, *La Grève des Bàttu* (Dakar: Les Nouvelles Editions Africaines, 1979).

28 Interview with Mouride *taalibe*, 9 June 1989. The final phrase in Wolof was "Tijan yi, dañu *civilisés* ba mu ëpp." A subsequent interview with other Mouride *taalibes* confirmed both the facts and this interpretation of it. Clearly, of course, at least some Tijans are capable of putting up tents, but this is irrelevant to the very real perception of difference among orders on issues of this sort.

29 Cruise O'Brien, *The Mourides*, 83–84.

30 There is of course a potential for the religious cleavage to become politicized, as occasionally seems to occur in specific local disputes in some areas. My observations in Fatick, however, were corroborated by numerous similar observations in Dakar and elsewhere in Senegal, indicating clearly the general non-politicization of this cleavage.

31 There is an occasional preference expressed for intra-*tarixa* marriage, but never as an absolute requirement. By contrast, cross-caste marriages are regularly dismissed as unthinkable.

32 This formulation is based on two examples from interviews on 15 and 18 February 1989, but the practice is quite common and I found innumerable incidences of this.

33 Interview, member of Qadir *daaira*, 10 October 1989.

34 Interview, imam of Ndiaye-Ndiaye mosque, 8 June 1989.

35 Mourides in Fatick have a separate prayer area, used only for these important feastdays. Otherwise no separation for prayers occurs. The justification for separate feastdays is rooted in the method for their calculation. The Muslim calendar is a lunar one, and religiously significant days – in particular the beginning of the fasting month of Ramadan – require visual confirmation of the new moon by competent religious authorities. While Tijans in Senegal follow the majority of the Muslim world in accepting the calculations of the *'ulama* in Mecca, Mourides follow the lead of their own *xalifa*. An elaborate story of a divine revelation by which Amadou Bamba was warned to beware of false moons which would mislead the unwitting serves as an ideological justification

for maintaining this distinction. Interview with Mouride disciple, 25 April 1989.

36 Interview with members of the Peulgha neighborhood *jàkka*, 25 January 1989.

37 Abdoul Aziz Sy Junior, in an interview with Debra Boyd-Buggs: "Entretien avec El Hadj Abdoul Aziz Sy, Jr.," in *Présence Africaine*, 148, 1988.

38 See Donal B. Cruise O'Brien, "Introduction," in *Charisma and Brotherhood in African Islam*, ed. Cruise O'Brien and Christian Coulon (Cambridge: Cambridge University Press, 1988) for a discussion of the application of Weber to African Islamic movements. Other articles in that work explore the applicability of the concept to particular case studies.

39 Abdoul Aziz Sy Junior, speaking at the *siyaare* organized at the feast of *Tamxarit* by the "Dahiratoul Moustarchidina wal Moustarchidaty" (see below) under the patronage of his ambitious nephew, Moustapha Sy. 13 August 1989. This ritual is discussed at some length in chapter 5.

40 Interviews with the marabout's son, an Arabic teacher in a local primary school, 7 November and 2 December, 1989.

41 These biographical sketches are based on several interviews with each of the marabouts, and supplemented with other sources over the year-long period of research in Fatick.

42 This is a pseudonym, as are the three that follow.

43 This is the family of *Shaykh* Sidiyya, the subject of Charles C. Stewart's, *Islam and Social Order in Mauritania: A Case Study from the Nineteenth Century* (Oxford: Clarendon Press, 1973).

44 See *Jeune Afrique*, 1404, 2 December 1987.

45 Bamba's exile there was spent with the same Shaykh Sidiyya family mentioned above (see note 43), who were themselves of the Qadiriyya order.

46 "Ndigel rëk wöor," in Wolof (his spelling).

47 Interview with local electrical contractor with some state ties, 20 November 1989. I could not, of course, verify this report directly. Yet even if the specifics are exaggerated or otherwise inaccurate, the story is nevertheless significant as an indication of the *modus operandi* of local Mouride representatives.

48 The *khalwa* is a mystical Sufi retreat, practiced in particular when seeking divine guidance. For a discussion of this practice in West Africa, see Jean-Louis Triaud, "Khalwa and the Career of Sainthood: An Interpretative Essay," in *Charisma and Brotherhood in African Islam*, ed. Cruise O'Brien and Coulon.

49 Diakhaté brought a copy of his alphabet to the Institut Fondamentale d'Afrique Noire (IFAN), the major research institute on Black Africa established in Dakar by the French during the colonial period. His innovative creation attracted the attention of researchers there, who interviewed him extensively about it and made copies of his original. To his knowledge, however, it was never exploited further, a fact about which he expresses some disappointment.

50 See Cruise O'Brien, *The Mourides*, 112 for a list of the most important of these. I follow Cruise O'Brien in the spelling of the names of the Mbacké marabouts.

51 Ibid., 120–121.

52 See ibid., 61–63, and 127–132, and, concerning the secret pact, 113.

53 This is according to Cruise O'Brien's account. See *The Mourides*, 112. Some Mouride *taalibes* whom I interviewed phrased it in terms of the eldest grandson of the founder – who is not necessarily the same as the eldest son of the eldest son. Though this may have been a simplification on the part of my informants, it

is nevertheless indicative of the complexity of succession and the inherent problems this transition will pose.

54 Cruise O'Brien listed Saliou as older than Abdoul Qadir (*The Mourides*, 131), as did Fernand Quesnot. See "Les cadres maraboutiques de l'Islam sénégalais," in *Notes et études sur l'Islam en Afrique noire* (Paris: CHEAM, 1962), 158. If there was any confusion about which of the two was the elder, however, it appears to have been resolved well before the 1989 succession. Again this is indicative of the potential difficulties of the system in a situation where there are many sons by different mothers and no records of birthdate.

55 Mouride marabouts do not observe the common limit on four wives found in most of the Muslim world. Bamba's offspring are also likely to have had an even more numerous progeny than their father given the greater security of their position.

56 *The Mourides*, 101.

57 See *Jeune Afrique*, 1416, 24 February 1988 for a discussion of this incident. The other dissident marabout mentioned was Dame Faty Mbacké, *xalifa* in the village of Darou Mousty.

58 F. Quesnot, "Influence du mouridisme sur le tidjanisme," in *Notes et études sur l'Islam en Afrique noire* (Paris: CHEAM, 1962), explores the influence of the Mourides on Senegalese Tijans. The similarities must also at least in part be attributed to the common influence of pre-colonial Wolof social and political structures on both orders.

59 An older son, Ahmed Sy, had died while serving in the French army in the First World War.

60 See the entry under "Mansur Sy" in Lucie Gallistel Colvin, *Historical Dictionary of Senegal* (The Scarecrow Press, 1981), 273–274.

61 Occasionally the Wolof "*bu ndaw*" (the younger/smaller) is used to distinguish this marabout from his uncle the *xalifa*. The English tern "Junior," however, is also very widely used in Senegal and I will adopt it in this work.

62 Baye Niasse's will and succession is briefly discussed in El Hadji Ravane Mbaye, "L'Islam au Sénégal," Thèse de doctorat de troisième cycle, Department of Arabic, University of Dakar, 1977, 523–525. Hassan Cissé, who was once a graduate student at Northwestern University and has inherited his father's position as imam of the mosque at Medina-Kaolack is particularly active in courting international ties. Under his leadership the family has developed a following in the United States. Some 50 to 60 American children currently live in Kaolack and are receiving a Qur'anic education there. Interviews with Cissé, 2 October 1989, and American *taalibes* of the family, 21 September 1989.

63 Former president Senghor once dismissed Ahmed Khalifa Niasse as "a little party-boy (*un petit fêtard*) who has left debts in numerous Arab countries." Léopold Sédar Senghor, *La Poésie de l'action: Conversations avec Mohamed Aziza* (Paris: Stock, 1980), 227. Niasse has since aligned himself closely with the ruling *Parti Socialiste*.

64 As reported in *Wal Fadjri*, No. 334, 9–15 October 1992.

65 For a recent analysis of El Hajj Umar Tall's movement, see Jon Ralph Willis, *In the Path of Allah. The Passion of Al-Hajj Umar: An Essay into the Nature of Charisma in Islam* (London: Frank Cass, 1990).

66 Interview with a nephew of the current *xalifa* and great-grandson of the founder, 12 March 1989. This nephew, a university student, has written a biography of the founder, which remains in manuscript form.

67 See the articles by Cruise O'Brien and Creevey on the emergence of the Mouride order, in particular the observation that Amadou Bamba was in many ways a reluctant participant in the development of the order and even, as Creevey puts it, "a factor despite himself," 300. Donal B. Cruise O'Brien, "The Saint and the Squire: Personalities and Social Forces in the Development of a Religious Brotherhood," in *African Perspectives: Papers in the History, Politics, and Economics of Africa Presented to Thomas Hodgkin*, ed. Christopher Allen and R. W. Johnson (Cambridge: Cambridge University Press, 1970); and Lucy E. Creevey (née Behrman), "Ahmed Bamba 1850–1927," in *Studies in West African Islamic History. Volume I: The Cultivators of Islam*, ed. John Ralph Willis (London: Frank Cass, 1979).

68 There is little information available on Badji's movement. I base this brief analysis mostly on interviews conducted during a visit to Sindian and the region in July 1986.

69 My description of this movement is based on an interview with the (female) president and another leading member of the *daaira* of Ngom's followers in Fatick, 8 December 1989, and on a two-page letter addressed "To the Attention of the Entire World" distributed by Ngom in 1987, a copy of which was made available to me by the *daaira* president. Beliefs in a *mahdi*, a leader who appears periodically to renew Islam or to herald the imminent arrival of the judgment day, are widespread in the Muslim world.

70 It is apparently not, however, unique. I am indebted to Mark Schoonmaker-Freudenberger for a photocopied "manifesto" by a group calling itself the *Communauté Islamidienne*. The group's female "*guide spirituel*," Madame Dieye, *Adja* Ndiaye Mody Guirandou, describes herself as a "Mudjadjida" (Arabic *mujaddida*, renewer), and espouses a message that is at once critical of the established Sufi orders in Senegal and incorporates various Sufi elements, claiming to receive, for example, various *zikrs* and *wirds* sent her by God via the intermediary of the angel Gabriel.

71 Interview with El Hajj Farba Diouf, 3 March 1989.

72 Interview, 5 November 1989.

73 Interview with the head regional doctor (*médecin chef régional*, a military officer) for Fatick, 11 June 1989.

74 Boyd-Buggs, "Entretien", 130.

75 Ibid., 132.

76 Interviews with Alpha, 17 November 1989, and Diakhaté, 5 August 1989.

77 Boyd-Buggs, "Entretien", 130. My italics.

5 THE MARABOUT–DISCIPLE RELATIONSHIP II: THE STRUCTURES OF ALLEGIANCE

1 The term comes from the Arabic word, *da'ira*, meaning "circle," so called because the role of host circulates, each member taking a turn at the position. My spelling corresponds to the Wolofized version of the word, but the term is also often written "dahira." It should not be confused with "dara" or "daara"

(from Arabic *daar*, house), which refers in Senegal to schools, notably Qur'anic schools in urban areas, or to Mouride agricultural settlements of young men in the service of a marabout.

2 See for example the introduction to Moriba Magassouba's work with the somewhat alarmist title: *L'Islam au Sénégal: Demain les mollahs?* (Paris: Karthala, 1985); Christian Coulon, *Les Musulmans et le pouvoir en Afrique noire* (Paris: Karthala, 1983), 139; and Christian Coulon and Donal B. Cruise O'Brien, "Senegal," in *Contemporary West African States*, ed. Donal B. Cruise O'Brien, John Dunn, and Richard Rathbone (Cambridge: Cambridge University Press, 1989), 157.

3 Senegalese communities abroad, in fact, frequently rely on the institution of the *daaira* for help in adapting to the demands of expatriate life. A Mouride *daaira*, for example, exists in New York City, and is responsible for organizing annual visits by important Mouride marabouts to that city. See "Muslim Leader Visits, and a Hotel is Reeling," in *The New York Times*, 1 August 1991, for a description of a visit by Cheikh Mourtada M'Backe.

4 Donal B. Cruise O'Brien, "Sufi Politics in Senegal," in *Islam in the Political Process*, James P. Piscatori, ed. (Cambridge: Cambridge University Press, 1983), 122.

5 Ibrahima Marone, "Le Tidjanisme au Sénégal," *Bulletin de l'Institut Fondamental d'Afrique Noire*, Série B: Sciences Humaines 32:1 (January 1970), 171–172. Marone dates the formation of this group from "one year after the death of El Hajj Malik Sy, that is in 1928." El Hajj Malik, however, died in 1922, so that there is a discrepancy in his account. Since he elsewhere refers to El Hajj Malik's succession in 1922, it seems most probable that there is simply a typographical error, and thus the date for the creation of this *daaira* would be 1923.

6 Interview, Tijan marabout, 17 November 1989. While I have no other source for corroborating this story, and do not know whether any copies of Ababacar's defense of *daairas* are in existence, I nevertheless know of no conflicting or alternative accounts for the origins of *daairas* in the literature on Senegalese Islam. This area represents a fruitful domain for further historical research.

7 Donal B. Cruise O'Brien, *The Mourides of Senegal: The Political and Economic Organization of an Islamic Brotherhood* (Oxford: Clarendon Press, 1971), 248–261. This work contains the fullest, and still highly relevant, discussion of *daairas*, although it deals only with the Mouride order. Christian Coulon's much more schematic treatment of the institution represents virtually the only other discussion of *daairas* in the literature. See his *Le Marabout et le prince: Islam et pouvoir au Sénégal* (Paris: A. Pedone, 1981), 132–136.

8 Cruise O'Brien, *The Mourides*, 250–252.

9 Cruise O'Brien, *The Mourides*, 257–260, and Coulon, *Le Marabout*, 132–134.

10 The most active of the two *daairas* did postpone its scheduled annual *màggal* (celebration), using some of the funds earmarked for that purpose instead to send a delegation to Touba to visit (*siyaare*) the new *xalifa* and inform him of the *daaira's* allegiance.

11 Interview, 14 March 1989. It is clearly unlikely that one could possibly be active in that number of *daairas*, given the frequency of meetings, etc. But the *taalibe's* insistence nevertheless underscores the lack of doctrinal barriers to multiple membership.

12 Interview, Tijan marabout, 17 November 1989. This marabout, who heads the most active *daaira* to the current *xalifa* in Fatick, recounted to me how the heads of other *daairas* in the region, predominantly to the defunct *xalifa's* descendants, had attempted to get him to join them in a "federation" of Tijan *daairas* in the area. He had refused, however, because of their ambivalence about recognizing the *xalifa's* authority.

13 Marone, "Le Tidjanisme," 172–174 discusses the organization of these superstructures beginning in the 1940s. Today these structures appear to do little more than hold occasional meetings. The president of a now defunct Tijan *daaira* in the Ndiaye-Ndiaye neighborhood of Fatick, for example, showed me a "convocation" from the president of the regional federation of Tijan *daairas*, calling all *daaira* presidents to a meeting in Fatick the following Sunday, but he shrugged off the significance of the meeting as being little more than social. Interview, 8 June 1989. In the case of Mouride federations, Cruise O'Brien notes the rather confused state of these organizations at the time of his research due at least partly to the suspicion that "officers saw the federation principally as a means of their own enrichment." *The Mourides*, 258.

14 Interview, 17 November 1989. See note 12 above.

15 Interview, "Vice chef de secteur" for the Dahiratoul Moustarchidina wal Moustarchidaty in Fatick, 11 May 1989. My description of the movement and its organization is based largely on this and a subsequent in-depth interview with this man, 11 August 1989, as well as other interviews and observations during attendance at the ritual celebration sponsored by the movement at Tivaouane at the occasion of *Tamxarit* (the Muslim new year) on 13 August 1989.

16 The marabout accepts the existence of *daairas*, but only for pragmatic concerns such as arranging for a vehicle to carry disciples to the *zawiya* at the occasion of religious celebrations. Interview with Ma Ansou Niang, 29 August 1989. This maraboutic movement will be explored further in chapter 7.

17 The listing in this paragraph is based primarily on one interview with a Tijan marabout in Fatick who elaborated on *all* of the reasons listed here, 17 November 1989. His answer, however, was by no means exceptional; other marabouts typically pointed to these same sources of the appeal of *daairas*.

18 Aili Mari Tripp, "Local Organizations, Participation, and the State in Urban Tanzania," in *Governance and Politics in Africa*, ed. Goran Hyden and Michael Bratton (Boulder: Lynne Rienner, 1992).

19 Immanuel Wallerstein, "Voluntary Associations," in *Political Parties and National Integration in Tropical Africa*, ed. James S. Coleman and Carl G. Rosberg (Berkeley, University of California Press, 1964), 318–339. Citation from 322. Wallerstein notes that his rubric includes a wide range of variation in the particulars of local organization, and that religious groups frequently share both functions and characteristics of such groups. The fundamental defining characteristics of these groups are that they "are 'voluntary' in that no one's membership was foreordained at birth, or automatic; they are 'associations' in that they were formalized groupings from the point of view of both the member and the society as a whole, and they were smaller than the whole society," 322.

20 Ibid., 320.

21 Personal communication. These issues are discussed in Geoffrey Bergen, "Trade Unions in Senegal: A Perspective on National Development in Africa." (Ph.D. dissertation, University of California at Los Angeles, 1993).

22 Interview, 12 August 1991. A photo album commemorating such activities is kept at the seat of the *Secteur de Fatick* of this *daaira*, and these examples are all drawn from this record.

23 The *Teysir* is a devotional poem composed by El Hajj Malik Sy, and which takes its popular name from the first line of the poem, "Alxamdulillah thi*teysir* yallahu."

24 Interview, Tijan *taclibe*, 23 April 1989.

25 At the time of research approximately 300 CFA francs were worth $1 USA. Different rates for men and women are also the rule. The DMWM sections, with their numerous younger members, tend to set dues on the order of 50 and 100 FCFA/month for women and men respectively. At least one of the other Tijan *daairas* in Fatick had dues set at the same rate as the Mourides, although another (ambitiously) set the rate at 500 FCFA month for all members. In this case, however, one member noted that if this presented difficulties, one could pay "50 or 100 francs per week." Interview 23 April 1989.

26 I can verify this most accurately in the case of the Mouride *daaira*, where I had the opportunity to examine the records kept by the organization. Payment of dues there is clearly very erratic; members were frequently several months, even a year or more, behind in their payments. At the same time, other people often paid many months' dues at once – either past due or future payments – when a windfall provided the means.

27 Interview with member of the Qadir *daaira*, 7 June 1989. It should be noted that although personalities were clearly important, at least part of the motivation for this split – which occurred quite a few years ago – must be seen in the two faces of the Qadiriyya in Senegal which was discussed in chapter 5. The former president represents the "venerable" tendency in the order, closely tied to a Moorish maraboutic family of which he is a *taalibe*, while the majority of *daaira* members identify more closely with its "popular" wing.

28 This anecdote is based on observation at the meeting in question, 13 May 1989. The only date available (barring an excessively long delay) was in July, after the normal start of the rains. Rain would have ruined the event, which is held outdoors. Interestingly, the women in the group seemed far more reticent to accept the argument, endorsed by several men, that ultimately it was all in God's hands, and that according to His will it could rain or not whether or not it was the rainy season, and that therefore the date should be retained. In any case, the death in June of the *xalifa-général* of the order resulted in the cancellation of the event, thus avoiding this test of God's will.

29 This description is based predominantly on an interview with an active member of the *daaira*, herself a nominal Tijan due to a change of affiliation at marriage, but originally a Qadir, 4 December 1989.

30 Interview, 29 August 1989, Sirmang.

31 Amar Samb, "Touba et son 'Magal'," in *Bulletin de l'IFAN*, tome 31, Series B, No. 3 (1969), 737. Samb gives the precise date of the first *màggal* as 19 October 1928. See also Cruise O'Brien, *The Mourides*, 63, and Quesnot, "L'Influence du Mouridisme," 120.

32 See Quesnot, "L'Influence du Mouridisme," 115 for a list of four of the most important of these *màggals*.

33 Although frequently referred to as *the gàmmu* (Gamou) at Tivaouane, and although there is a certain degree of unity in the family in presenting the event as

a single celebration, there are in fact two separate ceremonies held at this occasion in Tivaouane, one under the direction of the *xalifa*, Abdoul Aziz Sy, and the other presided over by the sons of the former *xalifa*, Ababacar Sy. Justified by the family as a simple pragmatic concession to the fact that the disciples are too numerous, and also said by Ababacar's descendants to be continuing a tradition begun when their father was given permission by the founder to sponsor his own celebration, this duality in the event nevertheless clearly reflects the rivalry between the two branches of this family.

34 Interview, Baldé, 7 February 1989.

35 The description which follows is based on attendance at the ceremony in two successive years, 1988 and 1989. There were no significant variations from one year to the next, despite the death of long-reigning *xalifa* Abdou Lahatte in June of 1989, and the fact that the *màggal* held several months later was thus under the auspices of the new *xalifa*, Abdoul Qadir. An indication of the extent to which this event has long been institutionalized and codified within the order is provided by the fact that it is still virtually identical in all significant respects to those attended by Amar Samb in the 1950s. See his very colorful description in Samb, "Touba et son 'Magal'."

36 The Catholic community, for example, holds an annual pilgrimage on the "Petite Côte" every year, the "Pélerinage national catholique de Popenguine." The village of Popenguine is the site of some of the earliest Catholic missions to Senegal.

37 This is clearly a prestige expenditure, with no clearly defined purpose. There have at various times been plans to build a "Mouride University" in Touba, and the library would presumably function as part of that still only hypothetical institution. For the moment the large and impressive building contains little more than numerous copies of the Qur'an and of the writings of Amadou Bamba.

38 The Wolof word *neex*, meaning "good" in the sense of pleasing to the senses, thus appears in discussions of the *màggal* at least as frequently as *baax*, implying morally good.

39 The discussion which follows is based on attendance at this *gàmmu* in February of 1989 in the company of "*Sëriñ* Diakhaté," the local marabout in Fatick who represents the branch of the Sy family which sponsors this *gàmmu*.

40 See *Le Soleil*, 28 January 1989. Although occasionally referred to in Wolof as Abdoul Aziz Sy *bu ndaw* ("the small/the younger"), as I have noted the English term "junior" is actually more widely used for this marabout to distinguish him from his uncle and namesake, the *xalifa-général* of the Tivaouane branch of the order.

41 This method of presenting cash gifts has become the norm, leading to the frequent use of the word "envelope" to mean an offering of money to a marabout.

42 This description is drawn from attendance at the *siyaare* in August 1989 along with the members of the local Fatick sections of the DMWM.

43 This gamble cost the movement in various ways. The 1993 *siyaare*, for example, was denied the necessary government permits on the pretext of various logistical problems but clearly for political reasons, and it had to be cancelled. It may have paid off in terms of Moustapha Sy's appeal to youth, however. The young

marabout was subsequently frequently to be found in the company of principal opposition figure Abdoulaye Wade, long the mouthpiece for the frustrations of the more urban and youthful population in Senegal.

44 Among the public figures thanked, in addition to President Abdou Diouf himself: General Waly Faye, Chief of the armed forces; The Commissariat Central de Dakar and the local *gendarmerie*; the directors of "Express Transit" and the SOTRAC bus company; The *Sapeurs-Pompiers* (Fire Department) of Dakar and that of the region; the directors of SENELEC and SONES, the state electric and water utility companies; the chief medical doctor for the region; and a special and effusive thanks to the Governor of the Thiès Region and the *préfet* of the Département of Tivaouane, with whom the family "always works closely for the development of the region and of the country as a whole."

45 As above, these brief descriptions are all based on attendance at the events discussed here. In addition, I was familiar in each of these local cases with the most important organizers of the events, and thus the implicit interpretations are also based on discussion with those individuals.

46 The then governor of Fatick is a Tukulor, and although he of course speaks Wolof he is not particularly eloquent in that language. It merits noting that at all other public events – the inaugurations of the Traditional Medicine Center or of the fabric shop discussed above for example – the governor spoke in French despite the fact that the majority of the audience would not understand him. At a religious event, however, it is inconceivable that he speak in anything other than Wolof, the undisputed language of religious devotion in Senegal.

47 A Baye Fall *taalibe* of the marabout identified the original founder of the line as a former soldier in the French military who, having returned to Senegal, made the *jébbalu* to Amadou Bamba himself and then worked for many years in his service before being directed to settle in Gaindiaye. In the tradition of the fantastic stories told about the history of the line, this *taalibe* recounts that when Amadou Bamba was imprisoned in the company of a lion (which of course did not touch him) during his exile in Gabon – a scene frequently portrayed in Mouride iconography – that lion was in fact none other than Baye Seck himself, transformed miraculously for the occasion. Interview, 7 November 1989.

48 Edward B. Reeves, *The Hidden Government: Ritual, Clientelism, and Legitimation in Northern Egypt* (Salt Lake City: University of Utah Press, 1990), 2.

49 The term *mulid* is of the same Arabic root as *mawlud*, ostensibly referring to birthdate but, as Reeves notes, in Egypt as in Senegal the term is no longer exclusively used for celebrations commemorating birth anniversaries. See chapter 6, "The Big *Mulid*" in Ibid., 113–134, for a discussion of this event, and chapter 7, "The Commemorative Festivals," 135–154, for other less important events.

50 Ibid., 4.

51 Ibid., 4–5.

52 Marc J. Swartz, ed., *Local-Level Politics: Social and Cultural Perspectives* (Chicago: Aldine, 1968). The quote is from the introduction to part II: "Politics and Ritual," 131.

53 As an indication of this, and perhaps of interest to the reader concerned with the epistemological questions concerning the manner in which the researcher may influence the object of research, it merits noting that my own attendance at

ceremonies was occasionally noted as adding to the marabout's prestige. At Abdoul Aziz Sy Junior's *gàmmu* discussed above, for example, my presence was included by the marabout in the public listing of "important" people who had made the trip to Tivaouane especially for the event. For local events this effect was even more pronounced. My reception at Gaindiaye by the Baye Fall marabout there indicated this clearly. Most significantly, this interpretation was also given by outsiders; one skeptical Fatick resident teased me about attendance at the Gaindiaye event, saying "That marabout must be really happy now. He's sure to be telling himself: 'Things are going really well now. Even *tubaabs* are showing up for my *màggal!*'"

54 William F. S. Miles, "The Rally as Ritual: Dramaturgical Politics in Nigerian Hausaland," *Comparative Politics* 21:3 (April 1989), 323–338.

55 Ibid., 328.

56 Ibid., 335.

57 Nit ku baax, ku amul kilifa, dotul nekk nit ku baax.

58 It is noteworthy in this respect that distinct icons, a simplified representation which makes identification relatively easy and rapid, have been developed for each of the most important marabouts in Senegal. Amadou Bamba, for example, is always represented in the same standing face-on pose, with the end of his white turban pulled over his face, and El Hajj Malik Sy always carries a black umbrella. Other marabouts have their own attributes by which they are identified.

59 Samb, "Touba et son 'Magal'," 751.

60 A difficulty which in any case is even further complicated by philosophical issues concerning how to quantify or evaluate such non-material benefits as increased sense of security or of community, or even of a belief in an increased likelihood of salvation in an afterlife.

61 Jean Copans, *Les Marabouts de l'arachide: La confrérie mouride et les paysans du Sénégal* (Paris: Le Sycomore, 1980).

62 Robert Fatton, Jr. *The Making of a Liberal Democracy: Senegal's Passive Revolution, 1975–1985* (Boulder: Lynne Rienner, 1987), 98.

63 Donal B. Cruise O'Brien, *Saints and Politicians: Essays in the Organization of a Senegalese Peasant Society* (Cambridge: Cambridge University Press, 1975), 59.

64 Coulon, *Le Marabout*, 112.

65 Cruise O'Brien, *Saints and Politicians*, 75. The entire second essay in this work, entitled "Land, Cash and Charisma: An Economic Sociology of the Mouride Brotherhood," is devoted to the issue of the exchange of goods between disciples and marabouts. He concludes this discussion with the observation that "The disciples over the years have been in a position to do their own unarticulated cost-benefit analysis of saintly leadership, and the balance up to now appears on the whole positive," 81.

66 Although the calculation of costs and benefits to disciples in this circumstance must take a long-term perspective, Cruise O'Brien argues persuasively that even then the benefits are positive from the point of view of an individual with few or no possibilities for securing access to land otherwise. See, ibid., 75.

67 One especially important such investment is in SOCOCIM, a large cement factory between Dakar and Rufisque in which the Sy family owes a controlling share. Other shares are held by the French firm, the Groupe Lafarge, which manages the plant.

68 In addition to the tent, lighting and amplification equipment, and other such hardware (most of which is usually rented) the payment to the lead singer at these events may represent a significant expense. At the Fatick Mouride *daaira's màggal*, for example, the singer was contracted for the extravagant sum of 125,000 FCFA. Some 200,000 FCFA were raised from the "envelopes" and other contributions during the event. Interview, *daaira* members, 10 October 1989.

69 A report on this contribution was made at the 13 May 1989 meeting of the *daaira* by the officer of the organization who had made the trip to Touba to deliver the envelope. The *xalifa* responded with a letter in "Wolofal" (Wolof written in the Arabic alphabet) which was read to the group and which thanked the Fatick *daaira* for its faithful support of the marabout's efforts. The marabout also sent a small package of sand from Touba which was carefully distributed to those in attendance at the meeting for its magico-spiritual value.

70 Coulon thus notes that "it is a fact of public notoriety that the richest merchants in Senegal are very close to the great religious chiefs of the country who use their influence with the authorities to procure easy access to credit or to public markets for them." *Le Marabout*, 114.

71 Cruise O'Brien thus notes of the Mourides: "A gift to one's *shaykh* is in material terms the most effective local form of insurance policy." *The Mourides*, 92.

72 This information is from an interview with Baldé, 3 November 1989. Although in practice the pattern he portrays may of course undergo some distortion, this model nevertheless clearly represents the ideal which the marabouts claim for themselves, and by which they will consequently be evaluated by disciples.

73 Miles, "Rally as Ritual," 332. Coulon likewise notes that the maraboutic ideal of generosity reflects the values of Wolof nobility. "As a 'man of honor' the marabout, just as the prince in the past, must demonstrate generosity towards his dependents. He must know how to give, just as he knows how to receive." *Le Marabout*, 112.

74 Interview, 15 March 1989.

75 Interview, 23 October 1989. This *taalibe* was among those present when the story was told by Abdoul Aziz Sy Junior.

76 Cruise O'Brien, *The Mourides*, 88.

77 Victoria Ebin, who has carried out research on Mouride commercial networks in Dakar, provides a fascinating discussion of how one family sponsors the "apprenticeship" of other Mourides in Dakar's Sandaga market in her article, "A la recherche de nouveaux 'poissons'. Stratégies commerciales mourides par temps de crise," in *Politique Africaine* 45 (March 1992).

78 Interview, 4 December 1989. This particularly interesting comparison was not elicited directly by questioning, but was offered spontaneously in the context of a discussion about her own switch at the time of her marriage. This was not, I believe, an effort to enhance her current affiliation with the Tijan order given that she also noted that it was actually excessively "heavy" (*diis*) for her, and she had consequently converted nominally but had not yet taken the Tijan *wird*.

79 Many of the variations that do exist can, I believe, be explained in terms of the historical evolution of Fatick. The greater likelihood of older people (50 years or over) to be Tijan reflects the fact that Fatick was originally heavily Tijan, and that the population growth due to migration in the past several decades is likely to involve mainly younger people, and thus dilute this concentration. A second

demographic trend, involving the influx of state functionaries since 1984, may account for the relatively high number of "other Muslims" in the 31–40 age group, and the significantly lower numbers in the higher age groups. State functionaries are more likely to belong to the two principal groups covered by this category: "secularized" Muslims without affiliation in the Sufi system, and members of the relatively small Layène order which is concentrated in the Dakar region. There does appear to be a modest shift from Tijan to Mouride in the 31–40 age group, but the significance of this is doubtful given that the percentage of both Mourides and Tijans in the 21–30 group is virtually identical to that of the 41–50 cohorts.

80 The specifics of this conversion are drawn from an interview with this man, 21 November 1989. "Thierno Tall" is a pseudonym.

81 Interview with a nephew of Tall's, also highly instructed in religion but an exception in his family in that he is not a *taalibe* of the Niasse marabouts, 4 December 1989. This nephew attributed the change in affiliation of other family members primarily to the aggressive proselytizing of the Niasse family.

82 Cited in *Jeune Afrique*, "Sénégal: le vote des religieux," 1416 (24 February 1988), 28.

83 One interesting analysis of these elections, which devotes only passing attention to the role of the marabouts, does argue that although the *ndigal* was not universally obeyed it was nevertheless significant. The authors point as evidence to the relatively higher percentage of the vote for Abdou Diouf in the official results for the region of Diourbel, the Mouride heartland. Given that this region has always been a stronghold of the ruling party, however, as well as the fact that voting irregularities in favor of the party are particularly likely there, this figure does not in itself contradict the argument that the *ndigal* was often ignored. See Crawford Young and Babacar Kante, "Governance, Democracy, and the 1988 Senegalese Elections," in *Governance and Politics in Africa*, ed. Goran Hyden and Michael Bratton (Boulder: Lynne Rienner, 1992). I am indebted to Donal Cruise O'Brien for an anecdote recounted to him in an interview with a Mouride from Touba which, though perhaps apocryphal, nevertheless indicates that both the disobedience of disciples and the prevalence of fraud were commonly believed to have occurred. When at the end of election day a lieutenant of the *xalifa* informed him that he had been "betrayed," that many people in Touba itself had ignored his command and voted for the opposition, the old marabout apparently shrugged and said, "It doesn't matter. I know who's going to win anyway." In a written summary of this interview (see note 87 below), Cruise O'Brien reports his informant's belief that the opposition PDS probably really won the election – in the city of Touba itself!

84 *Jeune Afrique*, "Sénégal: le vote des religieux." The frequency of this reaction was also often treated as common knowledge by both Mourides and non-Mourides alike.

85 Interview, Touba, 30 September 1988.

86 *Wal Fadjri*, No. 334, 9–15 October 1992, 4.

87 The single exception to this response was the marabouts of the Niasse family in Kaolack, who have many close familial and marital ties with Mauritania. The silence of the other marabouts was noted critically by various notables and important *taalibes* of the Niasse family in a group interview, Kaolack, 2 October

1989. This interview also included Cheikh Hassan Cissé, who serves as imam of the mosque in Kaolack. This was one of a series of focus-group interviews carried out as part of a research project on the attitudes of Senegalese Muslim elites toward the West, and sponsored by the Office of Research of the United States Information Service. The six other group interviews in this series were carried out in conjunction with Professor Donal Cruise O'Brien, who served as moderator. His written summary of these interviews is available in an unpublished report: "Islamic Attitudes toward the West: The Case of Senegal," R-3–90, USIA Office of Research (February 1990). These interviews will be identified in all subsequent citations as "Islamic Attitudes Project." Unless otherwise noted, however, my own notes rather than the report will serve as the source.

6   THE STATE–MARABOUT RELATIONSHIP:
    COLLABORATION, CONFLICT, AND ALTERNATIVES

1 Interview with El Hajj Farba Diouf, 8 March 1989. Most of the information in these paragraphs is drawn from this interview, supplemented by subsequent interviews with two of Farba Diouf's sons, including the one educated in Mauritania. About his own conversion Farba Diouf insisted that it was a *process*, not an event, and that consequently he could give no precise date. Martin A. Klein notes the ambivalent relationship between the *Buur-Siin* and Amadou Bamba in *Islam and Imperialism in Senegal: Sine-Saloum, 1847–1914* (Stanford: Stanford University Press, 1968), 226.
2 Their exact dates of birth are unknown, but can be rather confidently estimated. Lucie Gallistel Colvin gives the following dates for each of these men: Amadou Bamba, 1850–1927; Malik Sy, *c.* 1855–1922; Abdoulaye Niasse, *c.* 1850–1922. Lucie Gallistel Colvin, *Historical Dictionary of Senegal* (Metuchen, New Jersey: The Scarecrow Press, 1981).
3 F. Quesnot, "L'Influence du Mouridisme sur le Tidjanisme," in *Notes et Etudes sur l'Islam en Afrique Noire*, M. Chailley, et. al. (Paris: Centre de Hautes Etudes Administratives sur l'Afrique et l'Asie Modernes, 1962), 122–123, emphasis added. It should be noted that Quesnot, who thought little of the Mourides, saw this as a clearly regrettable tendency, since it involved a decreasing emphasis on morality and an "exploitation" of disciples by greedy marabouts. In contrast to the spirituality of El Hajj Malik's Tijaniyya, Quesnot says, we find ourselves with the Mourides "en plein vagabondage islamique," 118.
4 U.K. Foreign Office, *Peace Handbooks: Issued by the Historical Section of the Foreign Office* 17:100, "French West Africa (General)" (London: H. M. Stationary Office, 1920), 4.
5 Donal Cruise O'Brien, "Towards an 'Islamic Policy' in French West Africa, 1854–1914," *Journal of African History* 8:2 (1967), 304. For a more detailed discussion of this history, which takes roughly the same approach as Cruise O'Brien's, see Christopher Harrison, *France and Islam in West Africa, 1860–1960* (Cambridge: Cambridge University Press, 1988).
6 David Robinson, "French 'Islamic' Policy and Practice in Late Nineteenth-Century Senegal," *Journal of African History* 29 (1988), 434.
7 Ibid.

8 Harrison, *France and Islam*, 165. My discussion here of the period leading up to independence relies heavily on Harrison's work.
9 Ibid.
10 Ibid., 180–181.
11 Ibid., 194
12 On this period see William J. Foltz, *From French West Africa to the Mali Federation* (New Haven: Yale University Press, 1965), especially pp. 86–93; and François Zuccarelli, *La Vie Politique Sénégalaise (1940–1988)* (Paris: Le Centre des Hautes Etudes sur l'Afrique et l'Asie Modernes, 1988), 64–69. I draw from both of these sources in describing these events.
13 Cited in Zuccarelli, *Vie Politique*, 68, and in Christian Coulon, "Un Gaullisme Musulman: Les Marabouts et la Décolonisation au Sénégal," in *La Politique Africaine du Général de Gaulle (1958–1969)*, proceedings of a colloquium organized by the Centre Bordelais d'Etudes Africaines, le Centre d'Etudes d'Afrique Noire, and L'Institut Charles de Gaulle, 19–20 October 1979, Bordeaux (Paris: A. Pedone, 1980), 346–356. This article presents a superb account of the role of the marabouts in the referendum and the later efforts to coordinate maraboutic involvement in the new political system. A modified version of this discussion is included in Coulon, *Le Marabout et le Prince: Islam et Pouvoir au Sénégal* (Paris: A. Pedone, 1981), 209–218.
14 Ibid., 351, 355.
15 Ibid., 351.
16 The charter of the organization is reproduced in an annex in El Hadji Ravane Mbaye, "L'Islam au Sénégal," unpublished doctoral dissertation (*thèse de doctorat de troisième cycle*), (Department of Arabic, University of Dakar, 1976), 565–567. Mbaye discusses this document briefly, 519–520. See also: Coulon, "Un Gaullisme Musulman," 351–352. Mbaye is not entirely consistent on the wording, and there are several minor differences with Coulon's abridged version. My translation here is therefore intended to capture the essential elements, but should not be taken as an exact literal rendition of the original.
17 See Mbaye, "L'Islam au Sénégal," 521–522, on the continuity of the organization, despite a name change and an apparent minor shift in orientation.
18 Foltz, *From French West Africa*, 88–96. See also Coulon, "Un Gaullisme Musulman," 348–349. The information in this paragraph is drawn from these two sources.
19 Foltz, *From French West Africa*, 94.
20 See Coulon, *Le Marabout et le Prince*, 218–221 for a discussion of this event.
21 Ibid. See especially part two: "Les Marabouts et l'état." The essence of this discussion is also available in article form, in Coulon, "Les Marabouts sénégalais et l'état," *Revue Française d'Etudes Politiques Africaines* 158 (February 1979), 15–42. Coulon's work is certainly the most thorough existing examination of relations between religious and political leaders in post-independence Senegal, and throughout this chapter I build on his discussion of these relations at the national level in discussing the current situation from the perspective of Fatick. Lucy C. Behrman's study, *Muslim Brotherhoods and Politics in Senegal* (Cambridge: Harvard University Press, 1970) is an earlier work devoted largely to this issue.

22 It is interesting to note that the Senegalese government itself has not been the only agent to find itself obliged to consider the marabouts in such endeavors. International aid agencies have also explored the possible utility of working through maraboutic intermediaries. One example is provided by a report prepared under contract to the United States Agency for International Development (AID), which argues that "The question is not whether AID assistance and marabouts will interact, but how." Lucie Gallistel Colvin, "Marabouts, Agriculture and the Environment in Senegal: Issues in AID Agricultural Assistance," University Research Foundation Report #TR 83–0060 (November 1983), 11.

23 Virtually all analysts of the Senegalese political system have followed Coulon in emphasizing the exchange of services and the continuities with the colonial system. This despite the fact that Lucy Behrman's seminal discussion of the topic suggested (although it did not pursue) the argument I put forth here. In her words: "The French used the marabus [i.e., marabouts] because that was the easiest and least expensive way to rule Senegal; Senegalese politicians, in contrast, are in a more critical dilemma ... the Senegalese are weaker in regard to the marabus than the French were but they have a greater interest in undermining the power of Muslim leaders." Behrman, *Muslim Brotherhoods*, 107.

24 Coulon, *Le Marabout et le Prince*, 238 (in footnote) and 239. It should be noted that Coulon does not give the same interpretation to these comments as I do here. The first is cited only to support the simple observation that a policy of courtesy towards marabouts tended to include less important marabouts, while the second is part of a larger quote meant to illustrate quite the opposite – namely the respect by the state for maraboutic authority. Yet these interpretations are not necessarily incompatible; while the functionary in question clearly demonstrated a preference for not alienating the marabout on whom he had to rely in pursuit of his work, he also indicated the marabout's belief that he had something to fear from the state's longer-term efforts to promote development at the local level.

25 See Tidiane Diallo, "Pouvoir et marabouts en Afrique de l'ouest," *Islam et Sociétés au Sud du Sahara* 2 (1988), for a discussion of the very close ties between various West African heads of state and their personal marabouts, who at times become the real *éminences grises* behind presidential power.

26 Interview, 5 August 1989. Similarly, Diallo argues that: "African heads of state, Muslims or Christians, regardless of the official ideology which they proclaim, consult marabouts or seek their alliance with the goal of consolidating their power, of conserving it for as long as possible or for their whole life," in "Pouvoir et marabouts," 7.

27 Much of the information concerning Sëriñ Alpha's biography and his relations with state officials was accumulated over the period of fieldwork from various interviews and observations. In this section, however, I draw predominantly on one extensive, three-hour, interview with Sëriñ Alpha on 17 November 1989 during which all of the issues included in this section were discussed.

28 Sène has maintained important government positions. At the time of fieldwork he was serving as a diplomat, posted to Geneva.

29 Interview with Sëriñ Cissé and Mouride *taalibe*, 1 February 1989, later

corroborated by others. Although I was not able to determine the precise timing, Mamadou Dia only served as prime minister for the first two years of independence, until his removal after the alleged attempted coup d'état against Senghor. The lot granted to the Mourides has never been developed beyond the erection of a fence and a shed in which the Mouride casket is stored. It is nevertheless used as a prayer site on important feastdays when the Mourides pray apart from others, as well as occasionally for a ceremonial event.

30 Interviews, 11 June and 13 September 1989. The latter official at one point suggested that it would be more acceptable to work with imams, who *are* elected to their positions.

31 Due to its nature, this story is not one I could otherwise verify. Nothing about its telling, however, gave me any reason to doubt its veracity.

32 There are approximately thirty students per teacher, thus totaling some 30,000 FCFA per month in income, a sum insufficient even for room and board. The school went from four to three teachers and classes during my stay in Fatick, when one of the teachers received a salaried job in a state school, an offer which Alpha himself insisted the young man could not refuse.

33 Mamadou Ndiaye, *L'Enseignement arabo-islamique au Sénégal* (Istanbul: Centre de Recherches sur l'Histoire, l'Art et la Culture Islamiques, Organisation de la Conference Islamique, 1985). See especially chapter 8: "L'Etat sénégalais et l'enseignement arabo-islamique au Sénégal," which includes a discussion of the conditions established for the recognition of such schools, as well as lists of the established curriculum for each level. These curricula include both standard subjects (literature, history and geography, mathematics, English and French) and religious ones (tawhid, hadith, Maliki law, Qur°anic exegesis).

34 Interview, 8 May 1989.

35 Interview, 11 June 1989.

36 Interview, 21 October 1989.

37 Interview, 11 June 1989.

38 Abdou Diouf, "L'Islam dans la société oualoff," mémoire, Ecole Nationale de la France d'Outre-mer, Paris, 1959, 110. Cited in Coulon, *Le Marabout et le Prince*, 208. Diouf would of course distance himself totally from this remark today, and it merits noting that all copies of this manuscript, whether in Senegal or in France, have apparently been removed from public access.

39 Behrman, *Muslim Brotherhoods*, 104.

40 Interview, 9 December 1989. It bears noting that the prefect, a devout *taalibe* himself, also regretted the fact that the state was led to become implicated in religious questions. His belief in the equal undesirability of this again points to the strength of the ideology of secularism in the sense of separation of the two domains.

41 Behrman, *Muslim Brotherhoods*, 105.

42 Abdourahmane Konaté, *Le Cri du mange-mil: Mémoires d'un préfet sénégalais* (Paris: L'Harmattan, 1990), 181–188. This work is particularly interesting because, in the author's words, "it does not deal with the science of administration, on which numerous official documents expound. It leans instead towards the instinct of administration," 13.

43 Ibid., 184.

44 Ibid., 185.

45 Ibid., 187.

46 Coulon, "Les Marabouts sénégalais," 37. Robert Fatton, Jr., *The Making of a Liberal Democracy: Senegal's Passive Revolution, 1975–1985* (Boulder: Lynne Rienner, 1987), 99, cites from the same passage, translated somewhat differently.

47 Coulon, "Les Marabouts sénégalais," 37.

48 Interview, 11 June 1989.

49 One state official noted with irony that, in contrast to Tijan marabouts, Mourides were more variable in their support for political figures, but also far more likely to demand material favors from them. Interview, 23 October 1989.

50 Interview, 23 July 1989.

51 I quote here from an interview with the local reporter for the official government newspaper, *Le Soleil*, who works very closely with local officials at the *gouvernance*, where his office is located. Interview, 9 March 1989.

52 Group interview, Islamic Attitudes Project, Kaolack, 2 October 1989.

53 Interviews, 5 August 1989, and 3 November 1989.

54 I use the term "conformist" once again here in the sense suggested by Piscatori. See James P. Piscatori, *Islam in a World of Nation-States* (Cambridge: Cambridge University Press, 1986).

55 Piscatori, *Islam in a World of Nation-States*, 41.

56 See Mohammad Arkoun, "Algeria," in *The Politics of Islamic Revivalism: Diversity and Unity*, ed. Shireen T. Hunter (Bloomington: Indiana University Press, 1988), 172–174.

57 My discussion of this incident here is based primarily on Coulon, "Les Marabouts sénégalais," 31–34 and Mbaye, "L'Islam au Sénégal," 519–523.

58 Coulon, "Les Marabouts sénégalais," 32–33. Coulon cites a letter written by the Conseil which reads in part: "We are astonished to see that now, in Senegal, one wishes to introduce 'innovations,' not to say deformations, while the colonizers had accepted the Muslim Code and created special jurisdictions for Muslims."

59 This third document is included as an annex in Mbaye, "L'Islam au Sénégal," 568–569. It is unclear from his discussion why three responses were drawn up or why this third was chosen, though we can surmise that differences within the group complicated joint activity, and that the advantage of simply listing rejected articles without offering specific alternatives lay in the greater room for negotiation which it provided.

60 From annex in Mbaye, "L'Islam au Sénégal," 570–572, emphasis in the original.

61 Coulon, "Les Marabouts sénégalais," 33.

62 Ibid., 34.

63 Ibid., 33.

64 Amsatou Sow Sidibé, "Le Code sénégalais de la famille et son application," paper delivered to the conference "Etat et Société au Sénégal: Crises et Dynamiques Sociales," Bordeaux, Centre d'Etude d'Afrique Noire, 22–25 October 1991, 19.

65 Robinson, "French 'Islamic' Policy," 419–420.

66 Harrison, *France and Islam*, 171.

67 Interview, Official of the Fatick Chamber of Commerce, 31 August 1989.
68 Coulon, *Le Marabout et le Prince*, 275–277. This has historically been a very important act since it strikes at what was long the major source of state revenue, the monopolistic control over the peanut marketing system.
69 Harrison, *France and Islam*, 178. The discussion of *Shaykh* Hamallah is found on 171–182.
70 It should be mentioned, however, that as the colonial official also noted in the case of *Shaykh* Hamallah's practice cited above, this "silent aggression . . . also bears within itself the seeds of discord and sharp doctrinal quarrels between Muslims themselves." Ibid., 178.
71 Dale F. Eickelman, *Knowledge and Power in Morocco: The Education of a Twentieth-Century Notable* (Princeton: Princeton University Press, 1985), 114. This statement referring to Morocco is equally valid in Senegal. Various scholars of Senegal cited in this work have commented on the reformist tendency, but to my knowledge no in-depth research has been done on the topic to date. Of some note, nevertheless, is Christian Coulon's chapter, "Sénégal," in *Contestations en pays islamiques*, Bertrand Badie et. al. (Paris: CHEAM, 1984). A very good thesis (*mémoire de maitrise*) on non-maraboutic Islamic organizations in Senegal is that of Macodou Mohamet Horma Diouf, "Contribution à l'étude des associations islamiques du Sénégal," Department of Arabic, Université Cheikh Anta Diop de Dakar, 1988. More recently Muriel Gomez-Perez has begun research on Islamic organizations in Dakar, focused primarily on reformist groups. Some preliminary findings can be found in her paper, "Les Associations islamiques à Dakar," presented at the conference "Etat et Sociétés au Sénégal: Crises et Dynamiques Sociales," Centre d'Etude d'Afrique Noire de Bordeaux, 22–25 October 1991. Moriba Magassouba's work, *L'Islam au Sénégal: Demain les mollahs?* (Paris: Karthala, 1985) purports to address this issue but, despite some interesting bits of information, it is ultimately little more than a journalist's impressionistic overview of Senegalese Islam.
72 Momar Coumba Diop and Mamadou Diouf, *Le Sénégal sous Abdou Diouf: Etat et société* (Paris: Karthala, 1990), 69–81. This book provides the best available account of Senegalese politics in the 1980s.
73 Diouf, "Contribution à l'Etude," discusses the importance of Islamic organizations for Senegalese foreign policy, 126–129.
74 Ndiaye, *L'Enseignement Arabo-Islamique*, 146. Ndiaye finds that of 241 *arabisants* with advanced degrees, 180 (75%) were teachers in secondary education, while the remaining 25% were distributed in other sectors.
75 I heard such critiques, for example, made both by and about the director of the state-run Islamic Institute of Dakar. Interview with the director, 11 September 1989, Dakar, and group interview with Senegalese professionals, 27 September 1989, Dakar, Islamic Attitudes Project.
76 In Fatick, the Qur'anic school in the compound of Thierno Tall, one of the adjunct imams of the mosque, was under the guidance of a teacher who had studied in Mauritania at an Islamic Institute run by the World Islamic League. The organization had originally promised to help in the establishment of Islamic schools after the completion of studies. In this case, they had initially provided a large (and by local standards a rather impressive) painted sign in

French and Arabic indicating their sponsorship of the school. But, Tall said, that is virtually the only help they had ever given. Only one other time, Tall noted cynically, in response for a request for help, the organization provided the school with a few items of *fëgg-jaay* ("shake and sell"), discarded Western clothing sold in bundles. Interview, 22 November 1989.

77 Interview, Sidy Lamine Niasse, 6 April 1989, Dakar. Material in this paragraph is drawn from this interview, as well as from another with a cousin of Niasse's with closer ties to the marabouts in Kaolack, 15 November 1988, Dakar. See also Gomez-Perez, "Les Associations Islamiques."

78 An article entitled "An Islamic Cultural Revolution in Senegal," which appeared in the English language Iranian newspaper, *The Tehran Times*, 18 August 1985, notes the "blossoming" of an Islamic press in Senegal, including *Wal Fadjri*, and argues: "The Moslem press spontaneously adopted a revolutionary line and did not conceal its support for Iran's Islamic Revolution. This gave the French media and the pro-western Senegalese elite the pretext to accuse it of funding from Iran." I have no evidence on which to evaluate the validity of the claim concerning Iranian funding, but can only report that it is taken for granted by many in Senegal, including Niasse's cousin cited in the interview above.

79 Further indication of the strapped financial circumstances of the publication (a fate it shares with virtually all of the independent press in Senegal) is provided by the recent switch from a glossy-paged magazine format to that of a weekly newspaper.

80 This group is discussed briefly by Diouf, "Contribution à l'Etude," 114–115. My account of this particular incident is from an interview with a relative of the adjunct Imam of the mosque, 7 September 1989.

81 The *wazifa* (*wajifa* in Arabic) are chanted Tijan prayers recited around a white cloth spread on the ground, twice a day after each of the dawn and dusk prayers.

82 I thank Horma Dicuf for providing me with a copy of this document. It is dated 15 Ramadan 1406 (26 May 1986), and signed by the "Amir" in the name of the executive bureau of the organization. The group's headquarters are in the city of Thiès.

83 Diouf, "Contribution à l'Etude," 82–84. Diouf describes the attitude of the UCM: "It is a reality which we must admit: without those whom they call marabouts it will be impossible for us in the short run, or even for a long time, to really reach the masses," 83.

84 Behrman notes that such men as Ibrahima Niasse, Abdoul Aziz Sy, and Cheikh Mbacké all joined at various times, but argues that this was usually for political reasons having to do with anti-UPS sentiments. Behrman, *Muslim Brotherhoods*, 164.

85 Interview, Sërin̄ Diakhaté, 4 August 1989.

86 Cited in Diouf, "Contribution à l'Etude," 125. The director of the Islamic Institute in Dakar also indicated to me his belief that a significant reason for the UCM's survival was due to the fact that it is rather lucrative for its leadership.

87 The FAIS is discussed in ibid., 116–121, and an annex provides a detailed organization chart of the association.

88 Cissé is from a well-known maraboutic Tijan family in the village of Pire. He

was chosen by his father as a child to be educated in the French school system, allegedly after an incident involving the difficulty of various Tijan marabouts, including El Hadj Malik Sy, in having a letter from a colonial official translated. A highly laudatory article in *Le Soleil* of 1 December 1989 labels Cissé "le marabout diplomate," and notes in particular his role in the establishment of close ties between Senegal and the Arab Gulf states, while also distinguishing himself by his "defense of the principles of our Constitution, notably the secular nature of the State and its institutions."

89 Cited in Diouf, "Contribution à l'Etude," 118.

90 Interviews, Dakar, with Sidy Lamine Niasse, 6 April 1989, and with Daouda Diouf and other members of CERID, Muslim Attitudes Project, 28 September 1989.

91 Piscatori, *Islam in a World of Nation-States*, 127–138.

92 Individual *daairas* of the DMWM at the local level occasionally organize activities of this nature. One "talk" which I attended in Fatick, 27 May 1989, was sponsored by a local section of the DMWM and involved a long and well-prepared speech delivered by a young woman, a student at the high school, to a mixed-sex audience (though including more women than men) of some 50–60 people. A tent and chairs had been set for the occasion in an empty lot. The moralistic talk touched on numerous issues, including birth control, the secular state, and the "pornographic" nature of certain (Western) television programs shown in Senegal.

93 Interview, DMWM official in Fatick, 11 August 1989. Photos of the event are arranged in the album kept in the local seat of the DMWM sector in Fatick.

94 *Le Soleil*, 6 February 1989. Front page articles and banner headlines in *Le Soleil* discussed the conference every day from 6 to 10 February, 1989, although they give little insight into its proceedings or the reaction of the non-Senegalese participants. Two articles discuss panels on specific themes: the importance of women and a defense of Sufism. The articles do, however, give an indication of the state's role in the conference, and I draw on them in this discussion.

95 *Le Soleil*, 6 February 1989.

96 Interview, 5 November 1989.

97 Demba Koné, "Tijanisme et Pouvoir Politique au Sénégal (1950–1987)," Mémoire de maîtrise, Department of Philosophy, Université Cheikh Anta Diop de Dakar, 1988.

98 Coulon, "Sénégal," in *Contestations en pays Islamiques*, 76.

99 For a discussion of the political context of the 1993 elections, see Leonardo A. Villalón, "Democratizing a (Quasi)Democracy: The Senegalese elections of 1993," in *African Affairs* 93:371 (April 1994).

100 Interviews, 30 July 1993.

101 Koné, "Tijanisme," 108.

7   BUREAUCRATS, MARABOUTS, AND CITIZEN–DISCIPLES: HOW PRECARIOUS A BALANCE?

1 Donal B. Cruise O'Brien, "Introduction," in *Charisma and Brotherhood in African Islam*, ed. Cruise O'Brien and Christian Coulon (Oxford: Clarendon Press, 1988), 13–14.

2 Max Weber developed his concept of charismatic leadership in a series of essays, edited and translated into English as *Economy and Society* by Guenther Roth and Claus Wittich (Berkeley: University of California Press, 1978). An excellent collection of essays exploring the concept is *Charisma, History, and Social Structure*, ed., Ronald M. Glassman and William H. Swatos, Jr. (New York: Greenwood Press, 1986). The essays in *Charisma and Brotherhood*, ed. Cruise O'Brien and Coulon, all deal to varying degrees with the application of this concept to African Sufism, most systematically in Cruise O'Brien's "Introduction."

3 Lucy E. Creevey (née Behrman), "Ahmad Bamba 1850–1927" in *Studies in West African Islamic History: Volume 1, The Cultivators of Islam*, ed. John Ralph Willis (London: Frank Cass, 1979), 300, emphasis added. See also Donal B. Cruise O'Brien, "The Saint and the Squire: Personalities and Social Forces in the Development of a Religious Brotherhood," in *African Perspectives: Papers in the History, Politics and Economics of Africa presented to Thomas Hodgkin*, ed. Christopher Allen and R. W. Johnson (Cambridge: Cambridge University Press, 1970).

4 The phrasing is from Joseph Bensman and Michael Givant, "Charisma and Modernity: The Use and Abuse of a Concept," in *Charisma, History and Social Structure*, ed. Glassman and Swatos, 32.

5 See ibid., 31ff.

6 The term "pseudocharisma" for this phenomenon is proposed by Bensman and Givant, "Charisma and Modernity," in *Charisma, History and Social Structure*, ed. Glassman and Swatos.

7 Cruise O'Brien, "Introduction," in *Charisma and Brotherhood*, ed. Cruise O'Brien and Coulon.

8 The discussion in this section is based predominantly on interviews with the marabout and with various of his assistants, notably his son-in-law and personal secretary, carried out during two visits to Sirmang – a two day stay on August 29–30, 1989, and attendance at the *gàmmu* organized there at the occasion of the *Mawlud* (the Prophet's birthday), October 12–13, 1989. In addition I conducted numerous interviews with disciples of Ma Ansou Niang in Fatick, and attended many meetings of his *daaira* there.

9 As an example, one such song (in Wolof) sung repeatedly by the Fatick *daaira* on the road to Sirmang:

> Ansou Niang mii / boroom diine la
> ñówal! ma ñów / waa ja laay seet
> teral na lislaam / ca ay meloom

A rough translation might run as follows:

> Ansou Niang himself / He's a man of religion
> Come! I'm coming / I'm going to see the man
> He has honored Islam / In his actions

10 Equaling approximately $35,000, a huge sum by local standards.

11 Interview, 8 June 1989.

12 The pre-Islamic celebration, know as the *Jobaay*, involves a ritual hunt by the men of Ndiaye-Ndiaye, who wear disguises for the occasion. They return to Fatick at the end of the day with their "catch" (in the degraded ecological

conditions of today usually including only a few birds, a rabbit or two, and perhaps an iguana), and then gather in the arena for a session of drumming and dancing. The event continues to take place, but has lost importance in recent years, in part due to the death of the old man who had long organized it, but also due to the declining popularity of such clearly "pagan" rituals.

13 Jean-François Bayart, "La Revanche des sociétés africaines," *Politique Africaine* 11 (September 1983), 102.

14 René Otayek, "Muslim Charisma in Burkina Faso," 110 and Donal B. Cruise O'Brien, "Introduction," 12, in *Charisma and Brotherhood*, ed. Cruise O'Brien and Coulon.

15 Cruise O'Brien, "Introduction," in *Charisma and Brotherhood*, ed. Cruise O'Brien and Coulon, 13–14.

16 Patrick Chabal, "Introduction: Thinking about politics in Africa," in *Political Domination in Africa: Reflections on the Limits of Power*, ed. Patrick Chabal (Cambridge: Cambridge University Press, 1986), 13.

17 The phrase is Michael Bratton's, previously cited in chapter 1.

18 Donal B. Cruise O'Brien, "Ruling Class and Peasantry in Senegal, 1960–1976: The Politics of a Monocrop Economy," in *The Political Economy of Underdevelopment: Dependence in Senegal*, ed. Rita Cruise O'Brien (Beverly Hills: Sage, 1979), 226. I largely concur with Cruise O'Brien, and this assessment is central to my argument in this work, but it is important to note that other students of the Mouride order have interpreted it quite differently. Cruise O'Brien's famous (among students of Senegal) description cited here should be contrasted with the (equally famous) one proposed by Jean Copans and inspired by his understanding of religion as a hegemonic ideology which facilitates economic exploitation: "Abdou Lahat M'Backé proclaims in vain that all that which is not of the order is of the domain of Satan, it is the Mouride order which is an infernal machine." *Les Marabouts de l'arachide* (Paris: Le Sycomore, 1980), 258.

19 Michael Bratton, "Beyond the State: Civil Society and Associational Life in Africa," *World Politics* 41:3 (April 1989), 419. Bratton here is referring to a point made by Mahmood Mamdani in one of the works under review.

20 Donal B. Cruise O'Brien, *Saints and Politicians: Essays in the Organization of a Senegalese Peasant Society* (Cambridge: Cambridge University Press, 1975), 200.

21 Lucy C. Behrman, *Muslim Brotherhoods and Politics in Senegal* (Cambridge: Harvard University Press, 1970). See especially chapter 4, "The Political Parties and the Marabouts."

22 This troubling incident, unprecedented in Senegalese political history, took place on 15 May 1993 as the Constitutional Council was preparing to announce the results of the legislative elections of 9 May. Immediately after the killing several PDS officials, including Wade himself, were detained for questioning, though Wade was released within forty-eight hours. Allegations and counter-allegations about responsibility for the act, however, dominated political discussion in Senegal for months. The PS made every effort to implicate not only Wade, but also Moustapha Sy of the DMWM, who had sided openly with Wade after his public break with Diouf. Both Wade and Sy, in turn, elaborated a theory of a conspiracy by the PS government to kill Sèye because he was preparing to denounce PS electoral fraud. By the end of the year the controversy continued, and it appeared unlikely that it would ever be definitively settled.

23 Interview, 6 November 1989.
24 *Wal Fadjri*, 9–15 October 1992. The information and citations in this and the following paragraph are all from this source.
25 "The process of establishing a democracy is a process of institutionalizing uncertainty." Adam Przeworski, "Some Problems in the Study of the Transition to Democracy," in *Transitions from Authoritarian Rule: Comparative Perspectives*, ed. Guillermo O'Donnell, Philippe C. Schmitter, and Laurence Whitehead (Baltimore: Johns Hopkins University Press, 1986), 58.
26 A somewhat different version combined French and Arabic, reading: "C'est un fait de Dieu/Abdoul Ala Mbacké à Touba/Abdoul Aziz Sy à Tivaouane/Abdou Diouf à Dakar/Al Hamdullilahi Rabil Alamine [Thanks be to God, master of the world]/Le Sénégal est complet." "The Three Abdous" of the title is a pun of sorts, the term being used for a three piece traditional outfit for men worn in Senegal on formal occasions.

Select Bibliography

Abun-Nasr, Jamil M. *The Tijaniyya: A Sufi Order in the Modern World*. London: Oxford University Press, 1965.

Almond, Gabriel and Sidney Verba. *The Civic Culture: Political Attitudes and Democracy in Five Nations*. Princeton: Princeton University Press, 1963.

Anderson, Lisa. "The State in the Middle East and North Africa." *Comparative Politics* 20:1 (October 1987): 1–18.

André, Général P. J. *Contribution à l'étude des confréries religieuses musulmanes*. Algiers: La Maison des Livres, 1956.

Arkoun, Mohammad. "Algeria." In *The Politics of Islamic Revivalism: Diversity and Unity*, ed. Shireen T. Hunter, 171–186. Bloomington: Indiana University Press, 1988.

Arnaud, Robert. *L'Islam et la politique musulmane française en Afrique Occidentale Française*. Paris: Comité de l'Afrique Française, 1912.

Atlas National du Sénégal. Paris: L'Institut Géographique National, 1977.

Azarya, Victor. "Reordering State-Society Relations: Incorporation and Disengagement." In *The Precarious Balance: State and Society in Africa*, ed. Donald Rothchild and Naomi Chazan, 3–21. Boulder: Westview, 1988.

Azarya, Victor and Naomi Chazan. "Disengagement from the State in Africa: Reflections on the Experience of Ghana and Guinea." *Comparative Studies in Society and History* 29:1 (January 1987): 106–31.

Badie, Bertrand and Pierre Birnbaum. *Sociologie de l'état*. Paris: Bernard Grasset, 1979. Translated as *The Sociology of the State*. Chicago: University of Chicago Press, 1983.

Balans, Jean-Louis, Christian Coulon, and Jean-Marc Gastellu. *Autonomie locale et intégration nationale au Sénégal*. Paris: A. Pedone, 1975.

Baldick, Julian. *Mystical Islam: An Introduction to Sufism*. London: J. B. Tauris and Co., 1989.

Barker, Jonathan Shedd. "Local Politics and National Development: The Case of a Rural District in the Saloum Region of Senegal." Ph.D. diss., University of California, Berkeley, 1967.

"The Paradox of Development: Reflections on a Study of Local-Central Political Relations in Senegal." In *The State of the Nations: Constraints on Development in Independent Africa*, ed. Michael F. Lofchie, 47–64. Berkeley: University of California Press, 1971.

"Political Factionalism in Senegal." *Canadian Journal of African Studies* 7:2 (1973): 287–303.

"Political Space and the Quality of Participation in Rural Africa: A Case from Senegal." *Canadian Journal of African Studies* 21:1 (1987): 1–16.

Bates, Robert H. "Ethnicity in Contemporary Africa." Eastern African Studies papers XIV. Syracuse: Program of Eastern African Studies, Maxwell School of Citizenship and Public Affairs, Syracuse University, 1973.

Markets and States in Tropical Africa: The Political Basis of Agricultural Policies. Berkeley: University of California Press, 1981.

"Modernization, Ethnic Competition, and the Rationality of Politics in Contemporary Africa." In *Governing in Black Africa*, ed. M. E. Doro and N. M. Schultz. New York: Africana, 1986.

Batran, A. A. "The Kunta, Sidi al-Mukhtar al-Kunti, and the Office of Shaykh al-Tariq al-Qadiriyya " In *Studies in West African Islamic History, Volume 1: The Cultivators of Islam*, ed. John Ralph Willis, 113–146. London: Frank Cass, 1979.

Bayart, Jean-François. "Le Politique par le bas en Afrique Noire: Question de méthode." *Politique Africaine* 1 (January 1981): 53–82.

"La Revanche des sociétés africaines." *Politique Africaine* 11 (September 1983): 95–127

"Les Sociétés africaines face à l'état." *Pouvoirs* 25 (1983): 23–39

"Civil Society in Africa." In *Political Domination in Africa: Reflections on the Limits of Power*, ed. Patrick Chabal, 109–125. Cambridge: Cambridge University Press, 1986.

L'Etat en Afrique: La politique du ventre. Paris: Fayard, 1989. Translated as: *The State in Africa: The Politics of the Belly.* London: Longman, 1993.

Behrman, Lucy C. *Muslim Brotherhoods and Politics in Senegal.* Cambridge: Harvard University Press, 1970.

"The Islamization of the Wolof by the end of the Nineteenth Century." In *Western African History*, Boston University Papers on Africa series, vol. 4, eds., Daniel F. McCall, Norman R. Bennett, and Jeffrey Butler, 102–131. New York: Praeger, 1969.

Bendix, John, Bertell Ollman, Bartholomew H. Sparrow, and Timothy P. Mitchell. "Controversy: Going Beyond the State?" *American Political Science Review* 86:4 (December 1992): 1007–1021.

Bensman, Joseph and Michael Givant. "Charisma and Modernity: The Use and Abuse of a Concept." In *Charisma, History and Social Structure,* ed. Ronald M. Glassman and William H. Swatos, Jr., 27–56. New York: Greenwood Press, 1986

Bergen, Geoffrey. "Trade Unions in Senegal: A Perspective on National Development in Africa." Ph.D. diss., University of California at Los Angeles, 1993.

Boone, Catherine. "State Power and Private Interests: The Emergence of Crisis in Import-Substitution Manufacturing in Senegal." Ph.D. diss., Massachusetts Institute of Technology, 1987.

"The Making of a Rentier Class: Wealth Accumulation and Political Control in Senegal." *The Journal of Development Studies* 26:3 (April 1990): 425–449.

"State Power and Economic Crisis in Senegal." *Comparative Politics* 22:3 (April 1990): 341–357.

Merchant Capital and the Roots of State Power in Senegal, 1930–1985. Cambridge: Cambridge University Press, 1992.

Bourlon, A. "Mourides et Mouridisme 1953." In *Notes et documents sur l'Islam en Afrique noire*, M. Chailley et al., 53–74. Paris: J. Peyronnet and Cie., 1962.

Boyd-Buggs, Debra. "Entretien avec El Hadj Abdoul Aziz Sy, Jr." *Présence Africaine* 148 (Fourth Quarter, 1988).

Boye, Ibrahima. *Sayyidi Abdal Qadr Djilani: Imam suprême de la 'Walaya'*. Paris: Publisud, 1990.

Bratton, Michael. "Beyond the State: Civil Society and Associational Life in Africa." *World Politics* 41:3 (April 1989): 407–430.

Brenner, Louis. *West African Sufi: The Religious Heritage and Spiritual Search of Cerno Bokar Saalif Taal*. London: C. Hurst and Co., 1984.

   Reflexions sur le savoir islamique en Afrique de l'ouest. Bordeaux: Centre d'Etude d'Afrique Noire, 1985.

Brigaud, Felix. *Histoire du Sénégal: Des origines aux traités de protectorat*. Dakar: Clairafrique, 1964.

Brown, Nathan J. *Peasant Politics in Modern Egypt: The Struggle against the State*. New Haven: Yale University Press, 1990.

Burke, Edmond III. "Islam and Social Movements: Methodological Reflections." In *Islam, Politics, and Social Movements*, ed. Edmond Burke III and Ira M. Lapidus. Berkeley: University of California Press, 1988.

Callaghy, Thomas M. *The State-Society Struggle: Zaire in Comparative Perspective*. New York: Columbia University Press, 1984.

Caporaso, James A. ed. *The Elusive State: International and Comparative Perspectives*. Newbury Park, CA: Sage, 1989.

Carnoy, Martin. *The State and Political Theory*. Princeton: Princeton University Press, 1984.

Chabal, Patrick. "Introduction: Thinking about Politics in Africa." In *Political Domination in Africa: Reflections on the Limits of Power*, ed. Patrick Chabal, 1–16. Cambridge: Cambridge University Press, 1986.

   ed. *Political Domination in Africa: Reflections on the Limits of Power*. Cambridge: Cambridge University Press, 1986.

Chazan, Naomi. "Patterns of State-Society Incorporation and Disengagement in Africa." In *The Precarious Balance: State and Society in Africa*, ed. Donald Rothchild and Naomi Chazan, 121–148. Boulder: Westview, 1988.

Clarke, Peter B. *West Africa and Islam: A Study of Religious Development from the 8th to the 20th Century*. London: Edward Arnold, 1982.

Colburn, Forrest D. "Statism, Rationality, and State Centrism." *Comparative Politics* 20:4 (July 1988): 485–492.

Colvin, Lucie Gallistel. *Historical Dictionary of Senegal*. Metuchen, New Jersey: The Scarecrow Press, 1981.

   "The *Shaykh's* Men: Religion and Power in Senegambian Islam." In *Rural and Urban Islam in West Africa*, eds. Nehemia Levtzion and Humphrey J. Fisher, 55–65. Boulder: Lynne Rienner, 1987.

   ed. *The Uprooted of the Western Sahel: Migrants' Search for Cash in the Senegambia*. New York: Praeger, 1981.

   "Marabouts, Agriculture and the Environment in Senegal: Issues in AID Agricultural Assistance." University Research Foundation Report #TR 83–0060 (November 1983).

Copans, Jean. "From Senegambia to Senegal: The Evolution of Peasantries." In

Peasants in Africa: Historical and Contemporary Perspectives, ed. Martin A. Klein, 75–103. Beverly Hills: Sage, 1980.

Les Marabouts de l'arachide: La confrérie mouride et les paysans du Sénégal. Paris: Le Sycomore, 1980.

Copans, Jean, et. al., *Maintenance sociale et changement économique au Sénégal: I: Doctrine économique et pratique du travail chez les Mourides.* Travaux et Documents de L'ORSTOM 15. Paris: ORSTOM, 1972.

Cottingham, Clement. "Political Consolidation and Centre-Local Relations in Senegal." *Canadian Journal of African Studies* 4:1 (1970): 101–120.

Coulon, Christian. "Elections, factions et idéologie au Sénégal." In *Aux Urnes l'Afrique! Elections et pouvoirs en Afrique noire,* ed. D. G. Lavroff. Paris: A. Pedone, 1978.

"Les Marabouts sénégalais et l'état." *Revue Française d'Etudes Politiques Africaines* 158 (February 1979): 15–42.

"Un Gaullisme Musulman: Les Marabouts et la Décolonisation au Sénégal." In *La Politique Africaine du Général de Gaulle (1958–1969),* by the Centre Bordelais d'Etudes Africaines, le Centre d'Etude d'Afrique Noire, et L'Institut Charles de Gaulle, 19–20 October 1979. Paris: A. Pedone, 1980: 346–356.

Le Marabout et le prince: Islam et pouvoir au Sénégal. Paris: A. Pedone, 1981.

"Construction étatique et action islamique au Sénégal." In *L'Islam et l'Etat dans le monde d'aujourd'hui,* ed. Olivier Carré, 258–270. Paris: Presses Universitaires de France, 1982.

"Le Réseau islamique." *Politique Africaine* 9 (March 1983): 68–83.

Les Musulmans et le pouvoir en Afrique Noire: Religion et contre-culture. Paris: Karthala, 1983.

"Sénégal." In *Contestations en pays Islamiques,* ed. Bertrand Badie, et. al., 63–88. Paris: Centre des Hautes Etudes sur l'Afrique et l'Asie Modernes (CHEAM), 1984.

"Senegal: The Development and Fragility of Semidemocracy." In *Democracy in Developing Countries, Volume 2: Africa,* ed. Larry Diamond, Juan J. Linz, and Seymour Martin Lipset, 141–178. Boulder: Lynne Rienner, 1988.

"La Démocratie sénégalaise: bilan d'une expérience." *Politique Africaine* 45 (March 1992). Issue title: "Sénégal: La Démocratie à l'épreuve."

Coulon, Christian and Donal B. Cruise O'Brien. "Senegal." In *Contemporary West African States,* ed. Donal B. Cruise O'Brien, John Dunn and Richard Rathbone, 145–164. Cambridge: Cambridge University Press, 1989.

Couty, Phillipe. "Entretiens avec des marabouts et des paysans du Baol." Dakar: ORSTOM (Office de la Recherche Scientifique et Technique Outre-Mer), Febuary, 1968.

Creevey, Lucy E. (née Behrman). "Muslim Brotherhoods and Development in Senegal." *The Journal of Modern African Studies* 15:2 (1977): 261–77.

"Ahmad Bamba 1850–1927." In *Studies in West African Islamic History: Volume 1, The Cultivators of Islam,* ed. John Ralph Willis, 278–307. London: Frank Cass, 1979.

"Religion and Modernization in Senegal." In *Islam and Development: Religion and Sociopolitical Change,* ed. John L. Esposito. Syracuse: Syracuse University Press, 1980.

"Muslim Brotherhoods and Politics in Senegal in 1985." *The Journal of Modern*

African Studies 23:4 (1985): 715–721.

Crowder, Michael. *Senegal: A Study in French Assimilation Policy.* London: Oxford University Press, 1962.

Cruise O'Brien, Donal B. "Towards an 'Islamic Policy' in French West Africa, 1854–1914." *Journal of African History* 8:2 (1967): 303–316.

"The Saint and the Squire: Personalities and Social Forces in the Development of a Religious Brotherhood." In *African Perspectives: Papers in the History, Politics and Economics of Africa Presented to Thomas Hodgkin*, ed. Christopher Allen and R. W. Johnson, 157–169. Cambridge: Cambridge University Press, 1970.

The Mourides of Senegal: The Political and Economic Organization of an Islamic Brotherhood. Oxford: Clarendon Press, 1971.

Saints and Politicians: Essays in the Organization of a Senegalese Peasant Society. Cambridge: Cambridge University Press, 1975.

"Senegal." In *West African States: Failure and Promise: A Study in Comparative Politics*, ed. John Dunn, 173–188. Cambridge: Cambridge University Press, 1978.

"Langue et nationalité au Sénégal: l'enjeu politique de la Wolofisation." *Année Africaine* 1979: 319–335. Paris: A. Pedone.

"Ruling Class and Peasantry in Senegal, 1960–1976: The Politics of a Monocrop Economy." In *The Political Economy of Underdevelopment: Dependence in Senegal*, ed. Rita Cruise O'Brien, 209–227. Beverly Hills: Sage, 1979.

"Islam and Power in Black Africa." In *Islam and Power*, ed. Alexander S. Cudsi and Ali E. Hillal Dessouki, 158–166. London: Croom Helm, 1981.

"La Filière musulmane: confréries soufies et politique en Afrique noire." *Politique Africaine* I:4 (November 1981): 7–30.

"Sufi Politics in Senegal." In *Islam in the Political Process*, ed. James P. Piscatori, 122–137. Cambridge: Cambridge University Press, 1983.

"Wails and Whispers: The People's Voice in West African Muslim Politics." In *Political Domination in Africa: Reflections on the Limits of Power*, ed. Patrick Chabal, 71–83. Cambridge: Cambridge University Press, 1986.

"Introduction." In *Charisma and Brotherhood in African Islam*, eds. Donal B. Cruise O'Brien and Christian Coulon, 1–31. Oxford: Clarendon Press, 1988.

"Charisma Comes to Town: Mouride Urbanization 1945–1986." In *Charisma and Brotherhood in African Islam*, eds. Donal B. Cruise O'Brien and Christian Coulon, 135–155. Oxford: Clarendon Press, 1988.

"Islamic Attitudes toward the West: The Case of Senegal." Washington: USIA Office of Research, unpublished report number R-3–90 (February 1990).

"Le 'contrat social' sénégalais à l'épreuve." *Politique Africaine* 45 (March 1992). Special issue title: "Sénégal: La Démocratie à l'épreuve."

Cruise O'Brien, Donal B. and Christian Coulon, eds. *Charisma and Brotherhood in African Islam.* Oxford: Clarendon Press, 1988.

Cruise O'Brien, Donal B., John Dunn and Richard Rathbone, eds. *Contemporary West African States.* Cambridge: Cambridge University Press, 1989.

Cruise O'Brien, Rita, ed. *The Political Economy of Underdevelopment: Dependence in Senegal.* Beverly Hills: Sage, 1979.

Cudsi, Alexander S. and Ali E. Hillal Dessouki. *Islam and Power.* London: Croom Helm, 1981.

Cuoq, Joseph M. *Les Musulmans en Afrique.* Paris: Maisonneuve et Larose, 1975.
  Histoire de l'Islamisation de l'Afrique de l'Ouest des origines à la fin du XVIe siècle.
  Paris: P. Geuthner, 1984.
Davis, Eric. "The Concept of Revival and the Study of Islam and Politics." In *The
  Islamic Impulse,* ed. Barbara Freyer Stowasser, 37–58. London: Croom Helm,
  1987.
Dia, Mamadou. *Islam, sociétés africaines, et culture industrielle.* Dakar: Les
  Nouvelles Editions Africaines, 1975.
  Essais sur l'Islam: Tome II: Socio-anthropologie de l'Islam. Dakar: Les Nouvelles
  Editions Africaines, 1979.
Diagne, Pathé. *Pouvoir politique traditionnel en Afrique Occidentale: Essais sur les
  institutions politiques précoloniales.* Paris: Présence Africaine, 1967.
  Sénégal: Crise économique et sociale et devenir de la démocratie. Dakar: Sankore,
  1984
Diallo, Tidiane. "Pouvoir et marabouts en Afrique de l'Ouest." In *Islam et Sociétés
  au Sud du Sahara* 2 (1988): 7–10.
Diop, Abdoulaye-Bara. "Parenté et famille Wolof en milieu rural." In *Bulletin de
  l'Institut Fondamental d'Afrique Noire,* Série B, Sciences Humaines, 32:1
  (January 1970): 216–229.
  *La Société Wolof: Tradition et changement: Les Systèmes d'inégalité et de
  domination.* Paris: Karthala, 1981.
  "Les paysans du bassin arachidier. Conditions de vie et comportements de
  survie." *Politique Africaine* 45 (March 1992). Issue title: "Sénégal: La Démoc-
  ratie à l'épreuve."
Diop, Angélique. "Le Sine de 1859 à 1891." Mémoire de Maîtrise, Université de
  Dakar, Faculté des Lettres et Sciences Humaines, Département d'Histoire,
  1976.
Diop, Majhemout. *Histoire des classes sociales dans l'Afrique de l'ouest: II: Le
  Sénégal.* Paris: François Maspero, 1972.
Diop, Momar Coumba. "Les Affaires mourides à Dakar." *Politique Africaine* 1:4
  (November 1981): 90–100.
Diop, Momar Coumba and Mamadou Diouf. *Le Sénégal sous Abdou Diouf: Etat et
  société.* Paris: Karthala, 1990.
Diouf, Macodou Mohamet Horma. "Contribution à l'étude des associations
  islamiques du Sénégal." Mémoire de Maîtrise, Université Cheikh Anta Diop
  de Dakar, Faculté des Lettres et Sciences Humaines, Département d'Arabe,
  1988.
Diouf, Makhtar. "La Crise de l'ajustement." *Politique Africaine* 45 (March 1992).
  Issue title: "Sénégal: La Démocratie à l'épreuve."
Diouf, Mamadou. "Relations marabouts et administration dans le département de
  Thiès." Mémoire de fin de stage, Ecole Nationale d'Administration et de
  Magistrature (Dakar), 1977.
Doornbos, Martin. "The African State in Academic Debate: Retrospect and
  Prospect." *The Journal of Modern African Studies* 28:2 (1990): 179–198.
Dubois, J.-P. "Les Serer et la question de terre neuve au Sénégal." *Cahiers de
  l'ORSTOM* 12:1 (1975): 81–120.
Dumont, Fernand. *La Pensée religieuse d'Amadou Bamba.* Dakar: Les Nouvelles
  Editions Africaines, 1975.

Dumont, Pierre. *Le Français et les langues africaines au Sénégal.* Paris: Karthala, 1983.

Ebin, Victoria. "Mouride Traders vs. the State: Strategies for the Development of International Trade in a Time of Crisis." Paper delivered to the conference "Etat et Société au Sénégal: Crises et Dynamiques Sociales" by the Centre d'Etude d'Afrique Noire, 22–25 October, 1991.

"A la recherche de nouveaux 'poissons.' Stratégies commerciales mourides par temps de crise." *Politique Africaine* 45 (March 1992). Issue title: "Sénégal: La Démocratie à l'épreuve."

Eickelman, Dale F. *Moroccan Islam: Tradition and Society in a Pilgrimage Center.* Austin: University of Texas Press, 1976.

Knowledge and Power in Morocco: The Education of a Twentieth-Century Notable. Princeton: Princeton University Press, 1985.

"Changing Interpretations of Islamic Movements." In *Islam and the Political Economy of Meaning: Comparative Studies of Muslim Discourse,* ed. William R. Roff, 13–30. London: Croom Helm, 1987.

El-Zein, Abdul Hamid M. "Beyond Ideology and Theology: The Search for the Anthropology of Islam." In *Annual Review of Anthropology* 6 (1977): 227–254.

Ergas, Zaki, ed. *The African State in Transition.* New York: Saint Martin's Press, 1987.

Esposito, John L. *Islam and Politics.* Revised 2nd edn Syracuse: Syracuse University Press, 1987.

ed. *Islam and Development: Religion and Sociopolitical Change.* Syracuse: Syracuse University Press, 1980.

Evans, Peter B., Dietrich Rueschemeyer, and Theda Skocpol, eds. *Bringing the State Back In.* Cambridge: Cambridge University Press, 1985.

Fal, Arame, Rosine Santos, and Jean Léonce Doneux. *Dictionnaire Wolof-Français.* Paris: Karthala, 1990.

Fall, Mar. "L'Etat sénégalais et le renouveau récent de l'Islam: Une introduction." *Le Mois en Afrique* 219/220 (April-May 1984): 154–159.

Sénégal: L'Etat Abdou Diouf, ou le temps des incertitudes. Paris: L'Harmattan, 1986.

"La Question Islamique au Sénégal: Le Regain récent de l'islam, la religion contre l'Etat?" *Présence Africaine* 142:2 (1987): 24–35.

Fatton, Robert Jr. "Clientelism and Patronage in Senegal." *African Studies Review* 29:4 (December 1986): 61–78.

"Gramsci and the Legitimization of the State: The Case of the Senegalese Passive Revolution." *Canadian Journal of Political Science* 19:4 (December 1986): 729–750.

The Making of a Liberal Democracy: Senegal's Passive Revolution, 1975–1985. Boulder: Lynne Rienner, 1987.

"Bringing the Ruling Class Back In: Class, State, and Hegemony in Africa." *Comparative Politics* 20:3 (April 1988): 253–264.

"The State of African Studies and Studies of the African State: The Theoretical Softness of the 'Soft State'." *Journal of Asian and African Studies* 24:3/4 (1989): 170–187.

Foltz, William J. *From French West Africa to the Mali Federation.* New Haven: Yale University Press, 1965.

"Social Structure and Political Behavior of Senegalese Elites." *Behavior Science Notes* 4:2 (1969): 145–163.

Forrest, Joshua B. "The Quest for State 'Hardness' in Africa." *Comparative Politics* 20:4 (July 1988): 423–442.

Fougeyrollas, Pierre. *Modernisation des hommes: L'exemple du Sénégal*. Paris: Flammarion, 1967.

Où va le Sénégal? Analyse spectrale d'une nation africaine. Dakar: IFAN (and Paris: Editions Anthropos), 1970.

Fouquet, J. *La traite des arachides dans le pays de Kaolack et ses conséquences économiques, sociales et juridiques*. St. Louis du Sénégal: Institut Français d'Afrique Noire. 1958.

Froelich, J. C. *Les Musulmans d'Afrique Noire*. Paris: Editions de l'Orante, 1962.

Gamble, David P. *The Wolof of Senegambia, Together with Notes on the Lebu and the Serer*. London: International Africa Institute/Oxford University Press, 1957.

Gastellu, Jean-Marc. *L'égalitarisme économique des Serer du Sénégal*. Travaux et documents de l'ORSTOM 128. Paris: ORSTOM, 1981.

Geertz, Clifford. "The Integrative Revolution: Primordial Sentiments and Civil Politics in the New States." In *Old Societies and New States: The Quest for Modernity in Asia and Africa*, ed. Clifford Geertz, 105–157. New York: The Free Press of Glencoe, 1963.

Gellar, Sheldon. "State-building and Nation-building in West Africa." In *Building States and Nations*. Vol. 2, ed. S. N. Eisenstadt and S. Rokkan, 384–426. Beverly Hills: Sage, 1973.

Senegal: An African Nation Between Islam and the West. Boulder: Westview, 1982.

"State Tutelage vs. Self-Governance: The Rhetoric and Reality of Decentralization in Senegal." In *The Failure of the Centralized State: Institutions and Self-Governance in Africa*, ed. James S. Wunsch and Dele Olowu, 130–147. Boulder: Westview, 1990.

Gellner, Ernest. *Muslim Society*. Cambridge: Cambridge University Press, 1981.

Gilsenan, Michael. *Saint and Sufi in Modern Egypt: An Essay in the Sociology of Religion*. Oxford: Clarendon Press, 1973.

Glassman, Ronald M. and William H. Swatos, Jr., eds. *Charisma, History and Social Structure*. New York: Greenwood Press, 1986.

Gomez-Perez, Muriel. "Les Associations islamiques à Dakar." Paper delivered to the conference "Etat et Société au Sénégal: Crises et Dynamiques Sociales" by the Centre d'Etude d'Afrique Noire, 22–25 October, 1991.

Gravrand, Henry. *La Civilisation Sereer: Cosaan: Les Origines*. Dakar: Les Nouvelles Editions Africaines, 1983.

La Civilisation Sereer: Pangool: Le génie religieux Sereer. Dakar: Les Nouvelles Editions Africaines, 1990.

Gray, Christopher. "The Rise of the Niassene Tijaniyya, 1875 to the Present." *Islam et Sociétés au Sud du Sahara* 2 (1988): 34–60. Paris: Fondation de la Maison de Sciences de l'Homme.

Hale, Thomas A. and Paul Stoller. "Oral Art, Society, and Survival in the Sahel." In *African Literature Studies: The Present State/L'Etat Présent*, ed. Stephen Arnold, 163–169. Washington: Three Continents Press, 1985.

Halpern, Manfred. *The Politics of Social Change in the Middle East and North Africa*. Princeton: Princeton University Press, 1963.

Hamès, Constant. "Peintures et Images Islamiques au Sénégal." *Islam et Sociétés au Sud du Sahara* 2 (1988): 11–16. Paris: Fondation de la Maison de Sciences de l'Homme.

Hanson, John. "*Jihad* and the *Talibé* Colonization of Karta: the Genesis of a Dissident Tradition in the Umarian Movement." Paper presented at the 36th annual meeting of the African Studies Association. Boston, MA, 4–7 December 1993.

Hanson, John and David Robinson. *After the Jihad: The Reign of Ahmad al-Kabir in the Western Sudan*. East Lansing: Michigan State University Press, 1991.

Harrison, Christopher. *France and Islam in West Africa, 1860–1960*. Cambridge: Cambridge University Press, 1988.

Hesseling, Gerti. *Histoire politique du Sénégal: Institutions, droit et société*. Paris: Karthala, 1985.

Hirschman, Albert O. *Exit, Voice, and Loyalty: Responses to Decline in Firms, Organizations, and States*. Cambridge: Harvard University Press, 1970.

"Exit, Voice, and the State." *World Politics* 31:1 (October 1978): 90–107.

Hiskett, Mervyn. *The Development of Islam in West Africa*. London: Longman, 1984.

Hyden, Goran. *Beyond Ujamaa in Tanzania: Underdevelopment and an Uncaptured Peasantry*. London: Heinemann, 1980.

No Shortcuts to Progress: African Development Management in Perspective. Berkeley: University of California Press, 1983.

"Governance and the Study of Politics." In *Governance and Politics in Africa*, ed. Goren Hyden and Michael Bratton, 1–26. Boulder: Lynne Rienner, 1992.

Hyden, Goran and Michael Bratton, eds. *Governance and Politics in Africa*. Boulder: Lynne Rienner, 1992.

Hymans, Jacques Louis. *Léopold Sédar Senghor: An Intellectual Biography*. Edinburgh: Edinburgh University Press, 1971.

Isichei, Elizabeth. *History of West Africa since 1800*. New York: Africana, 1977.

Ismael, Tareq Y. and Jacqueline S. Ismael. *Government and Politics in Islam*. London: Frances Pinter, 1985.

Jackson, Robert H. *Quasi-States. Sovereignty, International Relations, and the Third World*. Cambridge: Cambridge University Press, 1990.

Jackson, Robert H. and Carl G. Rosberg. *Personal Rule in Black Africa: Prince, Autocrat, Prophet, Tyrant*. Berkeley: University of California Press, 1982.

"Why Africa's Weak States Persist: The Empirical and the Juridical in Statehood." *World Politics* 35:1 (October 1982):1–24.

Johnson, G. Wesley, Jr. *The Emergence of Black Politics in Senegal: The Struggle for Power in the Four Communes, 1900–1920*. Stanford: Stanford University Press, 1971.

Kamara, Cheikh Moussa. "La Vie d'El-Hadji Omar." Translated and annotated by Amar Samb. *Bulletin de l'Institut Fondamental d'Afrique Noire (Série B, Sciences Humaines)* 32:1 (January, 1970): 44–135.

Kane, Ousmane. "La Confrérie 'Tijaniyya Ibrahimiyya' de Kano et ses liens avec la zawiya mère de Kaolack." *Islam et Sociétés au sud du Sahara* 3 (May 1989): 27–40.

"Les mouvements religieux et le champ politique au Nigéria septentrional: Le cas du réformisme musulman à Kano." *Islam et Sociétés au Sud du Sahara* 4 (November 1990): 7–24.

Keita, Kélétigui S. "Maba Diakhou Ba dans le Rip et le Saloum (1861–1867)." Mémoire de maîtrise. Université de Dakar, Faculté des Lettres et Sciences Humaines, Département d'Histoire, 1970.

Keita, Maghan. "The Political Economy of Health Care in Senegal." Ph.D. diss. The African Studies and Research Program, Howard University, 1988.

"The Integration of Traditional and Modern Health Care Revisited." Paper delivered at the annual meeting of the African Studies Association, 5 November 1989.

Klein, Martin A. *Islam and Imperialism in Senegal: Sine-Saloum, 1847–1914.* Stanford: Stanford University Press, 1968.

"The Moslem Revolution in 19th Century Senegambia." In *Western African History*, Boston University Papers on Africa series, vol. 4, eds., Daniel F. McCall, Norman R. Bennett, and Jeffrey Butler, 60–101. New York: Praeger, 1969.

"Colonial Rule and Structural Change: The Case of Sine-Saloum." In *The Political Economy of Underdevelopment: Dependence in Senegal*, ed. Rita Cruise O'Brien, 65–99. Beverly Hills: Sage, 1979.

Konaté, Abdourahmane. *Le Cri du mange-mil: Mémoires d'un préfet sénégalais.* Paris: L'Harmattan, 1990.

Koné, Demba. "Tidjanisme et pouvoir politique au Sénégal (1950–1987)." Mémoire de Maîtrise, Department of Philosophy. Université Cheikh Anta Diop de Dakar, 1988.

Krasner, Stephen D. "Review Article: Approaches to the State: Alternative Conceptions and Historical Dynamics." *Comparative Politics* 16:2 (January 1984): 223–46.

Kritzeck, James and William H. Lewis, eds. *Islam in Africa.* New York: Van Nostrand-Reinhold, 1969.

Kurdi, Abdulrahman Abdulkadir. *The Islamic State: A Study Based on the Islamic Holy Constitution.* London: Mansell, 1984.

Lacombe, Bernard. "Etude démographique des migrations et des migrants relevés de 1963 à 1965 dans l'enquête du Sine-Saloum (Sénégal)." *Cahiers de l'ORSTOM* 9:4 (1972): 393–412.

Laitin, David D. "Hegemony and Religious Conflict: British Imperial Control and Political Cleavages in Yorubaland." In *Bringing the State Back In*, ed. Peter B. Evans, Dietrich Rueschemeyer, and Theda Skocpol, 285–316. Cambridge: Cambridge University Press, 1985.

Hegemony and Culture: Politics and Religious Change among the Yoruba. Chicago: University of Chicago Press, 1986.

Lawrence, Bruce B. "Muslim Fundamentalist Movements: Reflections toward a New Approach." In *The Islamic Impulse*, ed. Barbara Freyer Stowasser, 15–36. London: Croom Helm, 1987.

Leary, Frances Anne. "Islam, Politics and Colonialism: A Political History of Islam in the Casamance Region of Senegal (1850–1914)." Ph.D. diss., Northwestern University, 1971.

Le Chatelier, Alfred. *L'Islam dans l'Afrique Occidentale.* Paris: G. Steinheil, 1899.

Lemarchand, René. "Quelles indépendances?" *Pouvoirs* 25 (1983): 131–147.
  "African Peasantries, Reciprocity, and the Market: The Economy of Affection Reconsidered." *Cahiers d'Etudes Africaines* 113, 29:1 (1989): 33–67.
Lentner, Howard H. "The Concept of the State: A Response to Stephen Krasner." *Comparative Politics* 16:3 (April, 1984): 367–377.
Levtzion, Nehemia. *Muslims and Chiefs in West Africa: A Study of Islam in the Middle Volta Basin in the Pre-Colonial Period.* London: Oxford University Press, 1968.
  ed. *Conversion to Islam.* New York: Holmes and Meier, 1979.
Levtzion, Nehemia, and Humphrey J. Fisher, eds. *Rural and Urban Islam in West Africa.* Boulder: Lynne Rienner, 1987. First published as *Asian and African Studies* 20:1 (1986).
Lewis, I. M., ed. *Islam in Tropical Africa.* 2nd edn Bloomington: Indiana University Press and International African Institute, 1980.
Leys, Colin. "The 'Overdeveloped' Post Colonial State: A Re-evaluation." *Review of African Political Economy* 5 (January-April 1976): 39–48.
Lonsdale, John. "States and Social Processes in Africa: A Historiographical Survey." *African Studies Review* 24:2/3 (June/September 1981): 139–225.
Lukacs, John. *Confessions of an Original Sinner.* New York: Ticknor and Fields, 1990.
MacGaffey, Janet. *Entrepreneurs and Parasites: The Struggle for Indigenous Capitalism in Zaire.* Cambridge: Cambridge University Press, 1987.
  "Economic Disengagement and Class Formation in Zaire." In *The Precarious Balance: State and Society in Africa,* ed. Donald Rothchild and Naomi Chazan, 171–188. Boulder: Westview, 1988.
Magassouba, Moriba. *L'Islam au Sénégal: Demain les mollahs?* Paris: Karthala, 1985.
Manning, Patrick. *Francophone sub-Saharan Africa 1880–1985.* Cambridge: Cambridge University Press, 1988.
Markovitz, Irving Leonard. *Léopold Sédar Senghor and the Politics of Négritude.* New York: Atheneum, 1969.
  "Leopold Sedar Senghor: The Technicians' Politician." *Pan-African Journal* 3:3 (Summer 1970): 179–186.
Marone, Ibrahima. "Le Tidjanisme au Sénégal." *Bulletin de l'Institut Fondamental d'Afrique Noire,* Série B: Sciences Humaines, 32:1 (January 1970): 136–215.
Martin, B. G. *Muslim Brotherhoods in Nineteenth Century Africa.* Cambridge: Cambridge University Press, 1976.
Martin, Nicolas. *Senghor et le monde: La politique internationale du Sénégal.* Paris: ABC (Afrique Biblio Club), 1979.
Marty, Paul. *Etudes sur l'Islam au Sénégal.* Paris: Leroux, 1917 (2 vols.).
Maududi, Syed Abul A'la. *System of Government under the Holy Prophet (Peace Be Upon Him) with Discussion on the Method for Implementing it in Pakistan Today.* Lahore: Islamic Publications, 1978.
Mazrui, Ali A. "The Triple Heritage of the State in Africa." In *The State in Global Perspective,* ed. Ali Kazancigil, 107–118. Aldershot, England: Gower/UNESCO, 1986.
Mbaye, Ravane. "L'Islam au Sénégal." Thèse de doctorat de troisième cycle, Département d'Arabe, Université de Dakar, 1976.

Mbodj, Mohamed. "Le Sine-Saloum de 1914 à 1929: Le Développement de l'arachide et mutations sociales." Mémoire de Maîtrise, Département d'Histoire, Université de Dakar, 1975.

"Un Example d'économie coloniale, le Sine-Saloum (Sénégal) de 1887 à 1940: Cultures arachidières et mutations sociales." Thèse de doctorat de troisième cycle, 3 vols., Université de Paris VII, 1978.

McLaughlin, Fiona. *Noun classification in Seereer-Siin.* Ph.D. diss., The University of Texas at Austin, 1992.

Merad, Ali. "The Ideologization of Islam in the Contemporary Muslim World." In *Islam and Power*, ed. Alexander S. Cudsi and Ali E. Hillal Dessouki, 37–48. London: Croom Helm, 1981.

Migdal, Joel S. *Strong Societies and Weak States: State-Society Relations and State Capabilities in the Third World.* Princeton: Princeton University Press, 1988.

Miles, William F. S. "The Rally as Ritual: Dramaturgical Politics in Nigerian Hausaland." *Comparative Politics* 21:3 (April 1989): 323–338.

Mitchell, Timothy. "The Limits of the State: Beyond Statist Approaches and Their Critics." *American Political Science Review* 85:1 (March 1991): 77–96.

Monteil, Vincent. *Esquisses Sénégalaises (Wâlo, Kayor, Dyolof, Mourides, un visionnaire).* Initiations et Etudes Africaines series, No. 21. Dakar: Institut Fondamental d'Afrique Noire, 1966.

L'Islam noir. Paris: Editions du Seuil, 1971.

Moreau, René Luc. *Africains Musulmans: Des communautés en mouvement.* Paris and Abidjan: Présence Africaine and Inadès, 1982.

Morgenthau, Ruth Schachter. *Political Parties in French Speaking West Africa.* Oxford: Clarendon Press, 1964.

Mortimer, Edward. *Faith and Power: The Politics of Islam.* New York: Random House, 1982.

Myers-Scotton, Carol. "Elite Closure as Boundary Maintenance: The Case of Africa." In *Language Policy and Political Development,* ed. Brian Weinstein, 25–42. Norwood, New Jersey: Ablex, 1990.

Myrdal, Gunnar. *Asian Drama: An Inquiry into the Poverty of Nations.* New York: Twentieth Century Fund, 1968.

Ndiaye, Amadou Latyr. "70ème Anniversaire de la Commune de Fatick." Photocopied text of speech delivered January 1, 1988.

Ndiaye, Mamadou. *L'Enseignement arabo-islamique au Sénégal.* Istanbul: Centre de Recherches sur l'Histoire, l'Art, et la Culture Islamiques (Organisation de la Conférence Islamique), 1985.

Nelson, Harold D., et. al. *Area Handbook for Senegal.* 2nd edn Washington: Foreign Area Studies Division of American University, 1974.

Nettl, J. P. "The State as a Conceptual Variable." *World Politics* 20:4 (1968): 559–592.

Nguyen-Van-Chi-Bonardel, Régine. *Vie de relations au Sénégal: La circulation des biens.* Dakar: Mémoires de l'Institut Fondamental d'Afrique Noire, No. 90, 1978.

Nicolas, Guy. "Islam et 'constructions nationales' au sud du Sahara." *Revue Française d'Etudes Politiques Africaines* 165/166 (September/October 1979): 86–107.

Dynamique de l'Islam au sud du Sahara. Paris: Publications Orientalistes de France, 1981.

Nimtz, August H., Jr. *Islam and Politics in East Africa: The Sufi Order in Tanzania*. Minneapolis: University of Minnesota Press, 1980.

Nyang, Sulayman S. *Islam, Christianity, and African Identity*. Brattleboro, Vermont: Amana Books, 1984.

Nyang'oro, Julius E. "The State of Politics in Africa: The Corporatist Factor." *Studies in Comparative International Development* 24:1 (Spring 1989): 5–19.

Otayek, René. "Muslim Charisma in Burkina Faso." In *Charisma and Brotherhood in African Islam*, ed. Donal B. Cruise O'Brien and Christian Coulon. Oxford: Clarendon Press, 1988.

Paden, John N. *Religion and Political Culture in Kano*. Berkeley: University of California Press, 1973.

Peel, J. D. Y. and C. C. Stewart, eds. *Popular Islam South of the Sahara*. Manchester: Manchester University Press, 1985. Originally published as *Africa* 55:4.

Pélissier, Paul. *Les Paysans du Sénégal: Les Civilisations agraires du Cayor à la Casamance*. Saint-Yrieix: Fabrègue, 1966.

Peretz, Don, Richard U. Moench and Safia K. Mohsen. *Islam: Legacy of the Past, Challenge of the Future*. np: North River Press, 1984.

Pipes, Daniel. *In the Path of God: Islam and Political Power*. New York: Basic Books, 1983.

Piscatori, James P. *Islam in a World of Nation-States*. Cambridge: Cambridge University Press, 1986.

Piscatori, James P., ed. *Islam in the Political Process*. Cambridge: Cambridge University Press, 1983.

Poggi, Gianfranco. *The Development of the Modern State: A Sociological Introduction*. Stanford: Stanford University Press, 1978.

Popovic, A. and G. Veinstein. *Les Ordres Mystiques dans l'Islam: Cheminements et situation actuelle*. Paris: Ecole des Hautes Etudes en Sciences Sociales, 1986.

Przeworski, Adam. "Some Problems in the Study of the Transition to Democracy." In *Transitions from Authoritarian Rule: Comparative Perspectives*, ed. Guillermo O'Donnell, Philippe C. Schmitter, and Laurence Whitehead, 47–63. Baltimore: Johns Hopkins University Press, 1986.

Quesnot, Fernand. "Influence du mouridisme sur le tidjanisme." In M. Chailley et. al., *Notes et études sur l'Islam en Afrique Noire*. Paris: CHEAM (Centre de Hautes Etudes Administratives sur l'Afrique et l'Asie Modernes), 1962: 115–125.

"Les Cadres maraboutiques de l'Islam sénégalais." In M. Chailley et. al., *Notes et études sur l'Islam en Afrique Noire*. Paris: CHEAM (Centre de Hautes Etudes Administratives sur l'Afrique et l'Asie Modernes), 1962: 127–194.

Quinn, Charlotte A. *Mandingo Kingdoms of the Senegambia: Traditionalism, Islam, and European Expansion*. Evanston: Northwestern University Press, 1972.

"Maba Diakhou and the Gambian Jihad, 1850–1890." In *Studies in West African Islamic History, Volume 1: The Cultivators of Islam*, ed. John Ralph Willis, 233–258. London: Frank Cass, 1979.

Raufer, Xavier. "L'Afrique noire et l'Islam révolutionnaire: Développement visible, courants souterrains." *L'Afrique et L'Asie Modernes* 163 (Winter 1989–90): 93–105.

Reeves, Edward B. *The Hidden Government: Ritual, Clientelism, and Legitimation in*

Northern Egypt. Salt Lake City: University of Utah Press, 1990.

République du Sénégal, Ministère des Travaux Publics, de l'Urbanisme et des Transports, Direction de l'Urbanisme et de l'Habitat. *Ville de Fatick: Monographie.* Paris: BCEOM, 1974.

République du Sénégal, Ministère de l'Urbanisme, de l'Habitat et de l'Environnement. "Région du Sine-Saloum, ville de Fatick: Lotissement d'extension, rapport justificatif." Photocopied text, September 1978.

République du Sénégal, Préfecture, Département de Fatick. "Rapport de synthèse du Département de Fatick sur la charte culturelle." Photocopied text, March 1986.

République du Sénégal. "Plan régional de développement intégré de la région de Fatick: Synthèse du bilan-diagnostic et enjeux majeurs." Photocopied text, July 1987.

République du Sénégal, Ministère de l'Economie, des Finances et du Plan, Direction de la Prévision de la Statistique. "Les Principaux résultats provisoires du recensement de la population et de l'habitat du Sénégal." December 1989.

"Recensement général de la population et de l'habitat, mai-juin 1988: Résultats définitifs." 1990.

"Recensement de la population et de l'habitat de 1988: Rapport Regional, Résultats Définitifs: Fatick." September 1992.

Reverdy, Jean-Claude. "Une Société rurale au Sénégal: Les structures foncières, familiales, et villageoises des Serer." Aix-en-Provence: Centre Africain des Sciences Humaines Appliquées, Collection des Travaux du CASHA, n.d.

Robinson, David. *Chiefs and Clerics: Abdul Bokar Kan and Futa Toro, 1853–1891.* Oxford: Clarendon Press, 1975.

The Holy War of Umar Tal: The Western Sudan in the Mid-Nineteenth Century. Oxford: Clarendon Press, 1985.

"French 'Islamic' Policy and Practice in Late Nineteenth-Century Senegal." *Journal of African History* 29 (1988): 415–435.

Robinson, Kenneth. "Senegal: The Elections to the Territorial Assembly, March 1957." In *Five Elections in Africa: A Group of Electoral Studies*, eds. W. J. M. Mackenzie and Kenneth Robinson, 281–390. Oxford: Oxford University Press, 1960.

Roche, Christian. *Histoire de la Casamance: Conquête et résistance, 1850–1920.* Paris: Karthala, 1985.

Rockman, Bert A. "Minding the State – Or a State of Mind? Issues in the Comparative Conceptualization of the State." *Comparative Political Studies* 23:1 (April 1990): 25–55.

Roff, William R. "Islamic Movements: One or Many?" In *Islam and the Political Economy of Meaning: Comparative Studies of Muslim Discourse*, ed. William R. Roff, 31–52. London: Croom Helm, 1987.

ed. *Islam and the Political Economy of Meaning: Comparative Studies of Muslim Discourse.* London: Croom Helm, 1987.

Rothchild, Donald and Naomi Chazan, eds. *The Precarious Balance: State and Society in Africa.* Boulder: Westview, 1988.

Salem, Gérard. "Crise urbaine et contrôle social à Pikine. Bornes-fontaines et clientélisme." *Politique Africaine* 45 (March 1992). Issue title: "Sénégal: La

328   Select bibliography

Démocratie à l'épreuve."
Samb, Amar. "Touba et son 'Magal'." *Bulletin de l'Institut Fondamental d'Afrique Noire* Série B, Sciences Humaines, 31:3 (1969): 733–753.
Essai sur la Contribution du Sénégal à la littérature d'expression Arabe. Mémoires de l'Institut Fondamental d'Afrique Noire 87. Dakar: IFAN, 1972.
Sanneh, Lamine O. *The Jakhanke: The History of an Islamic Clerical People of the Senegambia.* London: International Africa Institute, 1979.
Sapir, J. David. "West Atlantic: An Inventory of the Languages, Their Noun Class Systems and Consonant Alternation." In *Current Trends in Linguistics* 7, ed. Thomas Sebeok, 45–112. The Hague: Mouton, 1971.
Schaffer, Matt. *Mandinko: The Ethnography of a West African Holy Land.* New York: Holt, Rinehart and Winston, 1980.
Schatzberg, Michael G. *Politics and Class in Zaire: Bureaucracy, Business, and Beer in Lisala.* New York: Africana, 1980.
The Dialectics of Oppression in Zaire. Bloomington: Indiana University Press, 1988.
Schumacher, Edward J. *Politics, Bureaucracy, and Rural Development in Senegal.* Berkeley: University of California Press, 1975.
Scott, James C. *Weapons of the Weak: Everyday Forms of Peasant Resistance.* New Haven: Yale University Press, 1985.
Searing, James F. "Aristocrats, Slaves, and Peasants: Power and Dependency in the Wolof States, 1700–1850." *International Journal of African Historical Studies* 21:3 (1988): 475–503.
West African Slavery and Atlantic Commerce: The Senegal River Valley, 1700–1860. Cambridge: Cambridge University Press, 1993.
Senghor, Léopold Sédar. *Congrès Constitutif du P. F. A. (Dakar, 1er-3 Juillet 1959): Rapport sur la doctrine et le programme du parti.* Paris: Présence Africaine, 1959.
Pierre Teilhard de Chardin et la politique africaine. Paris: Editions du Seuil, 1962.
On African Socialism. New York: Praeger, 1964.
Liberté I: Négritude et humanisme. Paris: Editions du Seuil, 1964.
Liberté II: Nation et voie africaine du socialisme. Paris: Editions du Seuil, 1971.
Liberté III: Négritude et civilisation de l'universel. Paris: Editions du Seuil, 1977.
La Poésie de l'action: Conversations avec Mohamed Aziza. Paris: Stock, 1980.
Liberté IV: Socialisme et planification. Paris: Editions du Seuil, 1983.
Ce que je crois: Négritude, francité, et civilisation de l'universel. Paris: Bernard Grasset, 1988.
Liberté V: Le Dialogue des cultures. Paris: Editions du Seuil, 1993.
Shepherd, William E. "Islam and Ideology: Towards a Typology." *International Journal of Middle East Studies* 19 (1987): 307–336.
Sidibé, Amsatou Sow. "Le Code sénégalais de la famille et son application." Paper delivered to the conference "Etat et Société au Sénégal: Crises et Dynamiques Sociales" by the Centre d'Etude d'Afrique Noire, 22–25 October, 1991.
Silla, Ousmane. "La Persistance des castes dans la société wolof contemporaine." *Bulletin de l'IFAN (L'Institut Fondamentale d'Afrique Noire)* 28, B: 3–4: 731–770.
Sivan, Emmanuel. *Radical Islam: Medieval Theology and Modern Politics.* New Haven: Yale University Press, 1985.

Skocpol, Theda. "Bringing the State Back In: Strategies of Analysis in Current Research." In *Bringing the State Back In*, ed. Peter B. Evans, Dietrich Rueschemeyer and Theda Skocpol, 3–37. Cambridge: Cambridge University Press, 1985.

Snyder, Francis G. *Capitalism and Legal Change: An African Transformation.* New York: Academic Press, 1981.

Snyder, Francis G. and Marie-Angélique Savané. *Law and Population in Senegal: A Survey of Legislation.* Leiden: Afrika-Studiecentrum, 1977.

Sow, Fatou. *Les Fonctionnaires de l'administration centrale sénégalaise.* Initiations et Etudes Africaines 29. Dakar: Institut Fondamental d'Afrique Noire, 1972.

Sow Fall, Aminata. *La Grève des Bàttu.* Dakar: Les Nouvelles Editions Africaines, 1979.

Stewart, Charles C. *Islam and Social Order in Mauritania: A Case Study from the Nineteenth Century.* Oxford: Clarendon Press, 1973.

"Introduction: Popular Islam in Twentieth Century Africa." In *'Popular Islam' South of the Sahara.* ed. C. C. Stewart and J. D. Y. Peel, 363–368. Manchester: Manchester University Press, 1985. (Originally published as *Africa* 55:4).

Swartz, Marc J., ed. *Local-Level Politics: Social and Cultural Perspectives.* Chicago: Aldine, 1968.

Swigart, Leigh. "Wolof, Language or Ethnic Group? The Development of a National Identity." Paper delivered at the 33rd annual meeting of the African Studies Association, Baltimore, Maryland, November 1990.

"Practice and Perception: Language Use and Attitudes in Dakar." Ph.D. diss., the University of Washington, 1992.

"Cultural Creolization and Language Use in Postcolonial Africa: The Case of Senegal." *Africa* 64:2, (1994): 175–189.

Sy, Cheikh Tidiane. *La Confrérie sénégalaise des Mourides: Un Essai sur l'Islam au Sénégal.* Paris: Présence Africaine, 1969.

Sylla, Assane and El-Hadji Mamadou Sakhir Gaye. *Le Mahdi: Mouhamadou Seydina Limamou Laye du Sénégal.* 2nd edn Rufisque, Senegal: Imprimerie Nationale, 1985.

Terray, Emmanuel, ed. *L'Etat contemporain en Afrique.* Paris: L'Harmattan, 1987.

Thiam, Iba Der. *Maba Diakhou Ba: Almamy du Rip (Sénégal).* Collection Grandes Figures Africaines. Paris: ABC, 1977.

Thomas, Louis-Vincent. *Les Diola: Essai d'analyse fonctionnelle sur une population de Basse-Casamance.* Volumes 1 and 2. Dakar: Institut Français d'Afrique Noire, 1959.

Triaud, Jean-Louis. "Le Thème confrérique en Afrique de l'Ouest: Essai historique et bibliographique." In *Les Ordres mystiques dans l'Islam: Cheminements et situation actuelle,* ed. A. Popovic and G. Veinstein, 271–282. Paris: Ecole des Hautes Etudes en Sciences Sociales, 1986.

"Khalwa and the Career of Sainthood: An Interpretative Essay," in *Charisma and Brotherhood in African Islam,* ed. Donal B. Cruise O'Brien and Christian Coulon, 53–66. Oxford: Clarendon Press, 1988.

Trimingham, J. Spencer. *The Influence of Islam upon Africa.* London: Longman, 1968.

The Sufi Orders in Islam. London: Oxford University Press, 1971.

Islam in West Africa. Oxford: Oxford University Press, 1959.

Trincaz, Jacqueline. *Colonisations et Religions en Afrique noire: L'Exemple de Ziguinchor*. Paris: L'Harmattan, 1981.

Trincaz, Pierre-Xavier. *Colonisation et Régionalisme: Ziguinchor en Casamance*. Paris: Editions de l'ORSTOM, 1984.

Tripp, Aili Mari. "Local Organizations, Participation, and the State in Urban Tanzania." In *Governance and Politics in Africa*, ed. Goran Hyden and Michael Bratton, 221–242. Boulder: Lynne Rienner, 1992.

U.K. Foreign Office. "French West Africa (General)." *Peace Handbooks: Issued by the Historical Section of the Foreign Office* 17:100. London, H. M. Stationary Office, 1920.

UNESCO. *Two Studies on Ethnic Group Relations in Africa: Senegal, The United Republic of Tanzania*. Paris: UNESCO, 1974.

Vaillant, Janet G. *Black, French, and African: A Life of Léopold Sédar Senghor*. Cambridge: Harvard University Press, 1990.

Vatikiotis, P. J. *Islam and the State*. London: Croom Helm, 1987.

Vatin, Jean-Claude.. "Popular Puritanism versus State Reformism: Islam in Algeria." In *Islam in the Political Process*, ed. James P. Piscatori, 98–121. Cambridge: Cambridge University Press, 1983.

Vengroff, Richard. "The Transition to Democracy in Senegal: The Role of Decentralization." *In Depth* 3:1 (Winter 1993): 23–51

Villalón, Leonardo A. "Léopold Sédar Senghor", in *Political Leaders of Contemporary Africa South of the Sahara*, ed. Harvey Glickman, 259–265. Westport, Connecticut: Greenwood Press, 1992.

"Charisma and Ethnicity in Political Context: A Case Study in the Establishment of a Senegalese Religious Clientele." *Africa* 63:1 (January 1993): 80–101.

"Sufi Rituals as Rallies: Religious Ceremonies in the Politics of Senegalese State-Society Relations." *Comparative Politics* 26:4 (1994)

"Democratizing a (Quasi)Democracy: The 1993 Senegalese Elections." *African Affairs* 93:371 (April 1994)

Wallerstein, Immanuel. "Voluntary Associations." In *Political Parties and National Integration in Tropical Africa*, ed. James S. Coleman and Carl G. Rosberg, 318–339. Berkeley: University of California Press, 1964.

Wane, Yaya. "Ceerno Muhamadu Sayid Baa ou Le soufisme intégral de Madiina Gunaas (Sénégal)." *Cahiers d'Etudes Africaines* 56: 14 (1974): 671–698.

Weber, Max. *The Theory of Social and Economic Organization*. New York: Free Press, 1947.

Economy and Society. Translated by Guenther Roth and Claus Wittich. Berkeley: University of California Press, 1978.

Willis, John Ralph. *In the Path of Allah: The Passion of Al-Hajj ʿUmar: An Essay into the Nature of Charisma in Islam*. London: Frank Cass, 1989.

Willis, John Ralph, ed. *Studies in West African Islamic History. Volume I: The Cultivators of Islam*. London: Frank Cass, 1979.

Wright, Bonnie. "The Power of Articulation." In *Creativity of Power: Cosmology and Action in African Societies*, ed. W. Arens and Ivan Karp, 39–57. Washington: Smithsonian Institution Press, 1983.

Yansané, Aguibou Y. *Decolonization in West African States with French Colonial Legacy: Comparison and Contrast: Development in Guinea, the Ivory Coast, and Senegal (1945–1980)*. Cambridge, Massachusetts: Schenkman, 1984.

Young, Crawford. *The Politics of Cultural Pluralism.* Madison: The University of Wisconsin Press, 1976.

"The African Colonial State and its Political Legacy." In *The Precarious Balance. State and Society in Africa*, eds., Donald Rothchild and Naomi Chazan, 25–66. Boulder: Westview, 1988.

Young, Crawford and Babacar Kanté. "Governance, Democracy, and the 1988 Senegalese Elections." In *Governance and Politics in Africa*, ed. Goran Hyden and Michael Bratton, 57–74. Boulder: Lynne Rienner, 1992.

Young, Crawford and Thomas Turner. *The Rise and Decline of the Zairian State.* Madison: University of Wisconsin Press, 1985.

Zubaida, Sami. *Islam, the People and the State: Essays on Political Ideas and Movements in the Middle East.* London: Routledge, 1989.

Zuccarelli, François. *Un Parti politique africain: L'Union Progressiste Sénégalaise.* Paris: R. Pichon et R. Durand-Auzias, 1970.

La Vie politique sénégalaise (1940–1988). Paris: CHEAM, 1988.

Index

Other books in the series